THE GREAT FAMINE

THE GREAT FAMINE

NORTHERN EUROPE IN THE EARLY FOURTEENTH CENTURY

William Chester Jordan

PRINCETON UNIVERSITY PRESS

PRINCETON, NEW JERSEY

LIBRARY OF CONGRESS CATALOGING-IN-PUBLICATION DATA

JORDAN, WILLIAM C., 1948–

THE GREAT FAMINE : NORTHERN EUROPE IN THE EARLY
FOURTEENTH CENTURY / WILLIAM CHESTER JORDAN

P.   CM.

INCLUDES BIBLIOGRAPHICAL REFERENCES AND INDEX.

ISBN 0-691-01134-6

ISBN 0-691-05891-1 (PBK.)

1. EUROPE—HISTORY—476–1492.   2. EUROPE—ECONOMIC CONDITIONS—
TO 1492.   3. EUROPE—SOCIAL CONDITIONS—TO 1492.
4. FAMINES—EUROPE—HISTORY.   I. TITLE.

D202.8J67   1996

940.1'92—DC20   95-26684   CIP

THIS BOOK HAS BEEN COMPOSED IN SABON

PRINCETON UNIVERSITY PRESS BOOKS ARE PRINTED ON ACID-FREE PAPER
AND MEET THE GUIDELINES FOR PERMANENCE AND DURABILITY OF THE
COMMITTEE ON PRODUCTION GUIDELINES FOR BOOK LONGEVITY OF THE
COUNCIL ON LIBRARY RESOURCES

THIRD PRINTING, AND FIRST PAPERBACK PRINTING, 1998

HTTP://PUP.PRINCETON.EDU

PRINTED IN THE UNITED STATES OF AMERICA

3   5   7   9   10   8   6   4

CONTENTS

LIST OF MAPS

ACKNOWLEDGMENTS

MANY PEOPLE have provided information on sources and other kinds of very generous help to me whenever I asked them: Hans Aarsleff, Peter Brown, Elspeth Carruthers, Michael Curschmann, Gerry Geison, Philip Katz, John Logan, Michael Mahoney, Julia Marvin, Stuart McCook, Vera Moreen, David Nirenberg, Mark Pegg, Gyan Prakash, Lawrence Stone, and Benjamin Weiss. I am also very grateful to the two anonymous referees who read the manuscript for Princeton University Press. I would like to express my gratitude as well to Lauren Osborne, Brigitta van Rheinberg, Lauren Lepow, and Sara Mullen, all of whom helped in various important ways to bring this book to publication. Mr. Chris Brest did a splendid job with the maps. Of course, I owe special thanks to a whole cohort of graduate students (beyond those included in the list above), many of whom are now professors and all of whom over several years have sat through my seminars while, together, we tried to make sense of the agricultural life of northern Europe in the High Middle Ages. It is to them that I dedicate this study. I must also acknowledge a particular debt to a few magical books that evoke the labor, joy, and anguish of preindustrial rural life, Thomas Hennell's *Old Farm* and Thomas Hardy's Wessex novels.

8 November 1994
Princeton, New Jersey

THE GREAT FAMINE

PROLOGUE

THE GREAT Franciscan chronicler and Italian talebearer, Salimbene de Adam, relates a macabre story of the year 1286. He tells of a man possessed by a "diabolic spirit" who believed that famine, like a dark cloud on the horizon, was about to cast its shadow over the land. Pretending to come on hard times, the man, a teacher of the Psalter to young boys, went about the streets of his town begging and singing. In the century and country of Saint Francis a holy pauper, with a repertory of sacred songs, could make a considerable living; with what this *poverello* earned he daily bought small amounts of grain and bread. At home during the evenings, he toasted the morsels of bread and put them aside against the dearth to come; but the devil, it was said, visited the *poverello* behind locked doors late one evening and suffocated him before he could enjoy his hoard. The body was found next day along with sacks of rotting flour and heaps of old toast. It was also discovered that the "poor" old man owned two other houses in the town, which the town fathers promptly seized into their hands.

Children (*pueri*), perhaps boys whom he had taught to read the psalms, carried out a grisly humiliation of the old man's corpse, stripping it, tying ropes to the cool, bony feet, and dragging the nude body through the town. Wearying of the sport, they commandeered a farmer's wagon to which they attached the mangled body. After dragging it a while longer through the streets, they dumped the grotesque burden from a bridge into the river below and then, to prevent it from drifting away, dropped scores of stones on it in a kind of mock burial. The whole episode, Salimbene tells us, gave rise to a proverb: "Beware, lest by your miserliness you provoke the madness of children."[1]

Fear of famine, in a year that Salimbene elsewhere describes as one of "great abundance of grain and wine," transformed the old teacher into a hoarder.[2] In the presence of a hoarder's corpse children were transformed into instruments of vengeance. For almost no one was reckoned worse than a hoarder, a person who profited from the misery of fellow human beings or reserved the earth's bounty for himself while the wretched went hungry. Few men deserved so humiliating a treatment of their remains. Resentment ran deep and strong; not even a year of abundance effaced it. Avarice was corrupting; it was made intolerable where the fear and ravages of famine weakened civility and decency, affection and trust. The history of the Great Famine that afflicted northern Europe in the early fourteenth century and encouraged just such transformations of community life is the subject of this book.

PART I

A CALAMITY "UNHEARD-OF
AMONG LIVING MEN"

1

THE BRINGERS OF FAMINE IN 1315:

RAIN, WAR, GOD

THE WORD *famine*, as used in this book, refers to a catastrophic subsistence crisis, the extreme limit of a wide spectrum of shortages that have sometimes been given the name in popular writing and speech. In adopting the more restrictive usage, I follow most other scholars.[1] Famines in this sense, like all extreme conditions, have been rare in history; yet their recent recurrence in postcolonial societies has stimulated politicians, relief workers, and economists to rethink their understanding of a phenomenon that at first seems more characteristic of the distant past than of the modern world. In turn, historians have reanimated their research into the origins and consequences of many ancient, medieval, and early modern famines, in large part to improve upon the somewhat caricatured Malthusian model of famine as a simple function of population growth's outpacing increases in food production. By far the most sophisticated and comprehensive historical work has been accomplished for early modern Europe.[2] But a distinguished tradition of study of other famines, particularly the "Great Famine" of the early fourteenth century, long predates this explosion of scholarship.[3]

The Great Famine deserves its name for at least two reasons. First, it was protracted: like the paradigmatic famine in biblical Egypt foretold by the young Joseph in Genesis 41, it lasted in many regions a full seven years, from 1315 to 1322.[4] Second, it was extensive: few medieval writers in 1315 were aware of how extensive, but gradually pilgrims, traders, and couriers brought sobering news from widely separated locations. Over time the reports grew worse; and as one unfortunate harvest-tide succeeded another and another, the catastrophe achieved mythic proportions. One contemporary chronicler would eventually declaim that "hunger" was abroad "throughout the seven inhabited regions (*climata*) of the world."[5]

More than a century later, Bavarians still invoked with awe the hunger and high prices that began in 1315.[6] A late German chronicler (ca. 1500) would summarize what he had read of the catastrophe's extent from earlier chronicles this way ("Duss geschichte findet man in vilen chroniken"): it was hard ("wart dure") in every country, "in Hessen, in Doringen, in Westphalen, in Sassen, in Missen, in Francken, an dem Ryne, in

Brabant, in Hollant, in Flandern unde durch alle lande, nicht alleyne in Tutschlant, sundern auch in Franckrich unde in andern vilen konnigrichen."[7] The information collected from various Low Country chronicle sources available to the Frisian scholar Ubbo Emmius around the turn of the sixteenth/seventeenth century led him to similar conclusions.[8] The historian and editor Johannes Lass in the early eighteenth century diligently studied perhaps an even greater number of chronicles (not all of which have survived to the present day). After doing so he came to regard the catastrophe of the Great Famine as unique among the disasters that had befallen "all Europe." He was particularly struck by the refrain in the chronicles to the effect that for a while not even the birds of spring heralded hope.[9]

Recent scholars, with fewer chronicles to consult but working more systematically than their predecessors over the documentary records, have been more restrained. Still, the evidence they have amassed is arresting in its implications. For Germany that evidence points to famine throughout the country, and along the Baltic to the borders of Poland. With this no previous medieval European famine could compare.[10] Northern France and the British Isles, with the exception of northern Scotland, were also hit with devastating severity.[11] The southern portion of Scandinavia, where grain was grown, was affected, perhaps only slightly less than the rest of the Continent.[12] By and large the line dividing famine-stricken northern Europe from territories of relative bounty further south ran westward along the Alps (most of present-day Austria was spared except for the region around Salzburg) into France through Lyons and the Forez, roughly, to southern Poitou.[13] A conservative estimate would be that the "Great Hunger" afflicted an area of 400,000 square miles with a population at the time, reckoned very roughly, in excess of thirty million.[14]

Serious modern investigation of the impact and consequences of this famine began with the work of the then unconventional German historian Karl Lamprecht in the 1880s. His discussion was part of a much wider, four-volume excursus into the economic life and the "material culture" of the Moselle country.[15] Lamprecht's grand vision, with its interest in the everyday and, in this case, the famine's impact on everyday life, was not unique, but it was peculiar given the prevailing norms in contemporary German historiography, which favored political and macroeconomic history. Whatever the genesis of Lamprecht's approach (and this is warmly debated), there is no doubt that he was committed to what we would nowadays call a form of historical anthropology that delighted in "thick description" and demurred from necessarily assigning narrative primacy to high politics.[16]

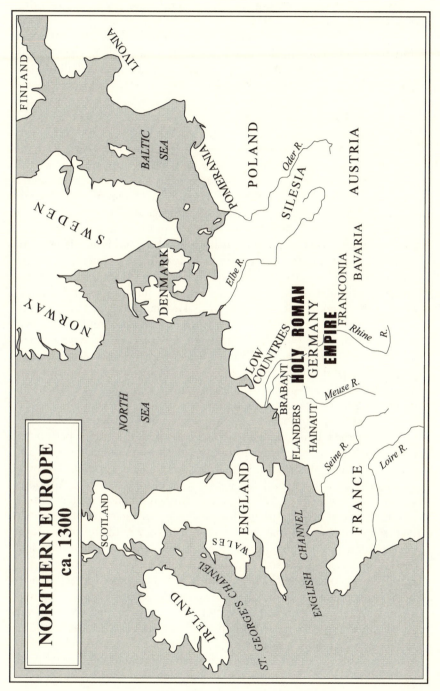

NORTHERN EUROPE
ca. 1300

FINLAND

LIVONIA

NORWAY

SWEDEN

BALTIC SEA

POMERANIA

POLAND

Oder R.

SILESIA

AUSTRIA

DENMARK

Elbe R.

BAVARIA

FRANCONIA

HOLY ROMAN

GERMANY

EMPIRE

Rhine R.

LOW COUNTRIES

BRABANT

Meuse R.

NORTH SEA

FLANDERS

HAINAUT

Seine R.

Loire R.

FRANCE

ENGLAND

SCOTLAND

WALES

ENGLISH CHANNEL

ST. GEORGE'S CHANNEL

IRELAND

Map 1

Fritz Curschmann, writing less than a generation afterward, was one of several gifted historians who recognized the magnitude of Lamprecht's overall accomplishment and applauded it publicly.[17] He also corrected some of Lamprecht's observations and in general went far beyond his predecessor in the geography of his concerns, which included all of German-speaking Europe. (French evidence, he decided, could not sustain the level of analysis of the German, assembled in the great project, the *Monumenta Germaniae Historica*.)[18] As background Curschmann covered and assembled the texts for the period from the year 700 to 1317 in Europe, a fact that has permitted scholars to compare the early years of the Great Famine, his principal interest, to what is recoverable on earlier ones. To this day the most satisfying treatment of the Great Famine and the most extensive collection of texts remain Curschmann's 1900 monograph, and we will return to it over and over again.[19]

Yet Curschmann's monograph is not the most widely cited study, at least not within Anglo-American historiography. That honor goes to an article by Henry Lucas published in *Speculum* in 1930. Lucas, an expert on the political history of the Low Countries, claimed somewhat unfairly in that article that the Great Famine "received but little extended treatment at the hand of Fritz Curschmann." Despite the slight Lucas's main contribution was his combination of Curschmann's accumulation of evidence with the then published evidence for France, the Low Countries, and especially England. For the last Lucas was extremely thorough. His close culling of the Patent Rolls, the Close Rolls, and the chronicles is as admirable (and labor-saving for subsequent scholars) in its way as Curschmann's work on the imperial sources.

Despite the appearance of several good studies on regions of France touched by the famine, many French scholars treat the famine perfunctorily or merely refer the reader to Lucas's work as the fundamental treatment.[20] For students of Great Britain, however, Lucas's primacy has been supplanted by the work of Ian Kershaw published in 1973. Although Lucas had thoroughly explored the published English sources (as of 1930), Kershaw in as thorough and welcome a manner comprehensively incorporated materials that appeared in print only in the following forty years. Moreover, he rooted some of his most interesting conclusions in a case study based in part on unpublished sources from the north of England. These conclusions have frequently been generalized by scholars to many other regions.[21] In fact, it is now possible to test Kershaw's findings against the abundant research, stimulated in part by his work, on the Celtic lands and eastern and southern England. Together these studies should permit a more trustworthy picture of the famine throughout Britain. Meanwhile, on the Continent, research on Denmark and other parts of Scandinavia, on the Hanse towns and their hinterlands, on the Low

Countries, and on important regions and estates in France (as remarked) makes it possible and desirable to put together a new synthesis of the causes, experience, and consequences of the Great Famine.

Curschmann, whom we shall follow at the outset, began his study with a consideration of words. Like the chroniclers whom he so thoroughly pillaged, he had a keen sense of language. He recognized that *fames* or a vernacular equivalent like *Hungir* was a strong word often employed for a genuine and general disaster the magnitude of which can occasionally be confirmed from other sources. Yet many medieval writers were loose in their use of the word, applying it to local shortages of brief duration; this is why confirmation or support from other sources was a necessary precondition to the acceptance of a single chronicler's report of a famine. *Caristia*, also with vernacular equivalents, had a larger semantic field than even *fames*. Usually signifying high prices, it did not necessarily imply famine conditions or even widespread declines in consumption; yet it too was fairly often applied to a period of acute or chronic lack of staples. Frequently, of course, the word or forms of it were used by writers in combination with *fames* to emphasize the general economic conditions during which a famine took place.[22] But again exaggeration on the part of any single writer was always possible. What Curschmann's work permitted historians to do was to cluster independent references to the same events. From a careful consideration of these reports and the geography of coverage, they were able to make good cases that famines, in the sense defined at the opening of this chapter, really did occur, but far less often than earlier scholars believed.

In the specific case of the Great Famine, there is no problem in assembling the cluster of appropriate chronicle reports. Numerous contemporary and near contemporary writers (far more than those known even to Curschmann) refer to *fames* and *caristia* in the years 1315–1322 even while they grope for the telling adjectives that might help describe the experience of life more vividly. The *fames* began as mere hunger, perhaps, but became ever more difficult, harsh, severe, terrible, finally intolerable (*groz, zo grot, valida, aspera, tanta magna, maxima, permaxima, intollerabilis*).[23] The *caristia* went from very high prices to unheard-of hard times (*tanta magna, maxima, permaxima; so dure tiid, groisse dure zit, grote und unhörlike dure tit*).[24]

That the Europe struck by this escalating *fames* and *caristia* from 1315 onward had achieved a precarious equilibrium by the end of the previous century seems a generally accepted conclusion. Demographic growth, to take one measure of the equilibrium, had slowed to zero in most regions after a long period of spectacular increases.[25] In the Moselle country, for example, where surviving data have made the relative measurement of population possible, there was a trebling from about the year 1100 up to the first half of the fourteenth century, before a tapering off or no-growth situation prevailed.[26] In medieval Gotland in southern Scandinavia the tenth century saw between 500 and 700 farmsteads in place; the year 1300, the peak of medieval settlement there, counted between 1,200 and 1,500, numbers that held firm thereafter.[27]

In absolute numbers (though these must be treated with caution), it would appear that German-speaking areas of the empire experienced a growth that resulted in a population of approximately fourteen million in the year 1300.[28] The number of Englishmen and women seems to have gone from 1.3 or 1.5 million in the late eleventh century to 5 million by 1300.[29] The population of France, defined by its present national borders, had risen from approximately 6.2 million to 17.6 or perhaps to as high as 21 million in roughly the same period.[30] Finally, there was the north. Denmark, with its wide medieval boundaries that included part of the Scandinavian peninsula inhabited by Swedes, saw its population grow from 850,000 to 1.5 million during the High Middle Ages.[31] Various estimates for Norway suggest a population in 1300 perhaps approaching 500,000.[32] Finland, finally, can stand for the various regions of the eastern Baltic. Its population can be estimated at between 200,000 and 300,000.[33] To be sure, the far eastern Baltic was not affected directly by harvest shortfalls, but it felt some of the economic, especially trade, repercussions of the famine.[34]

Almost all scholars believe that these figures, however problematic any single one of them may be, reveal a population under stress, because the economic growth necessary to sustain the standard of living had slowed long before the population itself leveled off. Precisely when the slowing occurred depends on what region we examine and what sector of the economy. The comprehensive picture is one of sluggishness in productivity in some sectors from the 1250s, more generalized sluggishness from the 1270s, and very slow growth from 1285 or thereabouts onward. Although the thirteenth century remained a period of economic growth right up to its close, the gap between demand and production steadily widened.[35] The famine took place in these conditions.

Certain similarities between these conditions and those observed in modern famines make it useful to look at and, in part, be guided by the systematic theoretical work that has emerged from studies of the latter. One of the most judicious of recent scholars, the social scientist David Arnold, argues for four possible scenarios for the onset of famine.[36] The first entails population pressure far beyond the productive means of the agricultural sector to provide a standard of living much above subsistence in the best of times. In a premodern economy of this type, where transportation costs are high and transportation networks very limited, even modest problems of production and distribution can cause famine. On the production side, the death of a small percentage of draft animals leading to a decline in available plows or manure, a brief period of unseasonable or severe weather that damages the crops, or an infestation of vermin that depletes the standing corn will issue in widespread malnutrition and death. On the distribution side, even a small breakdown—bridges out, roads temporarily impassible—might have devastating effects.

The second scenario, one common in the premodern world, is of a famine brought about by a *sustained* failure of appropriate weather. Only high rates and absolute quantities of storage and good distribution networks (modern conditions) would prevent malnutrition and increased mortality. Even with excellent modern storage facilities and transportation networks, famine is still possible in a third scenario, where crop specialization is widespread and the good health of the population depends on access to a large number of other markets: radical problems of distribution—war and civil war being common causes, but fuel insufficiencies and bureaucratic torpor also potentially contributing—render many regions liable to famine.

The most troubling scenario is the fourth. It sees peasant conservatism in the face of even modest but recurrent problems of production and distribution as a possible cause of famine when conditions worsen. Peasants, that is, help bring famine on themselves by their stubborn refusal to change their ways before crisis looms. Wisely Arnold does not see much independent power in this argument (peasant conservatism cannot cause famine in the absence of other factors), but it has been seized on and expanded exponentially in a recent book by Ronald Seavoy.[37] Basing his view on informal observations in south Asia, Seavoy has asserted that peasants are wedded to a culture of indolence (rest in preference to work), not leisure, which values rest after work. This is why, he continues, peasants live in a subsistence manner. To do otherwise would be to privilege work, which would be contrary to their ideological predilections. It is also why peasants have a great many children, whom, according to Seavoy, they mercilessly exploit by requiring them to care for them as they age. Then, when the children mature and beget, they themselves obtain the opportunity to exploit their own offspring and achieve indolence. Peasants also have no incentive to save or improve because they know that in poor harvests, other peasants (equally indolent?) will share.

There is, of course, really such a thing as peasant conservatism, but it is not the caricature that Seavoy makes it. His picture is immorally distorted for south Asia.[38] It would be equally grotesque if applied to medieval northern Europe, where excavations of rural cemeteries show the skeletons of mature peasants to be the last physical remnants of grievously hard lives (scarcely evidence of laziness whatever their ideology might have been): extensive arthritis, deformation of the spinal column, small bony growths and enlargement of joints from the excruciating labors of plowing, lugging forty-pound seed bags, and harvesting with the scythe. The skeletal remains show eburnation—the transformation of bone into dense, hard ivory-like material on the smooth surfaces—a result, again, of agonizing, yet regular and unavoidable, work routines in medieval rural society.[39] In the cemeteries of fishing villages on the northern coasts, one can hardly find a skeleton of an adult that does not reveal osteoarthritis of the spinal column due to heavy work routines on land and in cold, windblown open boats.[40]

One problem with all of these scenarios, so baldly stated, is that they evoke a passive rural society, acted upon but not acting. Yet every experienced adult in premodern Europe appreciated something of the danger of famine. Famine was a "hazard" and therefore necessitated risk management. That is to say, authorities and ordinary people knew that famines would come, since they had come in the past, but at no predictable time, and the probability of any specific year's having the hazard was relatively low. In other words, "uncertainty"—the inability to probabilize hazards—was not the case here. The aim of another major book, *Bad Year Economics*, is in part to generate models of how human beings deal with the hazard of famines when they do come, and how they modify their behavior afterward.[41] Stated differently, what is the potential for social change in dealing with hazards?

The editors of the book, in some ways nuancing and occasionally, if implicitly, challenging the emphasis of David Arnold's work, lay out four strategies of preparation for or reaction to food shortages, which may or may not be compatible at any one time. Producers might diversify, so as not to be dependent on one vulnerable crop. (Modern agricultural practice, especially in "developing" countries, under the pressure of the world economy to produce cash crops, does not typically indulge this strategy.) A political, social, and economic ideology favorable to mobility—movement to resource-rich regions—is a second strategy, but it is conditioned by ecology and by the existence of neighboring political authorities and social elites who may erect barriers to mobility and access to resources.

The third strategy involves storage. Any society that grows grain crops, even if it is so primitive that it lives from harvest to harvest (which was not the case in Europe in the High Middle Ages), must have sufficient facilities to lay up massive amounts of grain at harvesttime or massive amounts of grain converted to other forms (beer, for example, in the Middle Ages).[42] These stores would gradually be spent down until the next harvest. Usually these facilities or their capacity can be augmented to reap the bounty of an exceptional harvest (the barns can be stuffed to the rafters; attics can be commandeered to hold additional grain; barrels in use for other products can be reallocated to beer). It is hard to believe, however, that sufficient reserves for the population at large could be stored so as to last through two consecutive catastrophic harvests (following even a great cornucopia) in any premodern society. Of course, the storage facilities for governmental elites and the military might be of a size to protect against two bad harvests. The existence of such treasure-houses of grain under governmental authority (or, what amounts to the same thing, the capacity of a government to regulate retail sales in its interest) would furnish officials with the opportunity to correlate access to food according to the priorities of the ruling strata.[43]

The fourth strategy identified by the authors of *Bad Year Economics*, and one that was critical in primitive economies whenever food shortfalls were narrowly localized, was exchange, the routine exchange of goods producing the habit of cooperation, which could be exploited at times of dearth for the transfer of wealth to famine-stricken settlements from food-rich ones. Transportation networks, levels of organization and political authority, and other factors combined to diminish or expand the circumference of such exchanges.[44]

For historians the value of these models lies in the fact that they encourage a systematic and comprehensive set of questions on the subject of famine.[45] It may have been possible to generate the questions without resort to the models, but this is doubtful. Even the best researchers have hitherto been seduced by chronicle evidence into believing that the Great Famine of the Middle Ages was solely a production crisis caused by a massive failure of appropriate weather[46] and that there was nothing, or nearly nothing, that could be done about it. They have therefore ignored or barely mentioned other possible factors, like war and government policies. Of course, the Great Famine was in large measure precipitated by the production crisis to which the chroniclers bear witness, but much more was involved.

Let us begin with the question of attitude. One of the real disadvantages those affected labored under was a naive sense of the possibilities of natural disaster. That is to say, contemporary expectations about natural conditions were rosy from the beginning because the thirteenth century, with regard to climate—or, rather, long-term trends in weather—was so gentle.[47] A mid-sixteenth-century Low Country annalist of university background spiced book 14 (the long closing alphabetical catchall portion) of his chronicle with miscellaneous tidbits he had gleaned from earlier writers and from archives. Under *C* he recorded his findings on "High Prices" (*caristia*). He highlighted the years 1146 and 1197, then none for more than a century, then 1316. Nothing compared with that year for over two centuries more until 1530, 1546, 1557, and 1578—that is, the period of the Price Revolution stimulated by American silver flowing to Spain and in turn to the Spanish-dominated Netherlands.[48]

When the same scholar came to M, he put down his conclusions on the worst "mortality" (*mortalitas*) suffered in his region: 1315, 1316, 1318. Nothing compared at all before, and afterward he could find comparable reports only in 1458, 1483, and 1529.[49] Evidently, if at first somewhat surprisingly, not even the Black Death seemed to be as bad.[50] When he turned to rainy weather under P (*pluvia*), 1315 and 1316 got special mention; only one other year was singled out, 1567.[51] The impression is clear. For a multitude of simultaneous disasters tied to the weather there was nothing quite like and nothing quite so unexpected as the teens of the fourteenth century. A seventeenth-century humanist writer who made an even more thorough search of the chronicle records came to the conclusion that in his homeland of Frisia one would have to go back to the year 1069 to find a time when, in the chroniclers' eyes, it had been as difficult as it was in 1315 to make ends meet.[52]

What was going on? One or two recent scholars have argued for a steady deterioration of weather and a slight, progressive shortening in the length of the growing season in the north during the late thirteenth and early fourteenth centuries. This imperceptible deterioration culminated with the shock of 1315. Unfortunately, the evidence is not persuasive on the steady worsening of weather in the thirteenth century.[53] Pierre Alexandre, the most thorough of modern researchers—and, by far, the most trustworthy—would see a more or less uniformly gentle thirteenth century, indeed a secular warming trend from the twelfth century through 1350. Only one significant interruption in this trend occurred north of the Alps before 1350, a catastrophic dip that coincided with the onset of the Great Famine.[54]

Alexandre's observations, based on explicit references to weather conditions, merit particular respect for two reasons: first, because of his refusal to use his chroniclers' reports of famines, price inflation, and low yields (none of which *necessarily* depends on weather) as surrogates for information on weather conditions, and, second, because of his comprehensiveness with regard to available contemporary sources.[55] To be sure, Alexandre limits his investigation to the north Atlantic and Baltic Continental regions of western and central Europe (France, the Low Countries, and German-speaking Europe); he therefore ignores the British Isles, Scandinavia, and western Poland, which were affected by the Great Famine. Nevertheless, his information, culled from hundreds of narrative sources, provides the most satisfying picture yet available of the weather of medieval Europe; and it is relatively easy to supplement this picture for other relevant parts of Europe from the results of various historians of weather and of environmental economics published in the last several decades. What all these scholars agree on is that the epoch of the Great Famine saw some of the worst and most sustained periods of bad weather in the entire Middle Ages and that this was particularly unanticipated, given the mild thirteenth century.[56]

Two indexes prepared by Alexandre on the severity of winters and the incidence of rainy summers help make the point with greater clarity.[57] For reports of a continuous series of exceptionally cold winters there was nothing like the period 1310–1330. While the series of winters from 1160 to 1170 may have been the worst on record, that fact would have been ancient history to people in 1315. Moreover, for sheer length of time the succession of miserably cold winters in the years 1310–1330 was incomparable; and 1320–1330 was perhaps the second worst period for severe winters in the entirety of the Middle Ages.

Alexandre's index of the incidence of rainy summers also identifies the years 1310–1320 as one of the four worst intervals in the period from 1150 to 1420. Indeed, though it is difficult to be precise on relative rankings, the years 1310–1320 appear to be the second worst period for severe, sustained summer downpours for the Middle Ages as a whole.

Pierre Alexandre's conclusions can be tested against the independent evidence of dendrochronology. Mary Lyons has examined the northern Irish evidence of oaks, whose growth is very sensitive to rainfall. On the basis of tree-ring growth, it would appear that oak growth was 7 percent above normal in 1315 and 10 percent above normal in 1316. The year 1317 saw a growth rate near average (perhaps 2 percent below), which would suggest a tapering off of the rains in Ireland, a conclusion that, as we shall see, the chroniclers support. But in Ireland at least, the year 1318 saw another extraordinary spurt of tree-ring growth in oaks, 8 percent above normal. By contrast, the 1320s—based simply on dendrochronological evidence—appear to have been a period of attenuated growth, suggesting severe prolonged drought. The year 1324 witnessed tree-ring growth 22 percent below normal, and at least three other years in the 1320s had growth rates more than 10 percent below normal.[58] Study of oak-tree growth in Hesse on the Continent reveals similar patterns: the years 1310 to 1320 provide evidence of a devastating weather cycle.[59]

Striking and persuasive as are the general conclusions of Alexandre's, Lyons's, and other studies, they pale before the reports in narrative sources. We are not as fortunate as our Enlightenment forebears in terms of numbers of surviving chronicles, but what does survive fully supports their impressions. Texts as disparate as the Nuremberg *Annals*, a Flemish rhymed account for 1315, and a Breton chronicle for 1314 and 1315 declaim the unmitigated severity of the weather.[60] Others identify or dwell on specific aspects of the unfavorable weather. Nearly all contemporary or near contemporary authors emphasize the abnormal persistence of the rains in the opening years. They had already begun, at least in England and perhaps in Germany, in the summer of 1314.[61] Followed by a harsh winter and, of course, expected late-winter rains, which in this instance only compounded the problem, the unseasonable downpours recommenced in earnest in late spring and brought flooding in their wake.[62] These rains, with unusually deafening thunder and terrible displays of lightning in Scandinavia,[63] were steady ("inundatio pluviarum quasi continua") from Pentecost 1315 on in England, from mid-April in France, and from May Day in the Low Countries, and were heavy throughout the summer in Germany and elsewhere, including Ireland.[64] The winds and overcast skies made the whole summer abnormally cool ("frigusque aestivo tempore insolitum").[65] In October the rains were still falling in Britain: four mills on the usually gentle Avon, now swollen and clogged with debris, succumbed to flooding in that one month.[66]

The year 1316 was equally bad or worse.[67] It probably began with another severe winter during which ships were immobilized by ice as the Baltic froze over.[68] The chroniclers make clear that the rains following the severe winter weather came so frequently that the effects of the downpours could not be contained. Spring, summer, fall: they came when the seed had just been scattered, when what seeds remained in place sprouted and the shoots broke through the surface of the earth, and they came with equal severity at harvest.[69] "The whole world was troubled," wrote one chronicler from Salzburg, which had been at the southeastern geographical limit of the ruinous weather the year before.[70] Yet the chronicler could say the "whole world" in 1316 because as far as he knew, the devastation had spread far to the south and east, to Styria, for example, which suffered catastrophic flooding that swept away at least fourteen bridges on the river Mur.[71]

The downpours were somewhat less ubiquitous in 1317: western Germany was hard hit; its periphery less so[72]—in agreement with the dendrochronological evidence already presented. But the amelioration of conditions was brief. The harshest winter of all was 1317/1318.[73] In a *récit* by a French chronicler, winter was said to have been not only severe but interminable, with bitter cold continuous "from the feast of Saint Andrew [30 November] or thereabouts until Easter."[74] To an English observer it was the worst winter in a millennium: "A thusent winter ther bifore com nevere non so strong." No more benumbing punishment had ever been inflicted: "Com nevere wrecche into Engelond that made men more agaste."[75]

According to a number of chroniclers, improvement in conditions was more common after April 1318, but local conditions—those in Ireland, for example—were to make 1318 as bad a year in many villages as any of the years in which the disastrous rains were more widespread.[76] And though never again as general or as sustained as in the first three years of the famine,[77] conditions so often degenerated over large regions from 1319 to 1322 that it is no exaggeration to link these years with the earlier years of the catastrophe. Normandy was ripped by devastating wind-storms in 1319,[78] the equivalent of nor'easters on the Atlantic seaboard of North America, with the inevitable impact on flocks, herds, and fruit trees. Flanders was repeatedly punished by floods that hobbled the econ-omy and caused major property damage especially in 1320 and 1322.[79] Elsewhere—in England and on the Continent, as, for example, in the re-gion around Aachen—sustained periods of bad weather (sometimes com-pounded, the chroniclers tell us, by lengthy droughts) extended the fam-ine conditions even beyond 1322.[80] But a reasonable closing date for the long series of catastrophes is the winter of 1321/1322. It saw terrible and sustained cold, with the Baltic and parts of the North Sea frozen over and ships immobilized in icy prisons.[81] Norman chroniclers remarked the snow. It was everywhere; it was deep; it would not melt: "Nix maxima super terram et iterum fuit maxima ante mediam Kadragesimam."[82]

This tragic period was made more so by war. Although it cannot be said that war caused the famine, it intensified the deprivation by expand-ing a production crisis into a distribution crisis as well. No attempt will be made at this time to assess in detail the effects of the wars, a task that will be reserved for subsequent discussions of prices, wages, cost of living, mortality, and the like. Here we need only enumerate the conflicts and address a few of their most obvious and general consequences at the re-gional level in the principalities affected by the persistently bad weather.

In the north a tangle of complicated dynastic struggles kept the king-doms of Norway, Denmark, and Sweden at one another's throats in vari-ous alliances all through the famine, but especially until 1319.[83] These wars also had a disruptive, though not necessarily entirely unprofitable, effect on German-speaking towns and principalities all along the south-ern rim of the Baltic. Desperately needed resources were being diverted to military needs like castle building at the height of the famine.[84]

Among Germans proper the situation was no better. Locally severe flooding in 1312 and exceptional cold in 1313 had produced regional shortages and high prices in a number of places in the empire.[85] Exacer-bating these conditions, war broke out between Ludwig of Bavaria and Duke Frederick of Austria in late 1314 after the so-called double election to the German throne. In the Frankfurt area one chronicler describes how a "great multitude of men and horses" of the duke's army were already perishing from shortages in 1314.[86] Another delighted in observing in real life the topos learned from stories about knights, in this case hard up from the artificially induced shortages caused by marauding armies and siege warfare, selling their mounts in order to get food and drink. There is a mocking, tongue-in-cheek quality to the latter's report—on the eve of a dearth that would make the conditions he was describing seem almost desirable—and the tone betokens the naive character of expectations about the weather and war: "And what a wonder! Some knights who were sitting on a magnificently outfitted horse gave the horse and their weapons away for cheap wine; and they did this because they were so terribly hungry."[87]

As the wars and the famine conditions persisted, the time for mockery passed. There were numerous treaties, alliances, truces, regulations of tolls, and agreements with respect to suppressing disorder and modifying payments of debts to Jews in the years 1315–1322, especially in the Rhineland and southern Germany. It is probably wrong to conclude from this evidence that the country was in utter turmoil, since such agreements among towns, churches, and lay lords occurred at many other times as well.[88] Nevertheless, most historians seem convinced that the combination of wars and harvest failures convulsed the empire.[89]

An on-again, off-again war in Flanders in which French troops tried to bring the Flemings under their suzerainty bracketed the three major early years of the famine in that region and would be invoked by commentators as one factor (along with the taxation imposed in the preparation for and fighting of the war) that made an already difficult situation more difficult.[90] Even as the Franco-Flemish war affected the famine, the natural conditions that helped provoke the famine made the fighting of the war more arduous. In 1315 the steady, inundating rains ("the ugly weather") turned the roads into quagmires, trapped the riding and cart horses ("there was mud up to their knees"), immobilized wagons, and made supply of troops nearly impossible, as what seems like an infinite number of chroniclers relate.[91] And we are informed monotonously that the distress—and the postponement of combat which it necessitated—saddened the commanders, including Louis X, the king of France ("non absque displicentia et amaritudine cordis"), who craved nothing so much as a decisive victory in a war whose roots went back twenty years.[92] To the rebellious Flemings, of course, the ceaseless rains that stymied the king were the act of a beneficent God; the belief became a cliché, constantly repeated down the centuries in sources originating in the region.[93]

In the British Isles, too, war was everywhere. The Scots, in the aftermath of the famous battle of Bannockburn (1314) began to ravage large areas on the English borderlands and did long-lasting damage whose precise parameters, given the nature of the evidence, are difficult to assess with precision but appear to have been extensive and massive.[94] The English, in retaliation, were nearly as effective in ravaging the countryside of southern Scotland;[95] but the army that led the way in the raids was far less successful in fulfilling its major mission of bringing the Scots to heel. The difficulty of provisioning the army, together with disease, is said to have led to a greater number of casualties than did battle.[96] Moreover, in both countries border localities that were spared ravaging were affected in other ways as productive resources drained to the battle-scarred areas and the needs of the contending armies grew.[97] These issues will have to be pursued in greater depth in subsequent chapters.

Ireland and Wales, as intimated, also suffered from wars fought on their soil. The spring of 1315 saw the arrival of Scottish forces in Ireland led by Edward Bruce (brother of Robert Bruce); this was a kind of second front in the continuing war between England and Scotland already being played out on the borderlands of the two countries.[98] The mutual violence of the Scots and the Anglo-Irish lords and their supporters aggravated the evil conditions then beginning to be felt after the failure of the winter wheat harvest.[99] The disruptions continued through 1317 as the Scots, failing to enlist sufficient Irish support against English domination to overcome their enemy, went about hungry and harrying the island.[100] Killing in war, terrorism, and dying from the effects of the subsistence crisis went together.[101] Seizures of already much reduced crops are reported.[102]

In southern Wales, following the death at Bannockburn of the great English magnate and power in the Welsh March Gilbert de Clare, the earl of Gloucester, "men raised hostile insurrection in the form of war."[103] Such a power vacuum as that left by the earl's death might have served to persuade Welsh lords (in this case Llywelyn Bren) to rise, but most historians agree that it was the crop failures of 1315 which triggered the revolt against the English.[104] The economic effects of this rebellion were to be felt even in north Wales.[105] If we could not guess as much from what we know of their commitments against the Scots on the borderlands and in Ireland, chronicle evidence assures us that the English found their resources stretched to the limit by the insurrection.[106] It was to the great good fortune of the crown that the rebellion did not evolve into a general rising of the Welsh people and did not see the invasion of north Wales by Scots from Ireland, an invasion that Edward and Robert Bruce briefly contemplated.[107]

The weather, then, provoked a production crisis and complicated distribution. Wars and their destruction immediately before and during the onslaught of bad weather compounded the problems, especially that of distribution, in a major way. Other contributory explanations for the intensity and duration of the famine (some, like inordinate taxation, implicit in what has already been written) will be discussed at greater length in subsequent pages. Yet probably none of these explanations would have entirely satisfied most medieval men and women. For them, it was God

who was unquestionably bringing famine in order to mete out the legitimate recompense for sin ("pro sceleribus castigare").[108] Sin, hatred of the
visible Church, empty faith, and lack of loyalty offended God and explained why He permitted the foul weather to linger for such a length of
time.[109] It could only be God, as we are informed by one version of the
English poem "On the Evil Times of Edward II" (ca. 1320), who apportioned weather "so cold and unkynde"—out of its kind in the sense of
rupturing the natural order. As punishment for human pride God "sente
derthe on erde."[110] The text "he . . . sendeth rain on the just and the
unjust" (Matt. 5.45) confirmed this view: the punishment richly deserved
by the unjust had to be endured by the righteous as well, in the same way
that sunlight warmed both the wicked and the good. So, too, sickness
came on the battered and bewildered population of saints and sinners by
God's own ordinance in the "plaga divina."[111]

A merciful God, it must be added, gave fair warning of the disaster.
One schoolman, William of Wheatley, who had studied at Paris and later
became master of the grammar schools of Lincoln in England, claimed
that from things he had seen in the kingdom a good twenty years before
the time of high prices and hunger (1315, 1316, and 1317) he could have
predicted the catastrophe. He had seen similar signs again, he wrote,
while he studied in Paris fifteen years before the famine. William made
these claims in a treatise he later composed on the art and science of the
interpretation of signs.[112] Unfortunately, the part of his treatise where he
begins to talk about the particular signs that pointed to the famine was
never completed.[113]

Other observers were more revealing. The years 1315 and 1316 saw a
comet appear in the night sky.[114] (Observed not only in the West, the
phenomenon in question is also reported in the Chinese Annals as having
been visible from 28 November 1315 through 12 March 1316.)[115] This
heavenly manifestation was a clear counsel, as readers of earlier northern
European chronicles would have been led to believe, of the specter of
prolonged famine and death.[116] The Low Country chronicler Lodewijk
Van Velthem, who recorded that the comet was visible beginning on 21
December 1315 and whose narrative ended in late 1316 when he put
down his quill, was most insistent on this interpretation, adding civil
strife and widespread destruction to the litany of expected horrors.[117] Of
course, a few chroniclers saw in the comet other portents (the death of
Louis X in 1316, the general suffering of France) or nothing at all.[118]

Besides the comet other signs manifested themselves. Swedes observed
splashes of scarlet light in the heavens resembing showers of blood; these
were allegedly a herald of pestilence.[119] To the English this light, if indeed
the same light, made a ruby-red cross of blood as a token of future battle

deaths.[120] The traditional signs of the times also included a lunar eclipse (1 October 1316) and two earthquakes (1316 in northern and 1317 in western France).[121]

Like signs in general, the significance of the comet of 1315 and early 1316, the vermilion skies of that year or slightly later, and the other wonders could hardly have been determined with genuine confidence until the disasters themselves became evident: deeper want, pestilence, more casualties of war.[122] For embedded in the political economy of salvation was the notion that the power of the sign, whose *potential* significance was predictable from the memory of past patterns duly recorded, could be reversed by acts of contrition on the part of a sinful humanity.[123] Had the years from 1316 to 1322 been bountiful ones, the comet and the reddened canopy of heaven would have been regarded as that stimulus to conversion which brought disaster to a quick end, reconfirming at the same time the covenant between God and people.[124] Yet Lodewijk Van Velthem was certain when he finished the narrative portion of his chronicle in late 1316 that contrition would be too little and too late; the end of the world was near. At least this is the impression one gets from the fact that the terrible descriptions of 1315 and 1316 furnished by Lodewijk are followed by two long appended books on signs and miracles in which the chronicler-turned-exegete ruminates on the apocalyptic visions of the Book of Daniel.[125] Of course, as it turned out, Lodewijk was wrong. The great Day of Judgment did not come. Nonetheless, a severe punishment was inflicted by the Lord Most High for five more very long years—or so most men and women surely came to believe.[126]

2

THE HARVEST FAILURES AND
ANIMAL MURRAINS

TO MOST OBSERVERS the first major effect of the weather of 1315, 1316, and 1317 was the material devastation caused by the rains and the flooding that ensued: seedbeds sodden, crops and pastures under water, grain rotting, fish traps wrecked, dikes washed away, meadows too wet to be mown, turf too soggy to be cut, and quarries too swollen with the overflow to be worked for stone or lime.[1] Chroniclers occasionally report the devastation with an unsettling matter-of-factness. "In many places, as happens in a flood," writes one such annalist, "buildings, walls, and keeps were undermined."[2] Yet others, like the English compiler of the *Flores historiarum* under the year 1315 and a Salzburg chronicler portraying conditions in 1316, permitted themselves more dramatic expressions. Both quite naturally evoked the purifying deluge of Noah's day.[3] "There was such an inundation of waters," the German writer asserted, "that it seemed as though it was THE Flood."[4] Later chroniclers reading a wide variety of reports used words like "terrifying" and "gruesome" to sum up their impressions of the narrative record.[5]

Almost all chroniclers also mention the despoiling of good lands by these heavy rains.[6] By good lands they meant lands long in cultivation, from the assarting or clearing of woodlands, moraine, and bogs, since the eleventh century.[7] Leaving aside for the moment environments where pastoral farming, fishing, viticulture, and other specialized husbandries traditionally prevailed, let us look at the agricultural regime usually considered most characteristic of these medieval assarts, the large, unwalled, nucleated village with open-field farming.[8] This regime could be found in the central plain of England (midlands and lowlands), the plain of France (extending in a broad sweeping northern arc from the Loire to the Rhine), and the north German plain, that part of the great lowland plain that extended eastward from the North Sea along the Baltic coast, ever widening until it was gently interrupted on a longer than thousand-mile front by the Urals.[9]

The open fields with heavy soils plowed in long furrows were capable of absorbing enormous amounts of water; and drainage did not cause erosion. So the despoiling referred to by the chroniclers signifies the appearance of vast muddy tracts and sparse, beaten-down crops rather than the absolute ruining of the land. This was not the case in other areas, however, where so-called marginal lands with light soils had been converted to arable in the later thirteenth century and in the first decade or so of the fourteenth. On them, the disfigurement of the landscape was not only stark to the naked eye but alarming in its long-range implications. The sandy soils of parts of Bedfordshire, washing away, left behind seemingly interminable expanses of gravelly dunelike undulations on which nothing but scraggy rye could take root.[10] The descriptively named "Grits-and-Sandstones" region of south Yorkshire experienced a truly remarkable contraction of arable, perhaps by a proportion as high as one-half. The land, ravaged by the torrential downpours, became "terra frisca et inculta"—waste and unworked.[11] Taken together, the exposed rocky substrata (their thin topsoil also stripped in the unceasing deluge), the deep gullies, and the ruts made a moonscape of desolation. Only time—great lengths of time—would heal the violated terrain, when it could be healed.[12]

Even where the scars of nature's wrath were less visible, as, for example, where clays underlay thin topsoil, waterlogging temporarily inflicted equal levels of damage.[13] Two to five years might be sufficient for recovery. Over the course of that period, fertility would necessarily be low. The chroniclers talk of a "sterility of lands" and an "unheard-of barrenness" in Germany.[14] The Cistercian observer Jacques de Thérines described the estates of the Cistercians in France and lands in the northern part of that kingdom in general as succumbing to a *sterilitas* "hitherto unheard-of in the realm."[15]

It goes without saying that yields from all the terrains affected by the rains declined. How much? Even in the best of times and on the best of lands, yields were low as compared to those achieved under many other agricultural regimes.[16] Of course, medieval yields pale before modern ones of 200 or 300 to 1, induced by hybridization, promiscuous fertilization, and the use of pesticides, herbicides, and industrial methods of harvesting and threshing. But they also pale before those obtained in premodern societies where alluvial husbandry was practiced, such as in the ancient Nile Valley and Mesopotamia. In the Fertile Crescent in the third millennium B.C. yields of barley ranged from 20:1 to as high as 76:1.[17] Yet evidence from northern France shows that overall yields for grains rarely got as high as 10 to 1 (ten bushels for every one sown), and 3 to 1 was far more common in the thirteenth century.[18] Extensive data from England—the famous data from the estates of Winchester in the thirteenth century—suggest that wheat in England returned modally about 3:1 or 4:1, rye 4:1 or 5:1, barley in the range 3.5:1 to 7:1, oats 2:1 or 3:1, and beans and peas about 4:1.[19] Grain-growing areas in southern

Scandinavia in the thirteenth century, it is thought, seldom delivered much greater than 2:1; and agricultural historians of Poland agree that grain yields there were at best "somewhat more than 2 times the volume" of seed sown.[20]

Returns like these appear to be so inferior that a few scholars have refused to accept their typicality. It has been asserted, for example, that the "Winchester estates . . . were notoriously backward."[21] Or the quality of the land and nature of the management of the estates, if not "backward," still did not encourage improvement of yields.[22] Other scholars demur and cite in their support recent work on the Westminster Abbey manors. There the return was usually close to 3:1 for grains.[23] Even if the Winchester—and Westminster—figures are on the low side, there is very little evidence that far higher yields were being routinely achieved elsewhere. (The exceptions will be noted where appropriate.)

Why were yields so low? Of course, aggregate figures of the sort quoted for the Continent and England "invariably subsume a considerable diversity of experience."[24] Nonetheless, the long-received explanation is known as the "Postan Thesis," a neo-Malthusian interpretation based largely but not exclusively on evidence from the English midlands, but routinely generalized by almost all its supporters (even where the evidence is too meager to prove or disprove it) to the whole of late medieval Europe.[25] The assertion embedded in the explanation is not simply that yields were low but that they were lower than the naturally high levels (whatever those supposedly were) reached in the century before because the pressures of population growth had encouraged practices that decisively and dangerously decreased them. In the first place, intensifying demand for staples allegedly led to "cerealization," that is, the constriction of pasture in favor of arable, with a concomitant loss of manure from the contraction of herds. Thereupon, insufficient manuring of fields is said to have reduced yields. Expansion of arable into lands of marginal natural fertility supposedly further depressed average yields. Finally, and perhaps most important, overcropping (including inadequate fallowing) in the mad rush to increase production is presumed to have exhausted even good soil by the end of the thirteenth century.[26]

Recently and quite rightly, these arguments have come in for attack, though they continue to have devoted defenders.[27] The very idea of the primacy of the demographic push has been challenged by Robert Brenner, who argues for the key role of lordship and dependency (that is, class tensions) in the crisis—a point to which we shall have to return.[28] Brenner's critics, who denigrate or minimize the power of traditional Marxist class analysis to provide an alternative explanation, are numerous and serious as well.[29]

Another critique accepts the primacy of the demographic factor and the fact of depletion of nitrogen in old arable, but it argues that the conventional thesis needs revision on a quite different point. The contention—associated with Gregory Clark—has about it a kind of technological determinism. Farmers became conservative, given the high levels of demand and the decline in new assarts over the course of the thirteenth century. The benefits of heavy manuring,[30] or of enriching depleted arable by turning old fields effectively into pasture (it takes years with traditional methods) in order to return them to arable thereafter for a brief period, simply required too much time to be effective within the temporal calculations of medieval farmers.[31] This interesting contention needs considerably more elaboration before it can be accepted.

There are reasons, moreover, to wonder about the validity of some of Clark's leading assumptions. Indeed, consider the critical notion, that there was a long-term steep decline in soil fertility over the course of the thirteenth century, when overcropping to feed the burgeoning population led to the exhaustion of nitrogenous nutrients. This cannot be true. To begin with, there is the problem of how "natural" the very poorly documented but plausibly high twelfth-century yields were. Many of these yields were generated from newly assarted woodlands with heavy soils. These new assarts were superfertile for two reasons. First, vast amounts of enriching ash were plowed in after stumps were burned out. Second, the density of weeds in dark woodlands is relatively low; new assarts out of woodlands offered, temporarily at least, fields where competition between weeds and crops was also therefore relatively low. But it needs to be repeated that these were temporary advantages: the new assarts rapidly declined after a few years to what may more appropriately be called natural fertility as the benefits of the ash dissipated and weeds established strong root networks.

Moreover, it was more or less impossible to bring old fields back to the yields they had enjoyed as new assarts. Neither manure nor fertilizing ash of the proportions plowed under on new woodland assarts was ever available—year in, year out—for all fields. (What ash was available from village fires was regularly used in gardens; heavy manuring was always limited.)[32] And as W. Harwood Long has demonstrated incontrovertibly, medieval tools and animal power were chronically unable to clean or rid arable long in cultivation of the root systems of weeds (the cultivated crops' competitors) once these were well-established. This was the case even with the benefits of the heavy plow, one of the chief uses of which was to expose as much as possible of the root systems of weeds to the desiccating power of the sun. Crisscross plowing would have been more effective, but it was impossible, owing to the ridges and trenches created by the heavy plow.[33] Labor-intensive weeding during the growing season might have helped solve the problem of cleaning; and small plots, especially gardens, were subjected to this technique.[34] Given labor costs (children could not be trusted as effective weeders) it was not ordinarily a viable option for large open fields.

What farmers' customary techniques did accomplish was a *relative* cleaning of the soil. This fact, it turns out, had an indirect advantage. It meant that the fields could not be exhausted, because so many nitrogen-fixing weeds were regularly enriching it. Gorse or furze (*Ulex*) and broom (*Cytisus*) were common bushy weeds in England and on the Continent; they were legumes, nitrogen-fixers. And even weeds that were not legumes were plowed in; in rotting they returned nitrogen to the soil. Medieval farmers would not have been aware of the paradoxical advantages of weeds, so they continued to labor to reduce weed regrowth. Their most effective technique in the great fields was the use of heavy broadcast seeding before weeds reestablished themselves in recently plowed fields, but even this only cut into weed regrowth. It did not eliminate it.[35]

It is significant in this respect that no medieval manual says precisely how much seed ought to be sown. Rustics were quite aware that if they sowed too little, the yield would be down as weeds choked out the crop. They were also aware that if they sowed too much and the crop took root, yields would be down as the individual plants of the crop itself would choke one another out. They therefore had to strike a balance depending on the field. The balance was a comfortable range of seed corn to acreage, since up to a point a reduction in the amount of seed corn planted would allow the plants that did take root to branch and produce additional ears (grain). The overall yield per acre might decline very slightly but still remain quite acceptable (within a normal range). It would take steep reductions in the amount of seed corn planted before the precipitous fall associated with too light seeding occurred; and, vice versa, it would take spectacular increases in the amount of seed corn broadcast before the dramatic falloff in yields associated with too heavy planting resulted. Most important, the preferred balance always tolerated a significant amount of weed regrowth and, therefore, prevented exhaustion.[36]

While gross yield was most profoundly influenced by cleaning and seed-to-acre ratios, other factors influenced net yields even in basically good years:[37] hail at harvesttime that beat the grain to the ground and made it irrecoverable;[38] vermin and the supply of cats to control them;[39] smuts, molds, mildew, and rusts;[40] and the human factors that undermined at least *recorded* yields. These last included children's and scarecrows' ineffectiveness at keeping birds away from the fields immediately after the crops' ripening, as well as "theft and fraud . . . and [the quality of the] threshing gang."[41] In this potpourri of causes for poor yields, a questionable and at worst slight depletion of nitrogen was not decisive.

If medieval rustics could not have brought about the general exhaustion of the soil had they set out to do so, what explains rotation and fallowing, which are usually taken as proof of concerns over exhaustion? In the first place, one would have to show that rotation and fallowing significantly—indeed, steadily—increased in the early to mid–thirteenth century to compensate for exhaustion or, failing an increase in these practices, that new techniques were introduced which accomplished what increased fallowing and rotation were supposed to accomplish for lands *already long under cultivation.* One would also have to show that as demand continued to increase from the growing population, this "common sense" about fallowing was put aside in the misguided effort to meet demand and benefit from high prices. In fact, no one has persuasively made such a case.

Campbell and Stacey have suggested that the introduction into England of vetches (*Vicia*), a pealike crop or, rather, set of crops, was a thirteenth-century innovation.[42] If this had been the case, it could be argued that vetches were being employed to return nitrogen to the "exhausted" soil. (As a weed it was doing so independent of cultivation.) Unfortunately for this argument, Currie has shown definitively that Campbell and Stacey are in error. Vetches had been planted for a millennium in England.

It could still be possible that the already diffuse growing of vetches, "hitched, like the peas, on the fallow field,"[43] became more widespread and intensive in the course of the expansion of arable in the thirteenth century and, indeed, became sufficiently widespread and intensive to demand soil exhaustion as an explanation for its diffusion and its ever thicker hitching onto a contracting fallow. But that possibility remains to be verified. It certainly does not jump out from the estate or manorial records. Indeed, Campbell, in responding to Currie, more or less conceded that diffusion on the scale necessary to make this argument did not occur until after 1350, a period of catastrophic population decline.[44]

Rotation and fallowing were practiced, in fact, not primarily in order to preserve the long-term fertility of the soil, but to restore chemical balances that were temporarily upset by monoculture in particular fields. Farmers would not have explained their habits this way, but they would have said that sowing the same crop without respite made for "bad corn," that is, it gave rise to diseases or stunting which they could avoid by fallowing or planting a different crop.

To be sure, despite the unconvincing assertions about general soil exhaustion, a great deal of truth remains in the old orthodoxies. For example, proportional yields certainly did go down in the course of the thirteenth century (though not everywhere).[45] Partly this was a result of older, once superfertile, assarts' declining to their natural fertility; partly it resulted from changes in the balance of mixed (pastoral/arable) farming and the consequent decrease in available manure for certain of the newer fields (that is, those recently brought into cultivation) that were deemed to need and targeted for very heavy manuring.[46] But not all the new fields (even leaving aside converted pasture) were light-soiled, relatively infertile, and, therefore, in need of more manuring than land already in cultivation. Some of the new fields were carved out of lands with exceptionally heavy soils. These were oftentimes marvelously high in natural fertility and were made artificially higher by slash-and-burn assarting. The problem was to capitalize on this fertility, for these soils were even harder than existing arable to plow. Consequently, grain yields on both types of new lands were low.[47] When many of these lands were withdrawn from cultivation during and after the ecological disasters of 1315–1322, proportional yields obviously went up. Early scholars looking at the figures on yields alone believed that there must have been dramatic improvements in techniques of husbandry to account for these increases.[48] They were wrong.

By convention, the recently assarted lands of the late thirteenth and early fourteenth centuries (especially those with light soils) are referred to and have been referred to above as "marginal." Yet here again there is a danger, in the uncritical acceptance of the orthodoxies, of missing some significant complications to the situation. For example, in certain small, thinly settled regions of Gelderland, of the northern part of what is now Belgium, and of northwestern Germany, although the soil was not light, its physical quality was poor and its nutrients varied from poor to adequate. The problem was that there was no way to exploit the nutrients that were available (had the farmers realized they were there); good crops simply would not grow on the compacted mass. This seems a classic case of marginal land. However, farmers came up with an extraordinary technique, *plaggen* soiling, which probably would not have been possible in more densely populated regions where pressure on resources was greater. "Often annually" they overlaid the base soil "with a mixture of animal dung and heather turves, together with . . . grass sods, forest litter, peat, clay or sand." Over the years they literally created a carpet of new and far less marginal soil, though to maintain its chemical sufficiency required regular and very heavy manuring.[49]

Other lands deemed marginal in a production sense were also not necessarily "economically" marginal. For example, light, nutrient-poor soil near a rapidly expanding town could be used to grow a grain crop to supply the town (as long as the return on seed corn was greater than about 1.2:1 and prices were high), whereas rich soil, at a distance and with transportation costs high, might never be sown with grain until transportation difficulties and high costs were overcome, say, through the building of a canal or road or the suppression of tolls. Properly speaking, one should describe the relatively more fertile lands as economically marginal in or for grain production.[50] Other factors can marginalize lands of high natural fertility as well: (1) popular attachment to rural customs that in general protect rustics from exploitation but that also inhibit technological innovation (a variation on the suggestion that to some degree peasants help bring famines on themselves); and (2) atavistic lordship, which may have the same inhibiting effect or may insist on such high rents that rustics abandon their holdings.[51] An example of such atavism is the case of an agricultural regime that depends on corvée or involuntary labor for the cultivation of the lands (demesnes) held directly by lords. Laborers' resistance to the corvées at the very times their own lands need plowing or harvesting can marginalize demesne production.[52]

So, for many reasons, yields were low long before the heavy and persistent rains of 1315 began to wreak havoc on them.[53] It was not the case that the quality of the weather merely made effective planting and harvesting physically difficult or washed away the crops; the rain also leeched nitrates from the soil.[54] Depleted in this way the soil was less than ideal for effective crop growth. What the wet weather *was* ideal for was plant diseases—especially molds, rusts, and mildews—that were perennial, if usually less ubiquitous, problems.[55] If, because yields were already low, real disaster could have come from even modest proportional declines, the wet weather and its pathological consequences in 1315 and 1316 assured that the declines were anything but modest. According to one chronicler, crops simply did not ripen in 1315, and therefore, according to another, there was far less bread than usual to be had.[56] Several others used these or comparable words with conviction and horror about this and the next harvest.[57] Still others lamented the stunted crops almost as if there were no harvests at all.[58] And, of course, these and similar conditions persisted during most of the next twelve harvests—spring (for winter wheat) and autumn—from 1316 through the fall of 1321 and often beyond.[59]

Documentary evidence, though incomplete, is nevertheless copious and arresting. Let us begin with wheat in England and again the most famous data, those of the Winchester manors, assembled by Titow. They show that, after the long and relatively stable returns from old fields in the thirteenth century, wheat yields from 1315 and several years thereafter on the Winchester estates were usually far more than 15 percent below normal.[60] This means a reduction from 3:1 (if we take that as modal) to 2.6:1. Interpreting the Winchester data is not unproblematical, and scholars differ considerably on how to calculate yields especially during the famine; but all agree on the precipitous fall in the period. Slicher van Bath, who preferred to see a yield of 4:1 as normal for a wheat harvest on the eve of the famine, believed that the famine harvests fell to about 2:1 or 2.5:1.[61]

Data from the Winchester and Westminster manors (the latter returns being more fragmentary), aggregated by David Farmer, show wheat yields as 64.1 percent, 55.9 percent, and 87.5 percent of mean yields in 1315, 1316, and 1317 respectively, the 55.9 percent figure for 1316 being the lowest in the entire period from 1271 to 1410.[62] In East Anglian Breckland Mark Bailey documents a 20 percent drop in yields.[63] And in Cuxham, Oxfordshire, in 1316 and 1317 wheat yields were respectively 33 percent and 29 percent below the mean computed from available data from 1307 to 1323.[64] Computed decennially, aggregate yields during the decade 1310–1319 in Cuxham were 19 percent below the mean from 1289 to 1359, and 33 percent below the average yields of the decade before.[65] Finally, Ian Kershaw's study of Bolton Priory, a northern English house of Austin canons, provides evidence of a decline at times to yields below 1:1, less grain harvested than sown, with overall yields during the famine being reduced by 50 percent.[66] Returns of the tithe (paid in kind by rustics as a percentage of the harvest) suggest that peasants' harvests may have been even worse in the environs of the priory.[67]

So much for wheat, which one expects to fare badly from heavier-than-normal rain. Reductions in the yields of beans and peas from 4:1 to 3:1, and at some famine harvests to as low as 1:1, are also attested, the heaviness of the downpours and the inadequate opportunity for drainage causing the seeds to swell, float, burst above ground, and become susceptible to vermin.[68] Barley and oats might be expected to have fared less badly in the first three years than wheat and beans (they were typically more sensitive to drought than to rain), except that it was not a question merely of heavy rain and poor drainage, but, as noted, of *incessant* rain, which made it difficult for both barley and oats even to take root, let alone mature and be effectively harvested. Consequently, their failure, too, if not in quite the proportions seen in wheat, is recorded in these wet years.[69] Barley in 1315, 1316, and 1317 had yields of 86.9 percent, 69.7 percent, and 80.2 percent of mean on the Winchester/Westminster estates. Oats, to more or less complete the picture for major grains in England, had yields of 80.9 percent, 66.8 percent, and 78.3 percent of mean during these three years.[70]

It may be silly, as Henry Osmaston has chided, to try to calculate the probability of such bad grain harvests; and precisely for trying to do so Osmaston belittles G. H. Dury, who asserts that one could not expect so bad a year as 1316, the worst year, more than once every eight centuries.[71] But the point of Dury's efforts is worth repeating. England never saw a similar subsistence catastrophe in cereals during the whole of the Middle Ages.

The same may be said of northern Europe in general. Consider, for example, Germanic-speaking regions in Scandinavia and elsewhere on the Continent. Research on Norwegian corn harvests has had to depend on evidence from the payment of tithes rendered in kind; and there is no smooth extrapolation from such data to yields. Nonetheless, Kåre Lunden has argued strongly that with manipulation they do provide us with a good approximation of the curve of Norwegian yields, which turn out to have decided secular parallels with the Winchester yields.[72] It is less easy to be sure about year-by-year parallels for Norway and England, but a wider variety of evidence from the region around Braunschweig in central Germany points to a positive annual correlation of Continental and English production. This evidence has been meticulously assembled by Hartmut Hoffmann from the sources related to the holdings of the cathedral chapter of Saint Blasius of Braunschweig. His investigation led him to conclude that even if one were to consider average harvests of the first half of the fourteenth century as normal (although in fact they were far below by thirteenth-century standards), "the catastrophic harvest of 1316 stands out."[73]

A recent study of northern French Benedictine priories argues also in favor of a significant reduction in grain yields in 1315–1317. As in the case of the Norwegian and German evidence the argument turns, not on recorded yields, but on collections of grain from those who owed payments in kind. In any year a reduction in such collections from a "normal" mean might have nothing to do with a decline in yields per se. But in the absence of raiding parties or a breakdown in government, a truly calamitous decline in collections has a greater likelihood of pointing to a harvest shortfall. The region in the near north of Paris was subject to neither raiding parties nor a significant breakdown in government in 1316 and 1317; yet the evidence from the priory of Saint-Arnoul in this region suggests a decline in collections of grain of about 50 percent.[74]

Grains (along with beans and peas) were not the only crops that failed. The vintage, too, was far below normal. Ordinarily, of course, one cannot extrapolate from the harvest to the vintage, for what counts in terms of yield of grapes, and quality of wine for that matter, is sometimes only a few weeks, not necessarily continuous, of precisely appropriate weather—rainy at some times, sunny at others.[75] And whereas high grain prices usually relate to declines in production, population being constant, high wine prices may mask steady or even increased production that is more than compensated for by increased demand because quality is higher than normal.[76] This, however, was not the case during the Great

Famine. The rains were too steady and too hard.[77] Moreover, particular kinds of downy mildews specific to grapes "rapidly reproduce" in very wet weather and spoil yields.[78]

As even non-French chroniclers had heard, the weather in France (by which authors mean the north of the country) in 1315 and again in 1316 had ruined the vintage with regard to quantity. "There was a great failure of wine in France," wrote one chronicler under the earlier year.[79] "There was no wine in the whole kingdom of France," wrote a different commentator in describing 1316.[80] Bretons complained that the vintages were late and the resulting wines harsh.[81]

Contemporary Frenchmen themselves lamented the vintages. The vines "did not reach their proper maturity" is a sentence repeated time and again by contemporary and near contemporary reporters under the year 1315.[82] That the times saw a "complete and otherwise unheard-of failure of wine not only in quantity, but also in quality" is another sentiment shared widely by these narrative sources.[83] Everywhere, the chroniclers insist, the vintage was a disaster in France and its environs.[84]

Careful scholarly work has borne out these assertions. Thus the vineyards of the abbey of Vaux de Cernay, southwest of Paris, which had holdings in Vernon and Mantes in Normandy, in Jouy in the Beauce, and in a dozen other places on the southern side of the Seine and in the Gâtinais, suffered three bad vintages in 1314, 1315, and 1316; abundance did not return until the 1320s.[85] In the environs of the Benedictine priory of Saint-Arnoul—where grain yields, as we surmised, declined by 50 percent in the early years of the famine—collections of wine from those who owed levies in kind appear to have suffered an 80 percent decline by 1317.[86] The Benedictine priory of Coincy in the same region north of Paris evidences a similar story of decline.[87] Presumably, as in the case of grain collections, when we discount other causal factors (which, in these cases, do not seem to apply), such precipitous declines resulted from disastrously low production of grapes.

In 1867 a German antiquarian named Friedrich Dochnal began to publish the fruit of his researches into the local records of Neustadt on the Hardt, a small Palatinate town where wine was produced. Although he wanted to write an annalistic history of the town, his principal interest was in recording for posterity all that could be known about the "Weinjahre"—good and bad. Since 1867 Neustadt may not have suffered as much as have many German towns from wars and other depredations, but still much has been lost; so Dochnal's *Chronik* is a precious source.[88] The litany of troubles he incorporated from his sources from 1316 to 1322, and indeed until 1327, agrees with that in the contemporary records we have looked at from other regions: bitter winters, deep snows, long periods of dampness, high prices, famine, claims of deserted villages, abandoned fields.[89] But his discoveries about the vintage are equally informative. The year 1316 produced "a trifling quantity of wine"; 1317, "very little wine." The next year saw a brief recovery in quantity and quality, but in 1319 the wine was bad ("sour," as he put it), and it was bad again in 1320 when the whole year was wet, and prices rose and would not go down. If 1321 (and probably 1322) saw improvement, 1323 was devastating; the winter was so bitter that rootstocks died. It does not seem to have been until 1325, 1326, and 1327 that there was again an uninterrupted series of abundant vintages, but Dochnal's researches convinced him that in quality they were bad or worse than bad. Only in 1328, some six years after the famine in general had abated, could he summarize his sources with the words "very much and exceptionally good wine."[90]

While crops were failing, signs of a parallel crisis among flocks and herds began to appear.[91] Contemporary and near contemporary sources describe a situation in which the terrible weather (1315–1318) ushered in or laid the foundation for fatal diseases—"murrains," from Latin *mori*, to die—of epizootic proportions.[92] Among draft animals the murrains affected bovines and among food animals, sheep and cows. But how important were these murrains? In many parts of rural northern Europe where animal husbandry was the principal enterprise, they were critical, and even in grain-farming areas the murrains could have wide implications. In the latter, for example, the ox, a castrated bull (not a separate species of bovine as in parts of eastern Europe and beyond), dominated as the plow beast. With oxen yoked in pairs and up to four pairs necessary to pull the heavy plows, the plow teams were sometimes made up by the contribution of individual animals owned by several families who plowed their strips together (that is, practiced co-aration). In areas of dairy farming, pastoral agriculture, and mixed husbandry, the ox was frequently displaced by the horse, which was stronger, or by another equine. This development was possible thanks to the diffusion of an improved, nonstrangulating, horse collar in the eleventh and twelfth centuries.

The balance between the use of the horse and that of the ox was, however, based on a complex series of calculations. Oxen either grazed or ate hay and straw, far cheaper than oats, the preferred provender of horses even if they also grazed. Oxen lick themselves a great deal and are subject to hairballs, but otherwise are liable to far fewer diseases and pathological conditions than are horses, which have a particular susceptibility to colic. Oxen could be stubborn, but they were usually steady under the hand of a good plowman and his boy with a goad. Horses—that is, mares and geldings used in plowing—could be extremely temperamental. Finally, an old ox, no longer fit for the plow, was prized as food.[93] Turned out to pasture and fattened, it could fetch a price as high "as a healthy young one."[94] Broken-down nags, by and large, were not eaten by medieval rustics but could be slaughtered for glue (hooves), horsehair, hide, and dog and pig food.

Because of these considerations and others, oxen turned out to be more economical than horses for plowing on the demesnes of manors, where it was possible to discount hay and straw; and it was perceived so. Smaller farmers (peasant holders), however, particularly in regions of mixed husbandry, found the horse more economical, partly because they could not so readily discount hay and straw as a negligible expense (so the use of oats for feed was not fiscally irresponsible) and partly because the horse was a more versatile animal. Given the limited amount of plowing it had to do on very small peasant holdings and the speed with which it could do it, a horse was available and convenient for many other tasks that an ox could not accomplish so efficiently, especially hauling and personal travel.[95] Indeed, a good argument has been crafted that the substitution of horse hauling for other traditional forms of hauling helped spur economic growth over the twelfth and thirteenth centuries.[96] Finally, perceptive rustics who appreciated the economics of war knew that even a pretty miserable horse could fetch a fair price when armies on the march needed to replace wounded, exhausted, or dead animals. The point is that throughout northern Europe there were always to be found large numbers of both oxen and horses in the High Middle Ages. And this is critically important for the present discussion, since the particular diseases that characterized the murrains of the famine years had a differential impact on the two species.

The best work suggests that the initial and principal pestilential disease was rinderpest.[97] Another, less likely, suggestion is that it was anthrax.[98] However, pigs were not affected in the beginning; yet anthrax, characterized by malignant pustules of the skin, ordinarily numbers pigs among its victims.[99] Rinderpest, on the other hand, was a disease of ruminants (not swine or equines), and all the evidence indicates that ruminants made up the affected species. It was a terribly devastating disease, which ran its course in an infected animal over the period of a week or so. The animal initially manifests discharges around the nose, mouth, and eyes; these early symptoms (which sometimes are not conspicuous) are succeeded by astonishing stench, recurrent debilitating and explosive diarrhea (with consequent dehydration), and, perhaps most arresting, tenesmus—the painful struggle of the beast to defecate even when nothing remains to be voided. Death is followed by very rapid putrefaction.

It was hard to forgo salvaging the valuable hides of the dead animals before disposal, but fear of contamination was very great. A party to a dispute heard before an English court in the Hilary Term (January) 1316 grounds his defense in the expectation that judges and jurors would view his refusal to skin an infected animal as justifiable.[100] Burning, presumably, would be the preferred method of disposal of such carcasses. Burial, however, seems also to have been practiced where continuous rains made outdoor fires difficult to sustain. Sometimes infected animals were simply thrown into deep abandoned wells. England and Germany furnish examples of these methods.[101]

The decline in the ruminant population from the pestilence was compounded in the period 1315–1318 by two other problems. First, in many places the persistent dampness meant that even if it was possible to mow the meadows, it was difficult to cure (dry) the hay in the fields. On the one hand, to store uncured hay was to invite rotting and, worse, a buildup of heat and methane gas from the rotting hay, a buildup which by igniting any grain, straw, or hay that did manage to dry out would bring about the conflagration of wooden barns. (Even in normal periods grain in storage had to be turned as many as four times per year to prevent rotting and its consequences.)[102] On the other hand, there were no facilities adequate to cure the hay artificially in sufficient quantities. There is no doubt that in areas where overcast and foggy conditions were normally endemic, kilns, drying ovens, and curing houses had long been in use.[103] But under the circumstances of the famine these were used for damp or under-ripened grain rather than for animal fodder, as English, French, German, and Irish evidence indicates.[104]

The second problem compounding the loss of sheep and cattle from the pestilence was the terrible winter cold that endured for so long especially in 1317/1318. Stores of fodder were already low because of natural conditions; they were possibly artificially low because of severe economies.[105] When these ran out, animal food in general became unavailable. Consequently, strong animals that might otherwise have survived the pestilence grew weak from malnutrition or were put to pasture in warm spells that did not last. They froze on moors and heaths. "Evil was added to evil."[106]

If to some extent all herds, even nonruminants, suffered, sheep suffered uncommonly from this weather.[107] The perpetual rains encouraged liver-fluke, an infestation of parasitic worms, which has been shown to be "particularly closely related to the amount of rainfall between May and October." The cold, more especially the terrible cold of the winter of 1317/1318, had a devastating impact on mortality, as we might expect since good modern observations have shown that "temperatures during the first three months of the year are closely related to mortality in sheep flocks." Lambing is always difficult, but "prolonged snow and frosts in particular can cause mortality to soar and lambing success to fall away."[108]

In northern France one chronicler, appalled at the description of the rain and the harvest shortfalls that he had read and copied from one of his predecessors, was able to add that the great dying of the beasts was another of the calamities that beset his people.[109] In the north of England, the flocks of the Austin canons of Bolton Priory in 1316/1317 fell from over 3,000 animals to 913.[110] On manors in Breckland, East Anglia, by the early 1320s sheep flocks had declined as much as 25 percent or 50 percent owing to the unexpected damp and cold and also to the effects immediately thereafter of droughts and additional murrains.[111] Elsewhere sheep and goat flocks fell as much as 70 percent.[112] There was a "great pestilence of oxen and cattle," as the chroniclers sum up the crisis, in Germany, France, and England.[113] Temporarily, however, Ireland at least escaped.[114]

Later murrains that "endured a long time" (1319–1322) followed the wet-weather pestilences.[115] These were also basically cattle murrains and were as severe as the earlier scourges, or more so in some areas.[116] Rinderpest and whatever other diseases might have flourished with it from 1319 to 1322 caused another grievous decline in Bolton's herds: oxen declined from 139 to 53 and other cattle from 225 to 31.[117] Other figures accumulated by Kershaw show declines of herds from 54 head to 6, from 47 to 2, from 65 to 9, from 186 to 64, and from 80 or so to 27. Possibly not all of these deaths were from disease, but more than a fair number explicitly were. For example, in the herd reduced to 64 head from 186, at least 32 of the animals are explicitly recorded as having died from disease.[118] Cattle herds on some Breckland manors declined in similar proportions.[119] Recovery in the size of herds, however, was fairly quick in the middle and late 1320s, wherever stewards and peasant proprietors found the funds to invest in restocking.[120] Unfortunately, funds were not always available, and full recovery could be delayed ten or twenty years, or even longer.[121]

Near Ely, where animal mortality appears also to have been high, the fall in the number of draft animals and possibly the concomitant loss of animal fertilizer led to a reduction on one manor of from 12 percent to 17 percent of the arable under cultivation.[122] The manors of the great fief or honour of Tutbury in Derbyshire experienced a "severe shortage of stock" and a decline in arable (presumed from the decline in plow teams), but no effective compensation in pasture, because of the limited need of the depleted herds.[123] Ramsey Abbey manors in 1319 experienced catastrophic declines in the cattle herds: from 48 to 6, from 45 to 2, and so forth.[124] The size of sheep flocks also endured what has been termed a "considerable drop" on the manors.[125]

Evidence from Wales points also to a devastating attack of cattle murrain in these years.[126] And good evidence confirms the same for Ireland where the murrain, probably aggravated by anthrax in this instance, finally arrived in 1321, traveling from England or Wales.[127] There may have been severe localized outbreaks of cattle murrains in the thirteenth century but nothing so general or so ruinous as the epizootic described here.[128]

A last point. One of the most arresting consequences of the failure of the harvests and the depletion of flocks and herds was the disappearance in many manorial accounts (the examples come from England) of the entries known as *responsiones*, estimates of the coming year's yields of grain and other products, like milk. This important accounting technique, which made relatively long-term planning possible, disappeared from many manorial account books and rolls after the three melancholy years 1315–1317.[129] It had become presumptuous to predict a "response" to the laborious efforts of men and women to keep from starving.

PART II

THE ECONOMICS AND DEMOGRAPHY OF
THE FAMINE IN RURAL SOCIETY

3

PRICES AND WAGES

B Y THE EARLY fourteenth century prices and wages in the economy of northern Europe were genuinely responsive to supply and demand, despite the continuing ideological hegemony of the doctrine of the just price. One reason for the increasing importance of what might be called "market forces" over the course of the twelfth and thirteenth centuries was the development of the northern European economy into a far more integrated structure of exchange than had been characteristic earlier. The very existence of this structure implied that older, traditional notions of exchange were under stress. This was probably much more the case in the growing towns, where, for example, disputes about the right to charge interest were bitter, but it undoubtedly affected rural areas. For in the countryside, also, a much more sophisticated system of commercial exchange was emerging.[1]

Assessing the sophistication and level of integration of this system is not easy.[2] One set of attempts has been based on extrapolations from the transportation infrastructure. Based in part on references in charters to the travel of goods and people, efforts have been made to map harbors and coastal havens and the road, bridge, river, and canal systems of the Middle Ages in, among other regions, Britain, France, and Germany.[3] Measuring the topographical thickness and thinness of these systems over time allows scholars to identify regional patterns of trade and to chart the expansion or contraction of networks.

Robert-Henri Bautier has shown that there were systematic attempts to extend the length of navigable rivers in northern France in the thirteenth and early fourteenth centuries. The Seine, which was navigable for barges only to Nogent for most of the Middle Ages, seems to have been improved sufficiently to allow shipping to Troyes, an addition of well over fifty kilometers, during the first decade of the fourteenth century; the Durtain, a river of less significance in Champagne, was improved sufficiently to serve Provins effectively and thus further integrate the region during the same period.[4] In England, it has been argued, "few places [were] . . . more than 15 miles from the coast or a navigable river" in the High Middle Ages.[5] Although this conclusion has been challenged as an exaggeration, even the challenger allows that large parts of England, especially the populous eastern regions, enjoyed well-integrated water transport networks.[6]

As with river transport, so with bridges. Peter Goodfellow, in a study of Northamptonshire medieval bridges (terminal date 1500), finds that fully forty-five of the ninety or so bridges in that English county for which evidence has survived seem to have been in place before 1322. Although the data also reveal processes of deterioration and rebuilding (nothing was static), the lasting impression is of a well-bridged, therefore well-integrated, area.[7] The findings of a more general study of England demonstrate that many rivers were bridged every ten miles or so (largely obviating the traditional use of fords) and that the bridges were mostly of stone, well-constructed and wide enough for effective carriage.[8]

Of course, not every bridge was in constant use and not every navigable river was navigated at all times. Moreover, long stretches of coastline could be unfit for the collection or discharge of goods.[9] Consequently, it is good that evidence of infrastructure can be supplemented with voluminous information on tolls. This information, to cite the case of the Meuse River in the Low Countries as one illustration, points in the direction of widespread and intensive utilization of the waterways for transport of goods in the thirteenth and early fourteenth centuries—far in excess of that associated with earlier medieval commerce.[10]

Another common measure of economic integration draws on data documenting the proliferation of weekly or periodic markets.[11] In late Anglo-Saxon England, although there was a lingering "attachment to self-sufficiency," marketing seems to have been spurred by the impact of the Viking invasions, as the need to buy off or fight the invaders led to higher levels of administrative organization and economic cooperation among the indigenous peoples.[12] The configurations (spatial and temporal) of this Anglo-Saxon tradition of marketing partly laid the foundation for the geographical patterning of new markets in the twelfth century.[13] By the thirteenth century, however, these patterns were ruptured, if not entirely replaced, by a tremendous expansion of local markets (or, rather, grants of markets, since not all the markets that were planned succeeded).[14] According to one count "3,000 grants of markets were obtained from the Crown" in the thirteenth century, a fact that has been taken to be "a clear indication of the expansion of the rural economy."[15] The same author conjoins to this observation the fact that the period 1154–1250 witnessed the establishment of eighty-eight new (often seigneurial) towns in England, whose networks of exchanges of labor, goods, and money constituted central markets for rural areas even in the absence of formal confirmation.[16]

A study of markets in Essex reveals that of seventy-eight known markets in existence in the county before 1350, seventy-five were chartered or were in operation in 1322 or before. The siting of these markets, as we might well expect, was exquisitely coordinated with "main" roads and, to a lesser extent, coastal havens.[17] A mapping of chartered markets in Northamptonshire for the thirteenth century shows that if the catchment area for a market was approximately six and two-thirds miles, then perhaps as many as half the residents of the county had easy access to three different markets, and as many as 20 percent were conveniently situated to attend four.[18] The six-and-two-thirds-mile radius chosen in the Northamptonshire study was drawn from the great legal treatise conventionally attributed to Bracton. It intoned against too closely situated markets.[19] A wonderful court case from the midcentury shows that this theoretical reconstruction is by no means misleading: a farmer in Berkshire, in one breath, claimed that the raising of dikes in Sheford, presumably part of a reclamation effort, was a nuisance that prevented him from going from his home in Oakhanger to attend Lambourn market; their erection, he added in the next breath, also interfered with his traveling from home to Hungerford market. The court ordered the dikes cast down.[20]

What applied to markets also applied to fairs, the grand emporia to which merchants from much wider geographical circles traveled.[21] These, too, experienced a long spurt of new foundations in thirteenth-century England.[22] They had become so dense and so frequent by the time the economy slowed in the second half of the century that the English crown had to be stingier in its grants of new fairs.[23]

Ireland and Brittany experienced a similar, if more modest, expansion of markets. Research on Irish "towns" (a misnomer, in many cases, for villages writ large) has documented the existence of about 350 in the year 1300.[24] Only 25 of these could be classified as real urban centers. The others were hubs of rural marketing.[25] Although in a handful of cases these rural nodes of commerce went back to the pre-Norman or Viking period in Irish history, over 300 were Anglo-Norman foundations.[26] Their distribution was much more skewed than was the case in England. The heaviest concentration was in the southeast from the Shannon to St. George's Channel, although there was also a long string extending northward along the entire eastern seaboard by the year 1300.[27]

Apart from a handful of large coastal settlements, Brittany, before the eleventh century, had only ten "towns." As in Ireland these were not towns as we would classify them: they were rural market centers. The eleventh and twelfth centuries saw a startling expansion in the number of these markets in pace with the spread of castles and abbeys into the countryside. Fifty-seven new market towns seem to have been established in these years. Unlike the English pattern and, to some extent, the Irish, foundation of new centers fell off considerably in the thirteenth century, but most of the settlements already established by 1225 continued at least to function during the thirteenth century.[28] Brittany never became as well integrated economically as England or western Ireland in the Middle

Ages, but its economy by 1300 was not constituted from production and consumption in a handful of isolated self-sustaining fishing and farming hamlets.

The expansion of markets and rural fairs was typical of other parts of northern France as well,[29] although we know far less about the fairs than might be hoped.[30] In any case, Lucien Musset has shown that already by the end of the twelfth century "une population fondamentalement rurale" in Normandy "pouvait participer au mouvement général des échanges," thanks to the proliferation of markets.[31] The creation of these markets continued apace in the thirteenth century, before what seems to have been a complete cessation in the fourteenth.[32] The markets of Normandy—as well as of the county of Maine, as Robert Latouche demonstrated—were in part associated with the growth of *bourgs*, which despite the name were often rural rather than urban centers.[33] The growth curve of rural *bourgs* and markets is very similar.[34]

Another measure of the level of integration in the economy of northern France has sometimes been used, namely, the multiplication of rural communes. These communes, which proliferated in numbers in the twelfth and thirteenth centuries, were communities of relative self-government in the French countryside, much like the urban communes in the north. Their political purpose, like that of the towns, is obvious and needs no comment, but this should not distract us from their economic function. The rural communes, again like their urban counterparts, enjoyed charters of franchise that established the legal environment for economic exchange with restricted seigneurial privileges.[35]

There were, of course, isolated *pays* even within otherwise well-integrated regions of northern France, just as there were rugged regions elsewhere that were poorly served in terms of access to good thoroughfares and markets in the thirteenth century. Marshy regions were particularly isolated or only imperfectly integrated. Attempts at drainage and clearance were heroic but unequally successful because of technological limitations, and sometimes because of fierce resistance from the loners and rugged individualists who inhabited and exploited the wetlands.[36] The marshy country north of Saint-Omer is a case in point. Even though within the Saint-Omer region (and the whole Scheldt basin) there were extensive and intimate connections among castle towns, market towns, and villages, this particular *marais* down to the modern period remained cut off and economically self-sufficient, and its inhabitants remained endogamous.[37] The products of its husbandry—particularly fish and waterfowl—were less affected by the weather of 1315–1322 than was the produce of areas of grain husbandry and livestock raising.[38] Therefore, there was no *necessity* for the inhabitants to strengthen their economic connections with people living in villages beyond the great marsh. Nevertheless, in the absence of necessity, there were *incentives* for contact. Fishermen, for example, could benefit from the high prices at Saint-Omer in these years. Victims of the high prices might retaliate by poaching on the edge of the *marais*.

The German case—the expansion of markets in the west and their spread, and the spread of the infrastructure to support them efficiently in the east on the Slavic frontier—can serve to round off the discussion. In the western part of the country the process paralleled the expansion of seigneurial market towns (or villages) in England; there was probably a tenfold increase to perhaps as many as four thousand markets by 1300.[39] This implantation of tiny towns (*Kleinstädte*) in various regions resulted from an expanding economy and consolidation of economic and political lordship in the countryside.[40] In one tiny district near the Ruhr, Halver-Schalksmühle, only about seventy-five square kilometers, thirty-three new settlements were probably established between 1050 and 1200, and as many as twenty-four more in the thirteenth century. (The growth continued vigorously into the fourteenth century as well.)[41] Along with the establishment of the settlements went a dense network of roads.[42] In Westphalia thirty new "towns" (mostly rather small rural market towns) were certainly founded from 1180 to 1240, thirty-one more from 1240 to 1290, and thirty others (a great many of which were very tiny *Minderstädte*) from 1290 to 1322. These numbers might rise a little if new information comes to light on some doubtful cases; also they do not include an extremely small handful of failed foundations.[43] The impression of a densely settled rural landscape is inescapable.[44]

Further east on the ever changing frontiers German developments had some similarities with those in Ireland. In both cases, alien, sometimes conquering, minorities were transforming preexisting, often unsophisticated economic arrangements. The fundamental change was the diffusion of open-field agriculture[45] (whose social significance will be treated in subsequent chapters).[46] But also important and directly relevant to the discussion here was the transformation of indigenous road networks in the twelfth and thirteenth centuries. In western Poland, for example, the veritable obliteration of old networks took place in a process that began with the German *Drang nach Osten*.[47] As to markets the case is similar. The Slavic markets of the early Middle Ages in what became the duchy of Mecklenburg illustrate the point. They were infrequent and at substantial distances from one another. With Germanization came the proliferation of rural markets and market towns (as in Ireland, Brittany, and Normandy, despite the word, these tended to be very small settlements).[48] Also as with the English in Ireland, the Germans' creation of markets and their building of bridges tended to take place in fits and starts owing to political and military instability, not limited to that between Germans and Slavs but including internecine strife within Slavic lordships and among German lords themselves.[49]

Ultimately, though with modest exceptions even in older settled regions (such as parts of eastern Franconia),[50] Germans and western Slavs in general and in the Elbraum and Oderraum in particular managed to create a well-integrated economic system. The road network in Lauenburg (the once Slav-dominated territory bounded by the duchies of Holstein, Mecklenburg, and Braunschweig) grew dense and convenient for access to the three great towns of Lübeck, Lüneburg, and Hamburg.[51] In Brandenburg (particularly the districts around what became Berlin) over two hundred new settlements seem to have been assarted from woodland and moraine in the period concerning us; and the region's population rose from at most 10,000 in 1140 to 35,000–40,000 in 1240.[52] By the end of the century, this region was lightly embedded in international trade networks that, for instance, saw rye from the Berlin region available in Hamburg and for sale in Flanders.[53]

Suggestive as all this evidence is, it should nevertheless be treated with caution. As R. H. Britnell reminds us, the growing local integration does not mean that intermarket trade was being practiced in high volume; and not even all of the rural markets were fully monetized. Moreover, the expansion of rural fairs and the success of Brandenburg rye in the Low Countries notwithstanding, there was not much spin-off in developing interregional, let alone international, distribution networks. Insofar as these emerged, they usually tied together coastal towns. (The principal thirteenth-century exception was the network of fairs in inland Champagne, but there we are talking in part about urban, not rural, fairs.) Foreign merchants and foreign goods rarely visited rural fairs and almost never rural markets, except near large coastal towns.[54] A good many of the inconsistencies that may be identified in the responsiveness of prices and wages in rural society to the subsistence crisis from 1315 onward go back to the limitations and "immaturity" of the structures of exchange.

Let us now turn to details, beginning with prices, a subject about which far more is known than is known about wages. By and large, even correcting for what was a general rise in prices in the early fourteenth century,[55] the ascent that occurred during the Great Famine all over northern Europe is astonishing. In France this increase occurred at a time when, for two reasons, deflation might otherwise have been expected. First, the kingdom was suffering the effects of the crown's recent reversal of a policy by which the coinage had been overvalued; and, second, there was a net outflow of "silver and billon coinage" for the years 1312 to 1318 that was "said literally to have emptied the kingdom."[56] So the increase in prices is all the more remarkable.

The fundamental cause of the increase, of course, was the constriction of the harvests coupled with low disposable reserves. Schmitz is undoubtedly correct that storage was not a factor in stabilizing prices before 1200 and probably not much of a factor before 1300.[57] Yet storage of any harvest for gradual consumption in the period before the next harvest, and of at least part of the seed corn (though most planting, to be sure, was done with recently harvested corn), meant that reserves in granaries were massive.[58] Hence my use of the word *disposable*.[59] Perceptions, of course, of what was disposable varied according to circumstances and traditional expectations of local consumption.[60]

Other factors accentuated the rise in prices at specific times, such as the demand produced by war.[61] The requisitioning of food for armies elevated prices paid for whatever was still available to the sedentary rural (and urban) population.[62] In the event, few items were at all resistant to the rise in prices.[63]

Recent work on markets and harvest or grain distribution failures emphasizes the importance of these gross rises in prices as a positive factor in spreading the impact of the disasters. What high prices do is to force consumption among the vast majority of people downward to more modest levels and keep it there ("stabilize" it), so that available resources are more slowly depleted. High prices soon after a harvest failure or a distribution failure are also an economic good in that they provide consumers with an incentive to save, the counterpart of a reduction of consumption in the household. From this point of view, even hoarding or speculation—holding back grain to force prices higher—is an economic good; official intervention to discourage it permits "irrationally" rapid depletion of scarce resources.[64]

Three factors, however, complicate this picture. First, few families forced to reduce consumption can have softened their anger at high prices because of the alleged benefits arising from slowing down the depletion of resources; long-term economic trends are not appreciated under intensive short-term pressures.[65] Second, stabilization of consumption at "more modest" levels implies that normal consumption is capable of considerable reduction without biological harm. But if the population is already subsisting at or near the threshold of biological success, "the case in favor of stabilization . . . break[s] down."[66] It has been argued by most scholars that because of the demographic trends of the previous two centuries the northern European peasantry was fairly near that threshold in 1314, an issue to which we shall have to return.[67]

Third, and equally important, it is not merely that grain prices, if allowed to, rise in a general harvest failure; prices of consumables are almost always volatile—at least this was the case in the Middle Ages.[68] The political economy of milling, for instance, was such that in places where millers received a portion of the grain as remuneration for their work, it might be in their interest and power to manipulate supplies, forcing prices up.[69] Yet other factors could abruptly reverse or weaken the climb in prices. Governments try to cap prices (and may do so effectively for food requisitioned for armies) or force rollbacks; ships arrive from abroad with grain; a second crop comes in with middling yields; rumors particularly can cause prices to plummet.[70] Glut buying then ensues. Individual attempts to keep consumption down will persist during these temporary price slumps as a hedge against the need to purchase during price heights. Such attempts, if successful, might well perpetuate levels of undernourishment that can produce long-term negative biological consequences.[71] Presumably, dramatically visible consequences of low consumption, like swelling of the belly (hunger edema), would induce families to increase their daily allotments during price slumps, but only to the degree that these gross symptoms of hunger were alleviated. Less obvious conditions could persist under even this moderately improved regime of consumption.[72]

It should be evident by now that the price levels of staples, primarily cereals, were critical, not only to the overall functioning of the economy, but also and in much more subtle ways than we might at first have supposed to the health or apparent health of the population. Let us begin by focusing on France: by and large cereal (or bread) prices rose dramatically beginning in 1315, according to the chroniclers.[73] In 1316 the chroniclers also remark the "dearness of grain" in the kingdom.[74] In France, however, despite the Herculean efforts of Avenel, the price tables in his massive compendium give insufficient information for much precision on this matter during the famine.[75] A common guess is that the general rise in prices in the first three years of the famine may have been as much as 800 percent in the kingdom.[76]

We noted, however, that volatility of prices, not just price rises, had to be considered in any evaluation of conduct during the famine. It is extraordinary that the volatility and the behavior predicted above in response to it are documented by a selection of French chroniclers under the year 1318, that is, after the three years of extremely high prices just remarked. Prices also started out extremely high that year and in some places continued high throughout the year.[77] But several chroniclers, including the one just cited, noted a wild plummeting in prices, in many districts of 70 percent, when the rumor spread that the harvests were going to be better. (It must have been a rumor, for these chroniclers insist that the decline occurred before the harvest was in.) They attributed the decline to God's intervention—to a latter-day multiplication of the loaves—because it took so little bread to satisfy the hungry people. What this means, of course, is that stomachs had shrunk, and that the relative abundance of bread made the most obvious signs of malnutrition vanish.[78] Several of the chroniclers who tell the tale add a rhymester's concoction, a little vernacular ditty that went about the country. A translation that captures the exuberant flavor of the original seems almost impossible, but the sentiment is simple: in 1318, before the vintage and the threshing, our champion, God, beat down the high prices everywhere.[79]

Outside of France the general trends were similar. In Flanders, the Low Countries, and the entire lower Rhine region in 1315 and 1316 contemporary chroniclers alert us to the significant rise in prices: "there began a dearness of wheat . . . [and] from day to day the price increased."[80] The level of inflation was unheard-of.[81] Wheat, rye, and barley soared in unit price in Gelderland.[82]

In the late Middle Ages and deep into the early modern period Germans living as far apart as Bavaria and the Cracow region in modern Poland kept alive the memory of the high prices for grain that affected the empire beginning in 1315.[83] Compiling florilegia of their predecessors' accounts—many of which are no longer available—other chroniclers, like Heinrich Wendt who knew the Braunschweig sources thoroughly, noted vividly the extraordinary persistence of the inflation.[84] Extremely fragmentary data from even further east, the Rostock region, suggest that because of the harvest shortfalls of 1315, prices of grains (the example is rye) could not return to "normal" after the cessation in 1314 of the local wars that had been driving them up for three years.[85]

In England chroniclers also remark the price rise. For example, the Stoneleigh chronicler of the late fourteenth century, working from earlier reports, concluded that a quarter of grain had risen to a phenomenal price in 1316.[86] Fortunately, for England, too, details can be given to amplify the chroniclers' expressions. In this regard, the early accumulation of (mainly urban) price data by Thorold Rogers is still valuable.[87] Some additional, reasonably solid price data from estate *fiscalia* have also fairly recently been published, though skeptics about their reliability exist.[88] Much comes from the Winchester estates. Taken together the data appear to show that the years 1310–1320 (in the whole period 1170–1347) experienced the absolute peak for grain prices in general. Broken down for individual grains, the pattern is identical. Wheat prices from 1160 to 1347 peaked in those years. The same was true of a much less widely grown grain, rye, in the period 1210–1347 for which prices are available. Price series for barley (1190–1347) and for oats (1170–1347) manifest the same peak. Even the price curve for peas (1190–1347) has its crest in the years 1310–1320.[89]

David Farmer's sophisticated study of the data from the Westminster estates (aggregated with that of the Winchester estates) also demonstrates that the price of cereals in the years 1315 and 1316 was the highest in the entire period between 1271 and 1410. Significant relief started in 1317 and was profound in 1318, though with some reversals in the droughts thereafter.[90] Bruce Campbell's study of Coltishall in Norfolk finds barley dear in 1314–1317 (1316 grain prices being on the average two and one-half times mean levels), relatively cheap in 1318, and extremely expensive again in 1321–1322. These price fluctuations can be correlated neatly with independent evidence of the quality of the local barley harvests: 1314 saw what Campbell describes as a "partial" harvest; 1315 and 1316 experienced a "total failure"; 1317 continued to be "deficient." The rapid fall of prices in 1318 and the return to moderate price levels owing to better harvests were temporary phenomena, for 1321 and 1322 also saw crop failures.[91]

It is appropriate that we have been brought to the data on barley prices at the end of the previous paragraph. For, even broken down by grains, the price curves mask some differential rates of inflation, notably between wheat and barley (initial demand for barley being inferior, since it was "an aliment of substitution," in Hugues Neveux's words).[92] Tactics for dealing with the famine based on recognition of these price differentials, as well as of differential yields, were fundamentally important and will be occupying our attention when we discuss the cost-of-living crisis in the next two chapters.

If we turn our attention now from grain to other products, we will find similar patterns. For wine, it is usually difficult to coordinate production and prices with the general indications of weather given in medieval sources. Moreover, commercial activity has a much more stabilizing effect on wine prices than on grain prices since wine ships well and stores well (though vintages were not intended as they now are to be reserved over several years or decades).[93] All this being said, the Great Famine—which, as we saw in the last chapter, was characterized by catastrophes in grape production and wine quality—provoked a steep rise in prices commented on by the chroniclers.[94] Alain George (following Guy Fourquin on production in the Paris basin) remarks a peak in prices that was 300 percent above the lowest famine price.[95] But note that the comparison here is not with an abstracted average price. George's point is that a steep rise in prices could be followed by a similarly steep decline. As with grain there was significant volatility ("en dents de scie") in prices.[96]

Production of salt also suffered a shortfall during the early years of the famine.[97] Even in high summer in the north, the sun alone was usually insufficient, between high tides, to bring about full evaporation of salt pans, the shallow fire-hardened sand-and-clay depressions that caught the receding sea. Any evaporation that would ordinarily have occurred was, of course, limited in 1315 and 1316 by the exceptionally overcast and rainy weather. The ancient technique of stoking fires along the sides of the salt pan to quicken evaporation was fuel intensive in the best of times; in the drenching weather of 1315 and 1316 it was inefficient if not entirely ineffective.[98] Using shallow metal pans to boil brine collected from the sea was another, and perhaps more common, way to produce salt in the north. Whether employing peat or wood, this too was fuel intensive.[99]

Nevertheless, these sources of salt, along with some salt wells and springs relatively near the coast, were the main sources for much of north-western Europe. In the thirteenth century this salt was widely traded by locals along inland saltways from the coast and, in a pattern somewhat similar to that for grain, by Hanse merchants along the Baltic and the Continental shores of the North Sea.[100] Production costs were relatively low for panning, but shipping over long distances raised net costs signifi-cantly, at least relatively speaking. The product itself, cheap as it was at point of origin, was not very attractive; a good refining process, using the blood of healthy oxen, was not yet in use.[101]

What were the options? One was the exploitation of inland brine springs or wells. The latter required heavy inputs of labor supplemented by lead weights for lifting, and the water, once brought up, had to be transferred to cookhouses.[102] These might be at a considerable distance from the source, necessitating, as in Lorraine, the construction of wooden or earthen channels to carry the brine to the various cookhouses, each with (usually) one large pan measuring about seven meters by five me-ters.[103] Huge amounts of firewood were consumed in boiling away the water.[104] In Lorraine, again, so much fuel was being consumed by the mid–thirteenth century that the future resources of its woodlands were in doubt.[105] Salt produced in this way avoided price volatility because more and more sites came into production in the thirteenth century.[106]

Although the high inputs of labor in exploiting brine springs and wells made production seasonal, that is, calibrated it to those periods when labor could be spared from other tasks,[107] these sources of salt along with inland (rock) salt deposits with a purer product were more than merely local alternatives.[108] The bad weather of 1315 and 1316 complicated trade by turning roads into quagmires and bringing waterways to flood levels. Still, the disruption of inland production and transportation was probably far less severe than that on the northern coasts in 1315 and 1316. Thus, from what I have been able to determine, the myriad saltworks in Lorraine and in southern Germany and Austria experienced no precipitous production shortfalls in this period.[109]

In those regions supplied by the northern coastal salt industry, how-ever, times were hard. In Flanders the rise in the price of salt was already steep in 1315.[110] Similarly, from 1315 through 1317 the wet, leaden-skyed summers produced high prices for salt in France and England.[111] The number of chroniclers who noticed this phenomenon is startling.[112]

A discourse usually preoccupied with the deeds of kings, prelates, and warriors could not ignore the prohibitive price of such a commonplace necessity as salt, for as the authors of the *Agrarian History of England and Wales* point out, "this sharp rise in the cost of a normally cheap commodity" had wide implications. It "would have increased the cost of salting meat for winter" or even forced peasants and lords to reduce the amount of meat and fish kept aside for winter consumption—a fundamental shortfall if conditions did not otherwise improve. Moreover, the high price of salt, a necessary ingredient in dairying, would increase "the cost of making butter and cheese, marginally reducing still further the profitability of demesne farming."[113] Some regional economies were less dependent on salt than were others (rural Scandinavia is a case in point), but even in these regions it was a very important commodity.[114] Elsewhere it was an absolute necessity.

Given the implications of the price level of salt, it is of some interest to determine precisely how sharp the rise was. In the period 1220–1347 such data as have been accumulated on salt prices show that the peak years for the price in England were, as we might expect, 1310–1320. Indeed, the average price for that period was more than double that of the decade before.[115] Although a few prices are recorded in chronicle reports from other regions, there are, to my knowledge, as yet no comprehensive figures on the price rises for salt attested in narrative sources in France and northern Germany.

Before we turn to the question of meat and related prices, which also turn out to have been extremely sensitive to the deleterious weather, it should be admitted that not all prices were quite so responsive. Resistant to the generalized push toward *prohibitively* high price levels was wax, for example.[116] Essential for good-quality candles, for medicine (where it formed the base for most emollients and many emetics and purgatives), and for the sealing of documents and containers, wax was a very important product. Since bees continued to pollinate fruit trees, weeds, and flowers in even the briefest intervals of dry daytime weather, bee skeps continued to be exploited as a form of domestic husbandry by women. Wax and honey production, however, almost certainly declined, since as beekeepers are aware, bad "weather and moisture affect the nectar flow and colony growth" unfavorably.[117] Away from the hearth, and also probably with somewhat less success than in good weather, men exploited the hives of wild bees.[118] The modest declines in production meant that the products of beecraft, like wax, increased in price; and this increase was mirrored by increases for other items for which rainy weather hindered natural or man-made production: fruit, cider, and unfinished iron and steel (work at the forges being compromised by bad weather). Even so, the recorded increases were not so steep as those for grain, wine, salt, and, as we shall now see, animals (mammals) and animal products.[119]

The animals we are talking about include both draft animals (horses and other equines and oxen) and food animals (oxen and cows, sheep, goats, swine, as well as fowl, rabbits, and fish). It was remarked in chapter 2 that the diversity of draft animals paid great dividends during the early part of the famine. More specifically, although murrains were widespread, horses were not affected. While horses on the Bolton manors in northern England may well have declined in numbers by 40 percent during the early famine years, it is reasonably clear that the decline was from sales and cold, not from epizootic disease. And it is certain that their numbers held steady on Bolton's manors during the early twenties.[120] Presumably, the decreases in arable documentable from many estates would have been even more severe if there had not been the diversity of plow animals that there was.[121]

Contemporaries were obviously aware that horses were dying at slower rates than were ruminants, but they *were* dying (from other common diseases and from cold). Contemporaries would have been suspicious, therefore, when symptoms in an equine death overlapped with those of rinderpest, the chief killer: how else can we explain the dramatic elevation of horseshoe and horseshoe nail prices, except that, rather than retrieve them, people discarded the shoes and nails with animals presumed to be dead from the pestilence.[122] A decline in production at the forges, the alternative explanation, would have to have been extraordinary to stimulate such a rise in prices. But, then again, perhaps the decline was extraordinary in these nearly unimaginable years.[123]

Pigs were not affected in the least, either by the weather of the famine years or by the murrains.[124] Nearly all peasants had pigs.[125] They kept a few in sties near their houses, but they marked the others and let them loose in woods where they turned almost feral, like the lean, no-nonsense razorbacks that prowl the gloomy forests of the southern United States. The pigs ate acorns, beechmast, fungi, slugs, grubs, worms, carcasses of other animals, including other pigs—anything; yet with their small stomachs, they could not overeat. Amazingly resistant to disease—except skin lesions, which they protected against by mud baths—they provided an enormous array of products for the peasant household: tallow for cheap candles and soap, bristles, leather, food. And their bones were so soft that the stripped carcasses, bones included, could be boiled down into mush and served as slop to domestic pigs or, in a pinch, to humans.[126]

Every year in late fall or early winter swineherds did the dangerous work of gathering the half-wild woodland pigs (notorious for biting or eating children).[127] They then distributed the animals to their peasant or lordly proprietors, the unmarked younger animals being apportioned according to the number of marked pigs that had been admitted to the woods at the earlier "agistment" or reckoning. A number of animals were almost always then slaughtered, the others being returned (marked when necessary) to the woods. Or sometimes the swineherds drove huge herds to market. (The vast Burgundian herds were a byword.)[128] In normal times, the rate of slaughter or sale was calibrated to the traditional needs of the community and the market. There was a good deal of flexibility, since a few boars and two dozen sows could reconstitute a large herd very quickly. In difficult times, peasants and lords pushed this flexibility to the limit. The swine herd on Bolton manors, for example, declined in the first year of the famine by about 95 percent (to one boar and six sows) because the labor force of Bolton Priory tried to make up for the absence of bread, lamb, and beef in its diet by a gigantic increase in pork.[129]

This near annihilation of the swine herds was undoubtedly paralleled by the slaughter of fowl and rabbits as the subsistence crisis deepened. As with swine there was some play in the numbers of barnyard fowl that could be slaughtered. Geese, a monogamous species that was important in many rural economies, especially the English Fenland where gozzerds tended huge flocks, were slower to multiply than chickens.[130] In the case of the latter, however, a cock and a bevy of broody hens could rapidly bring numbers back to normal. There was some danger in reducing the village flock to a single rooster and a few hens, but it was a danger certainly worth the risk by 1316. Moreover, barnyard fowl, which in good times might be fed grain or peas, did not require such expensive food. They could scratch in the yard or in barns and henhouses for insects, seeds, and small plants; and geese, who could hold their own in the wild, might be pastured in woodlands and marshes.[131] All these birds got scrawny and laid fewer eggs, but they survived without very much investment of scarce resources. Even when they died, their feathers had a broad variety of uses.[132]

Pigeons, which were widely kept in northern Europe, also offered a valuable and very substantial food source. Archaeological evidence from Burgundy suggests that ordinary farmhouses almost routinely had dovecotes, and that seigneurial dovecotes of the thirteenth and fourteenth centuries sometimes had cells for up to 4,500 birds.[133] Again, as in the case of chickens, it was possible to cut feed substantially for these birds in scarce times. The birds would then feed on their own, but their nesting or homing instinct would bring them back to the cote. They would not have been the fat, succulent birds of good times. The death rate from bitter cold might have been elevated as well, and rates of reproduction would undoubtedly have declined. But the birds would still have survived in great numbers, and even scrawny pigeons made (and make) for tasty and nutritious eating either roasted or boiled.

There was far less flexibility or nutritional significance for rural society with regard to rabbits (coneys). We are wont to think of rabbits as ubiquitous. This was not the case in northern Europe until the early modern period, and in England not until the eighteenth century when winter forage crops and the extermination of predators (the same developments that made the introduction of pheasants feasible) allowed their population to explode.[134] It is true that a growing number of lords kept rabbit warrens.[135] These may originally have been quite large reserves on the scale of forests, at least in northern France, but it was soon discovered that it made more sense to confine rabbits in small, parklike, carefully enclosed, guardable warrens where predators and poachers did not menace. The rabbits could have escaped from these warrens, but lords introduced gravelly mounds that the animals could burrow into easily; and the rabbits adopted these as permanent homes. The presence of the mounds also made hunting very easy. A woman, one miniature suggests, could go out with a little dog or ferret on one side of the mound. The carnivore would scare the rabbit, who would escape from a different hole on the other side into a trap or cage held by a second woman.[136]

In the thirteenth and fourteenth centuries, if peasants kept rabbits, they kept them in hutches near home and fed them green plants. Prolific though they were in their natural habitat in the south of Europe—where they bore their hairless, vulnerable young in underground nests (an environment that lords tried to duplicate in building the mounds described above)—they bred poorly in the barely sheltered hutches fabricated by peasants. They were still valuable. They might make a tasty dish on festive occasions. And their fur could be used for ornamentation: outerwear "trimmed in rabbit fur" ("furratum de cuniculis") shows up in the records.[137] Nonetheless, even many thousands of rabbits, unlike the millions of swine, barnyard fowl, and pigeons, could not go very far in making up the shortfall in food production or distribution (owing to the rise in prices) during the famine. It may be significant that not one of the nine surviving English medieval household "diet" accounts known to Woolgar for the period before the famine makes reference to coneys.[138] To be sure, the accounts are fragmentary, but many are extremely detailed and informative. If coneys had already been important, this absence would be incredible.

Prices of all these animals eventually went up, both because of scarcities due to weather and murrain (oxen, cows, and sheep) and because of demand to make up these scarcities through surrogates (horses for oxen; swine and fowl for cows and sheep). However, even though the peak years for animal prices in the High Middle Ages were 1310–1320, individual prices did not go up all at once or necessarily at the same rate.[139]

Indeed, while prices for pigs and horses peaked early, prices for oxen, cows, and sheep, and for hides, fell for a time in England and very likely on the Continent, presumably because people were fearful of purchasing a diseased animal or the hide of one. Once the murrains were clearly over, prices began to rise "steeply . . . as manors competed for stock to make good their losses in the murrains."[140]

From the start, the poor were cut off from making up their loss of livestock by buying horses, which were too expensive, though they might risk buying a weakly ox, hoping against hope that it was not infected. Once the murrains seemed to pass their peak and prices of oxen rose, the impecunious had to turn to "stotts and affers" (or stots and avers, OED)—weaker, sometimes wind-broken, draft horses. We shall have to return to this point when we discuss the cost-of-living crisis in the next chapters. For now, it is important to record that the increased demand for stotts and affers stimulated a rise in prices for these animals, at least until the supply of oxen went up and prices for robust beasts came down again.[141]

From late 1315 on, steep rises occurred in the prices of animal products, like cheese and butter, grease and fat, and eggs.[142] No amount of substitution could do more than mitigate the price rises that were provoked by the enormous natural losses of productive animals. And some substitutions, like the overslaughter of fowl, created price rises, in this case the one alluded to above for eggs. We have already seen that estimated future yields, *responsiones*, for produce including milk disappear in several cases from stewards' account books, presumably because the yields of healthy milch cows were down from inadequate fodder and because many other animals had simply succumbed. Perhaps the change originally came about because unfulfilled *responsiones* reflected poorly on the stewards charged with administration of estates.[143] Soon their refusal to predict bespoke deeper uncertainties about the future.

The prices of butter and cheese were stimulated not only by the low production rates that the women and girls who ran the dairies had to endure.[144] It was aggravated, as noted earlier, by the increase in the cost of salt that was vital to the dairying process: salt was necessary in the extraction of liquid from cheese—pressing alone could not accomplish this—and as a preservative for cheese and butter.[145] As yet, the only good figures I have been able to find on all these animal products, including butter and cheese, come from England: they reveal that in the whole of the period 1190 to 1347 the peak years for the prices of animal products were 1310–1320, with 1320–1330 close behind. The curve more or less followed the curve of grain prices.[146] Interestingly, there was a commensurate rise in prices for several types of farm implements, presumably because many of these were destroyed—burned or buried—for fear of contagion. Wooden milk pails are an item in point: those used to collect from animals later identified as sick, or bespattered during an unexpected explosive discharge of half-liquid feces from a heifer not recognized as diseased until that moment. Prices for new milk pails rose.[147]

One of the most important animal products, wool, remains to be discussed. (Abundant evidence—illuminations, archaeology, husbandry manuals—on medieval sheep and wool types provides the context for exploring price fluctuations.)[148] The Winchester estates data, so valuable for grain yields and prices, furnish considerable information on wool production as well. The mean weight of a fleece in the thirteenth century seems to have been about 1.35 lbs., with wethers (castrated adults), who had denser fleeces, producing far above the mean, ewes nearer to it, and hoggs (two-year-olds) somewhat below the mean. Cold weather encouraged a heavier fleece, but, as we know, because of the pernicious effect on lambing, it also put strain on the capacity of the flocks to survive.[149] So, as we might expect, the average weight of a fleece, so far as the Winchester data permit us to say, rose sharply and its quality was luxuriant for sheep that survived during the famine (although the harsh conditions that provoked the famine, especially the terrifyingly cold winter of 1317/1318, did far more than decimate the flocks). The mean weight of a fleece rose to 1.93 lbs. in 1317. The estate data of several other manors that have now been studied confirm the pattern: maximum average per fleece yields were consistently reached in the years 1317–1319.[150]

Nonetheless, these increases in average yield per sheep did not offset the net decrease in production from depletion of the flocks. Wool prices, therefore, like many other prices, peaked in many areas of England around 1320. Indeed, in the entire period 1200 to 1347 the summit for wool prices in the country was the years 1320–1330.[151] It remains to be seen whether the rise in prices compensated sellers sufficiently to enable them to avoid bankruptcy or even mild impoverishment.[152]

Wages—the costs of labor—were more stable in rural society than were other prices, principally because in the demographic glut that was the thirteenth century's legacy to the fourteenth agricultural laborers could be said to be underemployed. This reservoir of underemployed laborers, coupled with the withdrawal of some arable because of erosion, had the effect of mitigating wage increases.[153] Nevertheless, once human sickness and mortality temporarily took a sharp upward turn in 1316 in some rural areas,[154] wages did experience an unmistakable rise, but still a rather modest one.

How modest? "Customary wages," unless they were still being paid in kind, were by definition entirely unresponsive to the shrinking of the labor market.[155] Piecework or occasional labor was different, although our information on the matter is almost embarassingly thin. In general, "payments to harvest workers on piece-rates" went up 18 percent and "wages for threshing and winnowing" up 6 percent in England and Wales in the famine years.[156] And overall the sharpest peak, though not all that sharp, in agricultural wages since the beginning of the thirteenth century was around 1320, decline setting in thereafter until the midcentury eruption of the Black Death.[157]

What the relatively abundant evidence on prices and the little on wages points to at bottom is a gap between the rate of price inflation and the cost of labor in the rural society of northern Europe during the Great Famine. That gap probably pales in comparison with the gap in towns,[158] but it was still distressing. The question we must now address is how much that distress, coupled with other pressures and constraints in the rural economy, transformed the lives of lords and rustics in the period 1315–1322. To answer that question, we have to deal with the thorny issue of the cost of living in the High Middle Ages.

4

THE COST-OF-LIVING CRISIS: LORDS

DID LAY and ecclesiastical lords benefit economically from the subsistence crisis of 1315–1322? Their record, as we shall see, was a mixed one, intimately linked to the changing fortunes of the rustic population in general (chapter 5). Moreover, the power of lords and the impact of the famine on them differed regionally and according to "status." The power of an aristocrat like the duke of Burgundy was incomparably greater than that of a castellan. The seigneurial authority, including the judicial power of life and death or of minting coins, vested in many a French lord went far beyond anything most English lords of comparable rank possessed, even if the latter were often wealthier. Yet German lords' extraordinary claims to military command and governance in eastern Europe or similar claims of English marcher lords on the Welsh border made French nobles' right of "private war" and banal jurisdiction seem almost insignificant in comparison. Less certain is whether within individual regions the exercise of ecclesiastical lordship and landlordship differed substantially from that exercised by lay lords, when the size and nature of estates or jurisdictions were roughly similar.[1]

Whatever the variants of lordship, did lords already face a "general economic crisis" in the thirteenth century? There were factors that pointed up the potential for such a crisis in that most lords—lay and ecclesiastical—were partly dependent for their well-being on fixed rents in a time of steady inflation and yet were burdened by increased commitments to an expensive style of living. Moreover, older ecclesiastical orders, the Benedictines in particular, were often overextended in terms of their properties; at the same time, they were no longer attracting the kind of largesse or other support that had earlier gone to them.[2] Newer orders, like the mendicants and the Celestines, were their competitors.

Nevertheless, genuine financial pressures with regard to falling real rents and declining eleemosynary grants cannot be said to have produced a general economic crisis for lords, because most prelates (and their institutions), as well as knights and barons, had other sources of income. It goes without saying that many ecclesiastical lords could count on pilgrims' offerings, tithes (in kind), fines for moral offenses, and similar income as their special sources. But they shared with lay lords access to perhaps diminishing but still significant direct and indirect royal and, in the German case, imperial largesse—gifts of money, chattels, franchises, offices, and (for lay lords) heiresses. They benefited too from the inflation when they marketed the produce of their demesnes.[3]

In the last area lay lords may have compensated for the slightly more restricted range of their sources of income: they seem to have been somewhat more sensitive or encouraging to the proliferation of markets in the thirteenth century. An interesting study of markets in the English county of Essex has established that of the seventy-five markets that may well have been functioning in 1322, forty-seven were possessed (effectively, owned), at the moment they first appear in the documentary record, by lay lords; and the pattern of lay ownership was becoming more pronounced over time.[4] The sheer increase in the volume of commerce taking place in these markets encouraged seigneurs of all types to seek benefits from regalian authorities, especially concessions of tolls, which substantially augmented noble and ecclesiastical profits. The situation on the Continent in the Meuse basin, explicated by Fanchamps, typifies this.[5]

In particularly difficult times there were other expedients as well. Squeezing their unfree dependents beyond customary limits or, alternatively, selling freedom to those dependents when resistance to further exploitation was too great or the need for ready cash urgent was one method.[6] Confiscation or taxation (tallaging) of the wealth of Jews held under seigneurial, royal, or imperial authority was another.[7] Converting from demesne farming to leasing, or vice versa, was a third.[8] Specific local factors might heighten the attractiveness to lords of one or another of these and various other options. Only free-market "renegotiation of the contract[s]" or leases where tenants of the same lineage had been in place for generations was usually unfeasible in the moral economy of rural life.[9]

In essence the thirteenth century was distinguished by a willingness and capacity on the part of landed elites to indulge various experiments to deal with the problem of the exploitation of agricultural resources in relation to changing conditions.[10] The experimentation was predicated on the belief that the conditions intermittently requiring new tactics were but brief interruptions in a generally favorable situation. We may talk about more or less conservative lordship, with ecclesiastical lords perhaps being the more conservative in the thirteenth century,[11] but there was no collective retreat from confidence within the landed elites in the course of the century. When the real challenge began in 1315, it is hardly to be wondered at that lords of all stripes thought back to the expedients that they had employed to weather temporary difficulties or at least mitigate them in time past.

The Empire (including Flanders)

In the empire, as elsewhere, certain lords profited handsomely during the famine. For example, the demand for salt at the high price it was commanding during the famine was beneficial to a great many ecclesiastical seigneurs. Of course, in Germany as elsewhere the record may be skewed in favor of large monastic enterprises,[12] but it seems to be the case that one of the favored endowments that, to their eventual regret, lay barons made to religious houses in the twelfth and early thirteenth centuries (a time of low salt prices) was the grant of salt making from brine springs.[13] In the event, lay barons came to have a very restricted influence on salt production and marketing in many regions, though they controlled a great many tolls and therefore indirectly benefited from the volume of salt traded in periods of high production and demand.[14]

The situation among religious establishments was much more favorable. Forty-six percent of all Cistercian monasteries in Germany came to be involved in some aspect of salt manufacture and commerce in the thirteenth century.[15] And although the Cistercians were "incontestably the most dynamic" force in salt production, other orders, collegial churches, and even bourgeois played a significant role in some regions.[16]

As competition increased, so did concentration. The bishops of Metz, responding to the escalating demand for salt as the population grew, managed in the course of the thirteenth century to carve out a virtual monopoly of salt production in the Messin, a region that had once seen rights distributed among more than seventy religious houses.[17] The high prices in 1315–1317 were, thus, a windfall for the bishop and chapter, to the extent that they had not farmed out production to various rustics for flat annual rents.[18]

There were regional variations in the level of windfall profits. The production falloff was less severe, and prices were thus lower, in those parts of the German interior with rock salt deposits.[19] Especially in the north German region, however, several lords, like the nuns of Kloster Ebstorf near Lüneburg, were situated to make out particularly well from the high prices. In Kloster Ebstorf's case, a goodly selection of the nuns were well-off already thanks to their family connections with the merchant oligarchy of Lüneburg.[20] That oligarchy controlled a large part of salt production and, with Lübecker carriers, the salt trade.[21] Moreover, the list of north German monasteries and nunneries involved in and unquestionably benefiting from the salt trade in this time of uncommonly high prices was enormous: Kloster Scharnebeck in the same region is another instance.[22]

If this evidence points to likely financial successes, it is only fair to say

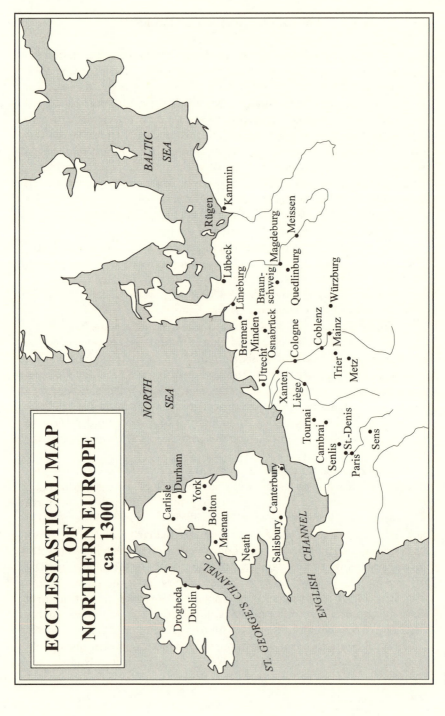

ECCLESIASTICAL MAP
OF
NORTHERN EUROPE
ca. 1300

BALTIC SEA

Kammin

Rügen

Lübeck

Meissen

Lüneburg

Bremen
Minden
Braun-schweig Magdeburg

Osnabrück Quedlinburg Würzburg

Utrecht
Cologne Coblenz Mainz

Trier
Metz

Xanten

Liège

Tournai
Cambrai St.-Denis
Senlis Sens
Paris

NORTH SEA

Carlisle Durham
York
Bolton
Maenan

Neath

Salisbury Canterbury

ENGLISH CHANNEL

ST. GEORGE'S CHANNEL

Drogheda
Dublin

Map 2

that they were the exception, not the rule, among lords. Much more common all through the empire were conditions that can only be characterized as deleterious. The difficult political situation, moreover, hampered lords' efforts to get the level of imperial support necessary to deal with local problems or the agrarian crisis in general. Not to mention local factions, the rival kings, Frederick III of Austria and Ludwig IV of Bavaria, and their noble supporters vied for power and largely ignored the pleas of badly stricken monasteries and regions. Insofar as the rivals distributed largesse, it was in strategically important districts whose political and financial support they were trying to assure; these might be but were not necessarily the areas hit hardest by the famine. Two Holy Ghost hospitals established by Ludwig IV in 1317 and 1319 in Amberg and Ingolstadt were a "loving" gesture to supporters and perhaps went some way to helping them cope with the sick.[23] How frequently such gestures occurred is an open question, but they were probably rare. The rivals' financing of their direct military efforts came first.

Many abbots and abbesses in the empire necessarily turned elsewhere, sometimes to rich local patrons, sometimes to the pope. The kindly Cistercian abbot Eylard of Aduard near Groningen who, we shall later see, was a devoted almsgiver to the poor and hungry during the famine[24] was also a friend to his less fortunate sister monastic institutions. One chronicler was particularly impressed that a Cistercian would take "under his care the poverty-stricken and desolate nunnery of Trimunt-bij-Marum, even though it was of the order of Saint Benedict"![25] In 1316 Kloster Reinbek, a house in the German-Danish borderlands, approached a previous lay donor and offered to "sell" him a village he had formerly possessed. The transaction promised a needed windfall for the inmates of the house. The sale went through on 19 November of that year. Graciously, the purchaser agreed to permit the abbey, if it were in a position to do so, to redeem the village for the same price after ten years.[26] (In fact, I have found no record that it was able to or did do so.) The nuns of Bernstein in the Oderraum were rescued by the bishop of Kammin after it became known in mid-1317 that "they could scarcely be sustained from their rents and income."[27]

Over and over again in 1316, 1317, and 1318, indeed down to 1322, monastic lords, like Kloster Ilsenburg in the region around Braunschweig, alienated rents and real property "because of the expensive times," retaining the chimerical hope of redeeming their holdings in the future.[28] The rural holdings of the cathedral chapter of Halberstadt seem to have been especially wasted by bad weather and local violence, with the result that it fell into grievous debt. Gifts from benefactors and sales made out of necessity helped but did not overcome the situation.[29]

Like Kloster Reinbek, the abbey of Paulinzelle in Thuringia also sold a village, Egelsdorf, to a wealthy local on 22 August 1316 to obtain ready cash; the buyer agreed that the abbey would be able to redeem the village at the purchase price within three years.[30] Evidence shows that the crisis continued. On 25 May 1317 the abbot of Paulinzelle, acting for the monastery, was forced to make another sale; then on 14 May 1319 he sold still another village, Bunsdorf. On these two occasions the purchasers were less amenable to offering redemption at cost, or at least they included no such clauses in the deeds.[31] The abbot and his monastery were not in a position to begin repurchasing property until 4 November 1320, more than four years after the initial sale of Egelsdorf and more than a year after the redemption date for that village had passed.[32]

These are not isolated examples of distress that might be found at any time in the medieval record. Already in October 1315 the abbess and convent of Saint Peter of Kreuznach near Mainz were alienating real property to the somewhat better off nunnery of Dalheim in order to raise the capital to pay off the convent's debts.[33] The bishop of Minden, in late December of the same year, acknowledged the "perpetual alienation of burgs" by the church on account of the "immense burden of debts."[34] In June of 1316 he was still complaining about the policies of his predecessors, whose carelessness in contracting debts had led him to despair whether recovery of the see's holdings would ever be possible.[35] March of 1316 saw the abbess and convent of the Lower Rhine house of Retters give their procurator the "authority and license of selling for our necessity" an array of properties to a Frankfurt burgher, "honest Wigand Freusch."[36] A year later honest Herr Freusch had joined a consortium that bought up a few more of the nunnery's properties.[37] Honest Wigand looks very much like a speculator coolly calculating how to benefit from the near bankruptcies all around. For, indeed, by 1317 bankruptcies and near bankruptcies were commonplace.

The mantra *nihil*, in phrases describing income as "nothing at all," recurs in the German documents. On 26 January 1317 officials at Kloster Möllenbeck in north-central Germany acknowledged that income for prebends, including allotments of bread and meat, were daily declining to nothing.[38] By February of the same year conditions near Xanten had become unspeakably difficult; property recently acquired by the cathedral was said, in a Job-like declaration, to have suffered over the previous year and a half from the effects of wars, wind, heat, and the swollen rivers.[39] Also in 1317 Abbess Jutta of the famous nunnery of Quedlinburg commenced a series of sales of rents, confessing that the action was undertaken out of lamentable necessity and for the "evident utility" of the house. The alternative was to allow the monastery to sink into "imminent and irrecoverable ruin."[40] By December the Hospitallers of Nieder-Weisel in Hesse were forced into similar disposals of property and justified them in almost the same words.[41]

The year 1318 continued this dismal story. On 5 April the abbess of Daimbach, a Cistercian house in the diocese of Mainz, chose to alienate a portion of its holdings to Kloster Eberbach on the Neckar west of Heidelberg. Her goal was the "reduction of the burdens of debts of our monastery, contracted by our predecessors," and she expressed the wish that by doing so, her nunnery would avoid being assailed by even greater dangers.[42] The Benedictine monastery at Kamberg in the diocese of Würzburg probably suffered those greater dangers and was obliged in late November to alienate large amounts of property. Yes, it was explained, "the heavy burdens of debts and not a few harms that went along with those debts" were compelling the action, but basically what had occurred was a "collapse," so that unless something was done very quickly, there would be no recovery. Here again was "urgent necessity" with a vengeance.[43]

Applying directly to the papacy for relief in 1319 was the Premonstratensian convent of Arnstein, situated near the confluence of the Rhine and Lahn not far from Coblenz. Over a long period of time in the late thirteenth and early fourteenth centuries the house had already suffered from a series of sell-offs of its rural holdings, rights, and rents (at places like Camberg, Dessighofen, and Heimbach) under Abbot Theoderich II. It would have been possible perhaps to continue down this route, but even Theoderich seems to have seen no hope in doing so.[44] There was some feeling that the deeds of sale already negotiated by Theoderich were unfair to the abbey and were tantamount to recognizing legalized theft (the abbot, who may or may not have been culpable, probably offered to resign as a result). The appeal to Pope John XXII did not bring largesse, but it did bring the Holy See's authorization of the use of ecclesiastical censures against those who had unjustly got possession of the convent's properties and rights.[45] Nonetheless, the situation really did not correct itself until after the agrarian crisis abated and stable leadership reemerged at the convent in 1323.

What looks to be a similar appeal to Avignon from a hospital in the diocese of Minden got similar results. Three representatives of the Apostolic See were persuaded in 1317 that a "copious multitude of the infirm, poor, orphans, and weak were pouring to the hospital." They "were received and sustained there," insofar as giving sustenance was possible, since "their own resources [that is, those of the religious] were insufficient." The only help the visiting prelates could offer—or the only help they did offer—was the grant of indulgences to those who visited and supported the hospital with their alms.[46] One could point to other examples of papal gestures toward the unhealthiness of the ecclesiastical situation in the north, especially where war subsidies compounded the difficulties of local churches in adjusting to the harvest shortfalls and murrains.[47]

All the cluster of pressures—war, poor leadership, harvest disasters, inadequate or belated concern from superior lords—culminated in an almost universal crisis for the northern European church. Occasionally some good came out of a bad thing, and, as Arnstein's story indicated, one should not underestimate even in this general crisis the importance of leadership or its lack in the fiscal prospects of ecclesiastical houses.[48] A quaint history of the Premonstratensian abbey of Obermarchtal in Swabia written by Friedrich von Walter, the last abbot, at the turn of the eighteenth/nineteenth century confirms the observation. Obermarchtal, according to the author (who had complete access to all the surviving documents), suffered much as had Kloster Arnstein from eight years (1314–1322) of "great want" caused by "disorder [over the political situation], hunger, and pestilence," which, documents convinced him, "consumed nearly two-thirds of the inhabitants" of the region. But two priors, Burchard II and Konrad III, who served in succession during the crisis brought the abbey careful administration and a splendid sense of the art of the possible; they not only helped Obermarchtal survive intact but most likely permitted it to do charitable work through the increasingly hard-pressed hospital it served at Marchtal. Of Burchard, von Walter could write, "he died as he had lived, pious and holy"—and, he might have added, solvent.[49]

Such heroic leadership in the awful circumstances was not everywhere decisive. Ecclesiastics in Flanders and bordering principalities, no matter how they struggled, were perhaps the most grievously affected. Occasionally the crises were short; that was about all one could realistically wish for. The church of Saint-Servais of Maastricht, for example, had gone through a terrible period in 1315–1316 forcing it into a series of gages that were virtually alienations of its rural properties, but by January 1322 it was successfully redeeming the gages.[50] Much more typical was the case of the Benedictine abbey of Affligem at Hekelgem in Brabant. It was already in bad fiscal shape by 1312, and the weather of 1315 and 1316 was ruinous as floods destroyed the polders that protected its lands. Annuities were draining its diminished funds as well, but the monks could think of nothing better, or perhaps they had no better option, than to continue debt financing in this way. The bishop of Cambrai gave his permission for a capital campaign of this sort in 1322.[51]

The case of the Cistercian abbey of Ter-Doest on the North Sea coast is somewhat similar. Around 1317 it was forced to seek approval from its immediate ecclesiastical overlords and *confrères* to alienate large portions of its holdings in order to pay off its debts; and at roughly the same time it managed to get permission from its lay overlord, the count of Flanders, to do the same thing, since he was convinced too that the monastery was overcome with debts.[52] Not content with these approaches to the monastery's problems, the abbot also sought and received the consent of Pope John XXII to establish life rents of up to two hundred pounds per year to stimulate investments that would help the monastery deal with its cash flow problems.[53] Even this was insufficient. And so we find Ter-Doest also turning to the count of Hainaut for help; he granted permission for the abbey to put at farm (that is, more or less, to mortgage) some of its properties held of him.[54] Despite all these efforts, Ter-Doest did not make a quick recovery, although it improved its situation. The enterprising Abbot Nicolas II de Lissewege got what credit was deserved for the partial turnaround.[55]

The scenario was depressingly similar with the abbeys of Eenham, Lobbes, Ninove, Val-Dieu, Argenton, with the house of Teutonic Knights at Siersdorf, and probably elsewhere.[56] Eenham's ecclesiastical superior, the see of Cambrai, authorized alienations of property on 28 May 1318; in July (in the wake of the authorization) we see the abbey, in a flurry of transactions, selling a farm and other rights and properties. The process was still going on in August.[57] Lobbes went the route of life rents. It sold one to the count of Hainaut on 23 December 1320 to raise money, but it was still so oppressed by debts that it turned to the count again in January, at which time he ceded a rent to the house on condition that at least a portion of it go to nothing else but the spending down of the debt, no new purchases.[58]

The dismal fiscal situation of the Premonstratensian abbey of Ninove in eastern Flanders almost brought it into receivership toward the close of the abbacy of Jean Scamp (d. 1318).[59] It was worse for the Cistercian house of Val-Dieu, also encumbered, as the general chapter of the order learned, with heavy debts. Its new abbot, Jean de Brust (1315–ca. 1328), sought permission to sell off lands and rents. The general chapter was dubious about the possibility of saving Val-Dieu but acquiesced. Jean's energetic efforts were aimed at recovering at cost productive properties earlier alienated. To this end he obtained seigneurial backing for the recoveries and various other kinds of help from the duke of Brabant and Limburg.[60] But it was not enough. King John of Bohemia, the heir of the abbey's founders, intervened to persuade the pope to take Val-Dieu into receivership on 21 July 1325 until such time as its debts were effectively liquidated.[61]

Similar to the monks of Val-Dieu, the nuns of Argenton, in the diocese of Liège, sought the permission of the chapter general of the Cistercian order and the "visitor" (or overseer) from the order to alienate some of its properties. These included an annual rent owed it by the abbey of Malonne. Permission having been granted, the sale was made on 2 February 1317 for a lump sum. The nunnery, "oppressed most heavily . . . by debts," took this course for its "utility" and under the "unavoidable and urgent necessity" of the dreadful year it had endured.[62] It was this and similar alienations, rather than any other devices, that presumably allowed it to survive.

To conclude this list of near bankruptcies in Flanders, we may turn to the Teutonic Knights of Siersdorf, who were forced toward the end of the famine to cede extensive properties, including arable, with the consent of the master-general of the order, to cover expenses occasioned by "storms, hail, and epidemic disease." These arrangements, originally made in October 1322, were confirmed in November. Two months later this was followed by official guarantees that those who purchased the properties would be secure in their possession, for, as we have seen, behind every alienation was the wish, if not the determination or possibility, to recoup the loss at cost in the future. Presumably the Knights' arrangements set them on a firm footing, and they were already considering ways of redeeming the property alienated in the autumn.[63] They too had been brought back from the brink.

Not so for some of the Flemish and other Low Country houses. The return on the efforts of the abbey of Saint-Martin of Tournai from exploiting its rural properties was so low during the abbacy of Gilles de Warnave (1308–1324) that "monastic goods [were] alienated and pledged to such an extent that nothing at all remained for the subsistence of the abbot and the monks and the carrying on of their business; it became necessary for the monks to beg."[64] Bad leadership caused the crisis, or so the reminiscing monk Gilles Li Muisit asserted thirty years after the fact, but the most thorough recent historian of Saint-Martin's, while acknowledging the inferior leadership, argued that the immensity of the harvest shortfalls was more significant.[65]

Toward the end of 1315 the Cistercian monks of the abbey of Villers at Tilly in Brabant, having endured famine and great mortality, called it quits and dispersed to other houses.[66] We should recall that troubles in the French-Flemish borderlands had long made the condition of the abbeys and the fiscal situation of lay lords precarious. Some abbeys, like Orval, a Cistercian house in the diocese of Trier, had been under threat of dispersion even before the famine. The famine only caused the authorities to renew the threat.[67] So the dispersal of the monks of Villers had not even been regarded as a really distant possibility; by no means did it come as a complete surprise. It is instructive in this regard that model letters were prepared for the monks who were to face the not unexpected eventuality. These letters, issued by Abbot ———— (fill in the blank for the name), described the debt-ridden state of the house. Giving its cause as war and crop failures, which had been permitted by God but had become too much to bear, the letter explained the difficult process (the "bitterness of heart") that had led to the decision to disperse. It called upon the charity of others to feed and clothe and shelter the shepherdless flock with their own until, God willing, they could be recalled to their forsaken abbey when conditions improved.[68]

The Cistercian abbey of Val Saint-Lambert, despite its "vast posses-sions" in the agricultural lands of the Liègeois and beyond, was also so profoundly struck by the economic conditions that the inmates dispersed to other, less impoverished, houses in what one of its historians calls the "devastating" wake of the famine in 1316. The monks were not to be reunited until the 1320s.[69] After the reunion they embarked on an effort to diversify their holdings. Not unlike other monasteries in the region (Orval is an example) they stressed mining, in their case surface coal min-ing, as a supplementary source of income.[70]

For the nuns of Porta-Celi (s'Hemelspoorte) in Zeeland, with little food and clothing, there was no hope of reconstitution and diversification as a protection against future disasters. Their prioress received permis-sion from Count Guillaume of Hainaut, heir of the founder, to dissolve the impoverished (*depauperatum*) priory in 1317. The nuns found succor at the convent of Reinsburg.[71] Porta-Celi disappeared.

The impact of a collapse of income was not limited to the internal well-being and integrity of lordly or monastic households; it had repercussions on tenurial arrangements as well. In the face of financial difficulties lords with small estates, for example, often retreated from direct exploitation and leased farms to the richer peasants who could or, at least in the earlier period of the agrarian crisis, thought that they could weather the difficul-ties and improve their long range financial condition. For a variety of reasons many lords had already commenced the retreat from direct ex-ploitation in the thirteenth century; the circumstances of the early four-teenth in a number of cases, like that of the abbey of Grand Hautmont near Avesnes in the imperial fief of Hainaut, completed the process.[72]

Yet even those ecclesiastical institutions that already collected much of their revenue from rents found only a temporary advantage over their peers engaged in direct exploitation of their estates. For example, the Rhenish abbey of Siegburg (to the southeast of Cologne), already heavily burdened with debts, could ill afford what appears to have been a sharp decline in rents paid directly to it and indirectly through its vassals from 1315 through 1318.[73] Another example: the cathedral chapter of Braunschweig, whose leaseholds were in the rural hinterland of the city, suffered acutely after the first year of the harvest shortfalls. By 1316 in-come had plummeted because renters could pay only part of what they owed (either in money or in kind) or could pay nothing at all. Having so little surplus of grain and such large obligations, in other words, the rent-ers (basically smallholders) were forced to dump their grain on the local market early before they could benefit from the price rises. Their decrease in income explains the abysmal returns to the cathedral chapter.[74]

The attractiveness of leasing, which seemed like a hedge against the economic effects of the bad harvests, now turned into a nightmare; and Braunschweig ecclesiastical institutions with rural properties in the hinterland were compelled to take the leaseholds back into direct exploitation or at least to provide the seed corn if any planting was to be accomplished. Important positions in the labor hierarchy, like that of steward, which gave status but also carried customary obligations (in the case of certain manors near Braunschweig, of providing seed corn) went unfilled because no one could bear the expense "on account of the dear times."[75] Not until 1321 had many aspects of the crisis in Braunschweig, which caused this flip-flopping in the cathedral chapter's tactics, abated.[76]

The situation everywhere and the plans for dealing with it were further aggravated by the impact of distant wars—or, to be more precise, the taxation necessary to plan, if not fight, distant wars. The papacy indirectly helped out the Premonstratensians of Arnstein and a few other houses, as we saw, but specific responses to these particularly importunate houses did not lead to a fundamental shift in papal priorities. The numerous papal calls for Crusade subsidies in the second decade of the century meant that northerners were obliged to send money south: the sees of Cologne, Mainz, Meissen, and Utrecht were put on notice of their duty in this regard in 1317; Cologne and Utrecht again in 1320.[77] These payments—which, in the event, never actually underwrote a general Crusade—were in addition to ordinary levies to which the papacy was entitled and which it never forgot to demand from places like Bremen, Kammin, Lübeck, Magdeburg, and Salzburg, ecclesiastical provinces hard hit by begging populations and the necessity to provide alms.[78] Exasperated northern churchmen lamented the papacy's failure to understand the gravity of the situation in the north and balked at the payments, which explains their arrears.

It was not solely religious establishments that were forced into impending bankruptcy and into creative ways of facing it. The evidence may be skewed toward these great record-keeping institutions, but the crisis was bleeding lay lords dry too.[79] Evidence on the plight of Prince Wizlaw III, the lord of Rügen, the largest of the enormous islands at the mouth of the Oder, is dramatic. The prince was obliged by the economic conditions and, it must be stressed, the almost unceasing wars to which he and the Rügen knightly class were committed[80] to sell or pledge huge properties, tolls, and rents. The method was a simple one. He would transfer the income of, say, a rent worth 10 marks a year to a purchaser for a payment of 100 marks. The purchaser would draw the income until the prince repurchased the toll at cost. There was no amortization of the purchase price.

In this way Wizlaw alienated properties at an alarming rate in 1316 and 1317, especially to rich burghers who saw splendid opportunities to expand and diversify their holdings in the countryside. The monies of account used to calculate the purchases were usually "Slavic" or "Wendish" marks. I estimate that the prince managed to acquire over 6,000 marks, the equivalent of between 1,200 and 1,500 English pounds, through these alienations in 1316–1317. Despite the incessant refrain giving him the option of repurchase, there is not much evidence that the properties were successfully redeemed.[81]

What motivated Wizlaw to do this on such a scale was an incentive for other lay people,[82] even great ones like counts, dukes, margraves, and rivals for the German crown in the same period, to think hard about their economic situation. Income for the count of Hainaut, for example, plummeted in 1316. Nothing, nothing, nothing is the seemingly endless refrain in the fiscal accounts covering the last half of that year and the first half of the next. In part the murrain was blamed.[83] Even as late as fiscal 1322–1323 full recovery had not been achieved.[84] So difficult was the situation for Duke Otto I of Pomerania and the margrave of Brandenburg in 1317 and 1318 that they went down the same road as did Wizlaw and disposed of properties with largely chimerical options of repurchase. Burghers from towns like Stettin (Szczecin) were the buyers.[85] Charters of 1315 and 1317 witness Duke Heinrich II of Braunschweig and a more local magnate as pledgers and sellers with four- and three-year redemption options.[86] Frederick of Austria, Ludwig of Bavaria's rival for the German throne, resorted to the same device when events were looking bad for him in 1320.[87]

Further east, near the border of Latin Christendom, where migration to new lands in the Oderraum was possible, conditions were different. The mortgaging and selling of villages to accumulative burghers was hardly an effective option. Nor was the arbitrary squeezing of tenants, who could readily take to the road and escape lordly power. For lords with holdings in the borderlands, the principal need was to maintain a labor force to grow food for the garrisons that protected their holdings from Slavic reprisals.[88] In 1315 the Teutonic Knights in the region of Lübeck "saved many of their dependents through the administration of doles of grain from the abundant reserves that had been amassed in the storage bins of their castles."[89] (Like all garrison towns and frontier villages, the castles of the Teutonic Knights tended to have large reserves to protect against the shortfalls of siege.)[90] During the year 1316 the Cistercian monks of Riddagshausen in the diocese of Magdeburg fed their workers/dependents, over four hundred per day, from Lent until harvesttime. Kind and considerate the monks may have been, but then they had no desire to be found shorthanded when the time to reap arrived.[91] For, surely, God would have mercy and restore abundance to the people.

France

As in the empire, so too in France on occasion great lordships benefited from the famine economy or at least held their own, avoiding budgetary crises even after conditions worsened in 1316. Although Guy Fourquin acknowledged that the famine years initiated the secular downturn in the economy of northern France, the fragmentary *fiscalia* for the estates of the richly endowed royal abbey of Saint-Denis, on which he depended for his analysis, led him to believe that the downturn initially had a gentle slope.[92] The problem with generalizing from the records of Saint-Denis is not merely that they are so spotty but that the abbey's income, as far as it can be ascertained, was so diversified, including, like that of a number of other neighboring lords (and individual proprietors and tenants), a substantial return from viticulture, which recovered faster than cereal husbandry.[93]

Thus work on the abbey of Les Vaux de Cernay, about twenty kilometers southwest of Paris, suggests the same conclusion about the nature of the decline and the possibility of relatively rapid recovery for lordships with diversified holdings in arable and, as the French would say, *vignoble*. Les Vaux de Cernay possessed numerous vineyards and significant associated rights in regions as far distant as eastern Normandy (such as Vernon and Mantes), the Beauce, and the Gâtinais, not to mention along the southern banks of the Seine.[94] The first two or three years of volatile wine prices were unsettling, combined as they were with an unstable grain market, but Alain George has concluded that the abbey's profits during the price rises—in wine prices specifically—were sufficient to compensate for the recurrent declines. When the vintage recovered earlier than the grain harvests, this further permitted the abbey to weather the agrarian crisis.[95]

Evidence on the rural estates of the cathedral chapter of Sens, the archiepiscopal see less than a hundred kilometers southeast of Paris, is a little bleaker, but it too confirms the impression from the Saint-Denis and Les Vaux de Cernay material. In the fiscal account of 1317, the cathedral scribe routinely alluded to the effect of the harvest shortfalls on the chapter's receipts in words like the following: "For two measures of oats owed at the farm of Le Nave. Nothing. The chapter forgave [it]." Or, again, "From Lord John the cellarer for the vineyards of Champigny. It was forgiven him." "The homestead at Monceaux. Nothing." "The house at Saint-Aubin. Nothing." From another house, "Nothing." From a bundle of rents in kind, "Nothing." From a group of meadows, "Nothing." From the customary levy owed the chapter when grain was transported from the viscounty of Melun, "Nothing"—presumably because there had been little or no grain to transport. From a mill, where there was insufficient grain to grind, "Nothing." Yet with all these "nothings" the scribe could still conclude that, "the deduction having been made of all expenses from total income, receipts exceed expenses by 817 pounds, 7 shillings, and 6 pence."[96] And the entries recorded as *nihil* that permeate the account show evidence of having been revised as soon as conditions briefly improved; the mill, for example, would soon show a small receipt.[97]

In two studies, one of Cluniac priories north of Paris and the other of the granges of the Cistercian abbey of Chaalis, Philippe Racinet and François Blary have been able to document similar conditions. Between 1310 and 1325, according to Racinet, many of the Cluniac priories witnessed an increase in indebtedness and a general weakening of their economic clout, which, in turn, exacerbated their problems in relations with other authorities.[98] In a number of houses, the style of life and level of well-being deteriorated, although these trends were not universal.[99] Good leadership, especially in liquidating debts, went a long way to mitigating the disaster's impact; so Racinet can conclude, as did Fourquin, that the era of the famine was the beginning of a long secular decline in the economic health of the region and its monasteries, but hardly an unqualified catastrophe in its own right.[100] Blary, more briefly, concludes that there was a break in economic equilibrium, with appropriate adjustments in management practices, but also not a profound catastrophe for the granges of Chaalis.[101]

I raised the question earlier whether this conclusion can be generalized for northern France. It is doubtful. Balancing the evidence of a brief sharp pain followed by rapid, if only partial, recovery is other evidence of lords suffering significant reversals and modifying their practices accordingly. This was especially the case for seigneurs who were already hard-pressed on the eve of the famine. The Cistercian monastery of Vaulerent near Senlis had endured a series of predicaments in the decade before the Great Famine. When the harvest shortfalls of 1315 became manifest, the monks, like some of their imperial counterparts, felt constrained to rush headlong into leasing.[102] A number of granges in this general area made the same transition in 1315 or thereabouts even if they were suffering less significantly from the economic crisis.[103]

Another device employed to assure the survival of impecunious institutions in France was the raising of cash (for the purchase of high-priced foodstuffs) from the sale of annuities or life rents. The Picard abbey of Saint-Amand went this route but still had to borrow right and left at high interest.[104] Indeed, the abbey needed to borrow partly in order to pay the return on the investments it had solicited, but the abbot probably went too far when, without the permission of any superior lords, he put valuable woodlands in the hands of the monastery's creditors, a fact that was revealed in mid-October 1320.[105] Shortly thereafter (probably 1321) the king, Philip V, acknowledged that the depredations of the Flemings "as well as the sterility of the fruits of [the abbey's] possessions over the preceding several years" had brought it to the brink of bankruptcy. He was particularly concerned at how the moneylenders were continuing to disturb and vex the luckless monks.[106]

Effects of the agrarian crisis on other French houses were equally deleterious and sometimes more dramatic. When the inmates of Deux-Jumelles, a Norman house, were officially visited in 1314 by a delegation of the abbey of Cerisy, the visitors found an institution in bad shape, poorly administered, with a physical plant urgently in need of repairs. They laid down careful instructions on how to rectify the situation.[107] The famine years that followed, however, were disastrous. It was not simply that Deux-Jumelles marked time for a while, as a visitation in 1315 makes clear.[108] It fell further and further into disrepair. In 1318 a panel of visitors reported that it had found complete chaos at the house. For lack of money, books that had already been lost in 1314 had never been replaced; clerical vestments were wanting; lighting was insufficient because there was no money available for candles. The altar of Saint Thomas was neglected, even though it was supported with "good rents" ("bonos redditus")—a rent paid in grain whose value increased with the dearth. (Other rents were just bad, that is, had failed.) The buildings continued in disrepair. With the number of employees cut, no one was tending the cemetery, and the bells were not even being rung. Something had to be done or the evils would multiply ("Fiat aut male erit"). With no money, no charity was being given.[109]

We saw earlier that despite problems on this scale, the papacy continued to make demands on the northern churches. In the most famous remonstrance to this fiscal exploitation, Jacques de Thérines, the abbot of the badly affected abbey of Chaalis and "the most prominent Cistercian of his day," composed a magnificent and moving lament of the famine and the misery occasioned by wars in progress and holy wars ever in planning.[110] An order in 1318 to the Cistercian fathers and to those charged with the visitation of houses had commanded them "to inform the Chapter General fully about the economic state of the houses they had visited."[111] In his letter to the pope roughly contemporary to this order Jacques reported that by this time the situation in France, where "the houses of the Order are most numerous," was one in which the abbeys were simply wasting away, surrounded by sterile fields and vicious lower nobles or minor gentry ("nobiles mediocres"), who were themselves up against the wall in the agrarian crisis.[112] The good monks turned to credit both to combat their penury and to provide themselves with the resources to feed the suffering poor.[113] Hardly possessing the income to pay off the loans, they were obliged to borrow to keep up the payments on the interest. Usury was gnawing away at the order's vitals.[114]

British Isles

In Britain as on the Continent, the initial shortfall in the harvest of winter wheat and then the shortfalls in the autumn harvest of 1315 were a temporary boon for large producers.[115] In Britnell's rather understated words, "large estates might be better able to hold out for the best prices, and there is good evidence that they did so."[116] Canterbury Cathedral Priory, for example, whose budget was in excess of £2,000 per annum, was running deficits from 1303 through 1314 that varied in size from £133 to £864. (There were only four years in this period with very modest surpluses—from £19 to £43.) Yet for 1315 following the explosion in prices, the priory enjoyed a £233 surplus in its budget.[117]

Let us focus our attention on the cathedral priory for a few moments, for its fate discloses a number of important aspects of response to the agrarian crisis. Though recording a sizable surplus in 1315, the priory plunged into debt soon after and had deficits of £591 in 1316, of £285 in 1317, and of £534 in 1318.[118] How can this be explained? In the first place the surplus of 1315 is somewhat misleading. It is certainly true that the priory benefited from the sale of its available grain in the first year. But in fact the wheat harvest had been so disastrous that the benefits were attenuated. Only fields with particularly good drainage produced sufficient grain for sale. The priory also managed to sell off supplies of oats, which were less brutally affected than wheat by the weather. No steward could have been entirely happy, therefore, with the returns from the estates; and, indeed, the priory accounts showed a surplus less from the benefits of the grain price rise than from huge oblations to the priory (over £500) as pilgrims prayed for the return of good weather.[119]

Then, as we know, the disaster renewed itself. Grain price inflation redounded on other products. Whatever grain products and hay and wine that the monastic labor force itself did not produce, or which tenants who owed rents in kind could not render, had to be bought at the inflated prices of 1316, even as production on the estates themselves plummeted during this, the worst year of the bad weather.[120] Mavis Mate estimates that expenses may have doubled as a result.[121] Moreover, Canterbury had a continuing upsurge in pilgrims, pilgrims caught now in the same cost-of-living crisis as was the priory itself. So offerings to the priory did not keep pace with the increasing number of pilgrims. Indeed, oblations seem to have declined by 50 percent. The poorer pilgrims, large numbers of whom were in orders, were now asking for relief; and the monks of the priory found it difficult to cut charity without undercutting the reputation of their house and thereby jeopardizing the likelihood of increased alms to it in the future. The large number of clerical pilgrims, incidentally, necessitated a twofold increase in the priory's expenditure for communion wine, since part of the devotional practice was repeated eucharistic service.[122]

The dismal situation affected the tenants of the priory too. Rents declined by perhaps 45 percent, so that the overall effect of the depression in income was a series of cost-cutting measures. Pensions were curtailed or respited. Measures that had been decided upon to improve the material fabric of the priory were delayed of execution. Costly litigation was postponed. Yet as far removed from the war zone as the priory was, royal taxation to pay for the war with the Scots ate up these savings. And even the phenomenally high prices for oats, which the priory estates still managed to produce in relative abundance, could not offset the downturn.[123]

After an improved harvest in 1319—to continue the story—the priory experienced a skyrocketing increase in oblations to it. The refusal to cut charity had been a wise one; and the feeling that God had again turned His face to the people inclined the less straitened pilgrims of that year to be extremely generous. Offerings reached £577. Relics given by clerical pilgrims had a value of over £426. We know this is so because relic-rich Canterbury Cathedral Priory saw no reason to keep the bones offered it by provincial religious and recorded the prices it got when it sold them off to other pilgrims. Finally in 1320 a murrain hit. In general the priory's flocks and herds had done well through the wet years, but the cattle murrain of 1320 was devastating, a fact that undercut dairy income as well.[124] Yet, interestingly, offerings from pilgrims edged up again during 1320, as they had in the first year of the Great Famine, in the desperate attempt of the pious to assuage God's anger and bring a quick end to the pestilence. Indeed, their offerings, in excess of £670 in 1320 alone, allowed the priory to surmount this disaster too.[125] Thus, generalizing, Mate can conclude that "this economy," namely, that of southeastern England, "was profoundly shaken, but not destroyed, by the agrarian crisis of 1315–22."[126]

For most lords, however, and despite regional variations,[127] the situation, even if it started out well or at least endurable, deteriorated rapidly, and there were no bonanzas of pilgrims' oblations to lessen the pain. To be sure, "our sources are neither ample enough nor sufficiently sensitive to register the precise effects of the famine" on many minor lords and lesser landowners.[128] Nonetheless, some very instructive data from an array of regions in Britain have survived. On the one hand, the stewards of lesser estates in England seem at first to have withheld quantities of grain from local markets in order to ship it to more distant ones where prices were significantly higher. On the other, the persistence and ubiquity of the severe grain shortfalls undermined these men's ability to sequester very much grain for shipping, explaining what appears to have been a marked decline in "carrying services" in the famine years just as we earlier observed on the estates of the Cathedral of Sens in France.[129]

Minor English lords also had less flexibility than the great landholders in discharging their financial obligations, so it was necessary for them to sell their crop earlier than the great lords did—that is, before the full effect of the price rises could be felt. The regional economy of East Anglian Breckland seems to have been peculiarly in disarray. A documentable 20 percent drop in crop yields of wheat, rye, barley, and peas in 1317–1318 must have been matched by a severe downturn in demand (otherwise mystifying in its causes), for there was no sharp rise in grain prices in the short run. This may explain the inability of the small manor of Fornham in Breckland to weather the crisis in production. So "severely disrupted" was grain production there in 1317 and 1318 that the "profitability of the manor turned into large deficits."[130]

To get around the fiscal difficulties, some institutions in Britain, as on the Continent, turned to corrodies.[131] These annuity agreements promised investors in the institution a fixed annual return of room and board. The corrodies were particularly seductive to the aged and to widows with small hoards of cash or inheritances but who might feel unable to weather the calamities of the harvest shortfalls and high prices on their own. Indeed, the device was a common one for ecclesiastical institutions to deploy in financial exigencies.[132] There was a harsh side to this practice, often emphasized by scholars, namely, the crown's right in England and Wales to nominate corrodarians. Nomination was a way of providing maintenance and a pension, free of government expense, for trusted but old royal servants, and such corrodies were established or perpetuated with minimum or no investment into the houses that received the pensioners. The Cistercian abbey of Maenan (Aberconwy) in north Wales, suffering exactions because of the Welsh rebellion of 1314–1316 and then bad harvests, with courage and determination refused to accept another corrodarian of this type during the famine.[133]

Another possibility under circumstances of collapsing profits was a direct cut in the paid labor force. Bolton Priory in Yorkshire dismissed more than half of its servants between 1315 and 1318; from a high of 100 or 120 the number declined to 35 or 36.[134] Temporary layoffs, such as of plowmen, also occurred, as, for example, at the manor of Meopham in Kent. There too, not unexpectedly, the cowman would be dismissed after murrain annihilated the herd.[135]

It might be argued that there were a number of complications in this approach to the difficulties lords were facing. For although, due to the large labor supply, underemployed servants and certain other types of workers might be dismissed with little net loss to the employers' aristocratic lifestyles, it could have been much more problematic to dismiss field hands, like plowmen and cowherds, even if they had been marginally underemployed in good times. Put another way, it was problematic to dismiss them if there was a strong possibility that they would migrate. In the beginning, of course, no lord anticipated that the small harvests would replicate themselves seemingly endlessly or be accompanied by equally sustained depletions of herds and flocks.[136] Consequently, employers desired at most to maintain access to the labor force needed to till, plant, and harvest the next (expected) crops and to exploit the restocked herds and flocks. Promises of extra beer and boon feasts were traditionally persuasive gestures both to attach labor to manors during periods of peak activity in nonfamine times, when competition among lords for free labor was high, and to make the workers feel that their intense work routines were worthwhile.[137] Perhaps as migration sharpened late in the famine, there was some concern even in the dense rural settlements of Europe about the labor supply, but if so it has left remarkably little trace in the records.[138]

An alternative or complementary way to hold down expenditures was by a restriction of household consumption and capital investment for improvement, repair, and renewal of depleted stores of seed corn, although investment was almost minimally low, less than 5 percent of profits among lords, even in the best of recent times.[139] For example, the priory of Durham, so far as its Bursar Account rolls indicate, typically received slightly more than its grain needs from its estates. In the early days of the famine, it therefore benefited somewhat from the high grain prices, but insufficiently, given the cumulative impact of the crisis on the absolute size of the grain harvest, on reserves of fodder, and on the size of herds and flocks. All of this was compounded by the English war with the Scots. Consequently, the priory suffered a "severe reduction" in income as the harvest failures persisted in 1316 and 1317. As a secondary consequence, there were bad harvests in 1318 and 1319 that must have been generated in part by the woefully inadequate supply of new seed corn. So low, indeed, were the quantities of grain harvested in these years that the subsistence needs of the priory could not be met without recourse to the high-priced market.[140]

An equally bleak situation developed among the Austin canons of Bolton Priory, whose estates never produced sufficient grain to feed the religious, let alone surplus that would permit them to benefit from the inflation of grain prices. They imposed strict limits of consumption and investment on themselves.[141] The canons then went further. Although their flocks were depleted and animal prices were, as we know, rather slower than grain prices to rise because of potential buyers' fears of purchasing diseased animals, the canons sold off some of their livestock at low prices to raise desperately needed cash.[142]

In the sometimes bad prefamine years that plagued certain long-established houses already suffering a falloff in largesse, many resorted to clever practices ("expedients," the editor of the cartulary of one such house, Daventry Priory in Northamptonshire, calls them) to supplement their endowments on the eve of the famine. When the harvest shortfalls came and problems of income became manifestly more severe, there seems to have been, in Daventry's case, a furious expansion of these practices, judging by the number of conveyances, quitclaims, and exchanges in the famine years, 1315–1322.[143] These expedients were but variants on the flip-flopping from direct exploitation, so-called high farming, to leasing and back again so characteristic of Continental lords and fully evidenced in the English records as well.[144]

One order, the Hospitallers, was given a golden opportunity to survive the agrarian crisis without resort to this sort of manipulation of the land market. The problem was how to exploit this opportunity to the fullest. Like most other major institutions the Hospitallers had come through the thirteenth century relatively strong, despite the continuous inflation. There were ominous signs, of course, especially the passage of the English Statute of Mortmain in 1279 and similar ordinances on the Continent.[145] Whatever its general impact on monasteries and churches (and the issue is debated), that statute and its Continental parallels put considerable limitations on the granting of lands to ecclesiastical institutions and appear to have had a devastating effect on grants to the Hospitallers. Almost no lay donors of lands or rents to the Hospitallers are recorded in England after 1279 for the next forty years.[146] Whether the decline in endowments was due solely to the effect of the statute may be doubted: after the loss of the last crusader outpost in the Holy Land (1291), it is plausible—although, again, this is disputed—that lay enthusiasm for endowing the military orders would have fallen off anyway.[147]

What seemed to the Hospitallers, however, to speak directly to its need for money, as the low rate of endowments persisted, were the arrangements surrounding the suppression of its great rival, the Temple, at the Council of Vienne in 1312. For the suppression of the Templar Order on an assortment of unproved charges, including sodomy and heresy, had as a corollary the transfer of Templar wealth and property to the Hospitallers.[148] This was the golden opportunity referred to above.

What we discover, however, thanks to the work of Michael Gervers, is that the agrarian crisis in the years after 1312 (though he does not say so explicitly) was anything but conducive to the efficient transfer of this property to Hospitaller control. While former Templar brothers awaited final punishment, the royal government charged the cost of their maintenance against the property, thus reducing its value. It ordered that cattle and other movables from Templar estates be given over to the crown. Moreover, the heirs of lay patrons and donors used the courts to argue that the order's dissolution broke the quitclaims that had accompanied the original endowments, so that they should revert to the heirs of the donors. Their pleas were made more urgent in those instances where the effect of the agrarian crisis was already lowering their own income. And what precisely were the endowments, anyway? The heirs of patrons and donors in the immediate aftermath of the suppression had often seized Templar manors and the records from those manors. Many of the records were destroyed, to the everlasting disadvantage of the Hospitallers.

The Templar estates were like a bleeding animal thrown into a bay full of hungry sharks. The crown could hardly be blameless in a period of widespread war when it was to its advantage as well to hold on to Templar properties. It was not until a parliamentary statute in 1324 (significantly, in the *aftermath* of the continuous harvest shortfalls and murrains and that of the long series of wars) that the king acted to rectify the situation, to the degree that rectification was possible.[149] The timetable looks the same in English-dominated Ireland: the crown could not effectively convey Templar property to the Hospitallers until about 1323.[150] Although the evidence is thin, the situation looks the same in Scotland as well.[151]

If the Hospitallers, presented with such a possibility of weathering the agrarian crisis, found it difficult to do so, how must it have been for other lords? Everywhere the sense of crisis seems clear: episcopal officials in Salisbury, suffering from a poor return on rents and ecclesiastical taxation, continuously lamented the difficulty of collecting ecclesiastical fines and subsidies from 1315 through 1322. The earliest of these laments, dating from 17 September 1315, associates the difficulties with the bad weather. Lean year followed upon lean year. Then the impoverishment got worse, not only because of the failure of harvests, but especially because of the murrain that affected the great beasts.[152]

Under these pressures the equivalent of bankruptcy became common. On some manors, although probably not the largest, the very calculation of profit (*proficuum* or *valor*) was suppressed.[153] Postles, who has drawn attention to this fact, shows that there were exceptions even on modest-sized estates, but he argues for the general significance of the development and the causative role of the bad harvests in it. The interesting thing to note is that the "perception of profit" was itself a rather new aspect of lordly mentality. The growth and increasing complexity of the thirteenth-century economy had helped transform lords and their estate managers from people who were satisfied to have abundance to people who wanted to maximize surpluses in order to cash in by disposing of the surpluses in rapidly proliferating local and regional markets. Stewards who were just beginning to routinize calculations of profit, albeit in crude and uncertain ways, began to avoid such calculations when the numbers revealed failures of such proportions as were generated during the famine. Sometimes the frustrations of the famine years are also revealed in the fiscal accounts drawn up at the far end of the crisis, say, 1323, "to assess the damage done" by the persistent agrarian disasters. This seems to have been the case with regard to the reckoning of the upland demesne of the De Lacy estate of Blackburnshire in England.[154]

We have already reviewed Continental evidence that monks, like those of Saint-Martin of Tournai, turned to begging alms.[155] Impecunious ecclesiastical houses in Britain petitioned great nobles and their own spiritual superiors to bail them out. The earl of Richmond through his good offices secured for the priory of Marrick a "pardon of more than £83 in unpaid taxes because of the poverty of the house," poverty resulting from the harvest failures and the depredations of the Scots. Another pardon or, rather, respite was secured following the murrain of the 1320s.[156] The nuns of Sinningthwaite (except for those rare few who flaunted their access to rich friends and relatives able to meet their personal needs—and were severely reprimanded for doing so) could not provide clothing for themselves. They went a-begging to the archbishop of York and prevailed upon him to provide help in the famine years.[157] House after house in the Anglo-Scottish borderlands complained in 1316, 1317, and 1318 of imminent collapse: Holme Cultram on the west coast near Carlisle, Armathwaite Nunnery in the hinterland southeast of Carlisle, Eggleston on the Tees about thirty kilometers southwest of Durham.[158] More generally, a peak in the number of royal grants of protection to ecclesiastical institutions in England occurs during the Great Famine—precisely because of their fiscal vulnerability.[159]

An inquisition on the value of lands and rights held by several lay lords in these same Anglo-Scottish borderlands reinforces the stark impression of the damage and the bankrupting force of the agrarian crisis. By the end of 1315 homesteads valued at 6s. 8d. were "waste." Arable, customary land and cottages held of the lords, and pasture were all "waste." The difficulty of exploiting the lucrative fishing on the river Tweed had reduced the value of fishing rights at various places—30, 50, 100 percent, compared with what peacetime and fair weather promised.[160]

Such a collapse of rents and evident abandonment or waste of tenements parallel to that observed on the Continent, in the Braunschweig hinterland, for instance, after the retreat from direct exploitation by its lords, finally ruined Bolton Priory.[161] The canons had to disperse to other houses of the Anglo-Scottish borderlands in order to survive.[162] The nuns of Moxby and of Rosedale, two other Yorkshire houses, had to disperse for the same reason, the bankrupting force of the harvest shortfalls and murrains and war.[163]

It is impossible to say whether the wars and their attendant taxation had a greater impact in some regions than did the harvest failures.[164] Yet for the English kingdom's "minor gentry" the fiscal crisis, exacerbated by war, was something of a turning point in their relations with the crown. The participation of the minor gentry in the rebellion of 1322 against Edward II has been attributed by Scott Waugh in part to the beating that they took from the economic effects of the famine and the war taxation. Waugh attributes the nasty edge and vicious quality of the rebellion, and its appalling toll on the common people, to the sense of frustration and betrayal inherited from the terrible years when the rains, the wars, and the taxation never stopped.[165]

The plight of lords in Wales was initially a little better. Take, for example, the pastoral economy of north Wales. Still imperfectly monetized, that economy was activated by a huge number of rent payments in kind. These included the characteristic butter rents that bondmen paid to lords. Because of production shortfalls, these rents were reduced in absolute quantity from what they had been in, say, 1314; even so, their collection would have cushioned other losses the lords were incurring.[166] For it would have been possible for the lords to take advantage of the high prices that butter was fetching in the marketplaces of garrison towns.[167]

Nonetheless, the combination of harvest failures, war, and murrains eventually wreaked havoc in Wales almost as terrible as that in the Anglo-Scottish borderlands. The ministers' accounts of Neath Abbey in the extreme south, where the Welsh rebellion was localized, describe the results in 1315 and 1316: tolls collected at Neath, the burg, were modest, and there were "no more because of the war." Rents from mountain tenements especially, but elsewhere as well, were uncollectible or off "because of the war"; many tenants were themselves dead. Mills were no longer in operation because they were burned or utterly (*omnino*) destroyed in the war. The disruption interrupted the work of the courts, so that profits from pleas crashed.[168] (A similar effect occurred in Ireland, where the eyre of Drogheda had to be suspended as late as November 1322.)[169] Smiths, potash makers, and potters left their forges, fires, and turners in the woodlands rather than risk injury from the war.[170] Yet despite all this disruption and the clear decline in production, the crown seems to have appropriated scarce grain in the region and put so much pressure on Neath Abbey to supply its troops that the religious severely depleted their herds: "sold in the war" is a refrain in the accounts.[171] When the mop-ping-up operation was completed, the crown inflicted a heavy fine on the adherents or supporters of the rebellion, but the king pardoned half of it—partly no doubt to show his grace, partly, it must be supposed, in recognition of the terrible effect of the war.[172]

The Cistercian monks of several Welsh abbeys made bitter laments about the destruction. Monks at Llantarnam Abbey, whose numbers had decreased from sixty to twenty by 1317, complained of having been forced during the rebellion to cede valuable properties to the rebels, and were concerned lest the king appropriate these to the crown lands after the rebellion was crushed and forfeiture of rebels' holdings decreed.[173] At the same time the government was requisitioning needed timber from the monks of Llantarnam, which they, to little or no avail, did not want to sell.[174] And, as if this were not enough, ecclesiastical taxation of the Welsh churches continued apace despite what verged on becoming a total economic collapse. The monks of poor Neath Abbey curtly summarized a widely shared attitude to ecclesiastical taxation: how could they pay when they had already "been plundered of their goods" in local wars?[175]

To Maenan (Aberconwy) Abbey, in the vale of Conwy about ten kilo-meters from the northern coast, the ripples of the southern rebellion and its suppression also reached. Mortgaging of many properties from their total of 40,000 acres or more was attributed to "lean years and debt."[176] The crown was engaging in any number of dubiously legal moves against the abbeys of north Wales to supply itself during the war and to protect against the possibility and success of a Scottish invasion of Anglesey and north Wales from Ireland.[177] It tried to compel the monks of Cymer near the western coast, for example, to finance needed bridge building, but they resisted.[178]

Some demographic data on the Welsh garrison towns (a misnomer for these essentially rural settlements) have survived. But because the English were given to gross resettlement practices, it is not possible to measure the overall impact of the crisis from this material.[179] The evidence of taxa-tion, however, showing revenues extracted by the English even in north Wales declining by 30 percent, does at least point in the direction of sig-nificant disruption leading to a major decline in production.[180]

Conclusion

Much, much more would have to be done before a fully satisfying picture of the economic condition of rural lords could possibly be painted. Un-doubtedly, the final balance sheet will see bright spots and large expanses of shadows in the history of seigneurial profit during the famine. Nonetheless, a few conclusions *seem* certain, although they, too, must be offered only as tentative interpretations of the data. First, on balance the fiscal situation in the countryside was negative for lords. Unless the high prices for a particular commodity they controlled—like salt, for instance, in the case of some Baltic lords—outweighed the effect of an absolute decline in production, even the greatest seigneurs with huge resources found it difficult after the first year or so of bad weather and bad harvests to maintain profit levels. Lesser producers, but still great men and great institutions, fared significantly worse. Yet the most horrendous fiscal experiences were those of minor lords whose profit margin was already low in areas hit particularly hard by a combination of bad weather, murrain, war, and taxation. Welsh and Flemish monasteries suffered prolonged and deep impoverishment. In England, Yorkshire looks especially bad, with canons and nuns of fiscally strapped houses abandoning their convents in something like despair, but similar abandonments occurred in Flanders as well.

In the Baltic area and in the rural hinterland of London, such abandonments do not seem to have taken place, but the severity of the situation is indicated by the many and ingenious devices employed in the effort to maintain profits or at least soften the fiscal crisis. Canterbury's sale of relics given as oblations is the most striking example, but the lord of Rügen's financial practices are almost as arresting. Prelates in the dioceses of Braunschweig, Lübeck, and Magdeburg, to name just three other examples, were equally active in seeking to mitigate the effects of the agrarian crisis on their rural estates—leasing demesne, recovering it, providing incentives to a dissipating workforce, and on and on. Thanks to these measures, neither lay lords nor institutional lords in these regions were ever in danger of disappearing or collapsing. It remains to be seen, however, whether the kind of pressures they responded to could be confronted with as much success by families and individuals. We have danced around this issue a bit already in this chapter. We must address it fully in the next.

5

THE COST-OF-LIVING CRISIS: RUSTICS

OBSERVERS NOTED and bemoaned the "crisis in the cost of living" (*penuria*) among ordinary people. Flanders, 1316: "Penury and high prices grew apace."[1] Würzburg, 1316: "The poor beset by penury and hunger were greedily eating the carcasses of cattle" dead from disease.[2] The region around Salzburg, 1317: it was the year of "penury and the severest hunger," the "greatest penury."[3]

In the case of England, it is possible to construct an aggregate decennial index of the disequilibrium between prices and wages, which constitutes a very partial measure of penury, from ca. 1260 to 1347. Because the compilers of the data lump together information on the wages of agricultural and building workers, it is difficult to correct for urban as opposed to rural penury. Nonetheless, overall—as we might have expected from the conclusions in chapter 3—there appears to have been an increasing disequilibrium in favor of prices from 1260 to 1320 with three dysfunctional peaks before 1347, namely, ca. 1270–1280, ca. 1290–1300 and, massively, 1310–1320.[4] Suggestive as this is, however, of a cost-of-living crisis, it is, as already remarked, only a very partial measure of penury. How important, after all, can prices and wages have been in determining the quality of life among rustics who consumed a great deal of what they grew and had only limited recourse to the market? To explore the question of penury among ordinary people in the countryside will require additional modes of investigation.

The Scholarly Debate

To begin with, two schools of thought seem to have emerged in recent decades concerning the economic well-being of rural society on the eve of the famine. Scholars partial to each have drawn support from the surviving evidence. At one extreme—though this is a caricature of sorts—we may imagine the thirteenth century in the north as something like a golden age. It was a period of growth in the economy as a whole; and even though growth gradually slowed, it did not stop.[5] The vast majority of rustics benefited from this growth and were not impoverished when deceleration occurred.

To sustain this view, we would need to show that typical holdings yielded far in abundance of what was needed for subsistence or were capable of increased exploitation when need arose. We would have to look askance at efforts to calculate rustics' productive capacity simply from grain growing, since there were many other products, less easily quantifiable from our sources than grain, but probably significant nonetheless. Since land prices were high (a fact accepted by everyone), there was an incentive to sell small plots. Indeed, there was an active land market among both free and juridically unfree rustics (all of whose entrepreneurial behavior, so it has been alleged, may mark them out as true individualists). Moreover, wages from doing all kinds of tasks supplemented home production and could have allowed rustics the opportunity of living in some comfort or, in the cases where home production fell below subsistence needs, could have put the rural dweller's "budget"—even the budget, perhaps, of the landless laborer and family—on a sound footing. There were bound to be individuals, one-parent households, dysfunctional families, even poorly run or marginal institutions that could not make do and isolated regions that failed to benefit, but in this view of things these would be exceptions, not the rule, during most, perhaps all, of the thirteenth century. In fine, the thirteenth-century European rural population was no "peasantry" at all in the sense of an abjectly oppressed, nonentrepreneurial, marginally subsisting mass of people without notions of private property in land.

At the other extreme is the view—again, slightly caricatured here to emphasize the differences—that, however idyllic the early thirteenth century was, the close of the century saw a concatenation of factors that pauperized the vast bulk of the peasantry (the choice of the word *peasantry* is deliberate). These factors reduced the peasants to a depressed economic condition similar to that of the eastern European peasantries of the early modern period. The demographic glut so far outstripped economic growth that Europeans were living from hand to mouth. Plots of land had become so subdivided that few families could produce their needs from their own holdings. Landless laborers became common. Service and wages were essential. Service—employment as a servant in an aristocratic household or ecclesiastical institution, or as a bondman on a lordly estate—offered some protection in return for the loss of autonomy and the degradation of personal status.

For free people wages meant the difference, not between comfort and modest living, but between hunger and living at all. Budgets were perpetually strained because wages did not keep pace with prices. Unemployment made life unendurable. The real entrepreneurial activity, activated by humiliation and the specter of bankruptcy and starvation, was resistance: appropriating the lord's harvest by theft; poaching in his forests, chases, parks, warrens, and fishponds, and from his dovecotes; using custom to thwart his fiscal exactions; plowing too lightly; working to rule.

Evidence has been amassed on both sides, but which of these two views is closer to the truth? On the resolution of this question hangs the proper interpretation of the initial impact of the bad weather and harvest shortfalls on ordinary people in rural society. If the standard of living was relatively high in the countryside and the normal "surplus" (food produced beyond the amount needed to prevent the obvious signs of malnutrition) was large, then "severe effects" from the harvest shortfalls should have been delayed or, in the rosiest scenario, never have materialized at all. In any case, the longer they were delayed, the more certain we could be that rural life before the famine was on the prosperous side. By severe effects I mean things like the extensive abandonment of homesteads, desertion of villages, widespread begging, and the kind of slashing of consumption that results in nutritional catastrophe, including, ultimately, a sharp increase in mortality. If any of these or similar severe effects occurred already by late summer 1315 and their causes cannot be explained by other means, we can be fairly confident in concluding that rural life was poised at the very edge of subsistence for the mass of families on the eve of the agrarian crisis. The later we find these kinds of effects beginning to manifest themselves, and the less significant they were at the outset, the greater the likelihood that the "average" rural household was relatively prosperous before the persistent harvest shortfalls and murrains began.

Rural Society

In order to make a judgment on these matters, we will have to explore any number of aspects of rural society—some obviously, some not so obviously, responsive either to the sorts of conditions that brought on the agrarian crisis or to the economic situation of farmers and laborers in general. Let us turn first to one of the most confusing issues, that of the significance of personal and tenurial freedom.[6] To begin with, why some people were free and others were unfree (serfs, villeins, and the like) in the thirteenth century or why there were degrees of freedom—if that is the preferred language—is not clear.[7] Most of the recent work on the origins of medieval serfdom is polemical in tone and not very enlightening.[8] It does establish that a transition occurred sometime in the ninth, tenth, or eleventh century, depending on the region, during which time the language of slavery was displaced by the language of serfdom.

The people whom we regard as juridically unfree in the thirteenth century may or may not have been descendants of the slaves of the old regime. Some certainly were, but others were the descendants of people who had commended themselves in the centuries of transition into the hereditary dependent relationships recognized by thirteenth-century lawyers as characteristic of unfreedom. Others were the descendants of men and women who had gone to live under the protection of or had accepted lands from lords who, as compensation, exacted perpetual services (later classified as servile) that were attached to the tenements or villages the rustics occupied. Free rustics in the thirteenth century could not necessarily claim any long ancestral lineage of their status either; many had only recently purchased their liberty or were the children or grandchildren of many thousands of others who had.[9]

In a number of regions, like Normandy and Scandinavia, few classic characteristics of juridical serfdom or servile (customary) tenure were at all prominent in farming villages around 1300, but other forms of dependency were strong.[10] In other regions, like parts of the so-called Celtic Fringe, clan-based bondage (like castes elsewhere in the world), though demeaning, encouraged strong kinship and village solidarities that, to some extent, mitigated its debasing and alienating character.[11] In still other regions, like the empire, where serf as a personal status did become firmly established, it could hardly be said to have degraded one's dignity or handicapped the achievement of financial well-being, at least not for many of the *ministeriales* who helped govern the country, intermarried with baronial families, possessed castles, made claims to knighthood, and had vassals.[12] In England and most of northern France, on the contrary, serfdom and villeinage and servile tenure were alive and well.[13] And in the Rhineland and elsewhere in the western parts of the empire many German-speaking farmers labored under the same obligations as serfs or occupiers of servile tenements in the kingdoms to the west; this was one reason so many sought freer tenures and free status on the Slavic frontier.[14]

With such a variety of juridical situations in rural society, it is hardly surprising that scholars have engaged in a number of (sometimes fruitless) disagreements about the quality of village life. Not all aspects of these disagreements are relevant to a discussion of the crisis of 1315–1322, but what the debate has shown is that even the hardest and fastest distinctions drawn by thirteenth-century jurists between servile and free status (whether focusing on personal status or on landholding) could be quite fragile or porous in social and tenurial reality.[15]

The question as to whether in England or northern France having to fulfill servile obligations undermined one's livelihood or one's feelings of self-worth has constituted a particularly sharp focus for debate.[16] While this issue cannot be fully resolved here, what seems to be a reasonable working hypothesis, based, for example, on magisterial work on Lincolnshire, is this: "[w]hen times were harder lords' immediate recourse was to their unfree tenants and to a more scrupulous exaction of customary dues and services."[17] What this suggests is that however equal the social and economic position of servile and free rustics was in good times, an agrarian crisis of the dimensions experienced from 1315 to 1322 would distort that equality to the considerable disadvantage of the servile population. Over and over again in the course of this chapter, we shall find indications of this differentiation as well as of parallel processes upsetting village equality or magnifying existing village hierarchies.

The social and natural landscape on which the famine wreaked its woe had emerged out of the process of land clearance and reclamation—assarting, for short. Assarting had been made possible on an enormous scale by a metallurgical revolution (dated about the millennium) that permitted the strengthening and reduction in cost of iron tools and the diffusion of the heavy plow.[18] Sometimes the difficult work took centuries, but the results were heroic.[19] Significant amounts of assarting were still taking place in the older lands of Latin Christendom in the thirteenth century, but the movement as a whole was slackening. By 1300 it was virtually complete.[20]

In the classic period of assarting, each effort, though usually sponsored by one or more lords and supervised by an agent (*locator*) or partner,[21] was also a collective undertaking of the rustics.[22] There was a tendency, therefore, after a "lordly portion" (demesne, from Latin *dominus*) was reserved to the lord himself, to distribute to the pioneers shares of the new arable in the regularly laid-out, big open (unfenced) fields around the village.[23]

Not every village (or *bourg*) that emerged culminated in this neat picture.[24] Some open-field farming regimes and villages were superimposed on ancient villages; there was no sense of starting from scratch and there was perhaps a less heady atmosphere of adventure and accomplishment when the destruction of existing resources to make the transformation undermined traditional social arrangements.[25] Some settlements were specifically intended to be forest villages; their close-in woods supplied raw material for the charcoal needed in the production of iron, without which the more typical villages (and towns) could not survive.[26] Others specialized in glassmaking and, therefore, were sited near otherwise poor, sandy land, but land with abundance of woods and fern (a source of potassium) and access to tin, lead, lime, and iron.[27] A number were cut out of upland areas that were much more amenable to mixed husbandries or to pastoral rather than cereal husbandry.[28] And whatever the planners' original intent, a number of the villages that were established came to be walled or moated because of unexpected but persistent recurrences of baronial violence, and these villages stayed small.[29]

Nevertheless, in the "typical" scenario, each household in the large unwalled village would have had shares in the open fields. These were allocated as bundles of strips, themselves scattered through the fields. One of many explanations for the scattering suggests that since hailstorms, a principal danger at harvesttime, usually wiped out small areas of fields without touching others and since soil quality varied so greatly in fields even over relatively short distances, scattering was a form of insurance guaranteeing that no one family risked total loss from a freak hailstorm or had a monopoly of choice land in the first distribution.[30] Perhaps the organizers of assarting and village settlements or the stewards serving the lords got double or triple shares,[31] but the thrust of property holding was egalitarian: common of pasture, common of waste, common of woods and water, and long well-distributed strips in the arable for each homestead.

The descendants of the villagers who undertook such a time-consuming enterprise maintained a sense of community.[32] They banded together in small groups to provide ox teams for joint plowing.[33] The masters of each holding constituted the "community of the vill," which issued regulations (known in English as by-laws, from *byr*, a Germanic word for village) on access to the commons, gleaning and pasture in the harvested fields, the planting of crops, and on and on.[34] Meticulous collective planning lay behind the most important aspects of village business.[35] Community was ritually reinforced by the practice of burying the dead in cemeteries rather than in separate family plots near the homestead.[36]

Lordship, to some extent, limited the autonomy of the community but could also serve to bind tenants together. Who other than lords normally had the capital to finance the building of watermills, or even the less expensive windmills, that provided a locus for community grinding?[37] Who else had the power to impose uniform weights and measures for clusters of villages under their control?[38] The balance is nicely illustrated with regard to the adjudication of disputes among villagers. This took place in courts monitored by the lord's steward, but run by village elders applying their essentially uncontested understanding of customs supposedly imposed by the lord; the court rolls that record the outcome of these disputes as well as register routine transfers of property within the village constitute our best, though certainly not our only, source on popular culture in the countryside[39]—and also on the effective absence of the powers of lordship in myriad aspects of village life.

There were ups and downs in village solidarity, of course.[40] And one among many reasons for this was that even the best-intentioned communitarian or collective efforts did not maintain the allegedly pristine economic equality of village life. In terms of status, if, as most historians believe, early 'servile" assarters ipso facto earned their freedom ("Rodung macht frei"),[41] the kinds of commendations into unfreedom described earlier could occur among debt-ridden former assarters and their descendants.[42] The need for protection against bandits and, on the eastern frontier, against pagans could induce some tenants to yield the privileges that their ancestors had obtained as a condition for clearing and settling the land. Even some of the original obligations imposed on homesteads or tracts in the assarting communities might come to be construed as servile by later lawyers.

In terms of holdings, the issues were more complex. Waste and pasture might be brought into cultivation by lords, to the benefit of certain rustics and not others. Woodlands might be transformed into game reserves intended to be exploited exclusively by lords and their friends. Villages that practiced partible inheritance sometimes saw strips subdivided into minuscule units that many scholars believe were incapable of supporting a young couple with children. Villages where holdings tended to descend intact—through ultimogeniture, exclusion of females, or, less often, primogeniture—often witnessed the creation of a class of landless rustics, who consequently had no voice in the councils of village elders and no access to whatever common rights survived.[43]

Those people reduced to very small holdings and those with no agricultural property to speak of were not necessarily impoverished. A few became village priests. Advantageous marriages might bring property to others. Supplementary agricultural labor, like that of threshers, was needed at critical times; and there were opportunities for occasional labor at almost all times of the year.[44] Craftwork, either as a vocation or part-time if rustics retained a few strips in the great fields, might provide additional income or the opportunity to lease additional agricultural property when the chance arose: "every rural society needed workers in wood, leather, metals and pottery, since objects made of these materials were essentials for agricultural production and for daily living."[45] There was also a place for quarrymen, herbalists, salt-workers, glazers, tailors, millers, hucksters, dairymaids, and domestic servants.[46] Finally, unless the seigneurial regime was extremely strict, youthful males, in particular, might seek their livelihoods elsewhere, and, especially for Flemings and Germans, in new villages being created on the Slavic frontier.[47] What seems certain—and what partly explains the continuing attractiveness of the eastern frontier to inhabitants of the Rhineland—is that the net rise in population in the oldest settled parts of Latin Christendom and the lack of rich assartable lands there by the opening years of the fourteenth century put significant stress on access to productive resources in village life. Towns helped siphon off some of the rural population but far too little to reduce the stress effectively.

What is the evidence of stress? There is a great deal; yet what should be the best and clearest evidence, that of size of holdings as an index of production and consumption, is the most frustrating of all. To be sure, historians are absolutely certain that the subdivision of parcels of holdings reached its zenith for the whole of the Middle Ages in the early fourteenth century.[48] But what was the average holding that resulted from this process: seven acres? eleven acres? fifteen acres? Who knows?[49] More relevant perhaps would be the median holding. But, again, no one knows what that was except in particular villages.

What could seven acres or fifteen acres produce? Again, no one can say with certainty. Not only were there quite gross differences regionally in quality of land, but, as we know, soil type changed rapidly even within a single open field. It therefore mattered profoundly what strips each household possessed. (Let us bear in mind that in 1300 there was no longer any "quasi-egalitarian" distribution of strips over all soil types as there may briefly have been in the remote past.) And, finally, is it only a matter of how much was produced by a typical rustic holding (presuming we could tell)? Or is it rather a question of how much remained after rents were paid to landlords, tithes to the church, and boons to helpers?[50] Medievalists should take some comfort that the best of modern economic historians of rural Europe cannot definitively answer questions such as these even for the eighteenth century.[51]

As a consequence of this realization, historians have adopted alternative strategies in assessing the quality of rural life around 1300. One involves access to common rights. If the "subsistence" crisis was real in 1300 for a large segment of the population, it would be all the more important for ordinary rustics to preserve their traditional access to common rights. Historians who have studied this issue closely have indeed concluded that competition for access was most severe and increasingly destabilizing around 1300. In England common rights of fishing were under tremendous pressure or "threat," to use John McDonnell's word, which prompted retaliation in the form of poaching as "commoners" sought to resist the lords.[52] Competition over common rights in woodlands, according to Jean Birrell, also "was at its height at the period of worst population pressure and greatest spread of arable farming at the end of the thirteenth and early fourteenth centuries."[53] The famine-induced demographic decline in some rural regions[54] "to a degree defused" the crisis in England.[55] In Continental regions as distant from one another as Lorraine and the northern Netherlands there is also persuasive evidence of considerable pressures on woodland resources in precisely the same period.[56] And in northern France, according to Elisabeth Zadora-Rio, the pressure of lords to extend their gaming privileges in woodlands led to a strong reaction from rustics who felt squeezed. The thirteenth century came to an end with lords actually retreating from claims to seigneurial warrens in forests.[57]

Partly, of course, this retreat was motivated by the lords' desire to shift to arable and capitalize on rising prices for staples in population-glutted Europe. It also reflected newly diffused practices in game management (such as the shift from large forest warrens for rabbits to small parklike warrens). But partly it was an indication of the tension between lords and rustics. By 1317—the date, during the famine, would seem to be significant—the French crown acted to control further claims to forest and warren by seigneurs seeking to exclude rustics.[58]

Another strategy for assessing the stresses in rural society at the height of its population has been to look at the evidence and role of rural indebtedness. The scholar who has made the most emphatic case based on this evidence is Guy Bois.[59] According to Bois, there threatened a structural blockage to accelerations in productivity during the period 1285–1315. The period, as we know, was marked by relentless and frequently brutal inflationary pressures,[60] including, following Bois, a shortage of specie, currency debasements, and the hoarding of precious metals. Rustics with larger holdings presumably managed to benefit from the inflation, while the vast majority of the rural population grew poorer. Even prosperous rustics sensed the precariousness of the situation and hoarded specie that might, invested, have stimulated higher rates of growth.

The disequilibrium allegedly "strained rural solidarity to the breaking point," making rustics as a whole powerless in the face of the lords, for the "abyss of poverty," again following Bois, is never "propitious for class struggle," only for class subordination.[61] Richer landholders looked upon their poorer counterparts as the threat. Some exogenous change would have had to come about by which village elites ("kulaks," in the vocabulary of a number of recent studies)[62] might be humbled in order for the condition or "atmosphere in the countryside to improve."[63] The inflationary pressures on the vast majority of the pauperized, dependent—and increasingly and unproductively indebted—rural population implied not only a politically divided and inert class but also, given the lack of investment, a stagnant rural economy.

The stagnation hurt the lords who had to face the twin perils of unmerciful inflation and the slackening of assarting that would earlier have brought additional productive lands under the plow; it in no wise ruined them, but it did impress upon them the need to extract further surplus from the pauperized mass (they had less clout over substantial farmers). Thus classic blockage emerged, in which every effort to maximize short-term benefits inevitably led to further pauperization, unproductive indebtedness, restricted investment, and the like. "Il est difficile d'imaginer une rupture plus importante dans une société rurale."[64]

Bois's conclusions have achieved something like general acceptance in France and have even penetrated rather popular books there.[65] Periodic negotiated redistribution, which would have been the most radical peaceful method for softening the distinctions among landholders, was rare in the extreme. Even if it had been practiced, there is no certainty that it would have been a spur to productivity. Indeed, there is some reason to think that it would have reduced efficiency and lowered productivity by removing large holdings from hard workers and risk-taking entrepreneurial types. So the blockage, if it really existed, persisted and was, as it were, relentless in its enervating effects on economic development.

Was this blockage general in northern Europe? Bois, who is a real expert on eastern Normandy, has suggested that it was, although it might not have been equally severe everywhere.[66] Yet there are problems with generalizing the picture.[67] In the first place, in many parts of the north there is precious little evidence of some of the central requirements of the thesis, like the hoarding of precious metals.[68] Second, all of this speculation on the blockage of the economy neglects several other factors. After all, rather than see themselves reduced to farming ridiculously tiny homesteads, many rustics forswore landholding, not for life in the towns, but for village artisanry and for lives as full-time agricultural laborers. And traditionally, as was earlier pointed out, many people with small holdings supplemented their income with part-time work. It may be that it is nearly impossible to assess the importance of these supplements to typical household budgets (since such budgets cannot be determined, anyway).[69] And it is not at all clear whether disbursements from this income would have retarded, encouraged, or had any effect on the various levels of blockage. The inability to evaluate these variables is a troubling factor in any overall assessment of Bois's argument.

There is a final, equally troubling, and more general consideration. Much of the work on the economic environment on the eve of the famine that has found widespread impoverishment of tenants generalizes from estates that fell squarely within the regime of open-field farming.[70] Even though Bois's material transcends some of the limitations implied by this observation, his work is more the exception than the rule. In trying to assess the quality of rural life from 1315 to 1322 in the pages that follow, I have attempted to keep to the forefront variations in husbandry and location that undoubtedly led to differential levels of seriousness in the effects of the famine. It mattered that an open-field village might be near the fenland in England or the vine districts of the Auxerrois or the fishing communities of the Atlantic, North, or Baltic Sea coasts. Whichever suffered less would attract the floating population of the neighboring community suffering more.[71]

The Famine

What, then, were the effects of the harvest shortfalls and murrains on the lives of ordinary people in a rural society already under the great, though not precisely measurable or evenly distributed, stresses of small family holdings, great swings in inflation, heavy indebtedness, declining investment, fierce competition for access to common rights—and, of course, as we saw in an earlier chapter, war and burdensome taxation? One of the most telling has always been taken to be the rapid "abandonment of villages" (*Wüstungen*), at least where villages were the normal mode of settlement.[72] Near contemporaries alleged that village abandonment occurred, for example, in the Lübeck region.[73] In fact, as a generalization this assertion is wrong, but it points us in the right direction. Significantly, the chronicler who reports it (like chroniclers of earlier famines faced with the same impression)[74] sets his allegation in the context of a large increase in the begging population. Rural beggars, in order to validate their activity, almost certainly did assert that whole villages were being deserted. But even if we assume that a number of serious depopulations and desertions actually occurred, prudence dictates that we regard most of them as temporary—in the absence of evidence to the contrary. (We shall have to return to the issue of vagabondage soon.)[75]

The one major exception to this picture may be Ireland, where, a good recent study has concluded, it "is probable that the nucleated settlements and open fields were deserted at this stage," that is, during the famine.[76] But the phenomenon in Ireland, which ought not to be exaggerated,[77] arose from a very complicated set of circumstances. The villages addressed by the authors of this study were Anglo-Norman "colonies" practicing a still new and—for Irishmen—alien form of open-field agriculture.[78] These villages were under multiple pressures: they shared with other villages throughout northern Europe the devastations of war, harvest failures, and animal pestilence; moreover, the English inhabitants, at least those who had not acculturated or made accommodations with native traditions, were deeply resented by the indigenous population working their estates. Finally, the government that should have been protecting them was under stress from its war with Scotland and for a while was ceasing to be effective in Ireland outside of a small area centered on Dublin and a few garrison towns. Increasingly, the English in Ireland, at least those living in poorly defended villages at some distance from Dublin and the coast nearby, were thrown on their own.[79] A noticeable increase in roving bands of beggars may indicate the depopulation of these villages.[80]

If a plausible case can be made for abandonment of certain kinds of villages in Ireland even though some modicum of control was returned to the English there after 1318,[81] no such case can be made elsewhere. Southern Wales, which saw the diffusion of nucleated villages and open-field agriculture under the Anglo-Norman conquerors and suffered many of the same problems as did Ireland during the famine, remained stable in its settlement patterns. Perhaps the reason is that this form of agriculture was less alien in southern Wales (there appear to have been a good number of pre-Norman instances).[82] Or perhaps the stability is explained by the fact that the destructive military situation in Wales never became as general as in Ireland during the famine years.[83] Whatever the case, neither in Wales nor elsewhere, as Wilhelm Abel's thorough studies in the 1950s revealed, was there any major wave of village abandonments at any time during the Great Famine.[84] More recent work confirms Abel's conclusions: certainly the abandonment of villages was not common during the famine in Flanders or the Low Countries in general,[85] or in Lower Saxony or elsewhere in Germany.[86]

In reacting to the perceived exaggerations of the chroniclers and of some earlier historians on abandonment, a tiny minority of recent scholars has gone too far the other way. It has been maintained, for instance, that evidence of renewed or continued assarting establishes that population in many areas was still growing during the harvest shortfalls, proof positive, in this scenario, both of the remarkable robustness of the agricultural regime in 1314 and, possibly, of the undiminished productive potential of the rural economy in general (even under constant technology). But this, too, is not convincing. A better explanation, based on research where the situation has been studied in depth, suggests that the upsurge in assarts documentable for some manors was a desperation move on the part of the rustics and/or of lords' reeves to find new fertile areas that might yield a bumper crop, or to renew "old clearances in order to boost manorial income at a difficult time."[87]

The truth, then, as usual, is between the extremes of collapse (widespread permanent village abandonment) and improvement (systematic new assarting of naturally fertile lands under the impulse of expanding population), though much more in the direction of the former than the latter. Recent archaeological investigations make a valuable contribution here. They show that abandonment of homesteads (*Hofwüstungen*), if not whole villages, in the early-fourteenth-century Low Countries occurred in numbers; such abandonment became a "relatively important" social phenomenon. Some figures can tentatively be offered to show the rate of abandonment in these relatively recently assarted ("marginal") lands. The sample is small, but it would appear that in some, perhaps atypical, villages in Flanders, from 10 percent to 34 percent of homesteads were abandoned around the time of the Great Famine.[88] Elsewhere in the remoter coastal regions of the Low Countries, it became a real problem to stimulate resettlement after the devastation that dike-breaking high waves and general flooding caused to farms and homesteads, animals and men.[89] The count of Hainaut on 20 October 1321 issued a general order that flooded and abandoned lands in Frisia be turned over to those with the wherewithal to dike them;[90] and evidence from January 1322 shows resettlement taking place and adaptation of sluices to the problems of flooding along the countless small streams and rivers, in this case the Demer, crisscrossing the flat land that had become so swollen as to ruin huge expanses of farmland in the famine's seven years.[91]

In rough country affected by war, like the Scottish borderlands, homesteads were abandoned for other reasons, but they *were* abandoned and in great numbers. It was easy for villagers to escape with flocks and herds to "fastnesses in the hills" in the Highlands whence they could return after marauding raiders had seized their already reduced crops and looted their homes. This kind of abandonment was ephemeral. What caused more permanent shifts was the fact that some inhabitants found pastoralism in the decade-long war a safer and, as wool prices skyrocketed, a potentially more prosperous way of life than cereal husbandry.[92] Many homesteads once occupied by these herders were permitted to remain at waste,[93] even though the villages in the main survived.

In any case, the newest of assarted settlements (open-field or not) were the most vulnerable to a high percentage of abandoned homesteads, because many of them were already so small: assarting in England, northern France, and western Germany in the late thirteenth century produced hamlets rather than territorially extensive settlements.[94] Here the work of John McDonnell is pertinent. In studying late-thirteenth-century assarting that took place on the "higher ground" in the northern enclaves of Bilsdale in northeast Yorkshire, he discovered that the rustics created a going concern in a generation or two, that is, a knot of small hamlets whose long-term viability seemed assured, given the "presence of foresters, a cooper, a carpenter, a cowman, and a tanner" among the residents. But all of a sudden the busy little hamlets grew less busy; they were moribund if not quite dead by the 1330s. As McDonnell tells us, "in the event climatic and economic deterioration, pestilence and Scottish raids, enforced a major scaling-down of the enterprise. Almost all the small communities of pioneers dwindled to single-family holdings, and so remained."[95]

A similar scenario might be argued for parts of Lincolnshire where newly assarted lands with light soils suffered a great deal from the rains and induced some rustics to withdraw them from cultivation for ages to come.[96] Still more corroborating evidence comes from relatively new assarts in south Wales, central Germany, and along the Baltic coast east of Hamburg. In south Wales, villages like Barry and Uchelolau ("Highlight") commenced the period that would leave them "shrunken": they had rapidly expanded their fields into areas with "heavy clay soils" in the thirteenth century, and the incredible rains of the famine's early years led to "increasingly waterlogged conditions" because of "the rise in the water table." Homesteads were temporarily (and, as crises continued, permanently) abandoned.[97] The German evidence is even richer. We may infer abandonment of new homesteads and hamlets from evidence like that from the records of the abbey of Scharnebeck on the Baltic which show the religious trying hard to prevent desertion with incentives precisely designed to keep new homesteaders (*coloni*) on their properties during the hard times of 1318.[98] But explicit evidence is not hard to come by either. Persistent heavy rains on villages near marshlands can be seen to have ushered in major adjustments of settlement patterns that meant some abandonment (but perhaps also rebuilding as well); there are examples from the German-Danish borderlands.[99] Finally, in 1319 or thereabouts Ropperode, a pottery hamlet not too far from Göttingen, and a small cluster of six upland homesteads on the crest of Salberg near Quedlinburg in Saxony fell victim to bad natural conditions, exacerbated in Ropperode's case by war, and were deserted.[100]

What all this evidence suggests is that beggars who in the midst of the famine would talk about village abandonment, even if they were guilty of exaggeration and self-justifying palaver in doing so, were not talking nonsense: the period of the Great Famine was indeed witness to a "long-term" increase in vacant land and "abandoned houses."[101] More work remains to be done to permit us to separate local crises that might have induced rustics to abandon their homesteads from the larger crisis of the bad harvests and war; and more precise dating of many of the abandonments than that provided currently by archaeologists would be most welcome. But the fact of widespread *Hofwüstungen* seems certain.

A close cousin to abandoning a homestead was yielding it or a portion of it to a person or institution better off. Many freeholders, a Flemish chronicler tells us, felt obliged to sell, mortgage, or sublease their farms in order to raise money to buy available food to eat, and this already in the first year of the bad harvests, for they were "reduced to the basest poverty."[102] Research in manorial court records and estate *fiscalia*, which describe among other things admissions to tenements and payments of rents, confirms and complements the chronicler's assertion. For example, Bruce Campbell's research on Norfolk in East Anglia, which exploits the court rolls of the manor of Coltishall, revealed a "three-fold increase in the number of land transactions," that is, of the yielding up of small parcels of land in exchange for money to buy food. This "rate of turnover . . . was only exceeded during the ensuing period of good harvests," when presumably the effort to recover patrimonial lands and reconsolidate holdings was in full swing.[103]

For a time, local conditions shielded some villages—including many outside of East Anglia.[104] As we might suppose, the presence of large towns with high demand for foodstuffs redounded to the benefit of agricultural laborers on big estates that had disposable surpluses of grain, and to the benefit of any villager who was a carter and who could buy up or hire himself to transport these surpluses. (Of course, as we saw earlier, when supplies dried up, so did cartage.)[105] The biggest towns, particularly those that were the seats of royal governments like London and Paris, had, up to a point, a very benign impact on their rural hinterlands, unless requisitioning replaced purchasing grain.[106] Paid laborers on the estates of Canterbury Cathedral Priory, for instance, profited from high demand for agricultural produce in London proper and its heavily populated suburbs. The economic explanation for this is simple. Despite a saturated labor market in good times, bad times accomplished two things. They induced young males to go to London, thus reducing the labor glut in the countryside. They also—at least in 1315 and 1316—increased the demand for labor: plowing and nearly all the other routine tasks of field work were more time consuming in sodden fields; yet the field work had to be done and intensively done if the priory's estates were going to reap the benefits (as they did) of London's high prices. Away from such an enormous market such developments did not occur, at least so dramatically, but wages for field hands—reapers and mowers—on Canterbury Cathedral Priory's estates rose significantly above the modest rise in piecework wages otherwise discernible in the period 1315–1322.[107]

The London catchment area was not, by the way, restricted to its immediate rural hinterland. Because of the city's siting at the mouth of the Thames, it drew food supplies in bulk from the eastern and southern coasts of Britain. Less populous areas like Cornwall in southwestern England, which might have greater per capita agricultural surpluses in normal years than other areas had, continued to supply some produce during the agrarian crisis to the larger population centers and thus, to a greater or lesser degree, escaped some of the more horrendous economic effects of the famine.[108]

Nevertheless, within two years most regions were experiencing severe economic and subsistence crises from the unseasonably wet weather. The vill of Kibworth Harcourt in Leicestershire is a case in point. The arrears of the steward or reeve reached an extraordinary peak in 1317 suggesting the magnitude of the tenants' inability to pay rents to their overlord, Merton College, Oxford. Calculated as best I can, the arrears in the famine years may have been three times as great as during "normal" years.[109]

Another example: on the manors of the honour of Tutbury in Derbyshire, rents fell some 30 percent from the fiscal year 1313/1314 to 1321/1322 because of vacancies "through poverty"; and new tenants were impossible to recruit. Then the civil war between Edward II and his barons (and minor gentry supporters) prolonged the famine—or delayed recovery—throughout Derbyshire. Land remained out of cultivation as waste or as grassland for years longer than natural conditions warranted.[110]

In Redgrave (Suffolk) a similar increase in turnovers in the period 1314–1317 was noticed by Richard Smith. But whereas in Coltishall (Norfolk) this bespoke a buyer's market (rich holders almost certainly exploiting the fiscal vulnerability of their less well-off neighbors), in Redgrave a great many of the turnovers seem to reflect "an expansion of intra-familial transactions concerning parental gifts to daughters among wealthy tenant families."[111] Such gifts, presumably, helped the daughters' families weather the famine years. Did they also, at least initially, permit these families to exploit to their benefit the high grain prices then in place? This is dubious. Small producers—and even "large" rural homesteads constituted small producers—could scarcely determine surplus or "excess" until the next harvest was in or nearly in. Ironically, therefore, they were in no position to exploit the market until prices seemed about ready to plummet. When the harvest turned out to be dismal and prices did not plummet, small producers had to hedge their bets still more and reduce consumption in the hope of reserving a portion of grain in order to make some profit in the market.[112] In the vill of Dry Drayton in the same general region as Redgrave, responses to the harvest shortfalls took a somewhat different approach, but they failed to make the lot of small producers any more tolerable than at Coltishall and Redgrave, as Jack Ravensdale's research on the "agony" of the famine in Dry Drayton suggests.[113]

It may be objected that the turnovers and surrenders of tenements, striking as they might appear to be, are not untypical of the period before the famine. I have already tried to suggest that the evidence is against this, but what has been marshaled thus far is admittedly patchy. Certainly it is the case that there was an active land market involving "sales" of freeholds, exchanges of leases, and subleasing of customary tenements in the thirteenth century.[114] This very active land market was sometimes obscured by euphemisms; the language of gift died hard: conveyancing of property was often expressed as "gifts in sale" and "gifts in lease" and so forth.[115] But the euphemisms notwithstanding, liberal rules of conveyancing evolved even at the manorial level and covered serfs and servile tenements clearly in recognition of an active land market.[116]

The extraordinary early studies of the Reverend William Hudson concerning the prior of Norwich's manor of Hindolveston in Norfolk (from which so much of the information in more recent English studies is pillaged)[117] allow us to poke around in the problem of conveyancing in much greater detail in order to distinguish between the "normal" land market and the peculiarities of the market during the famine.[118] Hudson first securely established the mean rates of turnover of tenements (surrenders by old tenants) and then calculated from the abundant information for Hindolveston the number of surrenders in 1316 and 1317. For the first of these years he found that the number of surrenders was 160 percent above the mean, and in 1317 it was 80 percent above the mean. Moreover, the rolls routinely report the cause: "pro magna fame."

Even more arresting was the distribution pattern of the surrenders: a few rich farmers bought out their poorer counterparts. Adam Carpenter, for example, in July 1315 acquired five parcels of land; in March 1316, six. In the totality of the court rolls he is revealed as having acquired forty-seven parcels and having surrendered only two. Robert Tubbel and William Tubbel were of the same sort as Adam, "though on a more limited scale." Robert appears in sixteen transactions, receiving land in fifteen; and William (possibly his brother) appears in eighteen, receiving land in seventeen. Finally, there is evidence of an aging paterfamilias surrendering part of his holdings to his children piecemeal up to 1315; but in that year and 1316, he was forced to give up land, again piecemeal, to Adam Carpenter and Robert Tubbel, including some that he had originally designated for his sons. By 1319, perhaps laid low by disease, most of this impoverished family was dead.

The Reverend Hudson, undoubtedly like some of Hindolveston's population, felt deep regret at discovering this landgrabbing activity based, as it was, on the pauperization of friends and neighbors. He seems to have regarded it as an unjust exchange of land for food, a violation of what we might now call the moral economy.[119] In a world where so many were suffering, it seemed depraved for a few people—landgrabbers—to benefit from that suffering. Something of this sentiment must also have been felt toward that fortunate minority of millers (or their lords) who, by custom, took a cut of the grain (or flour) as their fee for grinding.[120] If they chose to, these men could offer the grain for sale in the market at high prices and could harvest the fish in the millponds to the same end.[121] Something of the same must have been felt for those salters who paid fixed rents to the lordly owners of saltworks while making killings from the high market prices for their essential product in the years of heavy rains.[122]

What Hudson found is hinted at elsewhere—in the studies already examined and in a number of others. The overall conclusion now seems to be that the land market was volatile by the end of the first season following the initial harvest shortfalls in most places and skewed very briefly to a few rich holders during the famine, though the nature of the transactions differed from region to region depending on local customs of conveyancing, endowment of daughters, and so forth.[123] So in one region, such as Delftland in the Low Countries, the rich buyers of available farms became absentee landlords. They obviously attempted to consolidate holdings acquired in this still remote territory, which would have divested it of its character as a land of small farms. The count of Hainaut became so concerned at the rural depopulation of Delftland that he intervened, requiring all new acquirers of property there after 13 January 1316 to actually go and take up residence.[124]

Elsewhere the excitement of the land market is reflected in the frenzied buying up of subleases, as occurred in other periods of economic or financial crisis.[125] The implicit hope of sellers that improving conditions might allow them later to repurchase or re-lease their alienated properties explains the redemption clauses sometimes found in the records of transactions. In the manner of hard-hit monasteries, nobles, and burghers who had to dispose of property to their more fortunate compeers, an ordinary *famulus* and his heirs near Hameln in the north German plain also insisted as a condition of sale that they be given the opportunity to redeem their holdings from the local chapter.[126] In other regions, a wide variety of inter vivos land transfers, with very little or nominal purchase of subleases, characterizes the peak in turnovers in this period.[127] But everywhere the rich were the first to benefit, as, for example, in East Anglian Breckland where the "kulaks" (perhaps not the best word, but, as mentioned earlier, one or two scholars' choice) again reaped the benefits of an "unusually large" number of turnovers in 1316–1317.[128]

These facts suggest that even if, as Hallam writes, the "agricultural interests of the peasantry seem not to have differed materially from those of the lords," their tenurial interests most assuredly did, or, at least, that lords could see as much advantage as disadvantage in the further accumulation or concentration of property in the hands of the well-to-do.[129] Lords who authorized the waiving of entry fees to maintain holdings in production hardly cared if the persons to whom they were offering inducements had two, four, six, or ten recently acquired plots already under their belts. Stewards might have been more circumspect; uppity farmers could be hard to deal with. But ultimately stewards did what their bosses told them to do.[130] In Richard Smith's words, "there is certainly no indication of the manorial lord or his officials intervening to arrest the land grabbing activities of the village 'kulaks' . . . between 1315 and 1317."[131] It was the increasing number of the landless without customary rights who bore the heaviest burden. They cease to appear in the court rolls because, having no land, they had no homesteads to surrender in court. For them, in Jack Ravensdale's words, "things were never quite the same again."[132]

The effect of the land market's volatility on rural mentality may have been nothing short of dramatic: there appears to have been a decline in concern with the details of inheritance customs in the fourteenth and fifteenth centuries and a new obsession over conveyancing precisely because acquisition of land no longer needed to be delayed until inheritance, as had more regularly been the case during the perceived land shortage of the thirteenth century. This transformation would have received a major fillip during the Great Famine. Of course, there continued to be profound and pervasive interest in widows' rights since their existence inhibited the free market in land, but this was not *stricto sensu* an issue of inheritance.[133]

The ecological and social settings explored thus far represent with notable exceptions well-established communities with typical open-field agriculture. Of course, at a number of times we have had to discuss other kinds of communities, such as those living largely from fishing and hunting or from mixed husbandries. A few more words need to be addressed to these, however. We may begin with communities oriented toward grape husbandry; and, although it cannot be said to make interesting reading, Wilfried Weber's detailed tracing of the expansion of grape husbandry in the eleventh, twelfth, and thirteenth centuries is a useful introduction to the subject.[134]

The expansion of viticulture, Weber shows, was erratic, partly because wine shipped well, and so it was not always immediately necessary for new settlements to create vineyards. Also, long-term changes in weather transformed some regions from inhospitable to hospitable and back to inhospitable loci for grape production in our period. Some lands in grape production had been specifically assarted (from forest or marsh) for this use often as a joint enterprise of monasteries and consortia of lay people.[135] Others had been converted to viticulture from quite different husbandries. Consequently, people who produced wine sometimes lived in villages dominated by cereal production, in villages of mixed husbandry, or in outlying (almost rural) parishes of towns.[136] A viticulturalist might own or lease a house, storage cellar, small parcel of arable, kitchen garden, and plot growing some other cash crop.[137]

Nevertheless, like the typical farmer of wheat and other cereals, families whose livelihood came principally from vineyards found the early years of the famine very difficult indeed. High prices for wine offset the quantitative losses from the bad weather only where, as on big monastic and noble estates, the scale of production was vast. Ordinary family enterprises were not so fortunate. One such enterprise in the Rhine-Moselle region, worked by a husband-and-wife team, Wallefrandus and Levardis, can stand for many others. The couple made arrangements in 1314 with the church of Saint Gertrude of Nivelles to donate their vineyard to the church. The conditions were that they would sharecrop until their deaths and that the church would provide a loan up front to improve the vineyard. Expecting the best, the couple agreed to repay the loan at the next vintage.

The next vintage was the failed vintage of 1315, and then came the failed vintage of 1316. A charter of 10 November of the latter year describes the situation. The original arrangements were confirmed except that for the repayment of the loan, whose terms were reset to the benefit of the woeful sharecroppers. The reason is explicit: "because there have been grave and expensive times for the last two years." It was only the "patience" of Saint Gertrude that permitted them to stay on the land and face the future with hope.[138]

What was true of the ordinary family enterprise in viticulture was true also for small family farms that practiced pastoral husbandry. A splendid case where we can follow the impact of the agrarian crisis on tenancy on such farms is Denmark's. There free farmers who dwelt in small hamlets or isolated homesteads and who practiced intensive pastoral agriculture experienced in the early fourteenth century the transition from an "independent" farming class to a tenanted peasantry.[139] Although the series of exigencies inducing this transformation came to a head only in the 1330s,[140] the agrarian crisis of 1315–1322 already seems to have put sufficient pressure on many small proprietors that they sought the protection of (land)lordship and became tenants.

Their decision to do so may have been conceived as a temporary measure. Certainly, the negotiation of mortgages, as, for example, with Cistercian houses, which flourishes as a form of financing in Denmark in the early fourteenth century,[141] makes sense as a temporary device that perforce lingered on, despite the order's misgivings, as the northern agrarian regime received new shocks in the 1330s.[142]

Precisely the same scenario appertains to the strategies of farmers and monastery in the neighborhood of Haughmond Abbey in Shropshire and the abbey of Cîteaux in Burgundy. Shropshire rustics ("starving peasants," one scholar calls them) were advanced money in return for rents—classic mortgages—on arable and meadowland, with the terms for meadowland being especially favorable to Haughmond Abbey.[143] What began as a stopgap measure for the independent farmers of this extremely rugged and heavily wooded region, however, became a way of life. In Burgundy, Cîteaux enjoyed a feeding frenzy on the lands of rustics to whom, presumably, it had extended loans in the famine years but who were bankrupted as the agrarian crisis persisted much longer than anyone could have anticipated.[144] Landless villagers undoubtedly swelled the rural workforce as a result.

Conclusion

As in the case of lords, no final definitive picture of the condition of ordinary rustics can be drawn from the evidence presented here. Still, that evidence *is* substantial and covers a very large geographical area. Definitive it may not be, but the picture that emerges is certainly not a happy one. Whether the settlement pattern was classic nucleated village or not, whether the husbandry practiced was cereal production, grape production, or mixed farming, the agrarian crisis was severe. Thirteen fifteen, however, was not the turning point. Thirteen sixteen was. For the length of a year or so the various blows to rural society that we associate with the famine period (shortfalls, war, inordinate taxation) were parried with modest success, that is, without profound impact on the abandonment of homesteads, rearrangements of conditions of tenure, the volatility of the land market, or rural begging. But rural society was unable to maintain this fragile success any longer, given the extraordinary pressure on resources that was the legacy of two centuries of demographic expansion and the slowdown of assarting. Thirteen fifteen was the year the rains began, crops failed, prices rose, and people grew frightened. Thirteen sixteen was the year the rains continued, the crops fared even more poorly, prices seemed to know no limits, the animals wasted away, and the people grew close to despair. As we shall now see, it was also a year of prayer—one buffer against despair—as all the spiritual resources of rural communities throughout northern Europe were mobilized to petition God to relieve the suffering. The result, however, was unsettling. Sickness and death—unevenly, to be sure—began to claim their share of the rural population.

6

THE STRUGGLE FOR SURVIVAL

DESPITE measures to contain the effects of the famine, the calamity severely tested social cohesion. Many rural people—chiefly the poor—suffered the worst consequences of deprivation. Of course, the story is not one of unrelieved strife. Cooperation, *communitas*, was a deeply treasured ideal among villagers.[1] The real question is to what extent cooperation and mutual support could avert a fundamental breakdown in social relations or delay the worst effects of the harvest shortfalls—malnutrition, disease, and death. In this chapter we begin with the question of community and its limits, and we conclude with the evidence on rural demography that scholars have collected in attempting at least a partial answer to this question.

Community and Its Limits

The belief was widespread that churchmen should offer themselves in some sort of expiatory gesture for their communities in the period of dearth. Drawing on centuries of precedents the Benedictine monasteries of Saint-Faron of Meaux and Sainte-Colombe of Sens worked out a spiritual union in the crisis whereby common masses and common prayers were undertaken on behalf of the communities (many of them rural) for which they had a spiritual responsibility. This informal bond was formalized in 1324.[2] The abbey of Saint-Denis-en-Broquerie in Hainaut and its brother house Saint-Ghislain published their formal prayer union slightly earlier, on 23 June 1321.[3] For Saint-Ghislain this was one of a number of such spiritual unions that seemed appropriate in these difficult times.[4]

In Normandy and the Beauce processions of barefoot canons and priests took place on saints' days and Sundays; the clerics implored God, as their counterparts in the cities would do, to reestablish the normal rhythms of weather.[5] In the archidiaconate of Xanten, as early as the summer of 1315, a deeply scarred rural society was turning to the multiple display and parading of relics, with prayers and fasting; the local count, Dietrich of Cleves, added his voice to the clergy's in supporting these efforts, which he acknowledged were for the "common utility of all."[6]

Most historians have been skeptical concerning the translation of the virtue of cooperation into practice, despite evidence like the well-orchestrated and ecclesiastically controlled processions in Normandy and western Germany. Guy Fourquin asserted that it was the lower orders who took action in their own name. "Chiliastic hopes," he wrote, "became extremely strong" during the famine, "and whole processions of penitents sprang up. Prophecies foretelling a blood-bath and the massacre of the clergy and the powerful were rife."[7] These are exaggerations, but they should alert us to the fact that the surviving evidence does at least lend itself to apocalyptical interpretations. Indeed, it takes considerable effort to read any behavior during the crisis as evidence of philanthropy in the wide meaning of that term. Or, put another way, there is very little unequivocal evidence of philanthropy. And yet the situation was neither black nor white.

Consider charitable giving. Some producers, like monasteries, whose ideological justification for existence was their provision of religious and material sustenance to the poor in spirit and the poor in goods, did not benefit from the high prices. Where they did not benefit, they could not (or chose not to) enhance the eleemosynary dimension of their activities. Curiously, their restraint has sometimes been taken by revisionist scholars as evidence against the traditional picture of the famine's severity on the principle that if they did not give much more alms, there were not a great many more people who needed alms.[8] Surely the more appropriate conclusion is that the effects of the famine to some degree cut across class lines. Thus Bolton Priory, which was ultimately bankrupted in the agrarian crisis, actually held alms steady in the first year or so; but it felt compelled to cut its charity by almost 90 percent as the famine endured.[9]

Where the impact on institutions was less severe and perhaps where, as in heavily populated rural districts, the manifestations of distress were particularly visible, the monasteries came through with increased alms. In part, one can suppose, their decision was intended to keep the rural workforce in place. In part, it was an effort to forestall theft and acts of violence. But there is no reason to deny the possibility that theirs was also—as they said it was—a genuine response to suffering.[10] Such charity and reassuring gestures to the needy were said (in part self-servingly, of course) to have drained the treasuries of Cistercian abbeys in France "during the period of hunger and dearth" when "many more persons than in prosperous times flocked to the abbeys of the order for alms and shelter."[11]

Certain monastic houses made available or constructed special facilities to care for the rustic poor, while existing local charitable institutions, like scattered rural almshouses and hospitals, were mobilized for the eleemosynary effort of baking and distributing bread.[12] A giant pot was made in 1315 for Abbot Eylard of the Cistercian abbey of Aduard near Groningen, and in it beans and vegetables were cooked daily for the poor who were suffering from hunger during the famine. The pot became legendary: for centuries it was shown to visitors, who marveled at its size; the *ketel* seems still to have been on display like a quasi-relic at the Holy Ghost Hospital of Groningen as late as the eighteenth century.[13]

Lay lords were not immune from such sentiments or efforts, although it is always possible to give a materialistic or selfish interpretation of their actions as well. The lord of Dry Drayton in Cambridgeshire, the historian of that village writes, "as a matter of grace, to help the tenants in their poverty conceded to his tenants half of his fold-right" in the time of the famine.[14] A more cynical interpretation might make a case for his trying to buy off the possibility of raids on his granaries and herds.

Parallel to charity went credit. I have argued elsewhere that it is sometimes difficult to distinguish the two,[15] even though the received opinion appears to be that the class which provided credit to people in desperate circumstances like the agrarian crisis before us were not likely to be considered charitable by their debtors. No- or low-interest loans had a better chance of being regarded as evidence of decency than the high-interest loans typical of consumption lending in the Middle Ages.[16] Regrettably, we know little about friendly lenders, those "hoping for nothing again" (Luke 6.35).

A subset of creditors, pariah group lenders, always gets a bad press, deservedly or not.[17] Certain secular rulers felt the need to allow Jews to settle (and presumably provide credit to their hard-hit subjects), as Count John of Luxembourg did on 29 June 1316.[18] Certain clergy, meanwhile, took it as their special task to condemn and try to forbid the business dealings of Jews with Christians in the famine, as evidence (dated 13 May 1320) from Aschaffenburg and Babenhausen in the hinterland of Mainz testifies.[19] In France there is also evidence that the crown cracked down on Jewish "usury" in the famine years, but the French case is complicated by a number of factors. Jews had been readmitted to France in 1315, nine years after what was supposed to have been the commencement of their perpetual exile from the kingdom. There was a special provision in the charter of readmission that granted them the privilege of pawnbroking at high interest. Indeed, it was this provision that constituted a significant motivation for their returning at all. The provision proved embarrassing, however, after the famine set in; so the crown took steps to protect people especially hard hit by the harvest and vintage shortfalls from losing their property to Jewish pawnbrokers. It looked very carefully into interest rates in order to see whether the permitted limits were being breached, and it authorized respites of up to a year in loan repayments for some debtors.[20]

In any case, much of what the evidence reveals concerning moneylending by Christians or by Jews, skewed as it is toward bad debts and sharp lenders, is not pretty. "At Wakefield and other manors" in England studied by Christopher Dyer, "a flurry of pleas of debt" occurred during the Great Famine, both because the poor needed to borrow to buy food and could not repay and, interestingly, because old debts were being called in by creditors who were themselves in a pinch.[21] A similar flurry has been observed in the records of the manor of Brigstock in Northamptonshire: there the upsurge comes slightly later, in the immediate aftermath of the subsistence crisis, and may be a residual litigation effect of the methods employed by creditors to call in debts during the years of the famine itself.[22] The will of a Lombard lender (a citizen of Asti) who was active in the rural county of Burgundy (Franche-Comté) has come down to us from the year 1317. Remorsefully, the moneylender forgave or restored any number of outstanding debts to individuals. What is more fascinating is that he made restitutions to all the villagers ("omnibus habitatoribus villarum") of "Lure, Magny, Vounans, Abbenans, Melesey, Bouhans, Amblans, Velotte, Molans, Pomoy, Villemefroy, Calemoutier, Lievans, Cere, Autrey, Noroy, Borrey, Openans, Oricour, Eprey, etc."[23] The image of a whole region transformed by the economic crisis into debt peonage to a single man, an outsider, is arresting; the deathbed forgiveness of a whole region's debts—forgiveness arising from the fear of hell most probably—is equally so.

Local charity and credit—benign or with whatever intent—were modestly effective if limited responses to the deepening crisis in 1315 and even in early 1316. But by reporting the great and growing hordes of roving beggars in the latter year and during 1317, chronicler after chronicler unmasks the failure of local charity and credit to contain the misery.[24] Ireland saw small holders, who were at first able to offer charity to those less prosperous, reduced to poverty themselves (war was a contributory factor); and then it saw these same people leave their homes to search the countryside for alms.[25] Swedes, having suffered through two horrible years of natural disasters, 1315 and 1316, were subjected to the vagaries and terrorism of civil war thereafter: a funeral song for the princely victims of the strife laments in passing that the "rustics were impoverished" as a direct consequence.[26]

In Germany there is evidence that the rural indigent were making their presence felt by massing near towns; an example is their (probably menacing) presence at the postern and on the thoroughfares of Magdeburg in 1316.[27] A charter confirming the distribution of loaves and wine in January 1317 in the area near Mainz includes an extra provision (*hoc adiecto*) that foresees an increase in the number of people seeking free food. The charter tells how the same amount of food ought to be distributed, with the portions for each supplicant appropriately (*pro rata*) reduced.[28] Further north, people from western Germany were begging at towns all along the Baltic, such as Lübeck in 1317.[29]

The most intriguing possibility, hinted at before, is that elements of this massive vagabond population kept moving east and eventually became patriated in those eastern and southeastern German and western Polish lands being wrested from Slavic and/or pagan control. The pattern—famine in the west, migration to the east—was already familiar.[30] This in part explains why, whatever level of village and homestead abandonment may have occurred in western Europe during the worst periods of the late medieval economic crisis, the regions beyond the Elbe, with far larger individual holdings, were almost always far less troubled by desertion.[31] Little Poland, the area from Cracow to Warsaw and east, for example, saw the peak in the establishment of new franchises for small settlements in the years immediately after 1315. The granting of these franchises (the number was enormous) recognized the settlement of crowds of migrants who effectively turned villages into towns. What adds plausibility to the argument that it was the increasingly rootless, famine-motivated, and job-hungry immigrants from the west who helped swell these settlements is that the franchises under discussion were granted to vills "on important commercial routes."[32] Insofar as the roving begging populations had a goal (and it is misleading to think of them as lacking in calculation),[33] it was to present themselves at commercial centers either on the coast or, as that proved increasingly fruitless, in the more distant hinterlands of great cities like Magdeburg and Bamberg. Certainly, the memory persisted to the sixteenth century that the age of the Great Famine had seen many ruined householders from central and western Germany make their way "to foreign lands."[34]

Another indicator of the inadequacy of local charity and credit in the countryside was the increase in lawlessness ("the rising tide of crime"), specifically theft, and the sharpening of the determination to pursue its prosecution to the fullest.[35] Certainly German evidence coming from the lower Rhine region points in this direction, according to Günter Piecha.[36] In France the government reluctantly recognized the crescendo of attacks on merchants as a national problem in 1317.[37] In Lincolnshire the Great Famine is said by its most thorough and searching historian to have "led to a wave of petty crime," much of which resulted, not surprisingly, from the "inflated corn prices." The object of a great many of the thefts was grain.[38] Edward Britton has amassed evidence showing that the Broughton (Huntingdonshire) "community [was] unusually sensitive to theft during this period [1315–1317], particularly if it involved food stuffs."[39] Rarely anywhere in England was a jury lenient with thieves, even though their stealing was allegedly prompted or necessitated by hunger.[40]

Of course, some of the theft was arranged by men not for their own consumption but so that they might benefit from the high prices for grain and flour. The granary of the Norman abbey of Cerisy was the target of a conspiracy of three clerics determined to steal its hoard of milled grain in 1316. Although as clerics they would probably not have been suspected in the first instance, suspicions for some reason did turn to them. They were arrested and imprisoned in the abbey, and were released only when they found sureties to stand stiff bail for them.[41] Had they been successful and managed, undetected, to market a sizable portion of Cerisy's stock of grain through middlemen, they would have been rich and still respected men. As it was, their reputations were sullied forever.

It is virtually certain that this eruption of criminality was strictly circumscribed by type. The evidence is not good, despite Henry Lucas's assertion, for example, that murder rates went up sharply, for unfortunately he drew his conclusion from inadequate information in the Irish Annals.[42] It is also not surprising that there are few unequivocal references to riots. By and large, riots were an urban, not a rural, form of protest. The two factors that might have laid the foundation for rural riots were the hordes of vagabonds and the presence of well-supplied garrison towns in the midst of rural poverty.

In general, groups of beggars became dangerous when they massed, and this, as we noticed earlier, usually took place near towns. The town administrators offered them a little food in return for their moving on, and ordinarily kept the gates closed. Violence during these encounters can hardly be classified as rural. It is true that there were great waves of rural (and urban) discontent in France in 1320 and 1321, inspired in part by calls for a Crusade and directed in part against Jews and lepers; it would not be irresponsible to see the agrarian crisis as an important preliminary to the initiation of the disturbances. In the end the violence that did erupt as groups of discontented rustics wandered about was vented in towns—and largely, for the malcontents ranged widely, in southern France and Aragon where the forces of the crown in both kingdoms finally suppressed them. We will look more closely at 1320 and 1321 in France in our discussion of urban life and the state, in Part III.[43]

Garrison towns, too, may be better treated under the heading of urban life or the state's initiatives during the agrarian crisis, even though they were so often situated in otherwise remote, rural areas and had little of that autonomy and freedom of commerce we ordinarily associate with medieval towns. The embodiment of princely or lordly power in these garrison towns (English power in Wales, for example; German power in the Oderraum, for another) intimidated the often hostile and equally often ethnically distinct rural populations.[44] We have already seen that to some extent the administrators of these towns went out of their way to maintain the loyal part of the rural workforce, by doles if necessary.[45] With little or nothing to lose, natives who were suffering from the bad times and resented the incursions of English or Germans into their homelands made war, not riots; "racist" literature calling for a kind of ethnic cleansing by war would achieve a terrifying sharpness on the frontiers of northern Christendom in the wake of the famine.[46]

Rural Demography

So far in this chapter and its predecessor we have seen that the ordinary rural population suffered by having to pay unwonted prices, sink beneath an ocean of debt, surrender tenements, and go begging. We have seen, too, strong indications that the allocation of available foodstuffs to the needy was quite limited. The upsurge in rural crime is one sign of this limitation. In part it was precisely because of this failure to protect the weakest and most vulnerable part of the population that a significant number of rustics also fell victim to the cruelest forms of physical distress. The most deeply affected regions in rural society were those which suffered under the combined burdens of dense population, harvest shortfalls, murrains, and war—especially war. It is certainly likely that the rural population was already poised near the edge of subsistence.[47] But we must not exaggerate the extent of extreme adversity: in the absence of one or more of the additional burdens listed, rural society in fact came through the crisis with a far less intensive demographic shock than was the case, as we shall later observe, in urban areas.

For rural society the most disturbing and extreme allegations are those contemporary or near contemporary reports about people so hungry that they were reduced to eating corpses. One report describes how people went about the cemeteries digging up the newly dead and cooking the soft flesh in skulls.[48] Ordinarily historians regard such accusations (and the even more extreme ones associated with urban behavior during the famine) as fanciful.[49] This is certainly a possibility. On the other hand, the accusations, when of a rural origin, are not random. They tend to come from areas most deeply traumatized by war: the one cited is from Ireland where incessantly vicious combat had impoverished the countryside.[50] Moreover, similar behavior is documentable in recent war-intensified famines.[51]

Even if we assume that this kind of behavior did not take place in rural areas during the Great Famine, there might still be legitimate reasons for observers to report such actions as facts. For example, in the best of times grave robbing occasionally took place. It occurred all the more frequently during famines, wars, and periods of high prices when thieves were attracted by the possibility of finding coins, jewelry, or quality cloth and grave clothes that could be pawned.[52] In the morning light the physical evidence of grave robbing would look suspiciously like the desecration of cemeteries for food, especially if dogs or pigs disturbed the remains, as was their custom,[53] after the thieves departed. The Irish report might point to grave robbing, the illumination from the torches used by the robbers as they plundered the corpses being interpreted, from afar, as the light from cooking fires. No great leap of the imagination would be required to identify a skull or two, lying on the freshly disturbed earth of the desecrated graves or near a burned-out torch, as cooking pots or dishes.

It goes without saying that the psychological predisposition of people to make and to believe such reports was closely tied to the severity of the crisis they were enduring. Yet however much the psychological stress that gave rise to these allegations needs to be emphasized, it is the biological stress on the rural population that has left the best evidence. We begin with a point made obvious by the intensity of the cost-of-living crisis described earlier, namely, that there was undoubtedly a precipitous decline in average consumption among the rural population from 1315 on. The worst-off in the countryside—the "many paupers"—are said to have "gnawed, just like dogs, the raw dead bodies of cattle" and to have "grazed like cows on the growing grasses of the fields." The author who vouchsafes this information was troubled at the report. Was it right to bequeath testimony of such degradation to the world?[54]

His account points us in an important direction. Famine involves not only a net loss in the intake of food but also, granting the victims' attempts to make up the difference, the intake of "strange diets." Evidence from current famines attests to the presence in these diets of disagreeable plants, bark, leather, cloth, dirt, diseased animals and others—like grubs and vermin—not ordinarily considered palatable, and, in extreme cases, human cadavers.[55] According to J.P.W. Rivers, the significance for bodily health of the "dietary deviations of famine . . . received surprisingly little scientific attention [until recently] and yet they are most important in dictating the pattern of nutritional disease that occurs."[56] It is even possible to infer strange diets from the sorts of nutritional diseases that typify famines, because, however various these diets, they seem to have in common a short list of nutritional lacunae.[57] Or, at least, the diseases associated with recent famines and the nutrient deficiencies accompanying them duplicate to a large extent the diseases (deduced from the recorded symptoms) in historical famines,[58] thus adding weight to the notion that contemporary observers accurately recorded the adoption of strange diets, even if they laced their tales with picturesque metaphors (men "grazed like cows").

The phrase *strange diets* is a good one in that it captures both the psychological and the biological shock of being obliged to consume otherwise repugnant comestibles. But, to repeat a point made earlier, not all strange diets were equal. The range and opportunity of rustics to gather food only marginally inferior in quality if not in quantity to their normal diet far exceeded what the urban poor in big towns could command. And consequently the stress on the human body from strange diets was normally less severe in rural areas (always excepting those suffering the carnage of war) than in towns.

People in the countryside, therefore, were not in general "starving to death." (It is difficult to starve to death even when food intake is completely stopped, as in hunger strikes; and such complete cessation of eating is not characteristic of famines, when people look hard for something to eat.)[59] A few may have eaten fungus-infested rye grain (the damp conditions encouraged the parasite's growth); those who did so probably suffered painful paroxysms, became manic, and died from ergotism, the disease known in the Middle Ages as sacred fire or Saint Anthony's fire.[60] But the accumulated wisdom of the ages stopped most rural dwellers from utilizing spoiled rye, except in the most desperate circumstances.

Many, many more rustics, however, were *weakened* by the decline in caloric intake, by the diarrhea and dehydration that come from adopting strange diets, and perhaps by the decreased nutritional value of some of their substitute foods.[61] People were to die in significant numbers partly because of the increase in morbidity (susceptibility to disease) that resulted from this weakening. War played its role here—both by bringing alien populations (with their own diseases) into contact with rural people whose resistance was low, and by the sheer acts of killing and burning stores. The lethargy (or weakening), the disease, and, indeed, the fear, in turn, brought diminished productivity among rural workers, reducing overall output and therefore spurring on price rises.[62] Not all rustics suffered equally, of course. It was, rather, those among the rural poor whose food intake was most ruthlessly cut and whose diets were most radically altered for whom disease led to death. Presumably, this section of the population was composed principally of unemployed laborers and their families in the densest areas of rural settlement.

Modern work on the biology of malnutrition has established that the increase in morbidity is substantially more acute among newborns (even when they continue to nurse, for lactation, despite famine, persists in new mothers) and among young children than among adults, probably because of the low birth weight of infants and unintentional nutrient deficiencies in the food supplied to young, non-nursing children. What is adequate for an adult can be inadequate for a (potentially growing) child. By making energy intake so restricted and the dependence on strange diets so great, famine differs from traditional malnutrition in poor societies by extending the increase in morbidity, though not typically to the same high level, to members of additional age cohorts. After children, the next most vulnerable are the aged. Men are more vulnerable than women, who have more body fat and traditionally lighter energy needs. This vulnerability (differentially elevated levels of morbidity) is translated into differentially elevated levels of mortality when social-cultural factors fail to induce the leaders of communities and families to favor the distribution of scarce resources to the most vulnerable.[63] The significance, in terms of our evaluation of the famine's demographic impact, is this. The evidence on mortality, such as it is, almost all pertains to adult men. Where that evidence strongly hints at high mortality in *sedentary* populations, we must be prepared to imagine differentially higher, though unrecorded, mortality for newborns and children and perhaps for other groups as well. (High mortality among vagabond beggars, whose population is predominantly male, would not justify an extrapolation of this sort.)[64]

To be sure, although medieval commentators, like modern historians, talk routinely about death by starvation, the former, unlike many of their modern counterparts, were always well aware that the nature of the deaths they were recording differed considerably from person to person.[65] Opportunistic infections were at work, and although the chroniclers often used a simple singular word like plague or pestilence (*plaga*, *pestis*, *pestilentia*) to describe the situation in the Great Famine,[66] other remarks make clear their recognition that more than one disease was causing the deaths. The evidence of the Irish Annals is explicit on this point;[67] though late, they represent trustworthy traditions in this domain.[68] The chroniclers also recognized that a robust population had to be weakened considerably before it became susceptible to the kinds of diseases that could decimate whole regions. The spray of blood or scarlet light that rained down from the heavens warned them (or so hindsight suggested) that this level of weakness was reached among the Swedes only in 1316.[69]

There is other impressionistic evidence as well, like Edward II of England's letter to the bishop of Durham in 1316 where he records his distress that the "poor and beggars" were daily dying from want of food and from disease in the extreme northern borderlands of the war-ravaged kingdom.[70] But hard statistical evidence on rural mortality is quite

uneven. Let us take a closer look at England, and begin with lightly populated regions.

For these regions the evidence is equivocal to negative on high mortality. At best, one can get an impression of occasional problems. The records of Launceston Priory in Devonshire, for instance, hint that there
might have been an unusually high level of mortality in the region in our
period, for the priory had to fight a series of battles with local churches
over mortuary rights in these years. (The resolution of these disputes took
place during the famine years, on 30 November 1319 and 26 January
1320.)[71] This kind of dispute was characteristic of, though not by any
means limited to, periods when secular authorities, faced with a significant excess of deaths from infectious diseases, authorized rapid or mass
burials in available cemeteries without taking care to conform to standing
ecclesiastical regulations.[72] It is possible that Launceston's disputes originated in this scenario, since other evidence from the region also hints at
a possible contemporary surge in deaths. Nicholas Orme, in a study of
Clyst Gabriel Hospital near Exeter, about eighty kilometers away from
Launceston, identifies the years 1316, 1317, and 1318 as uncommonly
mortal ones for the hospital's inmates. Presumably, these old and sick
people were more susceptible to the complications caused by reduced caloric intake and modified diets than were healthy people. Of the twenty-
four or slightly more people who might have spent time at the hospital
during the period 1316–1318, eleven or twelve died in those three years.
Because this population is so small and was infirm to begin with, however, definitive conclusions cannot be based on his findings or those of
nearby Launceston.[73] And it remains the case that in general southwestern England, typical of relatively lightly settled regions, escaped the
"great mortality."

The evidence from heavily populated south-central and southeastern
England (Wessex, Sussex, Essex) stands in sharp contrast. There, heriot
payments, the equivalent of death duties on customary holdings, suggest
a relatively large increase in mortality.[74] "In 1316/17 the heriot payments
on some Winchester manors indicate a death rate nearly three times the
normal."[75] Using other available manorial records, scholars have established that in several villages of these Winchester manors and on various
Essex manors and in Halesowen there may have been a 10–15 percent
reduction in population in the years 1316–1318, a really quite staggering
figure.[76]

The English Midlands also provide some data that point, in Worcester-
shire, for example, to the famine's "severe effects" on the demography of
the rustics of various manors.[77] In Northamptonshire, seventy-five miles
north of London, on the manor of Brigstock in the forest of Rockingham,
where a diverse forest economy obtained, Judith Bennett has noticed a
decline in population between 1326 and 1340 that she relates plausibly to

the residual effect of the "famines and epidemics" between 1315 and 1322.[78] If this is so, it remains the case that in the Midlands countryside such mortality had a differential impact based on status. For Wiltshire, where aristocratic demography has been studied closely, research has been unable to identify any appreciable impact on the mortality of the upper class.[79]

If, exceptions aside, lightly settled areas escaped the great mortality, and some densely populated rural areas suffered grievously, it remains puzzling that the single most densely settled rural region in England, East Anglia, suffered only modestly, at least in demographic terms. The East Anglian data prove that the mortality was differentiated regionally as well as by status, for heriots in the region do not seem to have risen dramatically.[80] Hallam concludes, with some heat, that the idea ought to be "discredit[ed] . . . that the famines of 1314–22, which affected the wheat-eating gentry who wrote the chronicles and hated Edward II," had a significant demographic impact on "the barley-eating peasantry." According to him, rather than mortality, we should be looking at the demography of marriage. He suggests that rustics did little more than make short-term adjustments in family size by marrying late.[81]

Even though one can accept that there were differential regional rates of mortality, Hallam's conclusions in other ways seem to be in error. If he means that the "wheat-eating gentry" died in great numbers, he is wrong. At least there is no evidence that they did. If he means that they were adversely affected economically, he is probably correct, especially for the minor gentry.[82] But the attentive reader will note that the contrast Hallam makes is with the "barley-eating" peasantry, as if the barley harvests were not depressed by the rains and the ensuing drought—which is demonstrably false.[83] Finally, delay of marriage presumably occurred, but it would, again presumably, have occurred anyway, thanks to the economic situation, with or without increases in mortality; and since we know almost nothing of ages or dates of marriage, this is not a very profitable approach to studying the famine.[84]

Bruce Campbell, who has also studied the East Anglian evidence, can document no decline of population on the scale suggested by some students of south-central and southeastern England, and he insists that "great as was the distress which it caused," the famine was no "watershed" there. On the other hand, the picture he draws is not so simplistic as Hallam's: there was, Campbell shows for the East Anglian manor of Coltishall, an "increase in the proportion of non-filial heirs to 33.3% [from a normal 12–20 percent] during the years 1315–22 [that] probably indicates some excess mortality at this time; and the unusually large number of instances of inheritance by minors between 1312 and 1323 . . . invites the same interpretation."[85] Finally, Mark Bailey's study of Breckland, a region of light sandy soils in East Anglia, concludes that the mortality effect there of the Great Famine was real but "serious rather than critical." "Recorded deaths at Lakenheath," one of the manors investigated, he concludes, were "above average" in 1314, 1316, and 1322.[86]

A little less is known about rural France. The chroniclers assert that high mortality was widespread. The years 1315 and 1316 witnessed an especially large number of deaths, we are informed.[87] In the year 1316, wrote one chronicler, "there was a great mortality of people and most of all of the poor, many of whom perished from starvation."[88] In fact, although at least one of our many informants about the elevated death rate was a Norman monk,[89] the Norman countryside seems to have been spared the worst consequences of the harvest shortfalls. Its saving grace was probably its mixed husbandry, particularly the abundance of fruit in this heavily orcharded region, which supplied substitutes for the necessary decline in consumption of cereals and dairy products.[90]

Other regional studies paint a varied picture, sometimes similar to Normandy, sometimes quite different. There are reports of high mortality in the Parisian basin, although Guy Fourquin doubted that the levels reached those of urban areas like the Flemish towns or, one could add, some of the rural manors of south-central and southeastern England.[91] Work on Burgundy, on the other hand, where the rural population was very densely settled, shows the eruption of an epidemic in 1316 (probably occasioned by a disease introduced by a traveler recently in Italy) that in some villages caused the death of about one-third of the already weakened inhabitants.[92] Fossier, the most thorough student of rural society in northern France, is inclined, therefore, to regard the Great Famine as a demographic catastrophe in the countryside.[93]

The "great hunger" in the empire was already claiming many rural victims in the north who were felled by the "gruesome pestilence" in 1315; the chroniclers whose reports Peter Sax ransacked in the seventeenth century to construct his annals said that a third of the population was affected in one way or another.[94] One charter that refers to the widespread pestilence in the summer of 1315 was amended in a later hand (perhaps 1316) with the added words "and mortality," when disease began to take its grim toll on the weakened population.[95] The year 1316 was, indeed, by far the worst year in the countryside in the empire. It was the year of "the great death" in Gelderland,[96] and pestilence was rife in the nearby region surrounding Xanten as well.[97]

Occasionally, as we have seen in the case of Clyst Gabriel,[98] epidemic disease in the countryside seems to have penetrated the walls of a rural ecclesiastical house. The same can be surmised in the empire. For the nuns of Rijnsburg (Reinsburg) in coastal Friesland the *pestjaar* 1316 was a continuing tragedy. Abbess Elizabeth Van Wieldrecht died on 19 August 1316. Her successor, Abbess Ada Van Teylingen, a local lord's daughter, died the same year; and then her successor Abbess Ada Van Leyden, the daughter of another notable, died almost immediately thereafter.[99]

Such a cluster of deaths might not be related, but in fact the wonderful series of studies in the multivolume *Monasticon belge* permit historians to get some sense of the extent of the deaths of abbots and abbesses and of priors and prioresses in Belgium (roughly speaking) during the famine. Among Benedictines the year 1316 saw the deaths of Abbot Philippe Martin of Saint-Ghislain (Hainaut) and Prior Gillebert of Frasne-lez-Gosselies (Hainaut).[100] The Premonstratensians lost Abbot Gérard de Masny of Bonne-Espérance (Hainaut) and Abbot Guillaume Van Calsteren of Parc in Heverlee in Brabant (the latter is said explicitly to have died of pestilence).[101] The Cistercians counted among the dead that year Abbess Jeanne Persans of Val-Notre-Dame in the Liègeois, while the Augustinian Canons suffered the loss of Prior Baldwin of Val-des-Ecoliers (at Houffalize in Luxembourg).[102] We may conclude that the deaths of these heads of houses, if, like Guillaume Van Calsteren's, from pestilence, mean that a large number of monks, nuns, and canons suffered and perished as well.

The foregoing list in no way exhausts the evidence of the number of heads of houses in this region who died in the famine years. The problem is that sometimes only an approximate date of death can be given. An abbess, say, will appear for the last time issuing an order or confirming a contract on 21 August 1315. She will die sometime thereafter, certainly before 4 April 1317 when her successor is first known from charter evidence. This is not a hypothetical case, but that of Abbess Marie of La Ramée, a Cistercian house at Jauchelette in Brabant.[103] We would probably not be wrong to place her death tentatively with the others cited in 1316. More important, when we factor in all such cases of heads of houses in the region who died from 1315 to 1319, what seems bad enough in view of the explicit cases of deaths in 1316 turns out to be a tragedy of far greater proportions. At least seven more female and ten more male heads of houses, mostly in rural areas, met their demise. I list them here.[104]

Abbess Hawide of Salzinnes, Cistercian, Namurois, 8 April 1317 (1:106)

Abbot Jean of Frasne-lez-Gosselies, Benedictine, Hainaut, between May 1317 and March 1318 (1:301)

Former Abbot Gilles Moschons of Val-Saint-Lambert, Cistercian, Liègeois, 14 September 1315 (2:161)

Abbot Lambert d'Odeur of Val-Saint-Lambert, Cistercian, Liègeois, 28 March 1317 or 1318 (2:161)

Abbot Henri de Hermalle of Val-des-Ecoliers, Augustinian, Liègeois, 1318 (2:330)

Abbot Gautier de Tournai dit de Tollebeke of Saint-Barthélemy de l'Eeckhout, Augustinian, western Flanders, 20 June 1316 or 1317 (3:773)

Abbot Jean de Vlasschere of Saint-Barthélemy de l'Eeckhout, Augustinian,
western Flanders, 1318 (3:773)

Former Abbot Godefroid of Vlierbeek, Benedictine, Brabant, 1315 (4:92
especially n. 2)

Prévot Jean of Notre-Dame-de-la-Chapelle, Benedictine, Brabant, between
17 November 1315 and 21 August 1317 (4:154)

Abbess Ida de Cottem of Grand-Bigard, Benedictine, Brabant, 23 January
1318 (4:228)

Abbess Ida de Walhaim of Florival, Cistercian, Brabant, 1318 (4:431)

Abbess Clémence of Orienten, Cistercian, Brabant, between 29 April 1315
and 10 January 1319 (4:504)

Prior Jean de Troine of Val-des-Ecoliers, Augustinian, Luxembourg, early
April 1317 (5:312)

Abbess Beatrix Van Hallinckrode of Zwijveke, Cistercian, eastern Flanders,
1 July 1318 (7:478)

Former Abbot Jean Scamp of Ninove, Premonstratensian, eastern Flanders,
17 February 1318 (7:515)

Prioress Marguerite Dierwinne of Blijdenberg, Augustinian, province of
Antwerp, between 21 December 1317 and 31 January 1319 (8:544)

Prioress Marguerite Van Kersdorp of Sint-Margrietendaal, Augustinian,
province of Antwerp, 1315 (8:635)

In sum, during the early years of the famine (especially in 1316) a total
of twenty-four men and women, a significant proportion of the elite leadership of monastic institutions in what we now call Belgium and its environs, died. Without being too wedded to the precise accuracy of this tally,
one can still say that no other period, let alone single year, seems remotely
to have witnessed such mortality—at least before the Black Death.

Peter Sax, the seventeenth-century author earlier cited, added another
telling detail about the mortality encountered during the famine, based on
his reading of earlier reports. The terrible floods that followed the heavy
and incessant rains took thirty thousand people to their deaths. This was,
to be sure, an exaggeration. Nevertheless, to be induced to make such
statements the chroniclers on whom Sax depended for the information
must have seen drownings on a scale they had neither witnessed nor
heard of before.[105]

We can address only morbidity and mortality with reasonable confidence
in assessing the demographic impact of the famine on rural society, but as
the discussion of the famine's differential regional impact suggested,
other demographic factors (like age at marriage) would be relevant to a

full discussion of this issue.[106] Unfortunately, almost nothing has as yet been deduced from either impressionistic or documentary sources about these other factors. A little—very little—survives related to the matter of fertility during and after the famine. To interpret this material we may turn for guidance to work on recent famines, which indicates that in the duration of a typical famine or the year or two thereafter there is ordinarily a steep decline in fertility.

The causes of this short-term decline are somewhat uncertain and may in fact be voluntary (as we shall see in a moment), not physiological. Evidence for an actual decline over the short term in fecundity, the capacity to reproduce, is indecisive, though if a decline were to be documented, amenorrhea and reduced sperm counts could possibly be responsible.[107] Alternative explanations for the brief fall in the rate of pregnancy and the live-birth rate, therefore, include (1) lower frequency of intercourse owing either to a waning in the sexual drive caused by lethargy or to the absence of husbands who have taken to the road to find work or beg alms, (2) an increase in voluntary birth control, including self-induced abortions, and (3) postponement of marriage, which has already been remarked.[108]

We may infer a reduced birthrate during and immediately after the famine that conforms with this model in part from the existence of large transient male begging populations.[109] A very few medieval authors or types of evidence also point to a decline. Indeed, at least one author, Jacques de Thérines, writing in 1317 or 1318, appears explicitly to have noted the fertility decline in France.[110] Evidence that has survived from the manor of Cottenham in Cambridgeshire points faintly in the same direction. On that manor there was a reduction or excusing of leyrwite, the fornication fine, probably because of the poverty imposed by the Great Famine on the servile population. But a related fine, childwyte, was neither respited nor forgiven in the famine years because it involved pregnancy, threatening the community with still another mouth to feed.[111]

It is highly dubious, however, that the famine had a lingering negative effect on fertility. Recent famines have been followed after a couple of years by a return to normal fertility or even a decisive increase in the number of live births; very little convincing evidence exists showing any long-term impact on fecundity, the capacity for reproduction in the surviving adult population.[112] These observations make the little information suggesting a rural "baby boom" after the ebbing of the Great Famine all the more persuasive.[113]

PART III

TOWNS AND PRINCIPALITIES

7

URBAN DEMOGRAPHY AND ECONOMY

I N PART II we examined various aspects of the production and distribution crisis in rural environments where 85 to 90 percent of northern European population was concentrated.[1] Other considerations
now oblige us to turn our attention to the towns. It is, of course, no easy
matter to decide what a town was in the Middle Ages. In chapter 3, some
attempt was made to differentiate small towns from villages, but despite
the abundance of taxonomic work that has been done, the criteria suggested often seem arbitrary or conventional.[2] The same is true of the criteria used to distinguish the various sizes and forms of urban settlement
and, implicitly, the various "experiences of life" in different settlements.
Jürgen Sydow, for example, distinguishes big towns (*Grossstädte*), those
with populations above 10,000 (of which Europe as a whole knew from
fifty-six to seventy-nine examples in 1300)[3] from middling towns (*Mittelstädte*) having 2,000–10,000 inhabitants, and from small towns
(*Kleinstädte*) with 500–2,000 residents. "Dwarf-towns" (*Zwergstädte*), in
his scheme, are settlements with urban characteristics but with a population of fewer than 500. He also imputes a qualitative difference between
medieval *Mittelstädte* on either side of the 4,000 population mark.[4] Without commenting at this point on the persuasiveness of Sydow's particular
taxonomy (which has been widely accepted),[5] I wish to note that in the
course of this chapter I have tried to address factors like population and
metropolitan pull, as well as other criteria used to construct taxonomies
of the medieval town, to the extent that they seem directly germane to
the cluster of problems related to the onset, duration, and impact of the
famine.

But to go back to the original question: What compels a separate treatment of urban issues? First, the urban economy was in a sense the leading
(or transformative) component of the medieval economy as a whole.[6]
Men and women had increasingly, in the twelfth and thirteenth centuries,
come to see towns—old and new—as islands of economic opportunity.
Royal courts, though continuing to be peripatetic, had identified particular towns as their special havens or capitals. Two of these—London and
Paris—had grown tremendously in size, creating and structuring vast economic hinterlands that stretched from sixty to one hundred kilometers or
more in all directions.[7] Finally, across Flanders and the southern rim of
the Baltic coast, a group of towns had developed relatively sophisticated
economies and networks of trade.[8]

There is an ideological aspect to the centrality of urban life as well. Despite a lingering hostility toward commercial affairs among clerical thinkers, many other intelligent and educated Christians in the north had rediscovered or were reemphasizing the equation of the town and civilization.[9] This same reawakening awareness or stress on the emerging northern European town as the matrix of high civilization has also been documented in the work of contemporary Jews, such as the famous exegete Rashi of Troyes in Champagne.[10] For all these reasons—including the ideological ones—the urban crisis had wider ramifications than the actual proportion of medieval population living in towns might at first lead one to suppose.

A final consideration commanding particular attention for urban society can be much more briefly stated. It is that, although surpassed in total numbers by the population of the villages and hamlets, the towns and particularly certain classes of people within the towns suffered a great deal more and far longer than did their counterparts in the countryside.[11] The internal dissension precipitated amid the suffering often had, in turn, particularly persistent effects on the political and economic conditions of the towns. These effects were not uniformly bad, but they often influenced fundamental aspects of urban relations.[12]

Distribution, Population, Hinterlands

The year 1300 saw a very skewed distribution of urban centers in northern Europe. Ireland, Scotland, and Wales had a small handful of garrison and administrative towns, like Dublin, whose resident populations could not often have exceeded 3,000 souls and were ordinarily considerably lower. England had one truly great city, London, whose population in 1300 historians have traditionally put at about 40,000.[13] A new group of scholars led by Derek Keene and associated with the "Feeding the City" project, an attempt of the Centre for Metropolitan History to map the impact of London on its hinterland, now urges a figure closer to 100,000.[14] Although this figure is problematical at best, it has recently become de rigueur, being accepted in works by Richard Smith, Rodney Hilton, John Mundy, and R. H. Britnell, with, at most, the qualifier "perhaps."[15] A number of provincial English towns—Norwich and the port of Southampton, for example—were probably in the 3,000–10,000 range, despite the "recently encountered enthusiasm for urban population growth" among English historians that somewhat arbitrarily wants to bring that figure (in Norwich's case) up to 25,000.[16]

On the Continent, where the spread of major towns was more impressive, no such doubtful inflation of figures is necessary. To be sure, Scandi-

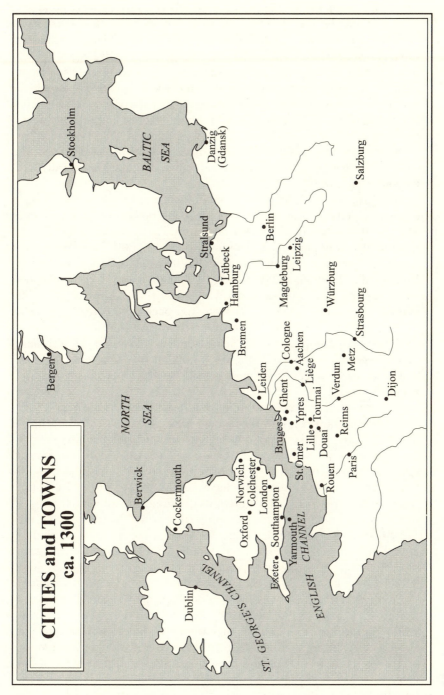

CITIES and TOWNS ca. 1300

Map 3

navia and the northern Low Countries had few serious towns. Guess-work imagines Bergen, the Hanse depot on the western coast of Norway, at 2,000–3,000, even 7,000.[17] The last figure seems high. The largest town in Sweden, Stockholm, it has been suggested, was of Bergen's order of magnitude.[18] To return to the example of Norway, even if we grant that, by the most generous definition, real towns existed in any numbers in that kingdom (fifteen is one figure suggested), the average size would be something like 1,300 inhabitants according to the best and still very questionable estimates.[19] The kingdom of Sweden, meanwhile, had only five other settlements, besides Stockholm, that have been classified as towns.[20] Each counted over 1,000 inhabitants, but these were hardly metropolises of note.[21]

Purer urban experiences were lived in Flanders. By 1300 or so, it had at least 25 percent, possibly as many as 40–50 percent of its inhabitants living in towns, many of which were enormous by medieval standards; the total urban population at a minimum was 180,000.[22] Ghent's population has been put at anywhere from 40,000 to 60,000, even 80,000.[23] Bruges tallied between 35,000 and 50,000 inhabitants.[24] Liège and Ypres could scarcely have reached the lower end of that range but were still sizable.[25] Saint-Omer and Arras were approaching but remained well under 20,000 by the end of the thirteenth century.[26]

In Germany important old Rhenish centers, like Cologne, also sustained large numbers of residents, say, 40,000 or so.[27] Of a lesser order of magnitude were other old settlements; both Aachen and Münster are estimated at about 10,000 inhabitants at their height.[28] But newer towns (the pace of foundation was extraordinary at least down to the year 1300) were an important factor in the demographic mix as well.[29] The Rhineland, for example, which had only eight towns in 1180, had fifty-two by 1250, and a few of these might have rivaled Aachen and Münster in size.[30] A number of inland towns of substantial size flourished as well. Strasbourg and Augsburg may have surpassed 10,000.[31] Würzburg seems to have reached 4,300–5,000, as did Freiberg and Görlitz in Saxony, and Memmingen and the imperial city of Nördlingen in the Württemberg-Bavaria borderlands. Magdeburg counted 6,000 inhabitants; Braunschweig, perhaps a few hundred souls more.[32] There were scores of other towns whose permanent population was in the range 2,500–4,000: Leipzig, Bautzen, Dresden, Marburg in Hesse, Zwickau.[33]

Although the Hanse towns and other settlements along the Baltic coast had grown rapidly as a result of long-distance and short-distance immigration in the thirteenth century, they were still modest in size relative to the larger Flemish and Rhenish towns. Yet several would have rivaled places like Norwich in England (based on sober-minded rather than inflated estimates of the latter's population). Hamburg, which quadrupled its population in the course of the thirteenth century, could have had about 5,000 souls in 1300; the received estimate for Lübeck is 6,000, although its most recent and thorough historian puts the number at 15,000 in 1300.[34] Other southern Baltic settlements, despite their economic vitality, were certainly smaller. Kiel, for instance, numbered only 1,500–2,000 inhabitants, and Oldesloe and Plön (two nearby settlements that have been classified as towns) could have had no more than about 1,140 and 720 permanent residents respectively.[35] In 1300 or so in most of the more easterly of these towns, as many as 20 percent of residents were recent immigrants from the Rhineland and neighboring regions; in many, immigrants from near and far constituted the vast majority of inhabitants.[36] And we are talking about large numbers of towns in these regions: in one of them, Mecklenburg-Vorpommern, approximately sixty-five new towns (a few on old Slavic sites) had been established in the period of assarting and colonization.[37]

Finally, we come to France. Paris, of course, dominated the scene. The lowest estimate of its population around 1300 is 80,000; the highest— and, according to the best modern research, the most accurate—is slightly over 200,000.[38] Lille, which came under French domination around the same time, probably had between 20,000 and 30,000 residents, depending on the multiplier one chooses to use in order to extrapolate from the number of houses to the size of the population.[39] Calais, which was also in the troubled borderlands of France and Flanders, had between 13,000 and 15,000 inhabitants.[40] Reims, more firmly linked to the kingdom, tallied between 12,000 and 18,000, perhaps even 20,000 residents, figures again extrapolated from the number of houses.[41]

The hundred years prior to the famine had been kind to most of these towns. To be sure, the last decade or so of the thirteenth century already was witness to a significant decline in economic vigor in some settlements,[42] but on the whole the century had seen expansion—economic, demographic, and spatial—and improvements that multiplied, after the crises of the early fourteenth century, the networks of trade.[43] Occasionally, there were transitions that marked new configurations of urban power without at all undermining the general picture of vigorous urban development. The town-based fairs of Champagne, for example, did not recover from the systemic weaknesses that affected their economic life in the thirteenth century, but the great emporia of Frankfurt-am-Main began to play much the same role as the fairs had once played.[44] The decline of the ports of Frisia, to provide another instance, was more than offset by the rise of the Hanse in the Baltic and the North Sea.[45]

Together with economic prosperity, there had been a relatively high degree of political stability in the towns.[46] Administrative arrangements worked out in the twelfth century (often with violence between seigneurs and sworn associations of burghers) grew hoary with age. Seigneurs retained ultimate control in many instances (Cologne is a case in point), but

for many towns such control was often token or only preserved in a payment from the town corporation to its lord. Even in England, where the
towns' independence from royal scrutiny was not pronounced, ordinary
government was virtually a monopoly of the burghers. There continued
to be islands of seigneurial, especially ecclesiastical, autonomy within
even the most burgher-dominated towns; and these were on more than
one occasion the cause of significant jurisdictional tensions.[47] But most of
these arguments were resolved in courts, not in street fights, and led to no
long-term disruption of economic production.

Serious exceptions to this picture affected the great capital cities, Paris
and London, and the towns of Flanders. In the case of the capitals, the
demographic, economic, and spatial growth was on a far greater scale
than in provincial centers. There were distinct immigrant neighborhoods
and suburbs; the immigrants even came from far-distant and linguisti-
cally distinct regions: Flemings to London and Bretons to Paris are merely
two examples.[48] Rural patches remained here and there in the city, but
they were in retreat as building campaigns multiplied.[49] In England London's tradition of municipal autonomy and the tendency to establish governmental institutions in Westminster rather than in the city proper made
it less dependent on the crown's efforts to stimulate supply.[50] In France,
where the seat of government was in the very heart of Paris, however, the
crown played an active role in monitoring, supplying, defending, and
governing the city.[51]

The second major exception to this general sketch of urban developments in thirteenth-century northern Europe touches upon Flanders.
There economic growth stalled in the late thirteenth century. In the same
period, northern French communes like Amiens and Beauvais (which
were of a size comparable to provincial towns in England) were experiencing something like a fiscal crisis caused by debt-financing and royal
taxation,[52] but theirs was not a crisis in industrial production per se as in
Flanders. David Nicholas, in 1976, categorized the Flemish situation as a
recession.[53] Like many recessions this one was the result of a series of
structural transformations, in this instance affecting the cloth industry.
According to John Munro, the military disruptions that characterized the
early fourteenth century encouraged the leaders of the textile industry to
go over to the production of luxury cloths and lessen their dependence on
cheap bulk exports.[54] The accompanying dislocation had grave consequences for artisanal and working-class families, and it elevated tensions
within the towns that led to recurrent revolts against the oligarchic governments and worsened the economic downturn.[55]

Not every town in Flanders or neighboring regions, of course, had an
oligarchic government whose very existence seemed to stand as a challenge to the workers' status and well-being. Mechlin, for example, man-

aged to develop a relatively stable government where representation on the council was widely distributed among social groups; but this was exceptional.[56] The general pattern, therefore, saw urban governments in Flanders suspicious of worker discontent, worried that the agrarian crisis in food production would lead to further disorder, and deeply concerned at what seemed to be a never-ending economic slump. Demographic catastrophe, as we shall see, only added to the somber mood.[57]

It has already been pointed out that it is impossible to consider great towns, like the capital cities, without constantly reminding ourselves of the mutual impact of metropolis and hinterland.[58] The same is true of ports and provincial towns. In the case of ports (like London), the catchment areas included distant regions, loops, as it were, at the ends of thin threads defined by the sea-lanes to them.[59] At times the impact of a port on its distant supply points was mediated by royal or baronial authorities.[60] The hinterlands of inland provincial towns were more coherent, like the protoplasm encircling the nucleus of a cell or, given the nature of road networks, like the area encompassed by the rim of a many-spoked wheel.[61] The area encompassed by the strong effects of metropolitan pull from a provincial town, wherever situated, could be quite extensive, and the efforts to capitalize on it (improving navigation was one way; further assarting was another) could be quite impressive.[62]

To judge from references to the places of origin of grain shipments within Devon to Exeter, its grain hinterland fanned out up to thirty-five miles (fifty-six kilometers) inland, not to mention to several far more distant supply districts along the sea-lanes to it.[63] This seems extraordinarily large, given Exeter's size (4,000–5,000),[64] but it may reflect the skewing of production toward oats in Devon: the town may have needed more distant imports to obtain sufficient quantities of wheat for the burghers' consumption.[65] Inland Nördlingen in Germany, with about 5,000 inhabitants, was commensurate in size with Exeter but had a much smaller and more typical hinterland with a radius of about seven kilometers.[66] The topographical evidence on all sorts of rural buyers and sellers at the markets of thirteenth-century Dijon, an inland city at least twice Exeter's size set in an area of rich and balanced agricultural production, suggests that its economic hinterland was just twenty-five kilometers in radius or, put differently, covered an area of about 2,000 kms. square.[67] One would have to get up to the size of Metz, toward 20,000, before typically encountering an inland town in a rich agricultural environment of mixed husbandries that had a grain hinterland as extensive as Exeter's.[68]

Artisans working in the nearer districts of the hinterlands of towns of any of these sizes and, of course, still larger ones were transformed by the urban demand: a lime-burner who might have been furnishing fertilizer in an isolated rural community was probably doubling as a potter if he lived in the shadow of a great town.[69] Rural tinkers and miners with access to sand deposits and fern (a source of potassium) contributed to a thriving glassmaking industry providing windows for large urban buildings like churches and town halls.[70]

A last and essential point: urban economies were not like estate economies in which employers of large numbers of people had to negotiate the trade-off between maintaining the workforce in hard times by doles or other acts of paternalism, on the one hand, and cutting costs, on the other. If they chose the latter, there were few institutions besides the household or begging to fill the gap in rural society. Of course, the household was the center of support in towns as well; and except in the most elevated of merchant households, homes doubled as workplaces, and work itself was a familial affair. Wives and daughters labored side by side with husbands, fathers, and brothers,[71] and with non-kin apprentices as extensions of the family. In the absence of family or because of disputes within families, hard times also stimulated begging in towns. But there were far more, if perhaps ineffective, alternative sources of support in towns than in the countryside.[72]

Among these were neighborhood and parish organizations (sometimes they were equivalent), like confraternities, almshouses, and hospitals. Guilds also served important welfare functions. When crises loomed, municipal governments themselves took a much greater interest in assuaging want, lest discontent lead to riots or rebellion. The crowns, too, became more active in assuring their capitals' and other important towns' welfare—by charity or repression—when other preservers of social control were not up to the task. Of course, none of the providers of social services was entirely disinterested. Work on the Bruges hospital network shows how much "class" tensions manifested themselves and led toward segregated institutions, and how rivalries for influence over these institutions might affect their administration.[73] But at least a large number of institutions existed in most towns from which help of some sort could be requested and, often, obtained.

Prices

As was true in rural markets, the years 1315–1322 according to the chroniclers saw a stupendous increase in prices in the towns. In Valenciennes, Liège, and Flemish-speaking Antwerp consumers were suffering "the dear times" and "the horrible expense" already in 1315.[74] In Germany, Magdeburg went through a "very dear time" in 1316.[75] Nuremberg endured similar inflation in that year, which persisted in the years to come.[76] The year 1317 saw prices shoot up in Stralsund; again, the high price level seemed intractable.[77]

Chroniclers in France tell a similar tale of the urban economy. While the general price rise is remarked for the kingdom as a whole in 1315, the dearness ("chierté") was noticed "especiaument à Paris."[78] The word *especiaument* is appropriate because contemporaries were also aware that Paris was usually well supplied with grain, and though prices varied, supply usually responded splendidly and kept prices short of the ceilings reached elsewhere. The crown was key here, but in 1315 even the crown was unable to effectively preclude steep rises in grain prices.[79] As for 1316, Paris is said to have endured truly skyrocketing inflation for wheat, barley, and oats.[80] The English chronicle record is ceaseless in its focus on the high prices and the especially bad situation in London. Almost no author seems to have passed up the opportunity to bemoan the distress—for centuries to come.[81]

Volatility was also as characteristic of urban prices as of rural ones, if not more so; there could be dramatic surges followed by steep declines. But the overall trend was decisively upward. Of course our price data are incomplete, and sometimes only general statements of this sort are possible. Statistical precision would in many cases be misleading. Nonetheless, the fragmentary information that has survived suggests that the pattern outlined was characteristic of the price curve in Bremen and Lübeck,[82] in Bruges and Ypres,[83] in Cambrai,[84] and in Valenciennes.[85] Indeed, if 1320 represents a temporary return to normal price levels in Valenciennes and Mons as well, two towns for which more detailed information survives, then the year 1316 had seen cereal prices in the former at twenty-four times and in the latter at thirty-two times the normal level. If, on the other hand, the price levels in 1320 are artificially low ("sy bas"), reflecting the volatility of the market, as a chronicler suggests,[86] then we could compare prices in 1316 with those in the more abundantly documented 1330s. This comparison would still show cereals selling in 1316 at almost eight times and almost five times the usual price in Mons and Valenciennes respectively.[87]

Around Louvain grain prices went up 40 percent in the month from All Saints' 1315 to Saint Andrew's Day (30 November). By Candlemas (2 February 1316) there had been a doubling. Easter witnessed prices 140 percent higher than at All Saints'; and by the Nativity of Saint John the Baptist (24 June), the price stood more than three times greater than at All Saints'.[88] Strasbourg, though on the southern rim of the famine area, also saw prices for products vended at its markets triple in the early years of the crisis.[89]

One can correct for the volatility in order to get some sense of the specific price rises as well in Strasbourg. Grain prices, in this instance, can be factored out and broken down by type in the critical periods. Let us consider rye, using prices in 1350 as an index (100): it can be established that the years 1310–1320 experienced price levels at 170. For oats similarly, the years 1310–1320 saw overall prices stand at 160. For wheat, unfortunately, the information is insufficient for this kind of comparison, but for barley, fragmentary data suggest that prices from 1320 to 1330 were, on average, more than 30 percent higher than in 1350.[90] This fact conforms well with what we know of the effect of the weather. The droughts of the later period of the famine, especially the 1320s, had a more deleterious effect on barley harvests than did the wet weather of the earlier period, and therefore the steepest price rises for that grain came after the first three years of the famine.[91] On the other hand, flooding brought on by severe winds along the North Sea coast and in the Low Countries in the 1320s also stimulated wild fluctuations in rye and oat prices.[92]

Price levels like these—especially in the first phase of the famine, when a portion of seed corn was available to be sold for food in anticipation that the harvest shortfalls would soon be reversed—induced small hinterland producers to try to skirt those established urban markets that had price controls in place. Since this tactic limited supplies in the marketplace even more sharply than what was expected as a result of the harvest shortfalls, middlemen and retail purchasers were seduced into dealing with traders outside the normal forums. Trading in this way, known as forestalling, was illegal and was usually a marginal activity in every way, but in famine years it did have greater economic significance. To be sure, that significance was even then less than contemporary commentators appear to have realized, but this misperception may be attributed to the sentiment shared by those commentators that exploiting the price rise of cereals was among the most immoral features of business behavior.

In mid-1315 the burghers of London, urged by a mandate of the king's council, "caused inquiry to be made on the oath of good men of the several wards as to forestallers."[93] In November of the same year there were further municipal efforts on the part of the London worthies to constrain traders to use established markets.[94] Smaller towns, like Exeter, were no less vigilant.[95]

It was hoarding and speculation, however, that, by withholding desired supplies and driving prices up, came in for the most criticism in urban as it had in rural society, despite their putative economic benefits.[96] The grain and bread market was, of course, the principal, if not sole, concern. Stories told of the famine in 1316 make the point vividly. In one a desperate woman begged bread of her sister, only to be rebuffed. There was nothing to share; as God was her witness (she said), there was nothing. To her distress the Lord did testify against her, changing an abundance of hidden loaves into stones, which later came to be treasured as a memorial of the divine wrath. A visitor could still see one of them and marvel two hundred years later in the Church of Saint-Peter in Leiden.[97]

Another hoarder, we learn,[98] filled his storage rooms to the fullest, intending to hold back the precious grain until prices were at their peak. The poor were as nothing to him. His antithesis was a devout widow who distributed what grain she had "with a free spirit and a cheerful face" ("libera mente, et hilari vultu"), thereby inviting the delight of God, who loves a cheerful giver (2 Cor. 9.7). In this way her supplies were very nearly exhausted. When a poor little girl (*paupercula*) and other hungry children begged pitifully at her threshold, she ordered her servant to feed them too. The servant was distressed. There was not enough for the children and for them. But miraculously when the servant opened the storeroom door, she found the chamber stuffed to the rafters. The grain spilled out on her with main force as a punishment for her hardness of heart. The children were fed. Poor people round about received portions. There was so much that even prices in the marketplace swiftly fell. Meanwhile, the miser, his stores so long reserved that they became unfit for man and beast, was ruined. In the end he dumped the grain, not on the market, but in the river. Thirteen sixteen was a very good year for such stories.

While grain was at the center of all concerns over prices, the decrease in the availability of salt also was a cause for alarm. Predictably, the shortage led to an increase in price from 1315; and big towns, like Paris and London, were hard hit.[99] Indeed, the cost was so great that no one could recollect and no search of the written records could turn up any similar increase.[100] The price rise in salt in turn led to elevated prices for the products for which it was used, not least salted fish, especially herring, one of the most important foodstuffs and a mainstay of urban communities on the North and Baltic seacoasts.[101] Rogers's aggregate prices for England suggest that the years 1315–1319 saw the peak in prices for herring in the entire period before the Black Death.[102] Local investigation of the herring market at Yarmouth, the bustling East Anglian port, confirms this impression: 1316 and 1317 were years of dreadfully high prices.[103]

The Cost-of-Living Crisis

Penury raised its ugly head, but it expressed itself in as many ways as there were levels of status and wealth in the towns. At the administrative or governmental level the best evidence of the impact of the crisis would at first glance seem to be fiscal accounts. If they were sufficiently full, they would tell us about defaults of taxes, for example, or adjustments in tax rates, declines in revenue, increases in deficits, adjustments with regard to expenditures, and the like. Unfortunately, although we shall have recourse time and again in this and chapter 8 to the wide variety of (usually fragmentary) accounts that have survived, few if any offer the really full picture that modern fiscal records provide.[104] And the myriads of other urban official records, though very valuable, will not completely fill in the gaps.

These limitations conceded, we may begin by looking at the Hanse towns. There are numerous, if sometimes indirect, indications of the profundity of the economic crisis.[105] One such indication emerges from a consideration of the fiscal records of Lüneburg, Dortmund, and Soest. They describe the admission of new burghers—a usually costly mark of high status—to the corporation of the towns. In Lüneburg the decline in admissions from 1311–1315 to 1316–1320 was from 136 to 116, with a modest recovery in the next five years to 122. Dortmund exhibits the same pattern: 116 admissions, then a precipitate decline to 68, then a partial recovery to 90. Soest shows a decline from 175 to 157 but not even partial recovery; the number of admissions in the years 1321–1325 decreased further to 127.[106] In Hamburg, such aggregate figures mask what was in fact another very troubling interruption of admissions, a fair indication of the inability of midlevel merchants to profit from the disaster. The diversity of economic interests in this relatively large town soon allowed them to make a recovery, however, which offset the earlier decline.[107]

Occasionally immigration compensated for the decline in admissions to burgher status. Ypres is a case in point. The demographic crisis was as profound in this town as anywhere in Europe during the famine.[108] Town properties would have been readily available for purchase by those who were profiting from high food prices. Ypres had a provision in its law granting bourgeois status to merchants who resided in it for five years, but this five-year rule was waived for those who directly purchased the status. David Nicholas found that the waivers and therefore admissions to burgher status in Ypres skyrocketed during the famine. This can probably be explained, according to him, by an increase in immigration.[109] Presumably, where the demographic crisis was less severe and where price controls were more effective, no such effects should be observed. As a matter of fact, the situation in Bruges seems to bear this out.[110]

Other indications of crisis abound. Labor shortages associated possibly with mortality, migration, and the weakness of the surviving population in Flanders[111] would have exacerbated a decline in textile production for the bulk export trade, which, we have seen, was already damaged by the Franco-Flemish wars. This seems at least to be the explanation favored by Gérard Sivéry to account for the decline in production (inferred from the decline in export) of finished cloth from Lille to northern Italy.[112]

For a different reason, the woolen industry of Cockermouth, a small town in the north of England, descended into crisis. The flocks that supplied the fleeces were simply devastated by murrains. The decline in production was so great as to bring about a depression. But, as in Flanders, the situation was compounded by war, in this case the Anglo-Scottish war. Accounts from 1316–1318 recall the effects of the "Scottish war." No lessee could be found for the fulling mill, which therefore fell out of use. There is evidence that "market tolls were also reduced because of destruction by the Scots." Rents for burgage tenements plummeted.[113]

The tenurial situation in Cockermouth was duplicated elsewhere. Dublin, the chief English garrison town in eastern Ireland, had evolved during the thirteenth century into something a little bit more than a garrison town. Indeed, according to Anngret Simms, "archaeological evidence and documentary material . . . show with detailed examples that the thirteenth century was a period of growth."[114] The Scottish invasion of Ireland, part of the second front against the English whom they were fighting in their borderlands as well, brought Dublin's prosperity to an end. Even though the English reasserted their dominance, there was emigration of some colonists to England during and after the troubles, and the taxation of Ireland by the English became inordinately heavy. The collapse of rents was remarkable in Dublin. By 1326 it was noted that "the burgagers of New Street used to pay 57s 6d a year for their burgages . . . now they pay only 32s 8d [a decline of 25 percent] because the rest of the burgages lie waste," that is, empty and abandoned. It was also lamented that "certain burgagers in St Patrick's Street hold houses and tenements, and they used to pay 45s 2d . . . they now pay 36s 2d [down about 20 percent] because the rest of the tenements lie waste."[115]

The English royal town of Hull mimics this pattern. It was already having difficulties on the eve of the famine.[116] A rental survey surviving from 1309–1310 reveals that 44 plots—28 percent of the total of 158 listed—had "decayed" rents, that is, were not being worked or were empty.[117] An investigation of 1315 showed "failure rates" of about 50 percent and 67 percent in two sets of recent rentals.[118] What the overall failure rate was has not been recovered, but presumably, given those for recent rentals, it was similarly high, exceeding the 28 percent rate of 1309–1310. A defective list tentatively dated by the editor to ca. 1315, when the investigation just referred to was carried out, and certainly before a crash program to fill the tenancies was inaugurated in 1317, reveals that this figure had risen to 32 percent.[119]

The information gathered in the investigation helped mobilize the effort to get new rentals. A roll of 1320 mentions at least forty times (in references to 164 plots) empty tenancies that had successfully been leased out in August of 1317.[120] How? The king's men managed this extraordinary feat by "ruthlessly reducing the rent" on the plots.[121] Yet in the same year, 1320, still another report castigates one of the men, Robert of Sendal, responsible for this turnaround for failing to maintain the king's income in other ways. That report specifically alleges that Robert destroyed sheepfolds and was dilatory with respect to reclamation work on the banks of the Humber.[122] One would like to know Robert's side. Was the destruction of the sheepfolds a measure associated with the murrain? Were the banks of the Humber undermined by the rains to such a degree that it was impossible to repair them with the marginal profits on rentals available to him?

Even small towns like Colchester, no more than 3,000 to 4,000 souls, seem to have suffered a crisis in tenancy.[123] The evidence in Colchester's case is circumstantial. More perfectly integrated into the rural context than a larger town would be, Colchester around 1300 showed the classic signs of rural rather than urban overpopulation—not unemployment, but stress on burghers' common rights in rural terrains abutting the town.[124] To be sure, even great towns, like Paris, endured similar stresses; the draining of the city marshes and their conversion to privately exploited arable led to a loss of common of pasture in the great capital that was deeply resented in the early fourteenth century.[125] But important as common rights remained in the metropolis, they were a more central concern in smaller towns. During the famine, the Colchester population "may have contracted" from abandonment of tenancies that could no longer be maintained by the combined income of household wages and the declining benefits of common rights.[126] The decrease in available grain also probably put one of the town's water mills out of service.[127] Not unexpectedly, there was an apparent reduction in ale consumption in Colchester as well.[128]

In several cases, particularly but not exclusively in "frontier" regions, the relenting of the subsistence crisis and of war led to a more or less immediate return to relative stability and prosperity.[129] As was the case with the rural world, however, this happened less often in well-established regions. The Colchester case suffers from lack of documentation but seems to point in the direction of a prolonged downturn.[130] Elsewhere the case is stronger. The debt-ridden peasantry that emerged from the famine saw its urban counterpart in Ghent, for example, in the enduring *penuria* of the laboring population: building accounts and wage statistics show that the so-called recovery years 1320–1321 and 1321–1322—after the hell of 1315–1319—were "highly problematical" and "difficult," putting the average workman right at the threshold of the continuing need for monetary alms to buy sufficient cheap (rye) bread for his basic nutrition.[131]

Beset by other forces, such as war and internecine strife, such towns, again with occasional exceptions,[132] suffered lengthy economic depressions. Lübeck, to cite one instance, continued to suffer through the period 1323–1327.[133] Bremen is another case. There internal violence disrupted trade and ultimately undermined Bremeners' capacity to maintain their former privileged position in the beer trade; Hamburg and Wismar took up the slack. For centuries this would be taken as an object lesson against the kind of self-destructive internal violence that had weakened Bremen during the famine.[134]

Morbidity and Mortality

The "people in many places began to eat less than sufficient bread, because they had no more," recorded a Fleming under the year 1316.[135] "The people were in such great need that it cannot be expressed. For the cries that were heard from the poor would move a stone, as they lay in the streets with woe and great complaint, swollen with hunger."[136] Bread and pottage made from types of grain, like oats, barley, and rye, that were credited in most towns as less good than wheat could make up some of the deficiency,[137] but the harvest of these grains was down significantly in the first three years and would suffer further in the 1320s.[138] Bread in Flanders came to be made—when it was made at all—from anything possible.[139]

The annalist of Bermondsey (London), a much later writer, envelops his descriptions on the English side of the northern seas with biblical prose; but he was giving expression (properly, he thought) to what he read in earlier sources. His emphasis, despite the scriptural language, is clear: men and women were scavenging.[140] Far more often than in the rural sources, the evidence here is, again, of "strange diets"—at least among the poor. The wide selection of foodstuffs imported or grown in the confines of the medieval town, after all, were differentially available in the best of times to the underclass—the destitute in general and discriminated-against minorities like Slavs in Hanse towns.[141] In the worst of times—and these were the worst—strange and otherwise repellent diets provided the only hope for many urban dwellers.

The strange diets of the urban poor, if their effect was like that in modern famines, resulted in a fundamental loss of energy. Muscles would have become slack; movements, slow and clumsy.[142] In this context the remark of a chronicler on the city of Bremen, who attributes to the famine a great languor or lethargy afflicting many Germans in 1316, loses some of its fantastic quality.[143] In severe cases of famine, body temperature is reduced, and anemia is severe. The skin becomes pallid because there is "reduced peripheral blood flow."[144] The poet who lamented the evil times of Edward II remarked the bizarrely pale complexions of English sufferers, men and women who once laughed with strong voices: "And thanne gan bleiken / here ble, that arst lower so loude."[145]

As we have already had occasion to observe, if the starvation deepens in intensity and consequently if the dependence on strange diets is amplified, the gut will malfunction and severe diarrhea and dehydration will ensue.[146] This pathology captured the interest of John of Trokelowe, the early-fourteenth-century monk of Saint-Albans and observer of the Great Famine: he noted that uncontrollable diarrhea followed upon the indiscriminate consumption of spoiled or "corrupted" food that poor people were reduced to eating. He remarked, too, that acute fever in some cases, lesions in the throat in others, accompanied the diarrhea attacks. His description of the London poor could be a modern clinical report of the effects of strange diets.[147]

Victims of famine weakened in this way find the cold especially painful, we are told, even though apathy sometimes inhibits their complaining.[148] This may explain why the medieval chroniclers of the Great Famine, interested though they always were in abnormally intense or sustained periods of bitter weather, yoke cold and hunger together ("propter gelu et famem"), referring repeatedly to the terrible winters endured by the famine victims.[149]

The weakened urban population—the poor—were, like their rural counterparts, now susceptible to disease (typhus has been suggested as a major culprit) and death, as prices continued to rise.[150] To the chroniclers the situation was overwhelming.[151] Thus the year 1315 saw a "great pestilence" at Cologne, a "great universal pestilence" as seen from Trier, a "pestilence [that] . . . raged especially" in *Germania* where, one writer tells us, "a third of the people were brought low, and within one day the infected began to fade."[152] The rapidity of enfeeblement once infection took hold, perfectly predictable from what is known of modern famines, is commented on by English and Flemish chroniclers as well.[153]

Much of the evidence presented thus far pertains to Flanders. Certainly there were similar developments elsewhere. Already, some English and imperial chroniclers have been cited whose observations for London, Bremen, Stralsund, and Rhenish and central German towns support this interpretation. One could add to this list the imperial "capital," Aachen, where documentary records from the autumn harvest of 1322 attribute the city's misery to "the tempests, hailstorms, and epidemics."[154] One can also add the great capital of Paris, which had experienced no "particularly violent famine" in the thirteenth century.[155] And the reason, in part, was that the city was always of primary concern to the crown: whatever the cost, whatever the sacrifice, "il faut que Paris mange."[156] Yet among the poor the record of Parisian success in protecting against the impact of famine began to erode after 1315. Then spent men and women began to clutter the streets of the city with their emaciated bodies as the urban crisis worsened.[157]

It is in the chronicles of the southern Low Countries, the most urbanized part of northern Europe, that the refrains are particularly insistent, however. The "general pestilence," the "bitter plague," the "death-dealing plague" is said to have "raised its hackles."[158] The men who recorded the history of the devastated Low Countries (in this case, Flanders and Brabant) accounted this "the greatest mortality, unheard-of in the last hundred years," "unseen hitherto," "unseen and unheard-of among the living."[159] Locutions of this sort, of course, like similar assertions about men and women dying in the streets, have a certain conventional ring to them and can be found in descriptions of many periods of dearth whether or not they were severe or recently preceded by similar calamities.[160] Yet the truth is that there had not been deaths from disease or general instability on this scale in living memory.[161]

Words for mortality (*mortalitas*, *sterfde*, and the like) constantly recur in the *récits* of the Flemish and other great towns. That which was unseen and unheard-of for such a length of time was difficult to describe. Always very emphatic declarations mark the reports of "the great mortality."[162] Sometimes slightly odd turns of phrase mark them as well. "There was no lack of death"; there was "most atrocious, savage death" and "tearful death." These miserable years engendered "inexpressible death."[163] People suffered to hear the lamentable cries of poor men dying: "A mannes herte mihte blede for to here the crie / Off pore men that gradden, 'Allas for hungger I die / up rihte!'"[164]

Not all the deaths were of the *urban* poor. Many of the dead were rural beggars who massed near cities and towns for alms. A particularly striking report from the Low Countries quoted earlier tells how in the countryside people were "grazing like cattle";[165] then they seem to have formed huge groups ("beggars without number") who "died in the fields, in groves and woods, and their bodies, without the benefit of Catholic rites, were taken to uncultivated fields for burial."[166] Large common graves seem to have been, as probably in this case, the simplest, most efficient way to dispose of corpses when a deadly disease had run through a dense, already weakened population like large concentrated groups of transient beggars.[167] These beggars, scavenging among the dung heaps that lay outside town walls, were particularly susceptible to parasitic diseases: several cities, we are told, from Trier to Tournai, hired laborers to gather up the corpses from the refuse heaps and public highways for mass burial. Good wages had to be paid these haulers and gravediggers.[168]

Perhaps the contagious diseases among the transients penetrated the densely settled towns through the immigrant neighborhoods that almost certainly provided havens for some of the rural beggars who sought help from kin there. The pattern was familiar. A report of the famine at Edessa around the year 500 makes many of the same points: emigration from villages, an urban population forced into strange diets, epidemics taking the rich, and on and on.[169] And from parish registers of a period later than ours, one can systematically watch pestilences in famines follow the same course, taking beggar after beggar—day by day, week by week— their names usually unknown, their bodies described for posterity merely as young or old, male or female.[170] The spread of the diseases was impossible to contain.

Yet however the epidemics began, they were common in towns in our period. "In all the towns of Brabant" the year 1316 was like a dying zone.[171] In Tournai in 1316 ("the year of the mortality"), "men and women from among the powerful, the middling, and the lowly, old and young, rich and poor, perished daily in such great numbers that the air was fetid with the stench."[172] Liège may have been suffering comparably.[173] One seventeenth-century compiler summed up his reading of the chroniclers of the famine in Ghent ("memorent historici") by concluding that pestilence and hunger claimed a third of the population.[174] Five of the twelve aldermen of Douai also succumbed, it has been suggested, to epidemic disease during the famine.[175] Other texts, again from heavily urbanized Flanders, address this *mortalitas* across social groups (rare in the countryside); and on such occasions they talk about common burial of people of all classes, "the powerful, noble, rich, those of modest means" who suffered the "marks of [famine's] cruelty."[176] This, too, was an extremely rare phenomenon in normal times: cemetery interments in medieval England, France, Norway—everywhere—were usually segregated by class.[177] But in a world beset by epidemics and where, as one report puts it, parish priests were so enervated from administering extreme unction that they no longer knew which way to turn, traditions of segregating the dead were temporarily suspended.[178]

A wagon from the hospital in Louvain "loaded with six or eight corpses twice or thrice a day continuously carried pitiable little bodies to the new cemetery outside the town."[179] Where possible, as at Saint Katherine's cemetery, Hamburg, the burial sites were extended in scope to meet the fantastic mortality.[180] But in many cases the existing cemeteries, hemmed in by urban development, filled up quickly.[181] Distinguished historians of Brussels, writing in the nineteenth century, were convinced by their research that at least two new cemeteries, set at a distance from the old town, were created for the common burial of large numbers of dead during the famine.[182] Recent scholarship accepts their conclusion.[183] Great common graves also had to be employed at Erfurt for the "innumerable cadavers."[184] Far to the east, at Bratislava (*Wratizlavia*), such "a great multitude" of inhabitants died that the "citizens had them buried outside the city," that is to say, outside the regular cemeteries. In remembrance of their deaths the citizens later raised a church on the site of the mass burial "to the honor of the Body of Christ."[185]

Impressed though they were by the magnitude of the calamity in the cities and towns, the chroniclers seem to have had little interest in precise computation. The death of any one of God's children might evoke their monkish lamentation. The death of many, not precisely this many or that many, deepened it, but the economy of salvation was not based on modern arithmetic and actuarial tables. It was enough that God signaled His anger with a punitive tour de force. There were many deaths from disease at Bremen in 1316 and 1317 and an "infinite number perished" in Lübeck,[186] because God could have caused an infinite number to perish; and in truth so many had died that the tribulation could only have been wrought by the hand of God acting beyond the understanding of men. In Metz, whose population never exceeded 20,000 or so in the Middle Ages, it was said that during just six months of 1316, 500,000 went to sleep with their ancestors.[187] The chroniclers were not showing their contempt for accuracy or their inability to count. They wanted to emphasize the immensity of their punishment and, by extension, the enormity of the sins that had brought the punishment on them.

The deaths were not always brought to a quick end by a "timely" arrival of foodstuffs. As we shall see in the next chapter, imports of foods did have a significant impact on the social stability and health of many towns;[188] but the immediate consequence of access to food by people already brought low by starvation was not always positive. It depended on how weak the population had become and what the food was. Broths and mush made from imported fish or beans could have a deleterious effect on people suffering advanced stages of hunger edema, who could not sustain (we now know) the ingestion of protein-rich foods.[189] One of our medieval commentators whose words were incorporated into a later compilation noted that just such people, after apparent recovery, died of strangulation or choking.[190] Probably, however, a far smaller proportion of the weakened population died in this famine or any medieval famine from such causes than in many twentieth-century famines, since ordinarily the timely import in the Middle Ages was grain rather than various protein-rich foods like those used to "rescue" famine victims in the 1950s and 1960s.[191] Gruel made from grain would not have caused this reaction.

Thus far we have depended mainly on the chroniclers and their sometimes lurid descriptions. What are the scholarly estimates of mortality, and on what evidence, in the absence of regularized reporting of deaths, are they based? Let us focus on Flanders. We have already seen that Flanders was suffering a recession in the beginning of the fourteenth century and a radical realignment of industrial production.[192] War was making it difficult for the region to come out of the recession, but David Nicholas sees a precipitate decline in town populations as another major factor in its inability to rebound.[193] The precise magnitude of this decline, however, remains elusive.

The received estimate is that Flanders as a whole suffered something like a 10 percent population drop in 1316 alone.[194] One might contest this figure since it is based on what we know of the population decline in Ypres. The size of Ypres in 1300 has been estimated, as we saw before, at somewhat below 30,000, even significantly less.[195] The summer of 1316 witnessed the deaths of approximately 3,000, hence the 10 percent estimate of mortality in the town. The Ypres figure, as far as absolute numbers go, is trustworthy, since it is based on aldermen's records of weekly burials from May through October 1316.[196] It is difficult—at least for me—to imagine what it was like to witness such levels of mortality over such a length of time: a town of 30,000 (the size of a large state university in the United States) recording deaths in one week of 54 inhabitants would be nothing short of incredible. Yet the account that informs us of these 54 deaths in Ypres tells us that the next week there were 173, then 146 more the week after that, then 101, 107, 157, 149, 155, 167, 158, 172, 190, 191, 130, 140, 148, 138, 124, 115, until finally the mortality abated, with the number of deaths in the last three weeks of the period covered being "only" 37, 27, and 15.[197]

Can we extrapolate from the Ypres figures? On the one hand, what they do not tell us explicitly is whether the burials included transients. If it were extramural beggars who were hit hard by disease and swelled the burial lists, it would be improper to think of the town itself as suffering demographic decimation—particularly across class lines.[198] On the other hand, the accounts that record the burials speak about the dead being picked up along the streets of the town ("aval les rues"), suggesting if not absolutely proving that the dead were residents.[199]

A more serious problem in extrapolating from the Ypres figure is related to the fact that the Bruges city fathers authorized a similar reporting. Bruges was larger than Ypres by several thousand souls; yet it suffered far fewer recorded deaths: 1,938, in a comparable period from the first week of May 1316 to 1 October 1316. As with the case of Ypres the weekly breakdown is known. Jan Bilherse "and his company" ("ende sinen gheselscepe") roamed the districts of Bruges picking up an average of 92 bodies per week, from a low of approximately 11 to a high of 165. The first weeks were by far the worst. More than 100 people succumbed every seven days from the beginning of the reporting (7 May) through the eleventh week of reporting (23 July). Thereafter the weekly mortality dropped off steadily: 95, 85, 59, 54, 30, 28, 19, 11, 11 (the last two averaged from the figure recorded for two weeks), and, finally, 16.[200]

Every "disposal" earned Bilherse and company sixteen pence. Along with a modest outlay (twenty shillings) to Boudine Berbise for making two temporary sheltering screens for the bodies, the Bruges city council allocated over 130 pounds for the gloomy business.[201] In the end the total number of dead (or, rather, collected) was about 5 percent, or a little more, of the population of Bruges.[202]

An estimate of Tournai's mortality can also be made on the basis of the yearly number of testaments inscribed in the town in the fourteenth century. A total of 4,952 were inventoried by Hocquet for the years 1301 to 1400.[203] The run may not be complete, but it is so large and diverse that it is not likely to mislead us.[204] The making of a testament was closely tied to expectation and fear of death and the occurrence of death in one's own family, and these were exacerbated in times of pestilence. In the years before the Black Death in Tournai (1301–1347) the yearly average of testaments was 36 (the median, 31). The year 1316, the year of pestilence, was unique, however, in this period in having the highest number of recorded testaments, 126—250 percent above the mean. Put another way, with the number of testaments used as a surrogate for rate of death, three and one-half times as many people died in 1316 as would normally have been expected to die in that year. Even if we average this out over the entire century (1301–1400) and take into account the surge of deaths associated with the Black Death and the repeated visits of the great plague in the second half of the century, the year 1316 was 212 percent above the mean in the number of testaments (and, arguably, mortality).

Moreover, one can, I think, go further and make a plausible case that as a proportion of the population of Tournai, about 10 percent died in 1316. This conclusion is based on the belief that approximately 30 percent of the population of Tournai perished in 1349 with the Black Death.[205] This figure is mirrored in a huge leap in testaments, to 570, as more and more people's families experienced death and expectations of dying surged. (The average year for the century would have counted only 50.) This means, again extrapolating from the number of testaments to the rate of mortality, a death rate eleven and one-half times the average. (The challengeable assumption I am invoking again is that more people were choosing to make testaments because more of their friends and members of their families were dying.) Since 1316 had a three-and-a-half-times surge of testaments (about one-third or so of that for 1349), one could even argue that the death rate was approximately one-third of that for the Black Death, or a little less than 10 percent. Although this is no more than a very crude method, yielding only a tentative estimate, the 10 percent rate falls in the range of the more reliable figures from Bruges (5 percent) and Ypres (10 percent). One thing is certain: the estimate lends credence to the chronicler's report already cited that in Tournai in 1316 "men and women from among the powerful, the middling, and the lowly, old and young, rich and poor, perished daily in such great numbers that the air was fetid with the stench."

The question remains, however, as to why one should extrapolate from Ypres's mortality (or Tournai's, if its figure is accurate) to that for Flanders as a whole, and not from that of Bruges (5 percent)? And it also seems reasonable to ask, Why extrapolate at all from the urban situation to the rural, even though we can feel reasonably certain that there were significantly elevated levels of mortality in the countryside?[206] Perhaps the safest conclusion is the following. The major towns of Flanders and its heavily urbanized borderlands probably suffered population losses in 1316 in the range of 5–10 percent. (The differences themselves need to be explained; we will return to this question later.)[207] Although only for Bruges and Ypres can we be confidently precise, we have seen that chronicle evidence and scattered data from other sources for Tournai, Antwerp, Ghent, Louvain, Liège, Douai, Bremen, Trier, Metz, and Cologne point in the same direction. And towns of modest size farther afield—Hamburg, for example, and Aachen, Speyer, Erfurt, and possibly Düsseldorf—appear to have endured similar demographic crises.[208] Maybe a few towns did escape epidemics,[209] but the evidence is still general enough to suggest an urban collapse of 5–10 percent in 1316, the worst year of the famine in terms of harvest shortfalls. Even without comparable losses in the countryside, urban losses of this magnitude for a region as heavily urbanized as the southern Low Countries constituted a demographic catastrophe.

The "proof" offered in the chronicle sources that social life and its undergirding morality were in jeopardy from the pain and suffering engendered by the urban crisis is the arresting allegation of cannibalism: Livonia, 1315; England, 1316; Poland, 1317; Silesia, 1317.[210] We have seen that there were a few of these allegations in rural areas, particularly those affected by the cataclysm of war, such as Ireland.[211] However, most of the accusations come from towns. "Many indeed consumed the flesh of gallows corpses," says one report about the Oderraum, where bands of criminal beggars were probably threatening the new towns.[212] One account tells us that in jails half-starved miscreants feasted on the flesh of other unfortunates. The chronicler who reports these events confessed that he found the narration of them an unhappy task.[213] Exponents of rationalistic explanations would say that such accounts originated from the sight of men, desperate for food, fighting among themselves for the small portions given them by jailkeepers. It was no hard thing after watching a spectacle like this to imagine the worst.

Urban observers regularly couple murder with cannibalism. "It is said [the reference is to Baltic towns] that certain people . . . because of the excessive hunger devoured their very own children."[214] "Mothers fed upon their sons" in this region.[215] "In many places [in the towns of the

Oderraum] parents after slaying their children, and children their parents, devoured" their remains.[216] Writing long after, the Bermondsey annalist—who, as we shall see, recorded *pauperes* in England eating pets and pigeon droppings—shared the information that the destitute ate their children too.[217] Such chilling descriptions were to be repeated endlessly.[218]

What possible reliability can be assigned to these reports? In 1930 Henry Lucas made no apology for accepting them at face value.[219] Most recent historians have tended to regard their inclusion, bad as the situation might otherwise have been in densely populated towns, as a literary topos. Certainly such allegations were well known in and after other such disasters.[220] From this point of view, to make a famine *real*, narratively speaking, the chronicler had to include cannibalism in the story. The less immediate the source, like the Bermondsey Annals or the German chronicle of Wigand Gerstenberg (ca. 1500), the more likely there will be an invocation of cannibalism, in the form of a cliché adorned in biblical prose: the Bermondsey annalist's reference to pigeon droppings and perhaps most chroniclers' references, contemporary and otherwise, to parents consuming their children in the Great Famine are direct, if perhaps unconscious, borrowings from Scripture.[221] Wigand Gerstenberg's parallelism between man eating man and dog eating dog is proverbial.[222]

A variation on this view, yet one that refuses to regard the cannibalism cliché as solely a topos, is that the invocation of cannibalism is a way of signaling to the reader the genuine emotional stress ("stark horror") of famine conditions.[223] The classic, frequently invoked, and quite extreme testimony to the stress is Pitirim Sorokin's moving reminiscence of the Russian famine of the early part of the twentieth century. He described a world peopled with victims who could think of nothing besides their hunger and in whom all mental activity was gradually deformed.[224] A strangely repellent book by the Italian writer Piero Camporesi, which appeared in English in 1989, perpetuates this view and is even less restrained: Camporesi dwells almost erotically on the loathsome details of "irrational" behavior, including self-devouring, imputed to famine victims.[225]

From the beginning there have been criticisms of this despairing portrait. Even David Arnold, who otherwise defends the "cannibalism-as-a-metaphor-for-stress" view, has deprecated Sorokin's interpretation of the irrationalizing, dehumanizing effects of famine. Observers/helpers (the makers of the famine narrative), he argues, may be constructing a view in which the residual and reasonable anger of victims at their plight is misleadingly read by the helpers themselves as irrational hatred of them.[226] Alternatively, the victims can deliberately provoke observers: by presenting themselves as deranged to the point of willingness to slaughter their own offspring, they may hope to intimidate the observers into giving up their own rations.[227]

Besides these opinions—that murder and cannibalism actually took place on a wide scale, that its invocation in the narrative is a topos, or that it is a metaphor of emotional stress—another view, one that was suggested above as well as in chapter 6, is that the reports are not unreasonable interpretations of observed behaviors. The tiny lanterns that flickered over urban churchyards, as at Marburg in 1320, from little niches on the exteriors of the buildings to ward off evil spirits were probably not an effective deterrent against poor men seeking a profit in linen cloth and silver pins in graves.[228] The pots of incense-sprinkled charcoal placed in open graves and burned also to ward off evil, to bring the blessings of heaven, and, since the pots and charcoal were subsequently covered by earth, to mark the places as sanctuaries to unsuspecting future excavators probably worked no better. After all, the pots, found usually in aristocratic or ecclesiastical graves, had some resale value.[229] As in rural war-torn Ireland,[230] the disordered grounds on the morrow could easily spur rumors of graveyard feasts. Another example: Arnold acknowledges the existence of family strife of only borderline rationality in modern famines.[231] The chronicle record for our famine also registers a profound weakening of filial piety,[232] a callousness that could have predisposed observers to think the worst—murder, even cannibalism—among parents and children when a family member suddenly died or left home unobserved (disappeared) to go begging or find work. The world of famine was a world of ignorance and shadows.

8

COPING IN TOWNS

THE AIM of this chapter is to explore the ways by which towns-men confronted the dearth and high prices and the sickness and death that accompanied them in the years 1315–1322. We need to remind ourselves that even though as a class the wealthy suffered higher-than-average mortality from epidemic disease in these years (a consequence of disease's spreading easily in densely populated urban spaces), the survivors continued to eat well and many among them prospered economically. Ecclesiastical institutions and burghers in Augsburg, Lüneburg, and Lübeck who controlled a large part of the local production and regional marketing of salt, townsmen in eastern Baltic towns of German settlement who controlled distribution, and various urban monasteries with saltern hinterlands, for example, could not help but do well.[1] The same was true of merchants in towns like Bonn, where the wine trade was the chief commercial enterprise;[2] the high prices in the first three years of the famine more than offset the decline in production.[3] Even the wars could be beneficial to town governments and well-situated monasteries and burghers. Not only could supply of troops be lucrative (at least where prices were not controlled),[4] princes themselves tried to buy municipal support. The civil war in the empire saw the town of Haguenau blessed with privileges bestowed by Frederick of Austria who sought to win its support; it received a similar blessing from Louis of Bavaria in his attempt to prevent it from entering Frederick's camp.[5] Strasbourg was in a virtual bidding war in 1315: Louis of Bavaria made an offer, Frederick a counteroffer; Louis of Bavaria, a little more, which Frederick matched; and so on.[6]

Of course, the successes of the great merchants and urban ecclesiastical institutions were not consistent. If a few tapped into the volatile annuity markets and made a killing, as evidence from Lübeck suggests,[7] more only muddled through and others descended toward bankruptcy (as the chroniclers assure us) in the manner of some of the hardest-hit rural abbeys.[8] It was always dangerous to pander to or accept special grants from rival princes at war. The line between clever politicking and outright treason was thin. Selling goods or making any friendly gestures to towns that did incur the wrath of princes was equally dangerous; on 1 September 1315 King Louis X of France conveyed this dictum to the abbot of Saint-Bertin of Saint-Omer, who was probably having some "conversations" with burghers of Bruges, Ghent, and Ypres in the midst of the Franco-Flemish war.[9] The warning to Saint-Bertin had repercussions. Abandoning its conversations, it began, even though royal fiscal demands were softened, to sink under debts and usury and was ultimately put into receivership for five years under the crown's tutelage in January 1319.[10]

The same variety of experience that the great endured touched urban merchants of middling status, smallish ecclesiastical establishments, artisans, and laborers. Everything depended on factors such as access to the rural economy. Did a burgher own property in the countryside? Did an urban priory collect rents in kind? Did unemployed laborers have families in nearby villages to whom they might appeal for help? Were some townsmen and women engaged in the kind of production that enabled them to continue to market sufficient quantities of goods, despite production downturns, so as to profit comfortably from the high prices?

Fending Off the Crisis

The evidence is varied about the ways that urban dwellers reacted to the economic instability. By and large, they resorted to methods and devices that had served them well in earlier times. In the Flemish and Hanse towns municipal authorities, seeing revenues undermined (Cambrésien *hommes d'affaires*, for instance, could not even pay the rent for stalls leased at the fairs of Champagne),[11] tried to stimulate investment by offering life annuities at good rates of return. These offerings were decided upon after thoughtful reflection about their usefulness to corporate well-being, as the town council of Dortmund put it in October 1316,[12] and were so attractive that they sometimes seduced burghers from other towns into investing.[13] Huon Lelarge of Reims is a case in point. He seems to have been drawn to make investments in the municipal "bond fund" of Cambrai around 1315. Unfortunately for him, the rates of return that were promised on the life rents, despite the thoughtful reflection, could not be satisfied, and Cambrai fell into serious arrears ("vies arrérages").[14]

Churches and hospitals were also traditional purchasers of annuities; that is to say, they invested relatively large sums of money in municipal bonds in order to receive annual fixed returns. Severe crises, however, that put inordinate demands on the expenditures of churches and hospitals exaggerated and transformed the pattern of their financial activity. Ecclesiastics in such circumstances either sold the annuities at discounts for lump sums or induced rich patrons among the burghers to give lump sums to their institutions in return for fixed annual returns. These lump sums, raised by whichever means, could then be used to help the institution weather the economic downturn.[15]

The Great Famine turns out to have been the most acute crisis in this respect. The lump sum investments presumably were immediately redistributed as charity or could be used to purchase grain and other commodities from a greater distance (when war did not make this impossible) for the needs of the clergy and for that portion of the urban poor whom they succored.[16] To give one example, a burgher of Stralsund made a sizable donation to Kloster Neuenkamp on 21 September 1316 in return for a life rent and, after his death, prayers for his soul. He also stipulated that specific sums be allotted at All Saints' Day to clothe the poor.[17] One example hardly proves the case, of course. Thanks to Klaus Richter's examination of Hamburg business ledgers, much more can be said with confidence. His analysis shows that the years of the Great Famine were a fundamental secular turning point (of "epochal significance," in his words) in the annuity market and the price curve of rents that was closely connected with it, with these rents, after an ephemeral recovery, becoming depressed and manifesting a persistent downward spiral soon after the famine.[18]

In the Hanse towns studied by Richter and others many holders of annuities—even those who were in a position to buy up discounted bonds early in the crisis—steadily sold off their bonds as the situation remained unstable. It was the purchasers of these bonds, as we have already noticed with regard to the Lübeck evidence, who would emerge fabulously wealthy from the crisis.[19] The presumption among historians of the urban annuity and real estate markets, however, is that the sellers are more typical, in that they "may have been trying to weather the storm by liquidating assets instead of going into debt." Moreover, those institutions and individuals who were obliged to *pay* annuities were, if their financial interests were not otherwise diversified, often unable to keep up with their disbursements except by further debt-financing. Stralsund repeatedly went this route, usually offering a 10 percent annual return on investment to be paid from rents or tolls or the like, and there are examples of other towns following suit.[20] Sometimes the towns pledged property, especially houses, as a guarantee of payment rather than, or in addition to, assigning income from rents. When they defaulted on payments in the Great Famine, a "conspicuous" result was their surrender of these houses.[21]

On the other side, although there was a regular business reflecting town councils' willingness to accept buyouts or lump sums for annual rents owed to them,[22] many communities wrote limited options for repurchase of the rents and tolls into the contracts (to be exercised in two, five, or six years).[23] They (and private persons) also did so when they sold other forms of property, like fields or gardens, rather than fiscal rights. A typical example is that of Dortmund's sale of a holding in November 1316 with a right of repurchase within four years.[24] Of course, since the municipalities had to pay back the full investment in order to repurchase, this in no way soured what was a very attractive deal to rich individual burghers. Not every purchaser profited. Some must have wished that municipalities and private persons would redeem properties that turned out to be less than lucrative.[25] Nonetheless, one can identify a number of crafty investors, like slick Konrad Witte, a burgher of Colberg, who serviced Stralsund and Greifswald and feasted in this market.[26]

The famine conditions and the high prices in general kept aggravating the housing market, driving municipalities and individual householders to dump more and more of their property on willing purchasers (or mortgagers) for the short-term gains in cash flow. This seems to have been the case in the Rhenish town of Andernach where so much property got into the hands of ecclesiastical institutions that a strict prohibition (6 December 1320) was put on conveyancing to the dead hand of the church.[27] This prohibition could just as well have been applied to rich and property-accumulating burghers. Widows with young children were particularly liable, according to Manfred Huiskes, to dispose of their homes for needed cash to these types in the "years of hunger especially 1316/17."[28]

One must wonder whether the extraordinary volatility of the annuity and housing markets in many Hanse towns and elsewhere during the famine and for many years thereafter occurred everywhere or even with equal intensity among the settlements where it did occur.[29] One must also wonder whether it had anything to do with the emergence of a much tighter and more closely regulated system of credit in the late fourteenth century that set urban Germany off from rural Europe. Of course, the famine could not have been uniquely responsible. Severe volatility was to recur in the era of the Black Death. The effect of the two shocks (famine and plague) probably explains the regulations.[30]

What churches and hospitals in the Hanse towns tried to achieve through manipulation of the annuity markets, charitable institutions there and in other urban milieus accomplished or tried to accomplish by different means. Few were as lucky as the Hermits of Saint-Augustine, whose houses were recipients in 1319 of the property of the Sack Friars, an order forbidden to admit new members after 1274 and almost extinct by the time of the famine.[31] Although the scale of the property transfer was nothing like that from the Templars to the Hospitallers detailed in an earlier chapter,[32] the benefits were undoubtedly palpable.

In the absence of such serendipities, the search for capital and support went on unremittingly. The hospital of Saint-Julien of Liège, for example, which was established not long before 1311[33] and which appears to have been overwhelmed by the number of poor, hungry, and sick it cared for in the Great Famine, turned to a campaign for increased donations. To some extent it was successful, at least judging from the securing of an indulgence granted by the pope at Avignon for everyone who visited the hospital and gave alms.[34] (Appeals to the pope from urban ecclesiastical institutions were common.)[35] The hospital of the Holy Spirit in Hamburg may also be seen intensifying efforts to stimulate endowments from those who could afford to give them "in order that they might comfort the poor."[36]

The Dominicans of Würzburg tried a quite different tactic to raise money. Undoubtedly of the opinion that they would soon see the end of the difficult conditions in the Würzburg region (attested by chroniclers and some charters dealing with transactions of cereals),[37] the friars decided in 1316 to place their precious glossed Bible into the hands of the vicar of Neumünster. The Bible was *obligata* to the vicar, which the editor of the registers of the Cistercian cloister of Bildhausen regards as simply a case of pawning the Bible.[38] In order to redeem the book, the friars had to repay the loan (whether with interest is doubtful). But, unhappily, the situation further deteriorated, and, either to persuade the vicar to extend them more money or simply to cancel their debt, they permitted him to sell the book. The Cistercians of Kloster Bildhausen managed to put together the cash to purchase it in 1317. The purchase price was 140 pounds *heller*.[39] The price—expressed in the language of a familiar currency and money of account in this region of the empire—was high (an indication of the Bible's quality): 5 pounds *heller* typically paid for an anniversary mass together with alms for the poor in memory of the deceased benefactor of a religious house; 50 pounds *heller*, let alone 140 pounds, constituted a major sum.[40]

There is no question that famine aggravated the need for credit in the towns, as this example suggests. Possibly motivated by the suffering he saw, Master Ralph Germeyn, the precentor of Exeter Cathedral, also "founded in 1316" a special chest, "for the purpose of making loans to poor scholars of [Exeter College, Oxford] . . . or for the college's corporate needs."[41] Ordinary transactions, however—like those between borrowers and traditional moneylenders or pawnbrokers—almost necessarily led to the deterioration of the already unstable social position of the moneylender, who seemed to be feeding off the misery engendered by the famine. We have already explored this phenomenon in a rural context. It has been observed and chronicled time and again in periods of great want in urban contexts as well.[42] Moreover, as has also been pointed out, the credit market in distress loans in many towns at this time was serviced by

Jews,[43] a factor that compounded social tensions between them and ordinary Christians.[44] Even nobles and municipalities, like Dortmund, fell into heavy debt to Jews in this period.[45]

We must recall, too, that throughout the famine years, preaching continued about the necessity of repentance. Charging usury was a mortal sin, and the most radical interpreters of usury called any moneylending at interest usury. Moreover, in the radical critiques of usury, it was also a sin to pay usury, because it encouraged the lender to continue in a sinful state that jeopardized his immortal soul. William of Rubio, a Spanish Dominican who was a student in Paris during the famine, must have seen or heard about countless incidents in which mothers and fathers were cautioned about going to moneylenders. He was not moved by their plight—or perhaps it is fairer to say that in the salvific economy to which he subscribed there was a clear hierarchy of soul and body. It was better to let the body die than to endanger the immortal soul. It could not have been easy for William to hold to these ideals in the misery with which he was surrounded in Paris, but they survived, and he wrote up his "bleak" views a few years later.[46]

Caritas: Appealing to God and Succoring the Needy

As the discussion of William of Rubio shows, coping with this crisis did not merely involve fiscal measures like discounting bonds, varying annuity portfolios, initiating capital campaigns, and heavy borrowing. There was a profound moral framework within which all actions were weighed. Moreover, on a more general level, since God was punishing a wayward people with the famine and testing them with moral dilemmas, it followed, to repeat a point made in an earlier chapter, that He was demanding a change of heart—true contrition and courage—as a price for the return of His blessing. What better proof of a change of heart could Christians offer than the putting aside of vanities ("dancing, games, songs, all revels") and the doing of other acts of penance[47] or the granting of charity? The plaintive appeal for relief by these gestures to God and the saints became a commonplace in the cities.[48] In Bynum's words, it is not "surprising that virtuoso fasts grew more common as famine and malnourishment began, from the later thirteenth century, to be noticeable aspects of European life."[49]

There were other gestures that pleased God and might induce Him to lift the scourge of famine. As in the countryside, so in the towns, one response to the ordeal was expiatory processions. "In this hour of need," wrote Henry Lucas, "the guilds and religious bodies in Paris often went forth barefooted, led by the clergy." An informative passage from the report of a contemporary French chronicler, an eyewitness, is arresting. He

saw a large number [of people] of both sexes, not only from nearby places but from places as much as five leagues away [from Paris], barefooted, and many, excepting the women, even in a completely nude condition, with their priests, coming together in procession at the church of the holy martyr, and they devoutly carried bodies of the saints and other relics to be adored.[50]

What was true of Paris was true of London as well, where the prelacy instructed monks and priests in the city to process barefoot every Friday from their churches to the Church of the Holy Trinity. The importance of the processions was also underscored by the requirement imposed on these English supplicants to carry with them consecrated Hosts and relics of the saints who were being venerated in their churches.[51] Elsewhere, as at Magdeburg, the archbishop made a special appeal for the veneration of the patron, Saint Maurice, in these trying times.[52]

The appeal to God's mercy was strengthened by acts of charity. In 1315 the Teutonic Order opened its grain stores "in its burgs" to the needy.[53] Similarly, there was a remarkable upsurge of philanthropy in the Low Countries. A contemporary spate of foundations of so-called Tables of the Holy Ghost in various Netherlandish towns undoubtedly relates to the famine's accentuation of the impoverishment of the underclass. The Tables of the Holy Ghost were lay parochial repositories of common funds (frequently in kind, and therefore constituting a sort of storehouse system) available to the poorest members of urban communities in distress.[54] Finally, dramatic gestures among wealthy individuals may have achieved spectacular results and helped keep the lid on violent discontent against the upper classes. Robert de Lincoln directed that one penny go to "each of 2,000 poor people" in London in 1318; Michael Coelian, a very rich man (*praedives*), gave up all he had to the Carthusians and, with the aid of a canon of Bruges, founded a Carthusian house in Ghent in 1320.[55] Much of Michael's wealth, given Carthusian rigor, would have been redistributed as charity among the desperately poor of Ghent.

A year before, a wealthy Würzburger patrician, Johann von Steren, had established a city hospital presumably for the famine victims in his town. As with so many of his counterparts in the Low Countries the dedication was to the Holy Ghost.[56] Indeed, there was a spate of hospital and hospice foundations in the years of the Great Famine that gives one pause. Perhaps not all of the foundations were direct responses to the famine, but the founders' timing could hardly have been indifferent to the suffering they saw about them. Some of the possible rural foundations and similar efforts at almsgiving were mentioned in earlier chapters.[57] Among urban foundations besides the one at Würzburg can be counted that of Guillaume Douloret, a Flemish seigneur, who made provision on 19 September 1316 for a hospice (admittedly to be established only at his death). Although the location, Hollain, where he had the property, was rural, the hospice was probably intended to serve Tournai, which was only a few kilometers south; and it was from his house at Tournai, where famine was causing horrendous levels of mortality, that he made his solemn promise.[58] Around January 1316 the lord and lady of Houdeng founded a hospital in their seigneurie that served the town of Mons; in June of the next year it merged with another local hospital.[59] Also to be numbered among these foundations are the hospice of the Trinity that opened its doors in Brussels in 1316 thanks to the gift of a pious bourgeoise, Heilwige Blommaert, known also as Bloemardinne,[60] and the hospital of Saint-Julien established at Lille, 31 October 1321, by Phane Denis, the widow of a bourgeois, Jean le Toillet.[61]

With a few exceptions the giving of charity was more characteristic of the early phase of the urban crisis than of its later period. As the cost-of-living squeeze began to affect many of the well-to-do, both lay and ecclesiastical, there was a retreat from private almsgiving, and it became increasingly common for municipal governments to act in the name of the general welfare. The most obvious thing to do was to replace private charity directly: a "bourse commune" was established at Douai when the situation in 1316 proved to be so difficult.[62] Another obvious undertaking was the importing of food. This was especially important for the inhabitants of Flemish towns whose hinterlands were not as diversified as other rural areas; there were, in the words of one historian, insufficient "secondary crops to tide them over when the grain harvest failed."[63]

To institute a policy of grain imports was not all that radical a gesture. As Naudé in his study of the Prussian grain trade asserted long ago, though with a touch of exaggeration, the only political authorities that can be said to have had a conscious, coherent, and sustained grain market policy in the Middle Ages were municipal councils.[64] Certainly, an array of documents supports the view that many municipalities and ecclesiastical authorities within towns admitted the need of a public grain policy.[65] Ordinarily towns in Flanders—Bruges, for instance—turned to Normandy, Picardy, or northwestern Germany to make up local shortfalls in the harvest in their hinterlands.[66] However, the Franco-Flemish war was disrupting transport in 1315, and embargoes made the situation worse for years to come.[67] That Normandy, Picardy, and the German regions bordering Flanders were also as severely affected by harvest shortfalls as was Flanders itself made unusual approaches to the grain crisis necessary in the years 1315–1322.

The municipal council of Bruges, according to evidence from April 1317, looked farther afield. It bought "considerable stocks of grain through various merchants," some of Mediterranean origin: two Genoese, a Venetian, and others, perhaps Spaniards.[68] Purchases, which in terms of cost were "of the same order of magnitude [as the] . . . ordinary expenses of the town," came to 19,636 hectoliters (over 55,000 bushels) of wheat, or 56 pounds per capita; plus 833 hl. of rye, or 2.4 pounds per capita—probably for a three-and-a-half-month period.[69] Blum estimated that eighteenth-century servile peasants, who may have had a more restricted diet than did medieval rustics and urban dwellers, consumed between 470 and 660 pounds of grain per year per head.[70] The grain imports to Bruges would have been the equivalent of about 30 percent, perhaps even as high as 45 percent, of what was required in the period covered, if normal consumption was comparable to that in the eighteenth century. In other words, the Bruges fathers made a stupendous contribution to the population's well-being. But where did this grain come from?

Scholars have suggested more than once that these Italian agents were bringing *Italian* or Mediterranean grain to the Flemish towns.[71] (The same suggestion, we shall see later, has been made about grain imports arranged by the crown in England.)[72] This is highly dubious. The sea-lanes from Italy, which necessitated navigating the Straits of Gibraltar in a westerly direction, were too uncertain for regular traffic in traditional carriers.[73] It is true that five sea voyages were undertaken from the Mediterranean to Antwerp and Bruges in 1317–1319 (a large portion of the total of eight known to have been undertaken in these years from the southern to the northern sea), but we have no cargo manifests so far as I have discovered for the vessels that made the trips.[74] With the possible exception of a few central or south German towns that might have got grain transported through the Italian mainland from Sicily,[75] overland carriage from Italy to northern Germany or Flanders for nonluxury goods was prohibitively expensive.

It is much more likely, therefore, that the Italians involved in the Bruges grain trade served as agents buying and shipping grain, in craft they owned or chartered, from regions closer than the Mediterranean ports. There was only one rational option, given the extensiveness and severity of the harvest shortfalls in the north: the Biscay ports of southern France and Spain, whose trade connections with northwest Europe and practice of using Italian factors were old and extensive.[76] Much of this trade traditionally brought wine out of the Bordelais northward.[77] Even though shortages of wine were significant in the north in the first two years of the famine and there is evidence of municipal concern about imports that would have come by sea or, in the case of inland towns like Strasbourg, by road,[78] grain was much more desperately needed.

The acquisition of grain, however, did not come without difficulties. In the first place, despite the money to be made, some authorities in southern France were wary of permitting unlimited exports, because local harvest shortfalls were certainly not unknown. In 1302 the entire south of France had been struck by a bad harvest, and 1303 and 1304, although the yields were less poor, are accounted bad years as well.[79] More to the point, local authorities put restrictions on exports of grain in those years, partly because available stores tended to be shipped to places within the region where prices were highest, not necessarily where subsistence needs were greatest, and partly because grain merchants with contracts to supply northern areas that happened to be in need wanted to fulfil their obligations and thus maintain their business connections for the future.[80] The years 1305 and 1310 saw equally bad harvests in the south and additional official action by local authorities to restrict the movement of grain out of the region.[81]

Nevertheless, the authorities would only invoke restrictive measures during grave hardships, so in general trade remained vigorous. There were a few local harvest failures here and there in southern France in 1312 and 1313 and drought in northern Castile in 1314–1315,[82] but there was no natural disaster of sufficient magnitude in the south in 1315–1322 to stimulate authorities to fully restrict the grain trade. There was, however, one factor that caused concern: everyone—not just Italian agents acting for Bruges, but agents of other Flemish towns, northern French towns, and the English crown—was clamoring for grain in southern France in these years.[83] French chroniclers insist that grain and wine imports from Gascony saved Paris from succumbing fully to the famine conditions.[84] But regional needs, even in the best of times, consumed the vast proportion of the harvests of the southwest. So local authorities had to be careful that purchases did not deplete stores below the anticipated needs of the local population.

Farmers in southern France undoubtedly benefited; rich merchant middlemen even more: this would have been a typical scenario.[85] It is documentable in the northeast as well. Grain exports to the Baltic towns, for example, from the hinterland of Berlin-Kölln appear to have been thoroughly dominated by a small clique of rich merchants until feudal authorities intervened in 1317 and 1319 to protect the interests of more modest merchants (called "poor" in the privileges granted); almost certainly, scholars agree, the intervention was meant to stymie internal urban strife.[86] The competition over access to the export business within the regions still capable of exporting large amounts of surplus grain from 1315 to 1322 testifies, not only to the windfall profits to be made, but to the reason stores of grain in those regions were nearly depleted.[87] This was not a failure of the medieval market system[88] but testimony to the relative efficiency of the responses it was capable of making, at least when the logistics it was exploiting were as hoary with age as were those between coastal northwestern Europe and southwestern France or between the Baltic towns and Brandenburg. "The maintenance of trade," after all, "when one side experiences a bad year is the critical test for a complex system."[89]

Not all towns that were importing foodstuffs benefited equally, of course. Interurban competition and strife could be awful, as revealed by incidents from 1317 and 1321 between Andernach and Nijmegen and between Koblenz and Nijmegen.[90] Let us, however, return to the figures on mortality during 1316 computed for Bruges and for Ypres and Tournai in chapter 7 as a way to probe more deeply into this issue. Van Werveke was disturbed by the significant difference between the two figures.[91] In Bruges about 5 percent of the population perished in six months in 1316; in Ypres (and Tournai) it was 10 percent or more.[92] It could have been the case that distinct diseases were affecting the different populations,[93] but Van Werveke favored a different explanation. The governors of Bruges, by long history and their town's situation near a port, routinely turned to seaborne imports in food crises. Moreover, offering some protection for the cargo carriers was a battle fleet, manned in the year 1316 by six hundred hands drawn mainly from the guilds (with conscription prorated according to the size of each).[94] Ypres and Tournai, inland towns, traditionally negotiated with food producers in their immediate rural hinterlands. As rapidly rising prices and insufficient supplies made this strategy tragically inadequate during the Great Famine, the governors of Ypres and Tournai would have looked farther afield, ultimately to southern France, and, given the prohibitive costs and uncertain fate of overland transport, they too would have tried to capitalize on seaborne imports.

Unfortunately, with war and its embargoes, and piracy all up and down the coast (involving Gascon and Flemish raiders of carriers of all *nationes*, and even preying upon ships at anchor in ports of call), importing was a very dangerous business in 1315–1322, and the Flemings in general suffered mightily as a result.[95] Thirteen sixteen, as we earlier observed, was the worst year.[96] Moreover, in the specific case of Ypres, her agents would have been latecomers to the negotiations going on at the Biscay ports, and whatever supplies they did manage to secure were debarked at northern ports already hungry for food. The difficulties in getting all of this grain to Ypres would have been very large indeed. Hoarders, speculators, and thieves on the inland waterways or on land were not averse to transporting grain to places where prices were off-scale even if what we might call the nutritional crisis was less severe in those places.[97] Already in 1315, for example, in parts of urban Flanders, "despite the need, large stocks of grain were in existence, yet they were not sold, but taken out to seacoast regions where prices stood still higher."[98] In the circumstances, Van Werveke felt that the governors of Ypres (and, we might add, probably of Tournai as well) fell short in meeting their citizens' needs. It compounded the problem that Ypres was a more industrial town than Bruges, more dependent on cloth manufacture, and, in the event, had a proportionally larger and depressed "proletariat."[99] For, as a result, there were a great many more cases of malnutrition, a great deal more morbidity, and, finally, a great deal more death in Ypres.[100]

Bruges, while doing better by its imports, was also careful about distribution of those imports. The "free market" was suspended. The just price and other tenets of the moral economy were strong ideological battle cries in famine times, despite or because of the activities of hoarders, speculators, and thieves.[101] The moral imperatives of the city fathers may have been reinforced by equally deep religious sentiments that explained the fall of man in terms of unchecked avarice—and even gluttony.[102] Whatever the reason, including self-interest,[103] for modifying municipal welfare policies, a wise distribution of the imported foodstuffs was desirable. The municipality decided to sell the grain at cost or even slightly below cost to licensed bakers, who made bread available at manageable prices to the distressed population.[104] It ceased employing this strategy only when it appeared that the dearth might come to an end, at which point the town council tried to make up the deficit before the market was glutted with grain.[105] What the town fathers of Bruges did was repeated in the actions of those of Ghent and Ypres, though with less adequate stores.[106]

The Breakdown of *Communitas*

The bakers licensed in the Flemish towns to distribute artificially low-priced loaves to the urban poor had their negative counterpart in unscrupulous bakers elsewhere where grain supplies were woefully depleted and prices incredibly elevated. A number of bakers in Paris, for example, were charged with adulterating bread: "When prices were at their highest that year [1316]," wrote the chronicler Jean de Saint-Victor,

> it was discovered that the bakers had put many disgusting ingredients (*immunditias*)—the dregs of wine, pig droppings, and several other things—in the bread that the famished people were eating. And in this way the bakers cheated the poor folk of their money. When the truth was known, sixteen wheels were placed on stakes in small fields in Paris, and the bakers were set upon them with their hands raised and holding pieces of the loaves so tainted. Then they were exiled from France.[107]

Petty theft as well as theft on a grand scale, it has been pointed out, were additional problems that had to be faced by municipal authorities who, like their rural and royal counterparts, wished to keep the worsening situation under control.[108] Migrants as well as natives could be a problem, since escalating "racism" between the two was characteristic of the frontier in these years.[109] The victims of choice were urban merchants and patricians or their agents who continued to do well even as the famine worsened for other social groups. "Murderers and thieves" began routinely to lie in wait near the Snellemarket in Greifenberg until drastic action was taken in early 1316 to clear the area and reestablish "security for each merchant and worthy man and for the good of the region."[110] It would be easy to multiply instances of theft in many towns,[111] although, of course, even a large number of cases would hardly establish the existence of a crime wave. More persuasive are documents like the so-called Peace of Fexhe, an agreement from 18 June 1316 that bound the lay, ecclesiastical, and urban authorities in the Liègeois to eradicate crime according to their various jurisdictional powers. The Peace is often looked upon primarily as a "constitutional" document, because it literally brought an end to a succession of nasty local wars in the jurisdictionally contested region of the Liègeois and provided the warrant for at least partial governance by assembly thereafter; however, it was also a response to the hitherto overwhelming level of crime and intimidation that suffused a region smitten with famine, runaway inflation, and, until its ratification, those seemingly ceaseless wars.[112]

Specific products were often targets of thieves. Salt was one such product. Suspicion in England that a large shipment was too lightly guarded encouraged malefactors there.[113] On the Continent officials in Bruges tried to run down offenders who had managed to get a huge cargo of salt into their hands. Purchased at Abbeville, the salt was supposed to come north to Bruges but seems to have been taken south to Harfleur at the mouth of the Seine. The record detailing the matter is dated 14 April 1317.[114] The salt was needed in part to prepare the herring catch, but also because Bruges was a major center of butter and cheese production and distribution. Quality control was exercised from the relatively new "Butter Warehouse" (*boterhuis*).[115] Retailing took place from private shops or, rather, stalls. In 1307 there were eighty-two of these; in 1310, eighty-four.[116] Salt was urgently required to sustain production on this scale.

As the famine worsened, the best efforts of good people proved unequal to the calamity. Terribly weakened men and women languished from hunger, we learn, in Bremen.[117] Or they despaired and, as at Lübeck, "victims of the famine who were yet alive entered the tombs that had been made in certain places for the multitude of those dead from the famine, in order that they might die in them and give an end to their pains."[118] Such gathering together of the poor and weak was evidently fairly common, perhaps at some familiar site where alms were or had once been distributed; sometimes the desperation led to pushing and shoving—and death.[119]

As time went on, forms of "irrationality" manifested themselves.[120] Protest poems written in the wake of the famine sometimes reflect this fact. The subject or, on occasion, the personification of gluttony commands the poets' shrillest condemnations, but with a twist: "falseness and trecherye" between father and son and daughter and mother, in one such poem, are seen to be rooted in an irrational and uncontrollable lust for food.[121] We find, too, "heretical" movements that seem to have drawn part of their inspiration from the psychological situation created by the food shortage. To the orthodox the heretics' behavior was also manifestly irrational.

Of course, heresy in this period in the north seemed more than merely irrational. It smacked of revolution. To be sure, not every heterodoxy that found expression in famine-stricken areas owed its *origin* to the famine conditions. But the social and economic tensions that accompanied the harvest shortfalls, high prices, and violence of war sharpened authorities' perceptions of heterodox believers as threats to the political and social order, both secular and ecclesiastical. Sectarians who had been suffered to exist, if not quite tolerated, for thirty years or more came to be tarred by those in power as diabolical and ripe for extirpation in the charged atmosphere of 1315–1322. It is also possible, perhaps even probable, that the sectarians themselves did become more radical because of the economic crisis. This set of hypotheses, at least, informs my interpretation of the persecution of a quasi-Waldensian sect in Schweidnitz (Silesia) that objected to swearing and to the superior efficacy of auricular confession to a priest. The sect had long existed, but in mid-1315 it came to be regarded as a serious threat worthy of concerted official action. Accused of worshiping Lucifer, impugning the morality of the Virgin, and practicing incestuous sex, many were condemned to the flames over the years 1315–1318, the worst years of the famine.[122]

One manifestation of the so-called heresy of the free spirit, attacked at Strasbourg in the years 1317–1319, provides another example.[123] The beliefs attributed to the heretics constituted a wide spectrum; some even contradicted others.[124] Undoubtedly the dossier of charges was influenced by what authorities expected to find, but one aspect of the movement seems directly pertinent. Beguines and Beghards (groups of laywomen and men living religious lives and dressing, to some degree, in habits) were the people accused of the heresy. It was said that they had been actively seeking alms on street corners and on thoroughfares and throughout the hinterland of Strasbourg. The name allegedly given the heretics—the popular name ("vulgus . . . nominat")—was "Brot durch Gott," an unexceptional phrase but one that seems to have reflected some sort of litany or mantra declaimed by the heretics themselves as they begged.[125] A phrase screamed so often that it named the group: what it evoked in the hearers—fear, pity, disdain—is impossible to recover. Yet in famine times loud cries of "For God's sake, bread! For God's sake, bread!" could not easily have been ignored by poor or rich folk observing the holy men and women in their wanderings.[126]

Where charity failed, warfare between the needy and their financial betters became a danger.[127] On the one hand, elite fears were in no way misplaced; grain riots did characterize urban life of the famine years.[128] High prices in Magdeburg, for example, in 1316 were to give rise to "spontaneous" demonstrations against food retailers.[129] On the other hand, elites themselves suffered cleavages in their ranks during the famine years. To pursue the Magdeburg example, the merchants targeted by mobs in 1316 were at loggerheads at the same time with the archbishop, who was determined to bring prices down by allowing imports and thereby to gain "popular" support in his own long struggle with the mercantile community for hegemony in the town.[130] The years 1316–1318 in Verdun and slightly later in Metz also witnessed clan violence admixed with class strife.[131] Provins would experience a revolt of its underclass ("rebellion des menuz ouvriers")—and systematic investigations by commissioners into the causes and extent of the violence—during the famine.[132]

In the towns of Flanders socially directed violence had already become common before the famine.[133] It would manifest itself furiously during the catastrophe, leading to draconian retribution—even in the case of Bruges, where food import policies had been relatively effective. It is impossible to say how closely tied the incidents in Bruges were to the economic and psychological conditions of the famine, but this much is known. Large-scale conspiracies swept the town. As a result of one of these, twenty-seven burghers who were implicated in a murder were banished, but an arbitrated settlement in which burghers of Ypres and Ghent took part "reconciled" commune and conspirators. People wounded in the murderous attack received compensation, and the banishments were lifted, effective All Saints' Day 1321.[134] No sooner was this reconciliation worked out than another (related?) conspiracy pitted the commune against a large number of inhabitants. In this case, twenty-one townsmen were banished for one hundred years and a day toward the end of the famine for "faisant conspirations pour destruire le ville et les personnes." Or so it was put in a letter (16 February 1323) to the municipal government of Saint-Omer. The letter urged Saint-Omer not to admit or succor the exiles.[135]

The most gruesome and well-documented instance of such violence associated with the famine occurred in Douai,[136] where earlier, as we have seen, a common fund was established to help mollify the poor and hungry urban underclass.[137] The uprising came at a time when matters should have been going better—that is, as the horrendous harvests of the teens were giving way to more abundant crops in the twenties. But some merchants and patricians were hedging their bets against a possible steep decline in their profits by creating artificial shortages to keep prices high. Or so many ordinary people believed. The explosion in Douai took place on the Thursday before All Saints' (28 October) 1322.[138] Two women, Jacquette, the wife of Jehan Espillet, and Margot Cauche, took to the marketplace to denounce the hoarders and incited the common people to take up arms. Inspired by the rising, Jehans de le Loge encouraged another group of malcontents to raid the granary of Collart de Mignot. Havius des Freres Meneurs and Jacquemins de Salau led raids on granaries and some heavily laden barges. Others rummaged menacingly in burghers' houses for sacks of grain. Some of the rioters came from outside Douai—from Hénin, for example, fifteen kilometers northwest, and Arras, about twenty kilometers to the southwest—a fact that suggests the regional impact of the hoarding. Intimidation—angry threats to kill, to behead, to get even one way or another—gave the town briefly to the rebels.

When order was restored, the reconstituted courts of justice handed down sentences against the perpetrators of the outrages. On 7 March 1323, because of the grain riots ("pour cause du ble"), the women were banished for all time; for their "evil and outrageous" words, their tongues were severed. Jehans de le Loge and Havius des Freres Meneurs, too, were sentenced to perpetual banishment, with a contingency sentence of beheading if they should ever reappear in Douai. Other rioters received lesser sentences made up of units of a year and a day of exile. Those considered most culpable (after the ringleaders) got twenty such units to run successively: twenty years and twenty days. A few were banished for ten years and ten days; five years and five days; three years and three days (the least of the punishments). Thus fell the curtain on the last act of the Great Famine in Douai.

9

THE POLICIES OF PRINCES

IT IS NOW appropriate to shift our focus to the initiatives undertaken by authorities who, if they did not dominate, at least claimed suzerain power over town and countryside alike. Medieval principalities (or states)[1] were notoriously ineffective in articulating economic policies and enforcing economic programs; yet none of the attempts by rural lords and urban patriciates and ecclesiastics to lessen the famine's consequences to their own advantage could be undertaken entirely independent of the concerns and monitoring of princely authorities. When stevedores unloaded grain and observed its transport to an inland city even as they themselves suffered the burden of high bread prices, they were bound to have feelings of resentment, which princely forces might help contain. The need to supply settlements of particular importance to princely prestige or regional defense was another factor that brought state power to bear on marketing in certain rural areas and on traffic along the sea-lanes. And one could go on.

The role of the state, then, was real, even if far less important overall than the efforts of local authorities to deal with the agrarian and urban crises. Princes tended to intervene in the political economy of famine relief most decisively (though with varying impact) in five areas: (1) regulation of access to productive resources; (2) control of speculation; (3) imports and exports—and their dangerous flip side, piracy; (4) the supply of garrison towns and of armies on the move; and (5) the repression of widespread popular discontent. Rather than consider each of these issues separately, let us explore the exercise of state power on a regional basis: first, France; then, England; last, the northern kingdoms.

France

The French crown was active both in attempting to moderate the differential impact of the dearth on people of modest means and in trying to prevent the exhaustion of productive resources in the manic competition for meat and grain. For example, efforts made by lords in the late thirteenth century to create protected areas for hunting had been fiercely resisted by rustics who felt—and correctly so—that these efforts would undercut long-standing common rights.[2] For a long time the crown's role in the struggle was muted, but it could not remain so once the famine intensified the attempts of both sides to press their claims. The best way to forestall violence was a moratorium on new protected precincts; and the best way to assure that local notables adhered to the moratorium was legislation requiring authorization for new warrens. In 1317 authorization by the crown became a requirement for the creation of "parcs à gibier."[3]

Of course, this intervention of the crown, though important in preserving social peace and economic equilibrium, was only part of its policy on the exploitation of game. In a period when the surplus from arable was down, the rustic population's access to woodlands and rivers encouraged overhunting and overfishing. In the case of the rivers, repeated incidents in the famine period moved the crown on 6 July 1317 to republish legislation that prohibited fishing with traps that took too-large catches; the traps, if found, were to be seized and burned. The crown also prohibited fishing in rivers from mid-March to mid-May in apprehension that the taking of inordinate catches of fry would undermine the future supply of food fish.[4]

As elsewhere, however, it was staples, like grain and salt, that were the key commodities. Grain reserves had already begun to shrink by the end of summer 1315, a situation that led to the importation of Gascon grain, acts of piracy against the carriers, and widespread speculation.[5] On 25 September the king stigmatized the "avaricious cupidity" of merchants who had cornered the market. Victuals of all kinds were being withheld; and merchants, in complete disregard of the fact that they were being cursed by consumers for doing so and unmindful that they would be blessed if they repented, kept them back in order to drive up prices still further. Or so the ordinance asserted.[6]

Indeed, speculation during the Great Famine was widespread.[7] Any benefits it had in lowering consumption and retarding the exhaustion of supplies[8] exercised precious little influence on the emotional fever of the infuriated population. The crown, as authorities had been doing for millennia, acted in its best political interest, therefore, when it cracked down on the hoarders.[9] The royal remonstrance mentioned above that contains the information on avaricious merchants describes the crackdown in detail. Concentrating on the shortage of salt, the king acknowledged the fundamental cause in the wet weather, but he again focused on the compounding sin of speculative, hoarding merchants. He ordered his officials in Paris, Rouen, and any other places where there were reputed to be large stores of salt to search out the merchant conspirators and, if necessary, confiscate all their goods and inflict whatever other punishments they deemed necessary to break their stranglehold on the salt market. Punishments were to be exemplary and harsh. Once the hoards were identified, the officials were to see to it that markets were supplied within a week at reasonable prices.[10]

The crown was genuinely concerned about the social consequences both of unrestrained competition for game and of hoarding and speculation; however, it was much more concerned about the problems of supply of foodstuffs for its troops in the field in Flanders, and about the possibility that supplies might be diverted to the enemy. Already in late summer 1315, at Soissons, King Louis X prohibited exports to the Flemings while encouraging merchants with grain, wine, and other victuals to vend them to agents of the royal army. He promised safe-conducts, along with freedom from road and wine tolls and other levies, to merchants who did so.[11] It is not clear that they did do so, at least with alacrity, since the merchants could get higher prices on the open market. Consequently, the export bans among French and privileged foreign merchants were repeated in November and December.[12]

As long as a state of war existed and windfall profits might be made, it was inevitable that some merchants would run the risk of purveying goods to the Flemings despite the prohibitions. At the very least, the desperate situation among the Flemish towns, especially the inland ones, described in chapters 7 and 8, encouraged the municipalities to use non-Flemish buyers as their agents in France to purchase victuals. The municipalities tried to get as much as they could from England as well, to the general consternation of the French; the English crown played dumb when questioned on the matter.[13] In the winter of 1316 the king took action. While at Rampillon in Champagne he prohibited merchants from Brabant from buying anything ("vivres, ne autres choses") in France for Flemings.[14]

Not even peace brought an end to the problems. The formal lifting of bans was tentatively accomplished in October 1316.[15] Considering the clandestine contacts before, the official English declaration of resumption (!) of trade with Flanders a couple of months later, in response to the French action, was disingenuous at best.[16] Confrontations and fear of a new general outbreak of hostilities led to the reinstituting of export controls by the French on 11 May 1322.[17]

What seems certain is that, threats and appeals to loyalty notwithstanding, there was throughout the famine a preference among many French merchants to trade in local markets or even to deal with agents of the Flemings for extreme profits rather than sell at lower prices to the benefit of the crown. Consequently, the crown increasingly requisitioned grain. The ramifications were profound. Merchants—presumably both honest and dishonest ones—were enraged; markets and marketers suffered; lords grew angry. As early as 18 November 1315, at Paris, Louis acknowledged the complaints and their truth, and he promised to rethink his policy to the extent that this was possible; but he reiterated his principal concern with keeping the war effort on course.[18] Complaints, therefore, continued. It was not until March 1317 that Louis's successor, Philip V, confirmed Louis's promises and gave them some teeth. In that month the king assured the clergy of the diocese of Paris, for example, that he would authorize the return of equivalent quantities (or the value in money) of grain, wine, and other supplies requisitioned for the war from clergy in the diocese.[19]

The subsistence crisis cannot be implicated as the cause, but it almost certainly exacerbated not only this elite but also popular discontent with the government, and it fed a disconcerting paranoia in society across orders. In 1320 the same king, Philip V, made known that he was planning a Crusade to the Holy Land. Expectations being aroused as the news spread, large crowds of volunteers, in part inspired by lower clergy or people who claimed the status, gathered together especially in the recently war-ravaged districts of French Flanders and northern France. In fact the king's plan came to nothing, but the excitement generated by the expectations could not easily be contained. What was originally conceived as a princely Crusade was quickly transformed into a plebeian movement comprising shepherds (hence the name, Pastoureaux), other rustics, artisans, and poor and outcasts of various sorts.[20]

The situation rapidly degenerated. Paris itself was temporarily penetrated by the "rebels"; so, too, were numerous other towns where the wrath of the malcontents, sometimes in concert with native disgruntled elements desiring to settle old scores, was directed against the rich and the Jews. Jews, who, as we saw earlier,[21] had only recently been readmitted to France from exile, were targeted not merely as religious rivals but as creditors mulcting the poor through pawnbroking. In the summer of 1315, about a month after the Jews had been readmitted to France, the king had sent out special investigators to inquire into and suppress "usury" (interest payments that exceeded the permitted levels), and they worked for months on end.[22] Yet in a sense the outrages in 1320 were a popular demonstration that their work had not been accomplished to the satisfaction of the Pastoureaux.

In the end, of course, the rebels were crushed by the forces of the crown or pursued south until they were chased across the Pyrenees into Aragon where, after a few brief episodes of violence, they were put down. But the shattering effect of the violence had a more durable impact on social relations, for hardly had the last vestiges of the Pastoureaux been vanquished when France saw additional "popular" violence against lepers and, again, Jews.

The year 1321, as is well known, was witness to the so-called leper scare.[23] Rumors of a plot to kill Christians in France by poisoning the wells spread wildly. The organizers of the conspiracy were believed to be Muslims, but their contacts in France were said to be Jews and their agents—the alleged poisoners—lepers. In the wake of the violence of the Pastoureaux, of the still incomplete return to good harvests, and, most important, of widespread disease, the idea of a plot seemed credible enough.[24] More and more "evidence" of the plot was gathered by torture, and authorities and vigilantes were ruthless in their judicial and extrajudicial attacks on the vilified groups. In the end large numbers of Jews and lepers were killed, many more beaten and otherwise humiliated, and many others saddled with oppressive fines by the state.

England

Already in 1315 the English under Edward II attempted by parliamentary action to impose price controls on livestock. There has been some hesitation among historians to consider this action a response to the Great Famine, since England would not see the first bad harvest associated with the famine before June; and prices could not really respond to that harvest until its true extent was widely known.[25] An alternative explanation, suggested by Mavis Mate, focuses on the money supply as a factor driving up prices and provoking the controls.[26] But no such explanation needs to be invoked, for we have already considered persuasive English evidence that the extremely bad rains started there in late 1314.[27] We also know that the usual winter rains were punctuated by periods of extraordinary cold. All this was followed by the renewal of drenching spring rains in 1315. Given these conditions, the first indicator of a subsistence crisis would have been a decline in herd and flock size from poor lambing and from diseases and infestations like liverfluke.[28] Though almost certainly not on the scale of the great murrains later in the famine, this decline would still have forced prices up considerably in London where the crown's focus of attention was riveted. Consequently—and this is decisive in the argument—the price controls were imposed not on grain or grain products in early 1315, but, as indicated, on livestock.

Because of the rapidly increasing magnitude of the shortages and the spiraling cost of fodder crops, the controls, for those who could benefit from the high prices, were worth getting around and proved unsuccessful. But although they were rescinded, the policy was reimposed and refocused after the harvests repeatedly failed. This time the controls were placed on products, like ale, that were manufactured from grain. The action on ale, in January 1317, reinforced that taken by the city of London in September of the year before.[29] Aggressive as the authorities were, however, no historian has argued that these price controls enjoyed any serious success.

The likely failure of price controls did not mean in England, anymore than in France, that the crown was willing to see prices artificially inflated by hoarders and speculators beyond the levels induced by the harvest shortfalls per se. Moreover, action against local speculation was a far easier policy to put into practice than were price controls; and it was far more popular, supported as it was by widely shared notions of the just price.[30] Consequently, speculation encouraged "draconian measures" on the part of the political authorities.[31]

In letters to various bishops in April 1316 the English king addressed the problem. Acknowledging that the horrors of bad weather and the poor harvests had been brought on his kingdom because of sinful humanity's disobedience, and "desiring therefore to provide for the salvation of our people by the ways and means that we can," Edward II urged the clergy to exhort the hoarders "with efficacious words" to offer their surplus grain for sale. They were to use other methods, presumably excommunication, if necessary, "lest the cause of such ruin and death be imputed to those having grain and refusing to sell it."[32] These ominous words obviously refer to the possibility of popular retribution. No king, least of all one like Edward II—at loggerheads repeatedly with his barons and involved in a war with the Scots—looked indifferently on the possibility of this sort of violence or its potential for getting out of hand and further hobbling his capacity to rule. Judging from the reaction of the bishop of Salisbury, the king's words were taken seriously. He immediately drafted orders to the clergy of his diocese to enforce the royal command.[33]

In addition to price controls and actions against speculators, the crown reacted to the famine in an entirely traditional way by offering incentives to merchants for the import of grain.[34] Just like town governments, however, the crown was faced with the problem that its neighbors and traditional trading partners were victims of harvest shortfalls and famine as well. Consequently, trade in grain with some nearby regions fell to almost zero. This was true with regard to the Baltic trade, which was still not a large grain source, anyway.[35] With just a little manipulation it can be shown to be probable with regard to English trade with Normandy, a better established trading partner, as well. Some figures on Rouen provided by Alain Sadourny make the point nicely. In 1301, by one measure, 38 percent of Rouen's commercial traffic on the Seine (with London as a principal destination of the city's exports) involved wine. In 1317 far more than 52 percent involved wine. These two facts suggest, if we can take 1301 rather than famine-stricken 1317 as a typical year, that the proportion and undoubtedly the absolute quantity of other products traded from the port declined precipitously.[36] This must certainly include grain, which appears to have made up a substantial part of commercial exchange in normal times. Already in 1306, for example, low grain supplies in Paris had induced the French crown to restrict exports, probably with the intention of requisitioning supplies at cost, but enterprising scoundrels were busy trying to keep shipments coming out of Rouen, a fair indication of its importance as an exporter of cereals.[37]

On the other hand, most historians cite Edward II's promises of safe-conducts to merchants as supporting evidence that princes took radical measures to feed their populations.[38] These merchants included Italians;[39] and this fact has led some historians to suggest that purchases or authorizations to purchase grain covered a catchment area that included Italy.[40] This suggestion must be treated with as much caution as was necessary in the consideration of municipal grain policies, however,[41] even though the attractiveness of responding to a buyer as powerful as the English crown would normally obviate comparisons with the pull of mere municipalities. In this instance, however, it is likely that the Italians, along with Breton and Norman carriers who were also active, were simply being encouraged to arrange imports of grain and wine from southern France and the Biscay coast of northwestern Spain.[42] Certainly the documentary evidence is rich on the activities of ethnically English agents in these regions who were given as much support as the crown could provide to help them procure grain.[43]

Yet because of the alleged power of the purchaser, the English crown, to stimulate mercantile activities that were decidedly extraordinary, we must spend a little more time on the issue of whether grain from the Mediterranean reached the Channel ports. The great economic historian Adolf Schaube argued the most tempting case for such grain shipments,[44] but all his evidence was circumstantial. He regarded two ships owned by Venetians and with Italian names off the English coast in 1316 as powerful testimony. However, we know something about the cargo of these ships, and it suggests a point of origin other than Italy: it included foodstuffs *and wine*; yet there was no significant market for Italian wine in England. Therefore, these ships almost certainly were plying the ocean from the Biscay ports to England.

Schaube also employed etymology in defense of his argument. He found the word *dromond*, a Greek word, being used to describe the ships coming to England and equated this with Italian *tarida*, an equation that is probably justified. The *tarida* or *dromond* was a very large, fast-moving ship. However, for an Englishman to call a big fast ship by a Mediterranean name does not establish that the ship came from the Mediterranean. A Genoese-owned ship designated a *dromond* came into port in northern England in April 1315; its point of origin was not Genoa but the Bay of Biscay.[45] Indeed, the word *dromond* was widely used in England from as early as 1191 (the word came back with crusaders who had seen such ships) even though there is almost no evidence of any ship whatsoever coming to England in this period after exiting the Mediterranean through the Straits of Gibraltar (an excruciatingly more difficult matter, as we have seen, given the currents and prevailing winds, than entering the Mediterranean from the Atlantic).[46] In sum neither the northern towns nor the northern crowns imported Italian grain.

Where the English crown did try to buy surplus grain, southwestern Atlantic Europe, its success depended on two factors, the competition with other buyers and the security of the seaways. The competition was fierce: agents of Flemish towns, buyers from northern France, and even local authorities in the southwest, who did not want to see stores there decline to perilous levels, were all playing an important part in affecting the market.[47] Presumably as agents of the man who was lord of Gascony, the English king's officials had a distinct advantage in exploiting the long tradition of export of foodstuffs—not just grain, but products as diverse as figs and walnuts—from the south.[48] In northern Castile, the strong and more purely economic pull of English demand also stimulated grain exports in 1317.[49]

The security of the seaways was quite another matter. Piracy was a continuing problem.[50] In the spring and summer of 1316 people attacked and seized stores from ships preparing to dock and unload food at ports in southern England.[51] One or two sailors and merchants appear to have been fatally injured in raids on ship stores and warehouses, for a royal mandate attempting to confront piracy refers to manslaughters done at sea.[52]

The documentary record is particularly rich with regard to the crown's attempt to supply its northern garrison town Berwick-upon-Tweed while the war with the Scots raged. As noted before, although some of the problems and issues affecting garrison towns did not differ to any considerable extent from those affecting towns in general, the paramount interest of state or princely authorities in garrison towns makes them appropriate to be treated here. Garrison towns, which were, almost by definition, in or near hostile territories, occasionally required special (princely authorized) food imports.[53] Berwick, by all measures, was of consuming interest to the crown in 1315. Right on the Scottish border (or within Scotland, some might say), the town could no longer be systematically supplied from its hinterland as raiding parties harried the district.[54] In April 1315, for example, five agents were trying to buy food for the town but seem to have been woefully inadequate to the task.[55] By October, indeed, famine raged, with the garrison itself appearing to be on the verge of abandoning the fortifications.[56]

Some desperately needed stores were jettisoned off the coast at the end of October, and seaborne supply continued to be dangerous in the opening months of 1316.[57] Meanwhile, the laments of the garrison and the permanent residents increased. February saw the formulation of a group of petitions that described for the crown's benefit the nature of the distress. The garrison was starving; there had been a foray into the countryside against orders, and the scavengers had been ambushed on their attempt to return. Desertions were becoming a problem. The remaining soldiers were reduced to eating their horses, a terrible calamity for a medieval company of mounted soldiers. Pity the poor Christians.[58] Further documents indicate that the number of horses may have fallen from three hundred to fifty under the impact of the hunger. The burghers, who were increasingly at odds with the garrison, plummeted into debt, with the possibility of starvation becoming as much a problem for them as for the troops.[59]

Even as the laments continued, acts of depredation in March and May of 1316 disrupted cargoes being shipped to Berwick.[60] Of course, it is presumed that some ships got through. (Certainly there are plenty of indications of very extensive commercial negotiations associated with efforts to supply the town.)[61] Still, the number of references to piracy is considerable. November 1316 saw another attack on the seas, and the years 1317 and 1318 were replete with incidents. Some of the attackers were Scots; some were freebooters. When ships from Gascony, for example, entered the North Sea through the perilously navigated Straits of Dover on their way north to Berwick, they became targets for Scots, English pirates, and even rogue Low Country and Hanse sailors operating from the Continental coasts.[62] Accusations against Lübeck, Stralsund, and Rostock crews were being made from at least February 1317 until December 1319.[63] Some of these accusations may have arisen from cutthroat competition among the various shippers,[64] but disruption of trade, whatever the cause, had the same ill effects on the garrison town.

In the circumstances, Berwick became a seething cauldron of tensions. The black market was in full operation in 1316; by 1317 accusations of speculation and fraud against the highest levels of the burgher patriciate were being made to the crown.[65] A sense of topsy-turvy reflected genuine reversals of authority and power when lower-class persons, including some butchers and even serfs who came to town, managed to make financial killings from the small surpluses they sold.[66] Hatred, especially between garrison troops and townsmen, also surged.[67] It was, in the end, an impossible situation. Berwick capitulated in mid-1318 through the treachery of native elements. Though the isolated garrison still had to be supplied as long as it could hold out, the main point is clear: despite all the best efforts of the crown to give safe-conducts to merchants and to keep the sea-lanes open, it was incapable of managing supply effectively.[68] At least one commentator knew why: the manifold sins of the English, his own people, were being punished.[69]

One obvious if partial answer to the litany of disasters was peace. Although piracy in the so-called truces caused extreme difficulties for honest traders,[70] genuine and long-lasting peace would have made possible a stretching of scarce resources to the limit, assuring a more equitable distribution of foodstuffs to the desperate population of northern England and Scotland. But this obvious and moral option yielded before the chimerical hope on both sides for a decisive victory. Lucas assembled evidence of the English crown's pressuring its officials to extract whatever possible from the already wretched peasantry. The pressure led to what he terms gross abuses of the peasantry, when the king's men confiscated grain and fodder under color of purveyance.[71] We know now that brutality became a condition of life, so that the hapless English crown found it difficult to control its own servitors, for whom even the highborn were easy pickings.[72] On the other side of the border, conditions were little better.[73]

A more general point can be made, however, for it was not merely in the war-torn areas or in the lands where troops were being mustered that the taxation, in the brutal form of purveyance, had an effect. Taxation of the peasantry of regions far distant from the war zones always had deleterious repercussions during periods of dearth. But in 1316 "prises and levies on movables were collected simultaneously" in England despite the famine, and in 1317 prises continued to be collected. The English peasant was typically assessed for taxation "only on the goods which he had for sale and not on those intended for his own domestic use," but every moment that saw the need for ready cash to pay other obligations like rents and tolls also saw agriculturalists reduce consumption in order to procure cash.[74] Reducing consumption under famine conditions was a considerable undertaking; yet English rustics who did so were then taxed on goods they could hardly afford to part with. Near the border with Scotland—in Cumberland, Westmorland, and Northumberland—the inhabitants petitioned the crown for a three-year respite on renders to the exchequer, but evidently with only mixed success at best.[75] It is not surprising that, as Maddicott writes, "the levy on movables was resisted most forcefully in the localities during the famine years of 1315–17."[76] Including the resistance to purveyors and middlemen that was a typical response of rustics under pressures such as those characterizing these years,[77] the difficulties facing the crown were virtually insurmountable.

Nevertheless, the resistance, as ubiquitous as it was, was insufficient to insulate the peasantry from the worst effects of these adverse times, for levels of effective taxation were still high enough to stimulate the sort of self-defeating behaviors that Guy Bois would see as contributing to the structural blockage dooming the high medieval economy.[78] Maddicott goes so far as to suggest, though with rather weak commitment, that the real turning point in the history of the English peasantry ought not to be associated with the harvest shortfalls or other natural disasters per se but with the onerous state-imposed taxation for the never-ending wars of the fourteenth century.[79] Again, a similar case can be argued for Scotland.[80]

The shortfalls in taxation compounded by a decline in customs on wool—resulting from corruption, war, smuggling, and animal disease[81]—made the English crown ever more creative in raising money. A government memorandum dating from the mid-teens and laying out the case for imposing a forced loan on international traders to make up for the financial shortfalls had interesting repercussions. Certain levies on merchants, in line with the recommendations of the memorandum, became harsh in 1317 and 1318; yet others that had been imposed in the first year of the famine were "withdrawn in September 1317 because of the practical difficulties encountered by merchants importing much needed foodstuffs into the country."[82] In this case, the crown's need for revenue came in conflict with the need to provision its garrison towns, like Berwick, and other large coastal towns, especially London, from abroad.

From the entirety of the discussion in the last several pages it might seem that the crown's reaction to the famine in England was a blend of grandstanding (the ineffective but appealing price controls and draconian measures against speculators), shortsightedness, bumbling, and, at times, almost criminal self-interest. But it would be amiss to ignore the image of his rule that Edward II wished to convey. His publicists represented him as the wise king, dealing with the famine with aplomb and moral rectitude, like the pharaoh who had put Joseph in charge of the granaries of Egypt in the time of the patriarchs.[83] Surely the effort to fashion this portrait was meant to counter the disappointment people felt with the king's leadership and his agents' activities. Perhaps it was also intended to embarrass the attacks on his counselors that had been characteristic of baronial opposition to him. (Where have all the Josephs gone? Answer: Killed by barons.) Yet if these were the goals, they were not entirely fulfilled. This curious image of Edward II as the good pharaoh never achieved much currency outside the circle of his sycophants and clients; and when echoes of it are discerned in texts originating in other circles, the comparison is not blithely accepted.[84] In the end, Edward failed in famine relief, and he failed to cover up his failure, too.

The Northern Kingdoms

Although on the northern side of the Baltic grain formed a far smaller proportion of agricultural output than on the southern side, both grain shortfalls and declines in meat and dairy production in Scandinavia ushered in a major subsistence crisis and a temporary diminution in collected taxes. As with the English king, no Scandinavian prince showed any immediate willingness to see his revenues decline or willingly adjusted his requests according to local needs. One consequence of this fact was an eruption of violence between princely agents and local farmers. In Swedish Norrland—the area of modern Sweden and Finland on either side of the Gulf of Bothnia—men licensed by King Birger II of Sweden in the winter of 1316–1317 attempted to ship provender as taxes out of the region to the area of densest settlement (whose access to Continental grain was costly and limited by the low supplies); they were met with stiff resistance, and the head of the taxing party was killed. When punishment came, it was swift and unmitigated: confiscation of goods and mass executions, as state power tried to reestablish itself in this sparsely populated region.[85]

The harvest shortfalls, outbreaks of pestilence, and this evident tax revolt were part of a cluster of other problems that affected Sweden and the north in general. The year 1317 provided a brief respite "after many difficulties and afflictions of wars and oppressions, of taxes and tribulations."[86] Nevertheless, we have already seen that additional fighting, indeed civil war, followed King Birger's execution of two princelings whose power he feared; after his own death in 1318 the power struggles continued, with wide-ranging results including the pauperization of the peasantry.[87] It was all the more necessary in these circumstances for whatever powers continued to exist to try to get needed foodstuffs to the northern countries.

There was, however, some competition. Whether it was significant or not is a complicated question. It is not impossible that Britons tried to obtain grain and other foodstuffs, like additional herring and stockfish, from Baltic suppliers to compensate for other shortages; stockfish (gutted, wind-dried cod), after all, was the principal import to Britain from the Baltic before the famine, amounting to more than 1,500 tons per year.[88] However, although British-Baltic trade networks existed, low grain production in the British Isles had not characteristically or preferentially evoked *grain* imports from the Baltic.[89] And the local cereal shortfalls in Scandinavia and the Hanse hinterlands would scarcely have encouraged any really radical modification of grain import policies. Moreover, as we have seen, importation of herring was at least closely tied to salt production, if not absolutely dependent on it. Without huge salt reserves, the attractiveness of increasing the supply of fresh fish diminished. Alternative preservation techniques—smoking and wind drying (the method for cod)—were either fuel intensive on the scale that would have been needed or difficult given the weather conditions.

I have deliberately used the word *Britain* rather than *England*, because fragmentary evidence indicates that shipping and trade contacts between the Scottish ports and the Hanse and the Scandinavian principalities were no longer entirely exceptional by the end of the thirteenth century. Even so, they were hardly routine either.[90] England itself was a pretty minor purchaser of Baltic grain at the most intense of times. Indeed, only in the fifteenth century was the major flow of the German grain trade, at least that in the control of Hanseatic League towns east of Hamburg, oriented westward to the Low Countries, Flanders, France, and Britain.[91]

All the same, it has been suggested that before the Great Famine there were occasional German exports to England during periods of peak prices.[92] The evidence is very thin. Is it really true that German merchants as far east as Danzig (Gdansk), for instance, were already in the thirteenth century coming into competition with southern English grain merchants when local conditions and high prices in the north of England or in the northwestern part of the Continent induced both to market their surplus grain in the ill-affected regions?[93] The fact of this competition—if it is a fact—would explain why in 1315 German merchants stayed abreast of famine-generated regional price differentials at the shire level in the English grain market—if they did stay abreast of them—and presumably targeted the areas where prices were highest.[94]

The cautious, not to say timorous, quality of the foregoing remarks arises out of uncertainty about the documentary basis from which the scholars concerned have made the case. Naudé, the leading proponent of these views, cited in his support a manuscript that I have not been able to verify. It reportedly was in the possession of a Danzig grain firm, still in existence in his day. N.S.B. Gras did not reject the evidence Naudé extracted from the Danzig manuscript, but argued that it showed a sensitivity not to harvest failure but to war policy, the English, one supposes, inducing the Germans to dump available grain in English markets rather than see it go to the Scots. Both arguments may have some truth, but in general it is probably wise to take Naudé and Gras with some circumspection.[95]

Moreover, even if Naudé and Gras were correct, with harvest shortfalls in Germany as well as in the British Isles in 1315–1322 the quantity of grain that could have reached England from this source must have been less than hoped, since no free market operated. Indeed, a few years before, in 1310, a modest rise in grain prices in the Continental northwest had provoked an increase in exports from a few Baltic Hanse towns stimulating, in turn, a steep rise in prices in the towns themselves. In a dither (itself evidence of the irregularity of grain export to the far west), municipal authorities in the Hanse towns of Wismar, Rostock, Stralsund, and Greifswald reacted by effectively banning the shipment of the needed grain.[96] It is not to be supposed that these authorities, let alone more important Hanse towns with nearer and more regular trading partners,[97] were less vigilant during the Great Famine when grain supplies from their own hinterlands, profoundly depleted by the bad weather, were so low.

Did grain come to the west from remoter locations—namely, Poland? A *fortiori* it is highly unlikely. What we call coastal Poland was a region that came under German domination, the domination of the Brandenburg ruling house and the Teutonic Order, by 1309.[98] This development was not looked upon with equanimity by other powers. As a result of a Danish-Polish alliance concluded in 1315, for example, a joint (if militarily inconsequential) invasion of the Brandenburg lands was launched in 1316.[99] The war would have made it quite difficult to export grain according to normal routines.

The grain that was being grown was limited in quantity, anyway. To be sure, in areas of German settlement and domination, grain production, despite periodic regressions, would increase over the course of the first half of the fourteenth century. Nonetheless, the region as a whole had not yet made the fundamental transition to grain husbandry that we associate with east central Europe two centuries later, and was, so far as the documents indicate, also suffering from the famine.[100] This is not decisive proof against the export of grain or other foodstuffs, of course, since traders were not loathe to send scarce supplies to regions that would pay the highest prices. But the orientation for these eastern German or Polish traders was traditionally northern or eastern (Scandinavia and Rus') where, because of the difficulty of growing native grain, there was a steady demand for German and Polish surpluses.[101] Smaller towns away from the coast (*binnenlandische Städte*) in central and eastern Germany and western Poland (Berlin, its twin Kölln, Magdeburg, and the like), when they had grain to dispose of, typically, if not slavishly, looked to the cold northeast for markets as well.[102]

Fear of inadequate access to Continental grain from the Hanse hinterland, then, was a long-standing sentiment informing the foreign policy not of English and Scottish authorities but of Scandinavian ones. Norway, it has been said, was particularly dependent on German (and to some extent English) grain.[103] To be sure, some historians may have a tendency to exaggerate this dependency.[104] Still, there is no doubt that grain was important in foreign-policy considerations.[105] Indeed, from the time of King Haakon IV, who reigned from 1217 to 1263, Norwegian foreign policy was predicated on keeping supplies coming from the German Baltic ports or even securing such a port (Lübeck was attractive) as a colony.[106]

In the face of resistance to the extraction of meat and dairy products from the pastoral hinterlands of the Scandinavian kingdoms to the more populous coastal settlements,[107] trade with Germany, no matter how costly, made even more sense than usual. Yet the Hanse towns, in whose hands so much of the trade was concentrated, could be ruthless and shortsighted in their economic policy when their stores were low, or even when they simply felt that the freedom of their merchants was threatened or the policies of their Scandinavian neighbors seemed at variance with their own political interests. Grain was a weapon in their intermittent cold war with the Scandinavians; the refusal of Hanse merchantmen to transport it or other goods could be devastating to the northern economies.[108] As recently as 1284–1285 a grain embargo organized by the Hanse (Lübeck) against Norway had been very effective.[109] Embargoes, of course, provoked retaliation in the tug-of-war between Scandinavian princes and Hanse merchant oligarchies.[110] This helps to explain an edict of King Haakon V of Norway in the midst of the Great Famine, 30 July 1316, that forbade the export of butter and stockfish except by merchants who imported grain and grain products in return.[111] Possibly Germans needed the products of the north, like herring and stockfish, more than the Scandinavians needed grain. Hamburg is a case in point, but even towns as far from the Baltic coast as Magdeburg (a good 150 kms.) consumed large amounts of Norwegian and Swedish fish purveyed out of Lübeck.[112] Bad feeling, the sadly low level of available German grain, and the German and Scandinavian murrains all combined to sour political and business relations along the Baltic: the economic recession they provoked on the southern shore of the sea from 1315 to 1322 has been characterized by Richter as nothing short of "catastrophic."[113] In fine, the "Great Hunger" prevailed.

EPILOGUE

ACCORDING to Jack Ravensdale what distinguishes the Great Famine from the Black Death, where the mortality, as is well known, was enormously greater, was that the famine perdured. In the Black Death "for a few months men died." In the famine "the agony was slow."[1] To some extent the resentment felt by the suffering population from this prolonged agony manifested itself in an outpouring of postfamine literature of social criticism. Among various examples of the poetry of "social protest of early fourteenth-century England," one representative specimen entitled "A Poem on the Evil Times of Edward II" (ca. 1320), quoted at various times in the course of this study, brings together the related themes of war (in this case the baronial rebellion against Edward II), the harvest shortfalls, and the animal pestilence. The lament, movingly describing pain, sorrow, uncertainty, rancor, and alienation from authority, captures a mood bordering on despair and sliding into hatred.[2]

How could this have been otherwise? The events of 1315–1322 were unspeakably difficult. Prices were high and volatile, making it hard, if not impossible, for people to plan for the future. Wages did not keep pace with the steep and nearly decade-long price inflation. Those lords who benefited from the high prices were far outnumbered by others who suffered economic crises and near bankruptcy. Rustics and burghers, with few exceptions, bore even heavier financial burdens—losing or abandoning homesteads, selling houses, going into heavy and unproductive debt. Sickness and death—especially in the towns in 1316—as well as erosion of civility and political stability, verging on and sometimes becoming rebellion, were the end product of a catastrophe until then "unheard-of among living men."

Credit, charity, and prayer, along with princely and municipal efforts to monitor and improve distribution of scarce resources, had gone some distance toward ameliorating the worst physical and spiritual effects of the famine in a few places, but they were insufficient to buffer the majority of the population. And so the collective memory was, for a time, one of failure, of a nightmarish world of child-murder and cannibalism. Poems like "The Evil Times of Edward II" were not intended merely as laments but as detailed sociologies of failure, carefully identifying and targeting the negligence and vices of specific social groups and classes.

It should come as no surprise, perhaps, that the men who wrote these poems were not usually of the highest rank in society or the church, which is not to say that the poems represent the unmediated voice of the lower orders. According to J. R. Maddicott's "provisional and tentative belief," the texts appear to have been "the work of clerks"—"possibly friars, possibly university masters, possibly the educated parish clergy," but not bishops or abbots or deans of chapters. The broad outline of the social experience of such writers is not difficult to imagine. While not of peasant origin, they would have been men who, on account of their immediate moral obligations as teachers of future priests or as clergy themselves in poor rural and urban parishes, "were familiar with what would later be called 'the condition of the people.'"[3]

The tradition of texts like "The Evil Times of Edward II" culminates, of course, in the late-fourteenth-century *Visio* of Piers the Plowman,[4] a work conventionally attributed to William Langland, a cleric in minor orders, the son of a country gentleman.[5] *Piers Plowman* is an extremely long and complex poem—a series of critiques in the form of visions of abuse of power in rural life—that has attracted many interpreters and interpretations.[6] Distinctive in its sympathetic concern for poor people rather than poverty in the abstract, even though it is a heavily allegorical work,[7] the poem has a much more striking impact than do many other protest poems. The character "Hunger," on which we may focus, is representative of a social indictment of shirkers in the fields in a period of much want[8] and takes on figurative dimensions as the character hungering "after righteousness," desiring the just judgment of those of status in society who shirk their social responsibilities.[9] There can be little doubt that Hunger's characterization is in part an echo of local elites' inability to confront the Great Famine successfully and their unwillingness—as perceived by farmers and laborers—to succor the poor who suffered.

The character of Hunger is also a salvational image. The "prophecy that Hunger will destroy the Wasters through water, flood and foul weather . . . recalls" the passage from the Gospel of Matthew (7.24–27) in which the man who obeys the words of Christ is likened to the builder of a house on a foundation of stone, rather than sand, which the rains, the flood, and the wind cannot destroy.[10] The evocation of the conditions of the famine years is powerful, in part because "wasters" (*wastoures*), in the medieval connotation of the word, comprise people who not only misuse available resources but also avoid working while at the same time consuming gluttonously.[11]

If Langland, like those professional keepers of memories, the chroniclers, preserves an echo of the afflictions of the Great Famine, it is merely an echo by the later fourteenth century. The poet of "The Evil Times of Edward II" remarks at how only a brief reassertion of normal conditions made most of his peers forget or perhaps want to forget God's "punishment and teaching."[12] He undoubtedly means that they abandoned processions and other forms of pious behavior that God's wrath had first inspired. A German stone carver in 1317 had wanted to prevent just this sort of backsliding; he was determined that his and future generations should never forget the misery of the famine or how it was brought to an end in his homeland. On a pillar of the Church of Saint Katherine in the Rhenish village of Oppenheim he inscribed on red sandstone a short sentence in the vernacular whose words recalled that the construction of the church, this *opus dei* as it were, had commenced in the year 1317 when men and women were paying "ein Haller" for bread.[13] He expected his audience to know and never to forget what he meant by this abbreviated reference to the common money of the region—that only good works and faith such as led to the foundation of Saint Katherine's could persuade an angry God to relent from punishment and restore an abundance of bread. We now know that the significance of the reference was effaced over time. Even early modern antiquaries, gifted though many of them were with an ability to penetrate the spirit of the past, were not quite sure what the carver meant by inscribing the *Hungerbrotstein*, as the block of sandstone is now known.[14]

How many generations after the carver his message would have become unintelligible or indifferent to the ordinary worshiper at Saint Katherine's cannot be recovered. What we do know is that neither the stony memorial in the church, nor protest poetry, nor mentions in chronicles were powerful enough reminders to make those in command encourage and carry through systematic practical adjustments in grain and related policies that might have lessened the impact of recurrences of harvest shortfalls. This slide into indifference might have been arrested if a famine on a geographical scale similar to that of the Great Famine had occurred in the late 1320s or early 1330s, but although there would be further crises of production in the decades to come, there was nothing remotely on the scale of that catastrophe. Consequently, rural investment continued weak or "light" even though larger barns and more drying ovens, to name just two possibilities, would have gone a considerable way to providing the facilities needed to mitigate future local calamities.[15]

That such calamities were only local, not general, has sometimes been a contested point. An older historiography imagined a Europe hobbled by the famine and afflicted continually thereafter until the savage years of the Black Death. In fact, the reality was quite different. In a good solid discussion of the agricultural regime in England from the Great Famine to the Black Death, based on a study of the estates of Canterbury Priory, Mavis Mate has demonstrated that overall recovery was relatively quick from the famine and that we cannot in any way justify a somber picture of rural society unrelievedly mired in a trough from 1322 to 1348.[16]

Other British researchers have come to similar conclusions. Cornwall "did not suffer a prolonged setback," according to John Hatcher.[17] Hallam here, if not elsewhere, can probably be trusted in his belief that the temporary demographic setbacks of southeastern England (Essex, Wessex, and Sussex), however severe, failed to usher in a decline over the long term, that is, until 1350.[18] Nigel Saul is cautious, too, about the long-term negative demographic and productive consequences of the famine in Gloucestershire.[19]

One can go further. Christopher Dyer has tentatively suggested, from data on the amount and kinds of food given to harvest workers on various English manors, that the significant but uneven decline in population as a result of the Great Famine may have led to a perceived improvement in diet—more meat, less dependence on bread, more ale, less cider—until 1348.[20]

Outside of Britain the picture looks similar. If towns suffered more and longer almost everywhere,[21] even their plight could come to be regarded in context as no more than a temporary setback—a few years of hardship with perhaps one summer (say, that of 1316) of terrible mortality. A few significant exceptions in Flanders aside, a full return to "normalcy" had taken place by the mid- or late 1320s. Evidence from Dresden points in this direction.[22] And evidence already provided on many other towns—Dortmund and Hamburg, to name two—reinforces the conclusion.[23]

The eagerness with which men and women put the bad years behind them and the gradual but steady recovery from the scourge should not blind us to one likely long-term consequence of the famine. It has often been suggested that the overpopulation of the early fourteenth century created persistent malnutrition, making the population as a whole more susceptible to the microorganism that caused the Black Death (1347–1351). In fact, what appears to be the case is that, if anything, the quality of nutrition improved over the period 1322–1346 or at least held steady. While not providing enormous "relief" on productive resources or completely breaking the financial "blockage" that characterized the economy at the turn of the century, the small but real declines of population in some densely settled districts, as well as the concentration of property holding among rich peasants in certain rural areas, introduced added economic efficiencies in rural agriculture. One may wonder whether the negative social consequences of the latter development outweighed these advantages by increasing tensions between haves and have-nots in villages. But even the have-nots of the 1330s and early 1340s—in villages and towns—probably ate better than had their counterparts in 1300.

Still, the high mortality of the midcentury plague, although it was not due to any persistent endemic malnutrition, did owe something to the famine per se. Let us return for the last time to the nutritional biology of famine. We have already seen that recent work establishes the existence of famine's differential negative impact on the mortality of children. There are also long-term effects on the children who survive famines, long-term effects that are considerably more severe than those on adults who survive starvation rations. The reason for this is that essential aspects of growth appear to be closely correlated with biological age; if growth or, rather, systemic development is inhibited, as it must be when energy intake is reduced substantially for any length of time at the critical age, recovery can never be complete.[24]

By *growth* nutritional biologists do not mean increases merely in gross weight or height, but the proper formation of specific organs and systems, especially the immune system, that need distinctive nutrients to function effectively and to develop the capacity to respond effectively to future infections. Extrapolation from animal studies may exaggerate the impact of the short-term absence of such nutrients, since all other mammals mature faster than humans and, for the former, even brief periods of malnutrition in infancy can have long-term and quite severe implications.[25] To put the point another way, a six-month deprivation for an animal whose preadult phase lasts one year would be much more significant than a nine- or ten-month deprivation in a human being whose critical preadult phase lasts up to thirteen years or so. But a famine (starvation rations) of three years—even in the absence of visible symptoms like distention of the belly—is of sufficient length to have devastating long-term effects on the future well-being of human infants: morbidity would almost always be increased over the long run because of the improper development of the immune system.[26]

By inference, the horrendous mortality of the Black Death in northern Europe in part should reflect the fact that poor people who were in their thirties and forties during the plague had been young children in the period 1315–1322 and were differentially more susceptible to the disease than those who had been adults during the famine or were born after the famine abated. Moreover, the group should have experienced a higher mortality than any "normal" population of thirty- or forty-year-old Europeans might be expected to experience. Conversely, those regions (the towns of Flanders stand out) that suffered epidemics in 1315–1322 in which large numbers of children died might have far lower relative rates of mortality in the period of the Black Death. Any research agenda for the Black Death should at least look into this possibility. Given the nature of the evidence and the complicating problem of migration, the theory will be hard to prove. But if it is true, it would help explain the astronomically high rates of mortality that we have come to associate with that catastrophe, as well as the exceptional areas, like many Flemish towns, that appear to have escaped.[27]

The region of Europe affected by the Great Famine was to see famines recur again and again in the centuries to come. Never of the extent or acuteness of the Great Famine, these were, with their implications for social instability, a constant reminder of the fragility of civil society. Such famines, however, became less frequent and less widespread over time, so that fear and concern about harvest shortfalls in particular in most parts of the north abated considerably by the nineteenth century. Improvement in agricultural techniques and therefore productivity had a great deal to do with this, but it had also become possible in the course of the early modern period to import staples from a wider range of food-rich countries, some of which, such as Poland and eventually Russia, developed specialized markets oriented to grain-hungry and once again heavily populated western Europe.[28]

The course of this development in northern Europe was not the same everywhere. Politics and prejudice played a clear role, as Jonathan Swift brilliantly satirized in *A Modest Proposal*, in putting some populations at risk longer than others. For England, the transition can be said to have occurred by the end of the seventeenth century. France was still experiencing intense local famines in the eighteenth. For Ireland, Swift's case, the transition would not occur until after the 1840s, about a century after his death. To be sure, war or the cold ideology of forced nonconsumption (to gain capital from exports in order to finance industrialization) has more than once brought about a repetition of famine in modern times. But the shadow of ineluctable famine, it is fair to say, effectively dissipated in northern Europe in the course of the nineteenth century.

It has often been conjectured that this waning of the incidence of famine, and of the fear of its inevitability, had its counterpart in a new attitude toward nature encapsulated in the term *Romanticism*.[29] Nature's impact on food production could be got around; and nature in her "feminine" wildness became, in turn, superbly admirable, with the poets writing her encomia. Yet Romantic adulation of terrifying nature never entirely displaced the older story. The very phenomena that fueled the most escapist aspects of Romanticism—industrialization, rapid urbanization, and rural improvements, including mechanization of agriculture, together with the increase in population that all of these encouraged—ushered in a variation on the ancient theme of fear.

Some commentators like Thomas Carlyle and Charles Dickens, in very different ways, gave themselves over to dark visions imagining a terrifying Malthusian world whose famine-end was only postponed by modernity. In his weirdly compelling essay/novel *Sartor Resartus*, Carlyle created the tragicomic Hofrath Heuschrecke (Counsellor Grasshopper), a man "so zealous for the doctrine [of Malthus], that his zeal almost literally eats him up." "Nowhere," according to Heuschrecke, as he surveys the macabre specter of modernity, "is there light; nothing but a grim shadow of Hunger; open mouths opening wider and wider; a world to terminate by the frightfulest consummation: by its too dense inhabitants, famished into a delirium, universally eating one another."[30] A reader would laugh but for the ghoulish and unsettling character of the locutions.

It is different with Dickens. One of the most famous passages of *A Christmas Carol* describes Scrooge's vision of the two children "Ignorance" and "Want" finding shelter under the skirts of the Spirit of Christmas Present.

> They were a boy and girl. Yellow, meagre, ragged, scowling, wolfish; but prostrate, too, in their humility. Where graceful youth should have filled their features out, and touched them with its freshest tints, a stale and shrivelled hand, like that of age, had pinched, and twisted them, and pulled them into shreds. Where angels might have sat enthroned, devils lurked, and glared out menacing. No change, no degradation, no perversion of humanity, in any grade, through all the mysteries of wonderful creation, has monsters half so horrible and dread.[31]

Scrooge's sympathy for the children's pitiable state marks one of the many steps in the old man's gradual redemption. And it reminds the reader how far the aged miser has come from the time, earlier in the novella, when the then unrepentant sinner had lauded the work of prisons and poorhouses and had encouraged death by poverty to "decrease the surplus population." For Dickens, at least in this tale, a moral reawakening among moderns, reinforced by knowledge (for it was Ignorance that he regarded as the more dangerous of the symbol-children), is represented with the capability of confronting and winning in the struggle to overcome privation and needless death.

That it is possible in our own day to cling to hopes for a similar moral reawakening, leavened by knowledge of the past and chastened by visions of the present, seems unlikely. We do not share the comforting fantasies of the Victorians. Badly managed nature and brutal wars perdure in unholy alliance against hope, and brief signs of promise are precious little in a landscape of persistent despair—in Africa especially, but elsewhere as well: "sad hungry faces / hoping, begging for one more day / tears rolling down their eyes."[32] They are the poor who are with us always.

NOTES

PROLOGUE

1. "Cavete vobis ne furorem puerorum propter vestram miseriam incurratis"; the translators of Salimbene's *Chronicle* render it, "You'd better watch out, the children's wrath will descend on your stinginess"; pp. 627–28 (for the Latin, see the Scalia edition [1966], pp. 905–6).

2. Salimbene de Adam, *Chronicle*, p. 621 (Scalia edition, p. 895).

CHAPTER 1
THE BRINGERS OF FAMINE IN 1315: RAIN, WAR, GOD

1. See, for example, Sen, *Poverty and Famines*; and Garnsey, *Famine and Food Supply*. I owe these references to my colleagues Gyan Prakash and Peter Brown.

2. Appleby, *Famine in Tudor and Stuart England*, addresses the sixteenth and seventeenth centuries; Post, *Food Shortage*, the 1740s. Rotberg and Rabb, *Hunger and History*, is a series of studies on various aspects of famine. Walter and Schofield, *Famine, Disease and the Social Order*, emphasizes problems of social control during early modern famines. Monahan, *Year of Sorrows*, is a case study of the famine in Lyon in 1709. This list could be multiplied almost endlessly.

3. Below, text to nn. 15–21.

4. Depending on when they wrote, where they were located, and how limited their interests were, chroniclers contemporary with the famine and even some later authors judge the duration differently. But in hindsight and after a thorough assessment of the records, it became clear to later authors that famine conditions had been very persistent; see, for example, Diemar, *Chroniken des Wigand Gerstenberg*, p. 238.

5. Curschmann, *Hungersnöte*, p. 216. See also Stoob, "Hansische Westpolitik," p. 8 (citing an array of chronicles).

6. Leidinger, *Veit Arnpeck: Sämtliche Chroniken*, pp. 284 ("Chronica Baioariorum"), 780 ("Chronicon austriacum").

7. Diemar, *Chroniken des Wigand Gerstenberg*, p. 238.

8. Emmius, *Friesische Geschichte*, 2:190.

9. Lass, *Sammelung einiger Husumischen Nachrichten*, pp. 21–22: "Wahrscheinlicher mag es aber seyn dass es 1315 gewesen denn zu der Zeit soll die Pest und Theurung in ganz *Europa* gewesen seyn: ja von dem ersten *May* biss Ausgang des Jahres soll es geregnet haben: der Hunger war gross woher auch annoch der *Vers* zu bemercken: *Ut lateat nullum tempus famis ecce CVCVLLVM.*" This weird little verse with its reference to the absent cuckoo (*cuculus*), the herald of spring and rebirth, appears fairly frequently in the sources (see, e.g., Diemar, *Chroniken des Wigand Gerstenberg*, p. 239; "Excerpta ex Nicolai Henelii . . . Chronico," p. 152). The letters of *CVCVLLVM* give the year of the famine's inception ($M = 1,000$, $2C = 200$, $2L = 100$, $3V = 15$; total 1315); Lass, n. f on p. 22.

10. Scholz, "Das Spätmittelalter," p. 405; Curschmann, *Hungersnöte*, p. 33; also, pp. 82–85, tables with the length and geography of earlier famines, back to the year 709.

11. Bois, *Crisis of Feudalism*, pp. 271–75; Kershaw, "Great Famine," p. 10 and passim. The exception of northern Scotland may be explained in this way. In terms of weather, prevailing winds there come from Scandinavia, not the Gulf Stream as in southern Scotland. Moreover, even if weather patterns had been the same as in the south, the effect would have been minimal on the diet since northern Scotland, an insignificant grain-growing region, was dependent on other foods. All this and a low density of population helped spare the region.

12. Cf. Lunden, "Korntienda etter Biskop Eysteins Jordebok," pp. 189–212. Like northern Scotland, northern Scandinavia (for similar reasons, above, n. 11) avoided the famine.

13. Lorcin, *Campagnes de la région lyonnaise*, p. 213; Carpentier, "Autour de la Peste noire," p. 1077. On the absence of the famine in most of Austria, cf. the silence of the entries in *Österreichisches Städtebuch*. Henry Lucas's effort ("Great European Famine," p. 373) to patch together bits and pieces of information to make a contemporary famine in the south was misplaced; Larenaudie, "Famines en Languedoc," pp. 37–38.

14. See below, text to nn. 28–34, for a partial breakdown of the population figure.

15. Lamprecht, *Deutsches Wirtschaftsleben*, vol. 1, pt. 1, pp. 589–602; pt. 2, p. 1551.

16. Chickering, "Young Lamprecht," pp. 198–214, has a psychologically based explanation for Lamprecht's peculiar approach. See also Lewald, "Karl Lamprecht und die rheinische Geschichtsforschung," pp. 279–304. More comprehensive—and treating Lamprecht's evolution and influence as a "cultural historian"—is Schorn-Schütte, *Karl Lamprecht*.

17. Curschmann, *Hungersnöte*, p. 2.

18. Ibid., pp. 6–8.

19. Ibid., p. 9. Often I will be citing texts from Curschmann's collection. This does not mean that I am indifferent to the continuing scholarly discussions about the authors and sources of the chronicles he excerpts. For example, the so-called Annals of Lübeck, which Curschmann excerpted extensively, have been thoroughly reexamined by Wriedt ("Annales Lubicenses," pp. 556–86), but despite some suggestions about improving the edition in *Monumenta Germaniae Historica*, Wriedt, like Curschmann, accepts the testimony of the Annals on the famine (pp. 560, 571). A great deal of work has also been accomplished on various Netherlandish annals since Curschmann's time (cf. Coster, *De Kroniek van Johannes de Beka*), but again my impression is that despite the ongoing debates, Curschmann was judicious in his selection. Where pertinent difficulties have been targeted by later scholars, however, I have noted their views and, when appropriate, adopted them.

20. Cf. Contamine, *Economie médiévale*, p. 293.

21. Kershaw, "Great Famine," followed by Miller and Hatcher, *Medieval England*, pp. 59–62, and Prestwich, *Three Edwards*, pp. 247–52.

22. Curschmann, *Hungersnöte*, pp. 10–11.

23. Ibid., pp. 208–11, 213–17; Hilton, *Stoneleigh Leger Book*, p. 75. Later, that is, noncontemporary, chroniclers naturally repeat this language; see, for example, "Chronijcke van Nederlant," p. 19, a sixteenth-century compilation.

24. Müllner, *Annalen der Reichstadt Nürnberg*, 1:368, 373; Valois, "Plaidoyer du XIVe siècle," p. 366; Meister, "Niederdeutsche Chroniken," p. 51; Baier, "Bruchstücke einer stralsundischen Chronik," p. 66; Curschmann, *Hungersnöte*, pp. 208, 210, 213–15, 217; Le Duc, *Histoire de l'abbaye de Sainte-Croix de Quimperlé*, p. 292; De Dynter, "Breve chronicon Brabantinum," p. 57. See also Nicholas, *Medieval Flanders*, p. 207, translating the chronicle of Jan Boendale. The published version of the "Continuatio Chronici Guillelmi de Nangiaco," p. 615, under the year 1316, has the phrase "caristia gravis," a misreading for "caristia granis," corrected by the editor of the "Chronicon Girardi de Fracheto," p. 45; see also "Chroniques de Saint-Denis," p. 698. Again, later, noncontemporary chroniclers repeat this language; see, for example, various late-fourteenth- through seventeenth-century Low Country chronicles: Borgnet and Bormans, *Ly Myreur des histors*, pp. 219, 222; "Korte Chronijcke van Neder-land," p. 64; "Brabandsche Kronijk," p. 50; "Chronijcke van Nederlant," p. 19; "Chronycke van Nederlant," p. 72.

25. On the historiography of the demographic movements, consult Hybel, *Crisis or Change*, pp. 3–4, 156–61, 228–30, 268–71. See also Contamine, *Economie médiévale*, p. 143.

26. Abel, *Agricultural Fluctuations*, pp. 21–22.

27. *Nordic Archaeological Abstracts*, p. 146, citing the work of Per-Göran Ersson.

28. Rösener, *Bauern im Mittelalter*, p. 41.

29. Other estimates in 1300 are 3.7, 4, 4.5, and 5.25 million; and after a brief downturn around 1315–1325 as high as 6.25 or 7.1 million in 1348. For the variety of estimates, see Abel, *Agricultural Fluctuations*, pp. 21–22; Rösener, *Bauern im Mittelalter*, p. 41; *Agrarian History*, 2:512–13, 537; Smith, "Demographic Developments in Rural England," p. 49; Mayhew, "Modelling Medieval Monetisation," p. 57; Britnell, "Commercialisation and Economic Development," pp. 9–12.

30. Abel, *Agricultural Fluctuations*, pp. 21–22; Rösener, *Bauern im Mittelalter*, p. 41. This, of course, includes southern France, which is not our concern, but it should be pointed out that southern Europe in general experienced similar if not quite so spectacular growth in the twelfth and thirteenth centuries. Italy, for example, went from 5 million to 7 or 8 million over these two hundred years, according to Abel.

31. Abel, *Agricultural Fluctuations*, pp. 21–22, summarizing various scholars in all his estimates.

32. Lunden, "Gardar, Bruk og Menneske," pp. 111–58, considers and rejects estimates of 400,000 and 455,000, preferring 500,000. Sandnes, "Ødegårds-prosjektet," pp. 397–410, offered criticisms of Lunden to which the latter replied with some persuasiveness; Lunden, "Øydegardsprosjektet," pp. 26–49. Helle, "Norway in the High Middle Ages," pp. 165–66, was unwilling to be more precise than 300,000–500,000. See also Gissel, "Agrarian Decline in Scandinavia," pp. 43–54, on the various methods used in coming up with these estimates.

33. Ylikangas, "Major Fluctuations in Crimes of Violence," p. 86.

34. Neither the Finns nor other eastern Baltic inhabitants on the northern and southern shores of that sea had as yet gone over entirely to permanent arable fields from slash-and-burn agriculture, a fact that afforded them a temporarily higher rate of yields on crops. For a full discussion of agricultural techniques and yields, see below, chapter 2, nn. 16–52.

35. For good surveys of the European economy and its constituent parts—by region or by sector—in the Middle Ages, the reader may refer to (from oldest to most recent): Bloch, *French Rural History*; Slicher van Bath, *Agrarian History of Western Europe*; Duby, *Rural Economy and Country Life*; Titow, *English Rural Society*; Postan, *Medieval Economy and Society*; Perroy, *Terre et paysans en France*; Hilton, *English Peasantry*; *Histoire de la France rurale*, vol. 1; Miller and Hatcher, *Medieval England*; Sivéry, *Economie du royaume de France*; Rösener, *Bauern im Mittelalter*; *Agrarian History*, vol. 2; Sivéry, *Terroirs et communautés rurales*; Genicot, *Rural Communities*; and Contamine, *Economie médiévale*. Naturally the authors differ on many issues and some of the older works have been supplanted in parts, but recency of publication is no guarantee of superiority of interpretation. Later, attempts will be made to adjudicate among the various views as these pertain to our understanding of the famine's causes and consequences.

36. Arnold, *Famine*.

37. Seavoy, *Famine in Peasant Societies*.

38. See the incisive and completely persuasive criticisms in Arnold, *Famine*, pp. 57–61, and Wardwell's review of 1987, pp. 835–36. Unfortunately, Seavoy appears to have learned nothing from these criticisms. His most recent effort, a study of East Africa, includes the same nonsense on the so-called subsistence compromise; Seavoy, *Famine in East Africa*, pp. 2–7.

39. Tahon, "Eglise Saint-Martin de Graçay," p. 53; Harman and Wilson, "Medieval Graveyard," p. 60; James, "Excavations in Wootton Wawen Churchyard," p. 44; James, "Excavations at the Augustinian Priory of St. John and St. Teulyddog," p. 155; Hodder, "Excavations at Sandwell Priory," pp. 134–35. These articles report French, English, and Welsh excavations from what seem to be "typical" rural cemeteries (those for burials of all the village dead). I have avoided referring to evidence from hospital cemeteries and from those which served a restricted monastic community (including domestic servants), since the estimates of deformities might be skewed—upward in the former case, downward in the latter: cf. Bishop, "Burials from the Cemetery of the Hospital of St. Leonard," pp. 32–33; Smith, "Excavation of the Hospital of St. Mary," p. 184; Butler and Evans, "Cistercian Abbey of Aberconway," p. 63.

40. See, e.g., Jansen, "Svendborg in the Middle Ages," p. 204.

41. *Bad Year Economics*, pp. 1–7. I owe this reference to Professor David Nirenberg. See also Newman et al., "Agricultural Intensification," pp. 118–21.

42. Theissen, "Das Leben in den Städten," p. 105: "Bier war im Mittelalter ein Grundnahrungsmittel, weshalb der Verbrauch besonders hoch war."

43. Cf. Amartya Sen, *Poverty and Famines*, pp. 45–51.

44. *Bad Year Economics*, pp. 3–5.

45. It may be appropriate here to refer to Townsend's *Medieval Village Economy*, which offers a sophisticated modeling of an agricultural economy and its

conditioning by the so-called expectation of famine, on the average, every twelve years. Townsend argues, using English evidence from the Middle Ages, that his modeling applies to medieval European village economies. I find many of his assumptions, though necessarily simple (simplistic?) for the modeling effort, dubious at best. Moreover, nowhere is there a discussion of famine per se. Rather, he accepts that any use of a word translatable as "famine" in a medieval chronicle—the Anglo-Saxon Chronicle, for example—can be taken at face value. In fact, as we saw above, one has to be circumspect on this matter. In addition, the chronicler may be reporting local conditions even if he generalizes to "the whole world." I see no persuasive evidence that individual villages were experiencing famine about every dozen years in the High Middle Ages.

46. Hofmeister's statement (*Seehausen und Hasenbüren im Mittelalter*, p. 161) is typical: "Witterungsbedingt war wohl die grosse Hungersnot der Jahre 1315/16."

47. This assertion seems generally accepted, but a few scholars have made extraordinary claims based on it: Genicot, for example (in his most recent, but not his best, book), claimed that the generally good weather, which he calls climatic improvement, "made previously infertile soils tillable"; Genicot, *Rural Communities*, p. 31.

48. De Ram, *Joannis Molani . . . Historiae lovanensium*, 2:846–48, bk. 14, no. 22.

49. Ibid., 865–66, bk. 14, no. 69.

50. Our author's ignoring of the Black Death is not, as with some late chroniclers (cf. "Vriessche Aenteyckeninge," pp. 46–47), a case of confusion or conflation of the Black Death with the famine. Rather, our author often depended on Brabantine chronicles in making the assessments mentioned (see, e.g., De Ram, *Joannis Molani . . . Historiae lovanensium*, 2:866, 870). Brabantine sources are simply thin on the Black Death. This fact has led later scholars to suggest, though not without some dissension, that the Black Death had a lesser impact on Brabant than elsewhere; cf. Despy, "Grande Peste Noire de 1348," pp. 195–217. Our author's failure to mention the mortality of the Black Death becomes considerably less surprising in this context.

51. De Ram, *Joannis Molani . . . Historiae lovanensium*, 2:870, bk. 14, no. 83.

52. Sax, *Nova, totius Frisiae septentrionalis, Descriptio*, p. 145. "Annis 851, 1006, 1051, 1062, 1069, 1315, 1403 . . . war eine tewre Zeit."

53. Cf. Dury, "Crop Failures" (1984), p. 417. On the methodological problems of studying climate and weather, especially in the absence of measured temperature data, see also Le Roy Ladurie, *Histoire du climat*, pp. 14–19, 212–15; Hallam, "Climate of Eastern England," pp. 124–32; and the collection of articles in the *Journal of Interdisciplinary History* 10 (1980).

54. Alexandre, *Climat en Europe*, p. 783. Some researchers refuse to acknowledge any return to the warming trend after the famine or backdate the end of the warming trend to years preceding the famine on the basis of local conditions they have studied. Alexandre is to be preferred, but cf. Lamb, *Climate*; Wright, "Barton Blount," pp. 150–52; Bailey, "*Per impetum maris*," pp. 184–208.

55. Alexandre, *Climat en Europe*, pp. 24, 38, 436–43. For the opposite ap-

proach, using famine and yield data to deduce the weather, see Lamb, *Weather*, p. 61 and caption to figure 4.7.

56. Schultz, *Das höfische Leben*, 1:127–40; Norlind, *Einige Bemerkungen über das Klima*, pp. 21–39; Schmitz, *Faktoren der Preisbildung*, pp. 12–27; Day, *Medieval Market Economy*, pp. 185–86.

57. Alexandre, *Climat en Europe*, pp. 781–85.

58. Lyons, "Weather," pp. 36, 63–64.

59. Palermo, "Carestie e cronisti nel Trecento," p. 355, citing the work of Huber and Niess on "Jahrringchronologie hessischer Eichen," in the *Büdinger Geschichtsblätter* 5 (1964), which I was not able to consult.

60. Müllner, *Annalen der Reichstadt Nürnberg*, 1:368, 373 (this late compilation draws on several earlier sources); Curschmann, *Hungersnöte*, p. 208, for the Flemish verse; and Le Duc, *Histoire de l'abbaye de Sainte-Croix de Quimperlé*, p. 292, for the Breton material. See also Curschmann, *Hungersnöte*, p. 209; Nicholas, *Medieval Flanders*, p. 207; Hofmeister, *Seehausen und Hasenbüren im Mittelalter*, p. 161.

61. Lucas, "Great European Famine," pp. 345–46; see also Kershaw, "Great Famine," p. 6; Müllner, *Annalen der Reichstadt Nürnberg*, 1:368.

62. See, for example, the contemporary Flemish chronicle of Lodewijk Van Velthem, *Voortzetting van den Spiegel Historiael*, 3:180; and *Monasticon belge*, 1:400, citing the chronicle of Jean de Sivry (d. 1320), prior of the Premonstratensian abbey of Bonne-Espérance in Hainaut.

63. *Annales suecici*, p. 372: "hoc anno [1315] multiplicata sunt plus solito fulgora et coruscationes" (also "Chronica Erici Olai, Decani Upsaliensis," p. 92). "Chronica Laurentii Petri, Archiepiscopi Upsaliensis," p. 90: "var så myckin tordöön och liungeld alstädes i landet at man slijk gräseligheet alrig näghon tijdh tilförende hördt hadhe."

64. "Continuatio Chronici Guillelmi de Nangiaco," p. 614; "Chroniques de Saint-Denis," p. 697; "Chronicon Girardi de Fracheto," p. 44; "Fragment d'une Chronique Anonyme," p. 151; "Excerpta e Memoriali Historiarum, auctore Johanne Parisiensi," p. 661; "Chronique Rimée attribuée à Geoffroi de Paris," p. 160; etc. Summaries of the evidence for parts of Germany and for Luxembourg are provided, respectively, in Götzelmann, *Hainstadt in Baden*, p. 28, and Lascombes, *Chronik der Stadt Luxemburg*, p. 148. It is important to refer here to contemporary or near contemporary chroniclers whose references to one hundred or more days of continuous rain are striking enough. In the retelling by later chroniclers the duration of the rains often gets even longer; cf. "Chronycke van Nederlant," p. 72, a seventeenth-century compilation.

65. "Continuatio Chronici Guillelmi de Nangiaco," p. 614; "Chronique Rimée attribuée à Geoffroi de Paris," p. 160. See also the sources cited in the preceding note.

66. Langdon, "Water-Mills and Windmills," p. 430.

67. Curschmann, *Hungersnöte*, pp. 208, 211–13, 215–16; Lucas, "Great European Famine," pp. 345–50; Cosgrove, *New History of Ireland*, 2:285; Crawford, "William Wilde's Table of Irish Famines," p. 5; Lyons, "Weather," p. 62. See also Norlind, *Einige Bemerkungen über das Klima*, p. 36, according to whom the situation was at its most injurious ("am drückendsten") in 1316.

68. Wriedt, "Annales Lubicenses," p. 571. (Because of medieval dating practices, a winter listed under one date, say, 1315, means the winter of 1315/1316.)

69. Curschmann, *Hungersnöte*, p. 215; Lodewijk Van Velthem, *Voortzetting van den Spiegel Historiael*, 3:210–11.

70. Curschmann, *Hungersnöte*, p. 215.

71. Redik, *Regesten des Herzogtums Steiermark*, 1:226, no. 849.

72. Lascombes, *Chronik der Stadt Luxemburg*, p. 150; Lucas, "Great European Famine," pp. 374–75.

73. Curschmann, *Hungersnöte*, pp. 216–17.

74. "Chronicon Girardi de Fracheto," p. 47.

75. Wright, *Political Songs*, p. 342, lines 410, 414.

76. Lucas, "Great European Famine," p. 376; Cosgrove, *New History of Ireland*, 2:285; Lyons, "Weather," pp. 62–63. And see above again (text to nn. 58–59) on the confirming dendrochronological evidence.

77. Cf., for example, Lascombes, *Chronik der Stadt Luxemburg*, p. 151, for a summary of the improved conditions in the Luxemburg region in 1319.

78. "Ex Uticensis Monasterii Annalibus," p. 483.

79. Prims, *Geschiedenis van Antwerpen*, vol. 4, pt. 1, p. 140.

80. The thrust of the English evidence is given in Kershaw, "Great Famine," p. 15; and Bolton, *Medieval English Economy*, p. 182. (Once more, see above for the parallel dendrochronological evidence.) German documentary evidence of tempests and hailstorms at harvesttime 1322 is quoted in Schmitz-Cliever, "Pest und pestilenzialische Krankheiten," p. 115.

81. Wriedt, "Annales Lubicenses," p. 571; Samsonowicz, "Das Verhältnis zum Raum bei den hansischen Bürgern," p. 32 (citing the Stralsund chronicle). Although probably referring to the same winter, the seventeenth-century humanist Peter Sax, after a review of chronicle evidence available to him, places the bitter weather under the year 1323; Sax, *Annales Eyderstadiensium*, p. 41: "Anno C[hristi] 1323 ist ein harter Winter gewesen, dass man über die OstSee, in Preussen hatt gehen können."

82. "Ex Chronico Sancti Stephani Cadomensis," p. 493; Lent (*Kadragesima*) was 14 March. See also "E Chronici Rotomagensis Continuatione," p. 349, which says that bitter cold lasted through mid-March and the abundant snow until mid-April; and Borgnet and Bormans, *Ly Myreur des histors*, 6:266, a later-fourteenth-century chronicle reporting information gleaned from earlier authors on the deep snows in Paris.

83. Hørby, "Fate of the Descendants of Christoffer I," pp. 227–29.

84. Jaubert, "Royal Castles during the Reign of Erik Menved," p. 219; the example discussed here is of the great Danish tower, Kärnan, in Helsingbor castle on the mainland of the Scandinavian peninsula (dendrochronologically dated 1317–1318). See also below, chapter 9, text to nn. 98–99 and 103–13, on further ramifications of the military situation in the north.

85. Ebendorfer, *Chronica Austriae*, pp. 238–39.

86. "Chronica de gestis principum," p. 80: "magna multitudo hominum et equorum ducis Austrie, cum essent in Frankhenfurt, famis inedia perierunt."

87. "Chronica Ludovici imperatoris quarti," p. 133: "Et mirum: milites, qui

sedebant in equo fallerato, dabant equum et arma pro rapato, et hoc pre nimia fame."

88. For the agreements of the years 1315–1322, see Ruser, *Urkunden und Akten der oberdeutschen Städtebünde*, vol. 1, nos. 58–62, 133–51, 188–89, 288–307, 402, 422–25, 446–47, 460, 476, 486, 495, 539; and Acht, *Regesten Kaiser Ludwigs des Bayern*, nos. 3–6.

89. Hahn, *Fürstliche Territorialhoheit und lokale Adelsgewalt*, pp. 56–57; Benker, *Ludwig der Bayer*, p. 95; Huber, *Verhältnis Ludwigs des Bayern zu den Erzkanzlern*, p. 38 n. 43.

90. Vincent, *Histoire des famines à Paris*, p. 39 n. 1.

91. Delcambre, "Chronique Valenciennoise," p. 59; Lemaître, *Chronique et Annales de Gilles le Muisit*, p. 87; "Rymkronyk van Vlaenderen," p. 816; Lodewijk Van Velthem, *Voortzetting van den Spiegel Historiael*, 3:206; Molinier and Molinier, *Chronique normande*, p. 31; "Continuatio Chronici Guillelmi de Nangiaco," p. 614; "Chronique Abrégée de Guillaume de Nangis," p. 652; "Chroniques de Saint-Denis," p. 697; "Chronicon Girardi de Fracheto," p. 44. Later compilations repeat the facts with relish; see, among others, Borgnet and Bormans, *Ly Myreur des histors*, 6:218–19, as well as their edition of the "Geste de Liège," 6:663–64; Kervyn de Lettenhove, "Chronique anonyme," 511–12, and his pastiche, *Istore et croniques de Flandres*, 1:305; and Sweerts, "Annales belgici Aegidii de Roya," p. 51. See also Nicholas, *Medieval Flanders*, p. 197; Lucas, "Great European Famine," p. 349.

92. "Continuatio Chronici Guillelmi de Nangiaco," p. 614; "Chroniques de Saint-Denis," p. 698; "Excerpta e Memoriali Historiarum, auctore Johanne Parisiensi," p. 662; etc., etc.

93. "Chronique des Pays-Bas," p. 141: "en celle saison, il plut si mierveleussement et si longhement, que par forche d'iauwes et de lait tams, il laissa le païs, et s'en revint sans bastaille, et disoit à ses gens que Dieus voleit esdier les Flamens"; this chronicle is dated to the fifteenth century (p. 13). See also Wielant, "Recueil des antiquités de Flandre," p. 362: the Flemings, desperate before the royal host, turn to God, and "il feisoit sy grand pluye que nulz vivers n'y pouvoient suyver." Wielant was also writing in the fifteenth century.

94. Waites, "Medieval Assessments," pp. 134–45.

95. Nicholson, *Scotland: The Later Middle Ages*, p. 106.

96. Mackay, *Chronicles of the Frasers*, p. 74. (These chronicles are a late and somewhat quaint seventeenth-century compilation, but they are based in part on now lost early sources; see pp. xix–xxi.)

97. Waites, "Medieval Assessments," pp. 140–42, 144.

98. Otway-Ruthven, *History of Medieval Ireland*, pp. 224–43.

99. Cf. Lucas, "Great European Famine," p. 356; Cosgrove, *New History of Ireland*, 2:285; Lyons, "Weather," p. 62.

100. Frame, "Bruces in Ireland," pp. 3–37.

101. Crawford, "William Wilde's Table of Irish Famines," p. 5–6. Frame, "Bruces in Ireland," in general follows Lucas, but see p. 25, especially n. 95, for additional information and commentary.

102. Frame, "Bruces in Ireland," p. 35 n. 149.

103. Hopkins, *Medieval Neath*, p. 66.

104. Smith, "Edward II and the Allegiance of Wales," p. 146; Thomas and Dowdell, "Shrunken Medieval Village at Barry," p. 97. Further on the crop failures, animal pestilences, and difficult political situation in the march along southern Wales, see Dohar, *Black Death*, p. 35.

105. Below, chapter 4, text to nn. 176–78.

106. Hilton, *Stoneleigh Leger Book*, p. 75.

107. Smith, "Edward II and the Allegiance of Wales," pp. 151–53; Morgan, "Barony of Powys," p. 21.

108. Curschmann, *Hungersnöte*, pp. 12–14; texts at 208–10; Hardy, *Register of Richard de Kellawe*, 2:1118–20. See also Nicholas, *Medieval Flanders*, p. 207.

109. "Chronique Rimée attribuée à Geoffroi de Paris," p. 160.

110. Ross, "On the Evil Times of Edward II," p. 186, line 225, and p. 187, line 236; Wright, *Political Songs*, p. 341, lines 391–92.

111. Weiler, *Urkundenbuch des Stiftes Xanten*, 1:310–11, no. 463.

112. Oxford, New College, MS 264, fol. 255 (col. a): "Propter quod ego W. tempore quo rexi scolas grammaticales Lyncolnie. Anno videlicet ab incarnatione domini. M°CCC°sextodecimo ad magnam caristiam qua illo anno ac anno precedenti proximo et consequenti viguit in regnis Anglie, Francie, Alamannie necnon in multis aliis regnis respiciens, ac cellule memoriali commendans quedam indicia famem precedentia que in regno Anglie vidi vicesimo anno precedente. Et etiam que vidi in regno Francie anno XV precedente predictos annos ab incarnatione domini quando steti in studio Florenti universitatis parisiensis." (The treatise was brought to my attention by Professor Monica Green of Duke University. Although I benefited from her tentative transcription and called upon the help also of my colleague Professor Michael Mahoney, any errors in the transcription are mine.)

113. After the passage quoted in the preceding note, William digresses briefly about his wonderful time in Paris and the worsening of education since his days as a student ("a quo studio sicut a paradiso procedunt quatuor flumina totum mundum rigantia. Sic inquam quatuor solebant procedere nationes videlicet natio gallicorum, picardorum, normannorum, et anglicorum quarum scientia omnium xpisticolarum gloriosa propago inebriebatur, illuminabatur ac perficiebatur. Que nationes modo arescunt et sterilitatem in aliis universitatibus magnam . . ."). Somewhat later he resumes the thread of his earlier discussion and promises to describe the signs foretelling the famine, but except for mentioning a shortage of beans he abandons the project and leaves a large blank space of a full column (half a page) instead: "Signa que vidi parisius anno supradicto et similiter que vidi bis in Anglia emergere tempore vite mee annis suprascriptis sunt ista videlicet, novem annorum defectio (?) fabarum."

114. The "Continuatio Chronici Guillelmi de Nangiaco," p. 615, dates the phenomenon around St. Thomas's day (3 July). See also "Chroniques de Saint-Denis," p. 698; "Chronicon Girardi de Fracheto," p. 45. Various other chroniclers, contemporary or near contemporary, report the comet's appearance at some other date (for example, around Christmas), or simply under the year 1315 or the turn of the year 1315/1316: "Ex Anonymo Regum Franciae Chronico," p. 20; "E Chronici Rotomagensis Continuatione," p. 349; Curschmann, *Hungersnöte*, p. 212; Borgnet and Bormans, *Ly Myreur des histors*, 6:219.

115. Williams, *Observations of Comets*, pp. 68–69.

116. Curschmann, *Hungersnöte*, p. 15. Southern European annalists in the fourteenth century concurred in this interpretation of comets; Palermo, "Carestie e cronisti nel Trecento," p. 351.

117. Lodewijk Van Velthem, *Voortzetting van den Spiegel Historiael*, 3:214–16, 218, 221.

118. The death of the king: "Continuatio Chronici Guillelmi de Nangiaco," p. 615 ("quae mortem Regis praenosticare videbatur"); "Chronicon Girardi de Fracheto," p. 45. The suffering of France: "Chroniques de Saint-Denis," p. 698 ("denonçant le detriment du royaume"). Without prediction: "E Chronici Rotomagensis Continuatione," p. 349.

119. *Annales suecici*, pp. 284, 306, 372: "Eodem anno [1316] in Ringstadhaholm pluit sanguis" (with minor variants in the texts). Ringstadhaholm was in East Gothland, the southeastern region of modern Sweden. (The texts are also available in "Chronologia ab anno 266 ad 1430," p. 27; "Chronologia Vetusta ab anno 1298 ad ann. 1473," p. 94; "Chronica Erici Olai, Decani Upsaliensis," p. 92.) See also "Chronica Laurentii Petri, Archiepiscopi Upsaliensis," p. 90. The annals of "remarkable happenings" ("Mårkvårdiga Håndelser i Sverige ifrån 1220 till 1552," p. 90) add the information about pestilence: "rågnade blod vid Ringstadholm. Samma år var pestilentia hår i Sverige." The so-called "Olai Petri Svenska Chronica," p. 263, posits God's role and the need for repentance: "Anno Domini 1316 regnade blod vijd Ringstadaholm, men ther fölgde mycken blodsutgiutelse effter, som man nu får höra. När Gud vill låta komma några plågor på land och städer plägar han gement någor underlig teckn låta skie tillförene, menniskiomen till en varnagel, att the skola vetta straff vara för handena, om the icke bättra theras lefverne." Although these Swedish materials are late compilations (fifteenth century and after), there is no reason to suppose that they transmit anything but reliable information on the general circumstances of the famine. Nonetheless, as was true of other late chroniclers (cf. "Chronijcke van Nederlant," p. 20, of the sixteenth century) hindsight permits them the luxury of showing no hesitation about the meaning of the signs. My friend and colleague Professor Hans Aarsleff helped me with the Middle Swedish. See also Lucas, "Great European Famine," p. 358 n. 1.

120. The Stoneleigh chronicler, writing at the end of the fourteenth century, records the appearance of the cross in a passage on the Anglo-Scottish wars, animal pestilence, high grain prices, and famine. The date of the heavenly apparition per se, however, may be 1319 rather than 1316; Hilton, *Stoneleigh Leger Book*, p. 75: "Et durante strage apparuit in aere super populum Anglie crux rubea ad modum sanguinis ad ostensionem martirii futuri in Anglia."

121. For the eclipse, see "Chronicon Girardi de Fracheto," p. 46. On the earthquake of (September) 1316 that affected northern France including Normandy, see "Continuatio Chronici Guillelmi de Nangiaco," p. 616; "Chroniques de Saint-Denis," p. 700 (dated wrongly 1317); "Chronicon Girardi de Fracheto," p. 46; "Excerpta e Memoriali Historiarum," p. 665; "Ex Uticensis Monasterii Annalibus," p. 483. On that of 1317 which affected Poitou, see "Chronicon Girardi de Fracheto," p. 47.

122. Curschmann, *Hungersnöte*, pp. 14–17; texts at 212–13, 215.

123. This commonplace was expressed by the twelfth-century chronicler and abbot of Mont-Saint-Michel Robert of Torigni in this way: "Prodigia autem portenta praeterita, quae famem vel mortalitatem vel aliqua alia flagella supernae vindictae pro meritis filiorum hominum, cum videntur, significant, ideo per litteras memoriae commendantur, ut si quando similia evenerint, peccatores, qui se iram Dei in aliquo incurrisse meminerint, mox ad remedia poenitentiae et confessionis, per haec Deum placaturi, festinent"; *Chronique de Robert de Torigni*, 1:92.

124. For a parallel case, see the manipulation of the meaning of an eclipse in the various texts studied by Paulmier-Foucart, "Histoire ecclésiastique et histoire universelle," pp. 98–99, 110.

125. Lodewijk Van Velthem, *Voortzetting van den Spiegel Historiael*, vol. 3, bks. 7 and 8.

126. "Prima vita Johannis XXII," in Baluze, *Vitae paparum*, 1:112–13: "tarde Deus . . . exaudivit."

CHAPTER 2
THE HARVEST FAILURES AND ANIMAL MURRAINS

1. For a vivid report, see Lodewijk Van Velthem, *Voortzetting van den Spiegel Historiael*, 3:182, 210–11. For general summations of chronicle reports such as that just cited, see Cosgrove, *New History of Ireland*, 2:285; Platts, *Land and People in Medieval Lincolnshire*, pp. 152–54, 161; Lucas, "Great European Famine," p. 346; Rogers, *History of Agriculture and Prices*, 1:468, 480.

2. Curschmann, *Hungersnöte*, p. 215: "more diluvii in locis pluribus subverteret aedificia, muros et castra."

3. *Flores historiarum*, 3:171. On the secular incidence of flooding (particularly coastal flooding) in England, see Bailey, "*Per impetum maris*," pp. 184–208.

4. Curschmann, *Hungersnöte*, p. 215: "inundatio tanta aquarum facta fuit, quod quasi particulare diluvium videretur."

5. For example, in the *Annales Eyderstadiensium* the seventeenth-century compiler Peter Sax wrote, "Anno C[hristi] 1316. Ist eine erschreckl: Wasserfluth gegangen" (p. 41). In the *Nova, totius Frisiae septentrionalis, Descriptio* the same author wrote, "Anno C[hristi] 1316 ist eine grawsame Fluth gewesen" (p. 155). In the eighteenth century, Johannes Lass's reading of the chronicle record caused him to conclude that 1315 was among the tiny handful of years when such enormous rains had occurred that it was worth highlighting the epochal flooding ("sind starcke Wasserfluten gewesen"); Lass, *Sammelung einiger Husumischen Nachrichten*, pp. 20–22.

6. Curschmann, *Hungersnöte*, pp. 208–10, 215–16.

7. Hybel, *Crisis or Change*, pp. 161–67, 186–87, provides useful summaries of the scholarly debates during the last hundred years or so on the extent and impact of assarting (which he calls "colonization") in England.

8. The standard study of the open fields is Ault, *Open-Field Husbandry*; see also Titow, *English Rural Society*, pp. 20, 22; and Baker, "Observations of the Open Fields," pp. 315–23.

9. McCloskey, "Open Fields of England," pp. 10–11. I will be using "open

fields," rather than "common fields," which has sometimes been employed, in order to avoid confusion with waste and pasture where common rights existed. (On the debate over nomenclature, see Titow, *English Rural Society*, pp. 20, 22; and Thirsk, "Common Fields," pp. 3–25.) The open fields were held in severalty, not in common, but ordinarily required community agreement about exploitation.

10. Baker, "Evidence in the 'Nonarum Inquisitiones' of Contracting Arable Lands," p. 524: "pro debilitate terre quia zabulosa."

11. Postles, "Rural Economy on the Grits and Sandstones," pp. 17–18.

12. Cf. Lincolnshire: Platts, *Land and People in Medieval Lincolnshire*, pp. 152–54, 161. On the overall question of abandonments, see below, chapter 5, text to nn. 72–101.

13. Thomas and Dowdell, "Shrunken Medieval Village at Barry," p. 97.

14. Curschmann, *Hungersnöte*, pp. 209–10, 216: "sterilitas terrarum"; "sterilitas inaudita."

15. Valois, "Plaidoyer du XIVe siècle," p. 366: "non . . . audita in dicto regno . . . a temporibus retroactis." Also King, *Finances of the Cistercian Order*, pp. 94–95.

16. Schmitz, *Faktoren der Preisbildung*, pp. 46–50, following Slicher van Bath.

17. Weiss, "Early Irrigation Agriculture," p. 1377.

18. *Histoire de la France rurale*, 1:451.

19. Titow, *English Rural Society*, appendixes A and B; Slicher van Bath, *Yield Ratios*, pp. 30–35, 72–74, 112–17, 152–57, 220.

20. The conclusions on both Scandinavian and Polish yields come from Piekarczyk, "Some Notes on the Social and Economic Situation of the Swedish Tenants in the XIIIth Century," pp. 192–216.

21. Hallam, *Rural England*, p. 13. For a summary of the long historiographical debate on English yields, including on the Winchester estates, see Hybel, *Crisis or Change*, pp. 127–29, 232–36.

22. Thornton, "Determinants of Land Productivity," p. 183; Biddick and Bijleveld, "Agrarian Productivity," p. 96.

23. Farmer, "Crop Yields," p. 152 n. 43; Farmer, "Grain Yields," pp. 331–48.

24. Cf. Campbell, "Land, Labour, Livestock, and Productivity," p. 174.

25. For its application to a German case, see, for example, Bentele, "Bietigheim im Mittelalter," p. 157; for a critique of its application to the sparsely documented Danish case, see Ulsig, "Pest og Befolkningsnedgang i Danmark," pp. 21–43. See also Bartlett, *Making of Europe*, pp. 155–56.

26. See Dury, "Crop Failures" (1984), p. 414, and Miller and Hatcher, *Medieval England*, p. 241, for these opinions (and variants), which go back to the work of Alan Baker, Jan Titow, Michael Postan, and even before (Hybel, *Crisis or Change*, pp. 56–58, 120–21, 124–27, 230–31; Campbell and Overton, "A New Perspective," pp. 42–43). On Malthus and the neo-Malthusian dimension of the Postan Thesis, cf. Smith, "Demographic Developments in Rural England," pp. 25–30.

27. For a judicious review of these controversial matters, see Harvey, "Introduction," pp. 4–11. One of the most insistent proponents of the Postan Thesis is G. H. Dury ("Crop Failures" [1984], 401–18). An unnecessarily ruthless, but brilliant and persuasive, critique of Dury may be found in Osmaston, "Crop Failures," pp. 495–500. Dury replied peevishly, but ineffectually: "Crop Failures" (1985), pp. 501–3.

28. Brenner, "Agrarian Class Structure," pp. 30–75. See also below, chapter 5, text to nn. 52, 61–62.

29. For a review of the Brenner Thesis and criticisms of it, see Harvey, "Introduction," pp. 16–19; and Smith, "Demographic Developments in Rural England," pp. 33–36.

30. Campbell and Overton, "A New Perspective," p. 89, make much of manuring; they certainly make it appear as if heavy manuring in the great fields was (or might become) routine, and they create an elaborate scenario in comparing more modern farm animal densities with those recoverable from the thirteenth and fourteenth centuries to justify their views. But on the point of manuring, at least, the evidence they adduce seems woefully thin.

31. Clark, "Economics of Exhaustion," pp. 61–84.

32. Thornton, "Determinants of Land Productivity," p. 199, discusses "intensive applications" of manure and concludes that "acreages manured were never very large, typically 10 acres per annum." Haphazard manuring—letting animals defecate promiscuously on fallow fields—was of limited value, since ammonium (the nitrogenous product) was "lost by volatilisation from animal manures" unless plowed in relatively quickly; Shiel, "Improving Soil Productivity," p. 59.

33. Long, "Low Yields of Corn," pp. 459–69. See also Mate, "Medieval Agrarian Practices," pp. 25–26; Farmer, "Grain Yields," p. 334; Farmer, "Crop Yields," pp. 133–34.

34. Cf. Postles, "Cleansing the Medieval Arable," pp. 130–43.

35. Mate, "Medieval Agrarian Practices," pp. 25–26.

36. Osmaston, "Crop Failures," pp. 495–97; Farmer, "Crop Yields," p. 122.

37. On the various important distinctions between gross and net yields and the arguments of some scholars on the greater relevance of the latter to a discussion of the rural economy, see Campbell, "Land, Labour, Livestock, and Productivity," p. 165.

38. McCloskey, "Open Fields of England, p. 34.

39. Spahn, *Untersuchungen an Skelettresten von Hunden und Katzen*, p. 67: "Die wesentliche Bedeutung der Katzen lag aber sicherlich in der Regulierung von Getreidevorratsschädlingen."

40. Schumann, *Plant Diseases*, pp. 44–45, 152–53, 217, 224, 227, 233–35. I owe this reference to the generous help of Mr. Stuart McCook of Princeton University.

41. Farmer, "Grain Yields," p. 334; Farmer, "Crop Yields," p. 122.

42. Campbell, "Agricultural Progress," pp. 26–46; Stacey, "Agricultural Investment," p. 930 n. 34.

43. Currie, "Early Vetches in Medieval England," pp. 114–16.

44. Campbell, "Diffusion of Vetches in Medieval England," pp. 193–208; at

p. 204 n. 58, Campbell acknowledges that Stacey "fails to appreciate the full time span that was involved."

45. Campbell and Overton, "A New Perspective," p. 74, see no decline in Norfolk, but Norfolk, with its emphasis on barley (p. 55), differed considerably from most regions where wheat was grown as the dominant crop.

46. Cf. Genicot, *Rural Communities*, p. 40; Farmer, "Crop Yields," pp. 136. Biddick's suggestion, which is the basis of her monograph *The Other Economy*, that Postan overstated this conclusion, too, is interesting, but her data, extracted from a unique and highly specialized pastoral environment that was not capable of much flexibility toward grain growing, may be irrelevant.

47. Long, "Low Yields of Corn," pp. 459–69.

48. Cf. Slicher van Bath, "Yields of Different Crops," pp. 26–106, for relevant figures.

49. Heidinga, *Medieval Settlement and Economy North of the Lower Rhine*, p. 92.

50. A marvelous cooperative study on the feeding of London, directed by Derek Keene, will very likely be exploring these issues in detail.

51. Bailey, "Concept of the Margin in the Medieval English Economy," pp. 1–17; Bailey, *Marginal Economy*, pp. 1–24; and below, chapter 4, text to n. 11, and chapter 5, text to n. 64.

52. Further on lordship and rustic dependency (serfdom), below, chapter 5, text to nn. 6–17.

53. In general, see Carpentier, "Autour de la Peste noire," p. 1075.

54. Shiel, "Improving Soil Productivity," p. 59.

55. Schumann, *Plant Diseases*, pp. 44–45, 235, 224.

56. "Continuatio Chronici Guillelmi de Nangiaco," p. 614; Delcambre, "Chronique Valenciennoise," p. 61; John of Trokelowe, *Annales*, p. 93. Later compilers summarized many similar reports from the period in their own chronicles. See, for example, Walsingham, *Historia Anglicana*, 1:145–46. Borgnet and Bormans, *Ly Myreur des histors*, 6:219, and "Chronijcke van Nederlant," p. 20.

57. "Chroniques de Saint-Denis," p. 697; "Chronicon Girardi de Fracheto," p. 44; Lodewijk Van Velthem, *Voortzetting van den Spiegel Historiael*, 3:181–82, 221.

58. "Fragment d'une Chronique Anonyme," p. 151; "Excerpta e Memoriali Historiarum," p. 661; "Chronique Rimée attribuée à Geoffroi de Paris," p. 160.

59. Above, chapter 1, text to nn. 73–82.

60. Dyer, *Standards of Living*, pp. 262, 265–66, summarizing the Winchester data.

61. Slicher van Bath, *Yield Ratios*, pp. 30–35, 220.

62. Farmer, "Grain Yields," p. 334; Farmer, "Crop Yields," pp. 122–27.

63. Bailey, *Marginal Economy*, p. 201.

64. Harvey, *Manorial Court Records of Cuxham*, pp. 739–40.

65. Harvey, *A Medieval Oxfordshire Village*, p. 58.

66. Kershaw, *Bolton Priory*, pp. 14, 39–42.

67. Ibid., p. 66.

68. For the figures, Slicher van Bath, *Yield Ratios*, pp. 30–35, 220.

69. Dury, "Crop Failures" (1984), p. 413; Kershaw, "Great Famine," pp. 16–17.

70. Farmer, "Grain Yields," p. 334; Farmer, "Crop Yields," pp. 122–27.

71. Dury, "Crop Failures" (1984), p. 407; Osmaston, "Crop Failures," pp. 495–500.

72. Lunden, "Korntienda etter Biskop Eysteins Jordebok," pp. 189–212.

73. Hoffmann, "Braunschweiger Umland in der Agrarkrise," p. 253.

74. Racinet, *Maisons de l'ordre de Cluny*, p. 73.

75. *Histoire de la France rurale*, 1:459; Schmitz, *Faktoren der Preisbildung*, 63–72; cf. Schultz, *Das höfische Leben*, 1:443–46.

76. Cf. Rosenthal, "Rural Credit Markets," pp. 301–2.

77. See, for example, Lodewijk Van Velthem, *Voortzetting van den Spiegel Historiael*, 3:211–12.

78. Schumann, *Plant Diseases*, pp. 44–45.

79. Curschmann, *Hungersnöte*, p. 208: "magnus defectus vini in Francia"; Lemaître, *Chronique et Annales de Gilles le Muisit*, pp. 89–90.

80. Curschmann, *Hungersnöte*, p. 211: "non fuit vinum in toto regno Francie."

81. Le Duc, *Histoire de l'abbaye de Sainte-Croix de Quimperlé*, p. 292.

82. "Continuatio Chronici Guillelmi de Nangiaco," p. 614: "nec vineae ad maturitatem congruam poterant pervenire." Also "Chroniques de Saint-Denis," p. 697; "Chronicon Girardi de Fracheto," p. 44.

83. "Continuatio Chronici Guillelmi de Nangiaco," pp. 614–15: "vini defectus universalis in regno Franciae aliàs inauditus, non solum in quantitate, sed etiam in qualitate." Also "Chronicon Girardi de Fracheto," p. 45.

84. "Excerpta e Memoriali Historiarum," p. 661; "Chronique Rimée attribuée à Geoffroi de Paris," p. 160; Delcambre, "Chronique Valenciennoise," p. 61. See also Lucas, "Great European Famine," p. 350.

85. George, "Vignobles de l'abbaye des Vaux de Cernay," pp. 40–41, 51.

86. Racinet, *Maisons de l'ordre de Cluny*, p. 73.

87. Ibid.

88. Dochnal, *Chronik von Neustadt*, "Geleitwort."

89. Ibid., pp. 39–40. Evidence on most of the issues has already been presented in this and the preceding chapter; evidence on prices and deserted villages will be treated in chapters 3 and 5 respectively.

90. Dochnal, *Chronik von Neustadt*, pp. 39–40: 1316, "Geringer Wein"; 1317, "sehr wenig Wein"; 1318, "Wein viel und sehr gut"; 1319, "Wein sauer"; 1320, "Wein sauer. Nasses Jahr, welches siebenjährige Theuerung nach sich zieht"; 1321, "Wein ziemlich gut"; 1323, "Kalter Winter, welcher die Reben tödtet"; 1325, "Viel, aber sauer Wein"; 1326, "Ziemlich viel Wein"; 1327, "Schlechter Wein"; 1328, "Sehr viel und ausgezeichnet guter Wein."

91. Lascombes, *Chronik der Stadt Luxemburg*, p. 150.

92. John of Trokelowe, *Annales*, pp. 104–5, 156–57; *Flores historiarum*, 3:343. Later chronicles incorporate this information; for example, Walsingham, *Historia Anglicana*, 1:252.

93. Hüster, *Untersuchungen an Skelettresten von Rindern*, pp. 32–37, 125–

26. Her study is in large part based on the evidence of 103,000 animal bones recovered in medieval Schleswig, 52,000 of which are cattle bones.

94. *Agrarian History*, 2:749.

95. Langdon, "Economics of Horses and Oxen," pp. 31–40.

96. Langdon, "Horse Hauling," pp. 37–66.

97. Kershaw, "Great Famine," pp. 24–26.

98. Lyons, "Weather," p. 43.

99. Ibid.

100. Arnold, *Select Cases of Trespass*, pp. 257–58.

101. An exhumation in Buckinghamshire of an immature bull or steer skeleton in a find from about our period (ca. 1300) is suggestive, since "it is unusual to recover articulated remains. Burial of a whole carcass is likely to be because the animal was diseased." In the carcass recovered in this exhumation, there was no evidence of butchering; see Allen, "Excavations at Bierton," p. 92. On the use of abandoned wells to dispose of infected animals in a southwestern German village that went into decline in our period, see Driesch and Kokabi, "Tierknochen aus einem Brunnen," p. 379; the finds indicate that the well was routinely used to dispose of unwanted puppies in normal times.

102. Small, "Grain for the Countess," pp. 60–61.

103. See, for example, Ewan, *Townlife in Fourteenth-Century Scotland*, p. 31 (despite the title, the evidence here is applicable to rural life); Thomas and Dowdell, "Shrunken Medieval Village at Barry," p. 114. See also Howell, *Land, Family and Inheritance*, p. 97.

104. Cf. Lucas, "Great European Famine," p. 351.

105. Kershaw, *Bolton Priory*, p. 76.

106. Curschmann, *Hungersnöte*, pp. 216–17 ("pabula animalibus defecerunt"; "malum malo additur").

107. Ryder, "Medieval Sheep and Wool Types," pp. 14–28; Bolton, *Medieval English Economy*, p. 183; Kershaw, "Great Famine," p. 14.

108. Stephenson, "Wool Yields in the Medieval Economy," p. 382. See also Kershaw, "Great Famine," p. 20; and Thornton, "Efficiency in Medieval Livestock Farming," p. 36. (Because of a woeful rate of survival of information for the period of the Great Famine, Thornton's otherwise wonderful article on the herds and flocks of Rimpton, Somersetshire, has proved less useful than one might hope.)

109. "Fragment d'une Chronique Anonyme," p. 151 n. 19.

110. Kershaw, *Bolton Priory*, pp. 14, 83–84.

111. Bailey, *Marginal Economy*, p. 201.

112. Cf. Kershaw, "Great Famine," pp. 20–22.

113. Curschmann, *Hungersnöte*, p. 215: "pestilentia grandis boum et pecorum"; also, Lodewijk Van Velthem, *Voortzetting van den Spiegel Historiael*, 3:211–12. See, too, Lucas, "Great European Famine," p. 358; Valois, "Plaidoyer du XIVe siècle," p. 366.

114. But cf. Lyons, "Weather," p. 43, who, unfortunately, invokes price data to prove the existence of murrain, otherwise unattested in Ireland in this period. In fact, as we shall see below (chapter 3, text to nn. 121, 130), the fluctuations of livestock prices are not a simple surrogate for fluctuations in the incidence of animal disease; cf. Schmitz, *Faktoren der Preisbildung*, pp. 33–37.

115. Hilton, *Stoneleigh Leger Book*, p. 75: "Eodem anno [1319] cepit morina animalium et durauit per longum tempus." Fraser, *Northern Petitions*, pp. 135–36: "sodeyn [ca. 1321] morin de[s b]estes."

116. Cf. Kershaw, "Great Famine," p. 14.

117. Kershaw, *Bolton Priory*, pp. 16, 97–98.

118. Kershaw, "Great Famine," pp. 24–26.

119. Bailey, *Marginal Economy*, p. 201.

120. Ibid.; Mate, "Agrarian Economy of South-East England," pp. 86–87; Hallam, *Rural England*, pp. 16, 47.

121. Raftis, *Estates of Ramsey Abbey*, pp. 137, 146; Mate, "Impact of War," p. 771.

122. Coleman, *Downham-in-the-Isle*, p. 94 and p. 130, table 11. See also Kershaw, "Great Famine," pp. 32–34.

123. Wright, "Barton Blount," p. 149, drawing on the work of Birrell.

124. Raftis, *Estates of Ramsey Abbey*, p. 137.

125. Ibid., p. 146.

126. Carr, *Medieval Anglesey*, p. 302.

127. Lyons, "Weather," pp. 43, 63–64.

128. Kershaw, "Great Famine," pp. 26–29.

129. Postles, "Manorial Accountancy of God's House," pp. 38–39.

CHAPTER 3
PRICES AND WAGES

1. See, for example, Britnell, *Commercialisation of English Society*, pp. 79–151; and also, though his assumptions about the eleventh century are suspect, Snooks, "Dynamic Role of the Market," pp. 27–54.

2. Although in the pages that follow the focus will be on a number of methods that have been employed to assess the density and quality of commercial networks on the eve of the famine, the methods discussed by no means exhaust the approaches that scholars have taken. Cf. Antonow, *Burgen des südwestdeutschen Raums*, pp. 62–65; Nau, "Währungsverhältnisse am oberen Neckar," pp. 190–220 and maps following p. 430; Blaschke, *Geschichte Sachsens im Mittelalter*, p. 249; Mayhew, "Modelling Medieval Monetisation," pp. 74–77; Britnell, "Commercialisation and Economic Development," pp. 7–26; Campbell, "Measuring the Commercialisation of Seigneurial Agriculture," pp. 132–93.

3. Britain: Harrison, "Bridges and Economic Development," pp. 240–61; Edwards and Hindle, "Transportation System of Medieval England and Wales," pp. 123–34. France: Derville, "Rivières et canaux du Nord/Pas-de-Calais," pp. 5–22; Derville, "Première Révolution des transports continentaux," p. 191, map (the region around Lille); Sivéry, "Variété des paysages ruraux dans le Hainaut," p. 19; Richard, "Passages de Saône," pp. 245–74; Dubois, "Techniques et coûts des transports terrestres dans l'espace bourguignon," pp. 65–82. Germany: Prange, *Siedlungsgeschichte des Landes Lauenburg*, pp. 41–55; Berner, *Siedlungs-, Wirtschafts- und Sozialgeschichte des Artlandes*, pp. 54–57; Blaschke, *Geschichte Sachsens im Mittelalter*, pp. 243–44.

4. Bautier, "Circulation fluviale dans la France médiévale," pp. 10, 24. See

also Contamine, *Economie médiévale*, p. 234 (which largely draws on the work of Bautier).

5. Edwards and Hindle, "Transportation System of Medieval England and Wales," p. 123.

6. Langdon, "Inland Water Transport," pp. 1–11, criticizes Edwards and Hindle's views. Edwards and Hindle have replied to the criticisms in a "Comment," pp. 12–14.

7. Goodfellow, "Medieval Bridges in Northamptonshire," pp. 143–58.

8. Harrison, "Bridges and Economic Development," pp. 240–61.

9. Edwards and Hindle, "Transportation System of Medieval England and Wales," p. 128.

10. Fanchamps, "Etude sur les tonlieux de la Meuse," pp. 214–32, 237–64, especially p. 230, map 2.

11. Schöller, "Der Markt als Zentralisationsphänomen," pp. 85–92; Britnell, *Commercialisation of English Society*, pp. 81–85. See also Hodges, *Primitive and Peasant Markets*, a synthesis that summarizes, if unevenly, much of the work on markets in various periods, including the Middle Ages.

12. Jones, "Transaction Costs," pp. 658–75 (the quotation is at p. 675).

13. Cf. Britnell, "English Markets and Royal Administration before 1200," pp. 183–96. More generally, on the debate about markets and an integrated economy in England, see Harvey, "Introduction," pp. 12–16; she deliberately conflates local periodic markets and the (conceptual) land market (on which, below, chapter 5, text to nn. 102–3, 111–28).

14. Cf. Masschaele, "Multiplicity of Medieval Markets," pp. 261–68.

15. Titow, *English Rural Society*, p. 33.

16. Ibid.; Unwin, "Rural Marketing in Medieval Nottinghamshire," pp. 231–51; Dyer, "Hidden Trade of the Middle Ages," pp. 141–57; Hilton, *English and French Towns*, pp. 32–41. See also on the necessity of thinking of peasant livelihoods in terms of regional networks, DeWindt, "Redefining the Peasant Community," pp. 163–207.

17. Britnell, "Essex Markets before 1350," pp. 15–19.

18. I am extrapolating from the remarkable map in Goodfellow, "Medieval Markets in Northamptonshire," p. 313. In his own words, "so liberal" was the distribution of markets "that there are few places without a theoretical choice of two, three or even more markets" (p. 312).

19. The implications of this "restriction" are addressed by Britnell, "King John's Early Grants," pp. 90–96.

20. Clanchy, *Roll and Writ File of the Berkshire Eyre*, p. 21, no. 50.

21. Schöller, "Der Markt als Zentralisationsphänomen," pp. 85–92, considers fairs merely a specialized type of market, establishing and/or tying into networks of long-distance trade and dealing in specialized products.

22. Britnell, *Commercialisation of English Society*, pp. 88–90.

23. In general, see Moore, *Fairs of Medieval England*.

24. Graham, "Definition and Classification of Medieval Irish Towns," pp. 20–32.

25. See the categories adduced in ibid., p. 24.

26. Ibid.

27. Ibid., p. 25, map.

28. On all these matters, see Bourde de la Rogerie, "Fondations de villes et de bourgs en Bretagne," pp. 71–73.

29. Hilton, *English and French Towns*, pp. 34–35. Although Campbell and Overton, "A New Perspective," p. 101 n. 185, rightly talk about the imbalance of work on the relation of markets and agricultural production in medieval England and France, to the advantage of the latter, unfortunately, they cite only an old study on France by Usher (1913) and two more recent (English-language) studies. The rich literature in French is ignored here and throughout their article; and the fabulously deep studies in German are never even mentioned—with the exception of one or two translated into English. As profoundly enlightening as much English work is, some of its conclusions, presented as great insights, were discovered long before and more substantially treated in Continental scholarship. The poverty of English scholarship with regard to the knowledge available from Continental work is lamentable. It is only fair to say that to some extent French studies are similarly "insular." Exceptions aside, only German scholars seem routinely to master the non–German language historiography.

30. Cf. Musset, "L'Ancienne Foire rurale de Saint-Georges-en-Auge," pp. 85–88.

31. Musset, "Foires et marchés en Normandie," p. 23.

32. Musset, "Peuplement en bourgage et bourgs ruraux," p. 205.

33. Latouche, "Aspect de la vie rurale dans le Maine," p. 61. Further on French *bourgs*, Contamine, *Economie médiévale*, p. 172.

34. Piletta, "Bourgs du sud du pays d'Auge," p. 211.

35. Fossier, "Communes rurales," pp. 258–59; *Histoire de la France rurale*, 1:488.

36. Cf. Sarrazin, "Maîtrise de l'eau et société en marais poitevin," pp. 333–54.

37. Cf. Legras-Martin, "Culture maraichère de Saint-Omer," p. 25. For other *marais* in the region, perhaps less isolated, see Sivéry, "Variété des paysages ruraux dans le Hainaut," p. 17.

38. The point, with regard to the early wet weather, should be obvious. The droughts of the later period were not so long or so severe as to parch the *marais*, which, after such persistent annual rains, would have had a great excess of water. At the worst of times (toward the end of the drought cycle), there would still have been swales, hollows in the marshy ground, that retained water. Fishing, indeed, was easier at such times, though getting to some of the swales in the center of the *marais* would have been a bit hazardous by then.

39. Dähne, "Marburg im Mittelalter," p. 20. On the problematic concept of "Stadt" ("In manchen Fällen ist die Grenze zwischen Stadt und Dorf fliessend geblieben"), see Eberl, "Die Stadt Blaubeuren im Spätmittelalter," p. 177.

40. Cf. Störmer, "Gründung von Kleinstädten," p. 564. See also Moraw, "Das späte Mittelalter," pp. 199–200; and Anderlik, "Entstehung und frühe Entwicklung der havelländischen Kleinstädte," pp. 383–402.

41. Jung, *Halver und Schalksmühle*, pp. 339–40, 342, 344–45. The number twenty-four given for new foundations in the thirteenth century is approximate; because of difficulties of dating, it is possible that one of these settlements occurred before and four after this period. The number of fourteenth-century settle-

ments is somewhere between thirty-nine and forty-three inclusive. See also the map of settlements and markets (pre-1200, 1200–1300, and 1300–1500) in Oexle, "Mittelalterliche Stadtarchäologie in Baden-Württemberg," p. 382; and the discussion in Eberl, "Die Stadt Blaubeuren im Spätmittelalter," p. 177, for what look to be similar findings in that region.

42. Jung, *Halver und Schalksmühle*, pp. 60–101, especially p. 69, map 20 (with careful indications of the chronology of road building).

43. Haase, *Die Entstehung der westfälischen Städte*, pp. 40, 74, 105, 224–25, and the maps at pp. 43, 75, 107. Haase's third period actually extends from 1290 to 1350. I have discounted the foundations in this period that are not attested in 1322 or before; there were fifteen of these postfamine foundations in the twenty-eight years from 1323 to 1350 (pp. 111–17, 120–21, 125–27), of which Haase classified nine as *Städte* and six as *Minderstädte*.

44. A similar impression arises from a study of Saxony and its 103 towns (again mostly rural market centers) in the year 1300; Blaschke, *Geschichte Sachsens im Mittelalter*, p. 227.

45. Schröder and Schwarz, *Die ländlichen Siedlungsformen in Mitteleuropa*, pp. 23–25; Richter, "Kulturlandschaft und Wirtschaft," p. 129; Meibeyer, "Rundling—eine koloniale Siedlungsform," pp. 27–49; Herrmann, "Cölln und Berlin," p. 26; Osten, "Siedlungsbild und mittelalterliche Agrarverfassung," p. 1. Schulze, "Die Besiedlung der Mark Brandenburg," pp. 42–178, is a comprehensive regional study of the process.

46. Below, e.g., chapter 5, text to nn. 18–25, 30–47.

47. Piskozub, "Czynnik Tradycji," pp. 19–40. Cf. also Fritze, "Entstehung und Anfänge von Berlin," p. 15, map.

48. Deppe, "Frühe Spuren der Stadtbildung in Mecklenburg," pp. 147–53.

49. Cf. Herrmann, "Cölln und Berlin," pp. 9–57.

50. Höhl, *Fränkische Städte und Märkte*, p. 93. See also Bockhorst, *Geschichte des Niederstifts Münster*, pp. 132, 145–47.

51. Prange, *Siedlungsgeschichte des Landes Lauenburg*, pp. 13, 41–55. Prange describes the premodern network in general, rather than dividing his reconstruction into shorter periods; but from what I have been able to deduce, the statement in the text is applicable for the road network on the eve of the famine.

52. Herrmann, "Cölln und Berlin," pp. 25, 27.

53. Schich, "Das mittelalterliche Berlin," pp. 181–83; Schich, "Entstehung Berlins im Urbanisierungsprozess," pp. 16–17.

54. Britnell, "Proliferation of Markets in England," pp. 209–21. See also Genicot, *Rural Communities*, p. 49; Farmer, "Two Wiltshire Manors and Their Markets," pp. 1–11.

55. Mayhew, "Money and Prices in England," p. 128; Prestwich, *Three Edwards*, p. 247; Prestwich, "Currency and the Economy," pp. 45, 51; Kershaw, "Great Famine," p. 6; Richter, *Untersuchungen zur Hamburger Wirtschafts- und Sozialgeschichte*, pp. 81, 84; Schmitz, *Faktoren der Preisbildung*, p. 98.

56. On the debasement and overvaluation of the coinage—the move from strong money to weak money and back—under Philip the Fair (1285–1314), see Strayer, *Reign of Philip the Fair*, 394–95; for a discussion of the outflow of specie, see Day, *Medieval Market Economy*, p. 125.

57. Schmitz, *Faktoren der Preisbildung*, pp. 56–59.

58. On granaries, their maintenance, and the work of laborers in assuring the integrity of the harvest against theft and spoilage, see Small, "Grain for the Countess," pp. 60–61.

59. Unfortunately, there is an unsatisfactory discussion of the problem of storage in Komlos and Landes, "Anachronistic Economics," pp. 36–45, and Komlos and Landes, "Alice to the Red Queen," pp. 133–36, with not entirely courteous criticisms of their views (which purport to be a critique of his) in McCloskey, "Conditional Economic History," pp. 128–32.

60. Under normal circumstances, for example, grain stores in garrison towns were not a readily disposable resource, since they were kept against the threat of siege; but famine altered the situation. See below, chapter 4, text to n. 89.

61. Cf., for Ireland, Crawford, "William Wilde's Table of Irish Famines," pp. 5–6.

62. Schmitz, *Faktoren der Preisbildung*, pp. 27–33.

63. But cf. below, text to nn. 116–19.

64. Jongman and Dekker, "Public Intervention in the Food Supply," p. 116. More generally—and perhaps more soberly—on the effects of speculation on prices, see Schmitz, *Faktoren der Preisbildung*, pp. 41–42.

65. Cf. Contamine, *Économie médiévale*, p. 319.

66. Ravaillon, *Markets and Famines*, p. 31.

67. Below, chapter 6, text to nn. 47, 69.

68. Waschinski, *Währung, Preisentwicklung und Kaufkraft des Geldes*, p. 102; Derville, "Draperies flamandes et artésiennes," p. 361 n. 68.

69. On the political economy of milling—a subject made complex by variations in the incidence of seigneurial monopolies (the ban of the mill or millsoke), geographical distribution and density of water and windmills, and the availability of "home" milling (with handmills and horsemills)—see Holt, *Mills of Medieval England*, 46, 52, 72, 78–79, and passim, in preference to Kealey, *Harvesting the Air*, which is full of errors. See also Given, "Economic Consequences of the English Conquest of Gwynedd," pp. 26–27; Langdon, "Water-Mills and Windmills," pp. 424–44.

70. Cf. Schmitz, *Faktoren der Preisbildung*, pp. 37–42, 111–25.

71. Ravaillon, *Markets and Famines*, p. 31.

72. See below, chapter 7, text to n. 26.

73. "Chroniques de Saint-Denis," p. 698; "E Chronico Anonymi Cadomensis," p. 25; "Chronique Rimée attribuée à Geoffroi de Paris," p. 161.

74. "Continuatio Chronici Guillelmi de Nangiaco," p. 615; "Chroniques de Saint-Denis," p. 698; "Chronicon Girardi de Fracheto," p. 45.

75. Avenel, *Histoire économique de la propriété*.

76. Cf. Abel, *Agricultural Fluctuations*, p. 39.

77. "Chronicon Girardi de Fracheto," p. 50: "toto anno isto [1318] durabit in regno Franciae caristia magna bladi."

78. "Continuatio Chronici Guillelmi de Nangiaco," p. 621: "Hoc anno [1318] renovavit Dominus antiquum miraculum de multiplicatione panum. Nam cùm jam esset caristia bladi pervalida undique in regno Franciae, ut sextarius bladi ascenderit ad quadraginta solidos in valore, ante omnem messionem et col-

lectionem fructuum redactum est ad valorem duodecim solidorum et circiter, Deo gratiam apponente sicut vidimus manifeste: nam panis qui vix ad unam horam parvam sufficiebat homini ad edendum, quinimmo quasi esuriens post comestionem surgebat, transactâ caristiâ copiose totâ die sufficeret pro duobus." See also "Chronicon Girardi de Fracheto," p. 51; "Excerpta e Memoriali Historiarum," p. 668.

79. The fullest version, which I have translated, may be found in the "Extrait d'une Chronique Anonyme," p. 128: "L'an mil trois cens quatorze et quatre, /Sans vendanger et sans bled batre, / Volt le cher temps du monde abatre / Cil qui pour nous se volt combatre." Other slightly different or abbreviated versions are reported in "Chroniques de Saint-Denis," p. 601; "Fragment d'une Chronique Anonyme," p. 152.

80. "Incepit caristia bladi . . . , de die in diem caristia augebatur"; Curschmann, *Hungersnöte*, p. 208, and also p. 212 ("blandorum caristia"). Also, Lemaître, *Chronique et Annales de Gilles le Muisit*, p. 89; and *Monasticon belge*, 1:400, citing the chronicle of Jean de Sivry (d. 1320) for Hainaut. See also Lascombes's conclusions, based on chronicle evidence, in *Chronik der Stadt Luxemburg*, p. 150.

81. Lodewijk Van Velthem, *Voortzetting van den Spiegel Historiael*, 3:181, 217.

82. Meister, "Niederdeutsche Chroniken," p. 51.

83. "Anonymi . . . Brevior Chronica Cracovie," p. 93 (ca. 1395): "Item anno Domini MCCCXV fuit caristia magna, quod mensura silliginis soluebat mediam marcam & mediam sexagenam"; Leidinger, *Veit Arnpeck: Sämtliche Chroniken*, p. 284 (fifteenth century): "facta est fames et caristia adeo magna, ut scaffa siliginis pro 5 libris 60 denariis Ratisponensis monete venderetur."

84. Wendt, *Geschichte des Welfenfürstentums Grubenhagen*, p. 428: "erschreckliche lange Theurung." Wendt's researches (mid–seventeenth century) persuaded him that this relentless inflation was in hand by 1317.

85. It was an uprising and other political disturbances in the Rostock region in 1312–1314 that made all prices rise considerably; Hauschild, *Studien zu Löhnen und Preisen*, pp. 171, 195. If prices for the years 1301 and 1303 were normal, then the year 1312 saw a unit price for rye at 267 percent the price in either of the normal years, in which case the unit price for rye in 1315 was 25 percent greater than in a so-called normal year. Of course, compared to the price rises during the uprising this was a considerable moderation of inflation for consumers. All of this goes, once again, to show the volatility of prices and the fact that attention to local conditions would result in the nuancing of all general conclusions.

86. Hilton, *Stoneleigh Leger Book*, p. 75. See also Lodewijk Van Velthem, *Voortzetting van den Spiegel Historiael*, 3:217.

87. Rogers, *History of Agriculture and Prices*, 1:197–99. For a critique of the applicability of Rogers's price series to small rural markets, see Howell, *Land, Family and Inheritance*, p. 148; but like all scholars of rural life she is obliged in numerous pinches to rely on them over and over again.

88. Cf. Derville, "Chaplains de Saint-Géry de Cambrai," p. 269.

89. *Agrarian History*, 2:734–37, tables 7.1, 7.3, 7.4; 757, table 7.6. See also Dyer, *Standards of Living*, p. 266; and Kershaw, "Great Famine," p. 8.

90. Farmer, "Crop Yields," pp. 122–27. In verifying my summary, the reader should note that Farmer expresses his conclusions numerically in what he calls "shopping basket" terms, rather than as he does with yield figures in terms of a deviation from a computed mean.

91. Campbell, "Population Pressure," pp. 112, 114.

92. Neveux, "Bonnes et mauvaises récoltes," p. 191.

93. Schmitz, *Faktoren der Preisbildung*, pp. 72–73, 79.

94. For example, "Chronique Rimée attribuée à Geoffroi de Paris," p. 161; Lodewijk Van Velthem, *Voortzetting van den Spiegel Historiael*, 3:181.

95. George, "Vignobles de l'abbaye des Vaux de Cernay," pp. 51–52.

96. Ibid., p. 51.

97. An unidentified fourteenth-century chronicler of Valenciennes, for example, makes this point ("fu faulte . . . de sel") under the year 1315; Delcambre, "Chronique Valenciennoise," p. 61. On the original date but the late manuscripts of the chronicle, see the editor's remarks, p. 2.

98. On the technique, which is known partly from archaeological finds, since the heating of the clay and sand hardened and preserved the pans, see Detsicas, "Salt-Panning Site at Funton Creek," p. 167. Holden and Hudson, "Salt-Making in the Adur Valley," p. 119, eschew the use of the word "salt-pan," in favor of "saltern," preferring to limit the former to the wide flat metal dishes used in southern Europe where evaporation was the preferred method of recovery.

99. Holden and Hudson, "Salt-Making in the Adur Valley," pp. 117–48.

100. On saltways from the coast (markers of the inland trade of salt), see (for Poitou, where these roads were called "charraux"), Sarrazin, "Littoral poitevin," p. 120; (for Normandy, where they were called "chemins sauniers"), Musset, "Voie publique et chemin du roi," p. 320. For the coastal trade, see Ferger, *Lüneburg: Eine siedlungsgeographische Untersuchung*, p. 85; and for a map of principal production sites in medieval Europe, Contamine, *Economie médiévale*, pp. 286–87.

101. Volk, *Salzproduktion und Salzhandel*, pp. 25–26.

102. *Westfälisches Urkunden-Buch*, vol. 9, pt. 2, Lieferung 3, pp. 662–64, nos. 1401–02, 1404, noting a "puteum salis" in operation in 1316 in Salzkotten, with a "domus salinaris" equipped "cum ponderibus plumbi."

103. Hiegel, "Sel en Lorraine," pp. 30–35. Such salt canals were known elsewhere: see, for example, Sarrazin, "Littoral poitevin," p. 120, on their use near the coast of Poitou.

104. Hiegel, "Sel en Lorraine," p. 37.

105. Cf. Ibid.

106. Ibid., p. 27.

107. Ibid., pp. 37–38.

108. Cf. the discussion of the trade network in Lorraine in ibid., pp. 39–40, and of saltways around Droitwich (Warwickshire) in Finnemore, "Saltway across Arden," pp. 128–30. As the latter study shows, it is sometimes difficult to recover the patterns of the salt trade.

109. Volk, *Salzproduktion und Salzhandel*, p. 26. For a good map of the extraordinary land and river routes over which salt traded (under the press of many tolls), see Wanderwitz, *Studien zum mittelalterlichen Salzwesen*, map 3.

110. Curschmann, *Hungersnöte*, p. 218: "incepit caristia . . . salis . . . , de die in diem caristia augebatur" (Lemaître, *Chronique et Annales de Gilles le Muisit*, p. 89).

111. *Ordonnances*, 1:606–8; Rogers, *History of Agriculture and Prices*, 1:458–59, 480. See also Prestwich, *Three Edwards*, p. 247; Kershaw, "Great Famine," p. 9.

112. "Fragment d'une Chronique Anonyme," p. 151; "E Chronico Anonymi Cadomensis," p. 25; and above, nn. 97, 110. See also Lucas, "Great European Famine," p. 351.

113. *Agrarian History*, 2:730–31. For salt's employment in the dairying process, below, text to n. 145.

114. Yrwing, "Salt och saltförsörjning i det medeltida Sverige," pp. 218–42.

115. *Agrarian History*, 2:757, table 7.6.

116. For wax prices, see Rogers, *History of Agriculture and Prices*, 1:417, 447, 454.

117. Dadant, *First Lessons in Beekeeping*, p. 10.

118. On wild beecraft, Steinhausen, "Waldbienenwirtschaft," pp. 226–57.

119. Cf. Rogers, *History of Agriculture and Prices*, 1:419, 471, 473, 480, 532–33.

120. Kershaw, *Bolton Priory*, p. 104.

121. Above, chapter 2, text to nn. 122–23.

122. Cf., for the prices, Rogers, *History of Agriculture and Prices*, 1:529, 531, 556, 560.

123. Cf. above, text to n. 119, and below, chapter 4, text to n. 170.

124. Raftis, *Estates of Ramsey Abbey*, p. 141.

125. Genicot, *Rural Communities*, p. 40; Howell, *Land, Family and Inheritance*, p. 102. Despite the ubiquity of pigs, pig bones are not as common in finds as we might think. In part this is accounted for by the bones' relative weakness and susceptibility to corruption; Lepiksaar, "Restes d'animaux," p. 92: "les restes de porc, en général, ne peuvent être considérés comme particulièrement resistants."

126. Lepiksaar, "Restes d'animaux," p. 92: "toutes les parties du corps de l'animal peuvent être utilisées pour la nourriture de l'homme."

127. Halard, "Loup aux XIVe et XVe siècles," p. 196.

128. Santiard, "Aspect du commerce des porcs," p. 106.

129. Kershaw, *Bolton Priory*, pp. 106–7.

130. For the importance of geese, whose "pair formation . . . lasts as long as both birds live" (Delacour, *Waterfowl*, 1:94), see Bolton, *Medieval English Economy*, p. 116.

131. "All Geese are hardy and easy to feed"; Delacour, *Waterfowl*, 1:95. Inhabitants of forest villages seem routinely and fearlessly to have put their geese out to "pasture" in woods; Bolton, *Medieval English Economy*, p. 116; Birrell, "Un Bois convoité," p. 73.

132. Of course, goose feathers—for quills and other uses—were regularly harvested from live birds.

133. Gross, "Colombiers bourguignons," pp. 57–59.

134. In "Rabbits: The Case for Their Medieval Introduction into Britain," pp. 53–57, James Bond synthesizes the available material fairly and confutes the

dubious assertions of John Warry ("Ancient History of Rabbits," pp. 13–15) on the widespread distribution of the rabbit in England before the eighteenth century. There is virtually no evidence of rabbits in medieval Scandinavia, but cf. Lepiksaar, "Restes d'animaux," p. 106.

135. Turner, *Select Pleas of the Forest*, pp. cxxix, cxxxiv; Zadora-Rio, "Parcs à gibier et garennes à lapins," p. 134.

136. Zadora-Rio, "Parcs à gibier et garennes à lapins," pp. 133, 137–38.

137. Jordan, "Jewish-Christian Relations," pp. 52–53, nos. 195, 208.

138. The first mention is in an account of 1336–1337; Woolgar, *Household Accounts*, 1:204.

139. *Agrarian History*, 2:757, table 7.6.

140. Ibid., 747, 748 (table 7.4), 749. Kershaw, "Great Famine," p. 10; Rogers, *History of Agriculture and Prices*, 1:401, 432, 451.

141. *Agrarian History*, 2:749; Mate, "Impact of War," p. 771.

142. Below, n. 146.

143. Above, chapter 2, text to n. 129.

144. On dairying as women's work and the organization of the dairies, see Vanja, "Frauen im Dorf," pp. 147–59.

145. Fussell, *English Dairy Farmer*, pp. 205, 224–25, with extensive discussion of production (and the role of salt in production) in the early modern period. The processes do not seem to have varied from the Middle Ages. See also Biddick, *Other Economy*, p. 96.

146. *Agrarian History*, 2:757, table 7.6; Rogers, *History of Agriculture and Prices*, 1:405, 409, 411, 432, 452–53.

147. Rogers, *History of Agriculture and Prices*, 1:526; cf. also pp. 529, 556, 560, 567.

148. A good summary of this contextual material may be found in Ryder, "Medieval Sheep and Wool Types," pp. 14–28.

149. Stephenson, "Wool Yields in the Medieval Economy," pp. 382, 385.

150. Ibid., pp. 370, 378, 385.

151. *Agrarian History*, 2:730.

152. In general, see below, chapter 4.

153. *Agrarian History*, 2:720. Cf. Day, *Medieval Market Economy*, p. 188, and Kershaw, "Great Famine," pp. 32–34.

154. Below, chapter 6, text to nn. 74–76, 88, 92, 95–97, 99–104.

155. Cf. Goose, "Wage Labour on a Kentish Manor," p. 210.

156. *Agrarian History*, 2:720.

157. Ibid., p. 767, graph 7.9. See also Goose, "Wage Labour on a Kentish Manor," pp. 211–12.

158. On penury in the towns, see below, chapter 7, text to nn. 105–34.

CHAPTER 4
THE COST-OF-LIVING CRISIS: LORDS

1. The complicated question of the power of lordship in its various guises may be explored in Bloch, *Seigneurie française et manoir anglais*; Fossier, "Land, Castle, Money and Family," pp. 159–68; and Fourquin, *Lordship and Feudalism*.

2. Wisplinghoff, "Beiträge zur Wirtschafts- und Besitzgeschichte," pp. 87–98;

Wisplinghoff, "Beiträge zur Wirtschaftsgeschichte," pp. 133–36; and D'Haenens, "Crise des abbayes bénédictines," pp. 75–95. But cf. Racinet, *Maisons de l'ordre de Cluny*, for a long rebuttal of this view. Racinet does acknowledge the existence of problems (see below, text to nn. 98–100), but no sustained crisis.

3. Cf. Carpenter, "Was There a Crisis of the Knightly Class," pp. 721–52; Thomas, "Subinfeudation and Alienation of Land," pp. 397–417; Hiegel, "Sel en Lorraine," pp. 40–45. For thorough regional studies of the changing nature and fortunes of ecclesiastical and baronial landlordship, see Rösener, *Grundherrschaft im Wandel*; and Bittmann, *Kreditwirtschaft und Finanzierungsmethoden*, pp. 54–110.

4. Britnell, "Essex Markets before 1350," pp. 15–17. Most of the other twenty-eight markets were possessed by ecclesiastical institutions or by the king; in two or three cases the original possessor is unknown.

5. Fanchamps, "Etude sur les tonlieux de la Meuse," pp. 214–32, 237–64.

6. Jordan, *From Servitude to Freedom*, pp. 28–33; Platts, *Land and People in Medieval Lincolnshire*, p. 66; Fourquin, *Campagnes de la région parisienne*, p. 165; Sée, *Classes rurales et le régime domanial*, pp. 253–55. Cf. Guérin, *Vie rurale en Sologne*, p. 211.

7. Jordan, *French Monarchy and the Jews*, pp. 29, 64, 66–69, 95–96, etc. (with references to the French royal and other cases).

8. Below, text to nn. 72–76, 102–3, 143–44.

9. Reed and Anderson, "Economic Explanation of English Agricultural Organization," pp. 134–37.

10. Mate, "Farming Out of Manors," pp. 331–43; cf. Titow, *English Rural Society*.

11. Cf. Raban, *Mortmain Legislation*, p. 6.

12. Cf. Sarrazin, "Littoral poitevin," p. 121.

13. Hiegel, "Sel en Lorraine," pp. 21–23.

14. Cf. Fanchamps, "Etude sur les tonlieux de la Meuse," p. 261.

15. Volk, *Salzproduktion und Salzhandel*, p. 148; Hiegel, "Sel en Lorraine," p. 13; Romhányi, "Role of the Cistercians," p. 185.

16. Hiegel, "Sel en Lorraine," pp. 11, 17, 24; Sarrazin, "Littoral poitevin," p. 121.

17. Hiegel, "Sel en Lorraine," pp. 40–46; cf. also pp. 47–48.

18. Cf. below, chapter 5, n. 122.

19. On the production process from seawater and brine springs, above, chapter 3, text to nn. 97–107. Production in south Germany is addressed in Wanderwitz, *Studien zum mittelalterlichen Salzwesen*; also above, chapter 3, text to nn. 108–9.

20. Jaitner, *Urkundenbuch des Klosters Ebstorf*, p. 5.

21. Ferger, *Lüneburg: Eine siedlungsgeographische Untersuchung*, p. 85; Witthöft, "Mass- und Gewichtsnormen im hansischen Salzhandel," p. 39; Hiegel, "Sel en Lorraine," p. 24. On the changing fortunes of the so-called Lüneburg saltern from the Middle Ages through the nineteenth century, see Waldow, "Rise and Decline of a Saltern," pp. 581–600.

22. For the years 1315–1322, Brosius, *Urkundenbuch des Klosters Scharnebeck*, pp. 116–17, nos. 160–62; 132–34, nos. 191–94; 136–38, nos. 298, 200–201.

23. Laschinger, "Das Spital in Amberg," p. 153; Wagner, "Das Heilig-Geist-Spital," p. 132.

24. Below, chapter 6, text to n. 13.

25. Brugmans, "De Kroniek van het Klooster Aduard," p. 55: "monasterium sanctimonialium in Tribus montibus, cum esset ordinis Sancti Benedicti et ad extremam devenisset paupertatem et desolationem, sub cura sua suscepit." Dead in 1329, Eylard presumably did this in the late teens or the 1320s.

26. Hasse, *Schleswig-Holstein-Lauenburgische Regesten*, 3:182, no. 340. On the nature of so-called *Kauf/Wiederkauf* contracts, see Bittmann, *Kreditwirtschaft und Finanzierungsmethoden*, pp. 116–19.

27. Heinemann, *Pommersches Urkundenbuch*, 5:308, no. 372 (dated 9 June 1317): "de redditibus et proventibus suis vix valeant sustentari."

28. "Propter tempora cara"; Hänselmann and Mack, *Urkundenbuch der Stadt Braunschweig*, 2:443–44, 449–50, 458, 470–71, nos. 789, 798, 806, 826; 4:479, no. 313 (with correction at p. xiii).

29. Schmidt, *Urkundenbuch des Hochstifts Halberstadt*, 3:142–43, 175–76, 179–80, 186–90, 198–99, nos. 1970, 1972, 2015, 2020, 2031–33, 2048–49. These constitute a small selection of an enormous series of transactions, many of which employ the language described in the text ("malum terre statum"; "ecclesia . . . depressa guerrarum continuis molestis"). They date from 30 January 1317 to 11 March 1321.

30. Anemüller, *Urkundenbuch des Klosters Paulinzelle*, 2:173–74, no. 171.

31. Ibid., pp. 176–78, nos. 174–75.

32. Ibid., pp. 179–80, no. 178.

33. Baur, *Hessische Urkunden*, 2:771–72, no. 771.

34. *Westfälisches Urkunden-Buch*, 8:362, no. 1001: "ecclesiam nostram inmenso debitorum onere multipliciter pregravante, alienationem perpetuam castrorum ipsius ecclesie" (see also p. 382, no. 1056).

35. Ibid., p. 382, no. 1055: "bona premissa a nostris predecessoribus adeo fuerunt graviter obligata laycis, ut eorum recuperatio nostris temporibus posse fieri minime speraretur."

36. Menzel and Sauer, *Codex Diplomaticus Nassoicus*, vol. 1, pt. 3, p. 98, no. 1603, dated 25 March 1316: "auctoritatem et licenciam vendendi pro necessitate nostra quinque mansus terre arabilis iacentes in Sundelinch et in Wilebach discreto viro et honesto Wigando dicto Vroysch civi Frankenvordensi pro decem et ducentis marcis."

37. Ibid., p. 102, no. 1626 (dated 26 March 1317); the Frankfurt burgher's name is spelled Wiglo Froyhs in this record. The property was three manses in Sundelingen; the purchase price, 110 marks Cologne money.

38. Engel and Lathwesen, *Urkundenbuch des Klosters Möllenbeck*, 1:101–3, no. 83: "prebenda, que in pane et carnibus cottidie ministrari solet, de die in diem perit et annichilatur."

39. Weiler, *Urkundenbuch des Stiftes Xanten*, 1:324–26, no. 487: "de novo conparatis, que tot et tantis bellorum, ventorum, caumatorum, fluviorum pluribusque aliis privatis subiacent periculis registrandis." The charter that makes this declaration is dated 28 February 1317. The earliest reference to the deleterious conditions of the famine in the Xanten charters dates from 23 June 1315 (1:309–10, no. 462); hence my conclusion that the lament in 1317 sums up about

eighteen months of disasters. The use of the phrase "Job-like" is a comment on the word *cauma* (in the oblique *caumatorum*) in the quotation; this relatively unusual word is used in the Vulgate, Job 30.30.

40. In the original, the phrases summarized and quoted are "necessitate, proch dolor, ardua compellente," "in evidentem ecclesie nostre utilitatem," and "cum monasterium nostrum ad ruinam propinquam et irrecuperabilem dispositum videremus"; Weirauch, "Güterpolitik des Stiftes Quedlinburg," p. 173

41. Baur, *Hessische Urkunden*, 5:227, no. 255: "ob evidentem domus nostre in Wisen predicte necessitatem ac utilitatem."

42. Ibid., 2:814–15, no. 815: "ad minuendum nostri monasterii onera debitorum a nostris antecessoribus contractorum, necnon imminentibus et dampnabilibus periculis per varios euentus ingruentibus obuiare volentes."

43. Ibid., 1:265–66, no. 372: "ipsum monasterium nostrum propter grauia debitorum onera et dampna non modica, que ex ipsis debitis prouenerunt, adeo in temporalibus sit collapsum, quod nisi sibi celeri remedio succurratur, nunquam adiciet vt resurgat, volentes indempnitati dicti monasterii precauere." The date given for this document in the heading is 24 December 1318, but the text itself says 9 Calends December, which would be 23 November; the mistake is corrected in the index volume (5).

44. Krings, *Prämonstratenserstift Arnstein*, pp. 137, 511, 513, 523.

45. Ibid., p. 138. The evidence of resignation is equivocal; see p. 588.

46. *Westfälisches Urkunden-Buch*, 8:410, no. 1122: "ad dictum hospitale infirmorum, pauperum, orphanum et debilium confluat multitudo copiosa, qui ibidem recipiuntur et sustentantur, ad quod tamen proprie non sufficiunt facultates."

47. Saint-Génois, *Inventaire analytique des chartes des comtes de Flandre*, p. 305, no. 1336: among others, the churches of Thérouanne and the abbey of Saint-Jean-au-Mont in French-speaking Flanders may be cited.

48. This is not to say that leadership was all-important. We should not fall into the habit of some later chroniclers who tend to reduce rather complex issues to the simple dichotomy of good versus bad leadership; see, for example, the remarks of Adrien De But (ca. 1480) on the fiscal measures of the abbots of Dunes in the early fourteenth century (*Cronica et cartularium monasterii de Dunis*, pp. 13–14), and below, text to nn. 49, 55, 60, 65.

49. Walter, *Kurze Geschichte von dem Prämonstratenserstifte Obermachtal*, pp. 111–13.

50. Wauters, *Table chronologique*, 9:35; cf. 8:578.

51. *Monasticon belge*, 4:41–42.

52. Wauters, *Table chronologique*, 8:672; 9:62.

53. Ibid., 9:72.

54. Ibid., p. 108.

55. *Monasticon belge*, 3:340; he was remembered as the man "qui usuras varias deposuit."

56. Besides those examples to be discussed in the text, see also Mazerand, "Histoire de l'abbaye de Sainte-Marie-au-Bois," p. 116 (a Lorraine house).

57. Wauters, *Table chronologique*, 8:681, 684–85, 690.

58. Ibid., 749; 9:3.

59. *Monasticon belge*, 7:515.

60. Wauters, *Table chronologique*, 9:45.

61. The whole story of Val-Dieu is told with perhaps a shade too much verve in Vandekerckhove, *Histoire de l'abbaye du Val-Dieu*, pp. 80–84.

62. Brouette, "Chartes et documents de l'abbaye d'Argenton," p. 373, no. 28: "utilitate et inevitabili et urgente necessitate nostri monasterii pensata, pro solutione debitorum nostrorum quibus monasterium nostrum gravissime premebatur ac instantis anni gravaminibus urgentibus."

63. Wauters, *Table chronologique*, 9:67–69, 76.

64. D'Haenens, "Crise des abbayes bénédictines," p. 82: "Bona monasterii alienata et obligata in tantum quod nichil omnino pro victu abbatis et monachorum et negotiorum sustentandorum est reservatum et monachos mendicare opportebat."

65. D'Haenens, *Abbaye Saint-Martin de Tournai*, pp. 103–6, 121–23.

66. *Monasticon belge*, 4:380.

67. For the confirmation in 1315 of an overseer's power, originally conferred in 1313, to require the monks of Orval to disperse if necessary ("si necesse fuerit . . . quod utilitati dictae abbatiae viderit expedire"), see Goffinet, *Cartulaire de l'abbaye d'Orval*, p. 646, no. 593.

68. Kervyn de Lettenhove, *Codex Dunensis*, pp. 489–90, no. 343. The form letter (undated, naturally) is among documents of roughly the famine period. It is worth quoting in full. "Universis praesentes, etc., talis abbas salutem et gratiae quantum sibi. Opprimente graviter intollerabili sarcina debitorum ac pensionum domum nostram propter guerras et defectum segetum et alia infortunia quamplurima, quae permissione divina diu sustinuit et adhuc graviora sustinet hiis diebus, de licentia capituli generalis, ad dilectas et devotas nostri ordinis abbatias, proprios filios avulsos ab uberibus matris suae, non sine multa cordis amaritudine et pressura, dispersionis gratia compellimur destinare. Quare Caritatem Vestram requirimus humiliter et rogamus quatinus in Christo fratri . . . . . . dyacono, monacho domus nostrae, latori praesentium, ad domum talem proficiscenti gratia comedendi, cum per vos transire contigerit, caritatis et humanitatis beneficia cum vecturis necessariis benigne et favorabiliter impendatis. Sane venerabili et in Christo karissimo patri domino abbati dicti loci cum reverentia offerimus preces nostras ut fratrem nostrum antedictum cum suis ovibus retineat, donec processu temporis, meliori fortuna, favente Domino, arridente, eumdem et alios poterimus revocare. Datum, etc."

69. Van Derveeghde, *Domaine du Val Saint-Lambert*, pp. 100–101; Poncelet, "Herstal et Vivegnis," p. 86.

70. Van Derveeghde, *Domaine du Val Saint-Lambert*, pp. 132–48. Orval's interests were in iron mining; see Grégoire, "Abbaye d'Orval," pp. 51, 53–54.

71. Miraei and Foppens, *Opera diplomatica*, 4:265–66.

72. Prévôt, "Grand Hautmont," p. 46: "Peu à peu, toutes les grandes exploitations appartenant à notre abbaye vont être affermées et au XIVe siècle, l'evolution est achevée."

73. Wisplinghoff, *Urkunden und Quellen zur Geschichte von Stadt und Abtei Siegburg*, 1:367–71, 373–74, nos. 238, 240–41, 243, 247.

74. Hoffmann, "Braunschweiger Umland in der Agrarkrise," pp. 187 n. 47, 189–90, 205–6.

75. "Propter tempora cara"; ibid., pp. 205–6, 255–56.

76. Ibid., p. 243.

77. On these demands "pro subsidio terre sancte," see Bock, "Studien zur Registrierung der politischen Briefe . . . Johanns XXII," pp. 182–85.

78. Ibid., pp. 187–88. The examples date from 1317 and 1318. The papal orders are in every case, except Lübeck's, addressed to the archbishops or bishops; the order to Lübeck is addressed to the consuls of the city.

79. See also below, text to n. 154.

80. One of the most impressive treaties intended to end these wars—impressive for the sheer number of seals pendant of the contracting parties—is that between Stralsund and the Rügen nobility (1316); see the splendid photograph in Fritze, "Entstehung, Aufstieg und Blüte der Hansestadt Stralsund," p. 53.

81. Heinemann, *Pommersches Urkundenbuch*, 5:262–65, 269–71, 294–95, 297, 305, 307, nos. 3009, 3011, 3013–14, 3020, 3022, 3051, 3055, 3066, 3070. To calculate the exchange rate, I have used Spufford, *Handbook of Medieval Exchange*, pp. 210, 281. Around the year 1300 four Wendish marks were equal to three Lübeck marks, according to one source; a little earlier five Wendish marks could be exchanged for four Lübeck marks. An English pound in the mid to late thirteenth century could be exchanged for fifty-four Lübeck shillings (3.375 marks).

82. See below, chapter 5, text to n. 126, and chapter 8, text to nn. 23–24.

83. Smit, *Rekeningen der Graven en Gravinnen*, 2:423: "want die sterfte van den biesten do was."

84. To establish this, one needs to compare the accounts from fiscal 1316–1317 until fiscal 1322–1323; ibid., 423, 427, 430, 433, 436, 439, 442.

85. Heinemann, *Pommersches Urkundenbuch*, 5:293–94, 352, 354, 363–64, nos. 3050, 3144, 3147, 3163.

86. The usual phrase is "moghe we wider kopen" or a variant. See Jaeger, *Urkundenbuch der Stadt Duderstadt*, pp. 17–18, nos. 15–16; Meinardus, *Urkundenbuch des Stiftes und der Stadt Hameln*, pp. 125–26, no. 184.

87. Stievermann, "Biberach im Mittelalter," p. 215.

88. Even villages on the Slavic frontier had small permanent military annexes; see, for example, Gühne, "Nennewitz—Eine Wüstung des hohen Mittelalters," p. 424: ". . . ensteht eine dörfliche Siedlung und parallel dazu eine Wehranlage."

89. Curschmann, *Hungersnöte*, p. 210: "Fratres vero domus Teotonicorum multos suos homines salvarunt per amministrationem annonae habundantis reservatae in loculis castrorum suorum."

90. The very word *garrison*, etymologically speaking, evokes the sense of "place where supplies are stored."

91. Curschmann, *Hungersnöte*, pp. 79–80, 214. On the migration in or, rather, from the area around Magdeburg, see below, chapter 6, text to nn. 27–34.

92. Fourquin, *Campagnes de la région parisienne*, pp. 191–94, 199; there are notable lacunae in the accounts for the period 1305–1320.

93. On the importance of viticulture for a comparably wealthy abbey, Saint-Germain-des-Prés of Paris, in the rural hinterland, see Le Bacon, "Vignoble

d'Issy," p. 110. For an extremely detailed look at the varied rural (agricultural) and urban holdings as well as the "industrial" enterprises of a monastic lord, see Blary, *Domaine de Chaalis*.

94. George, "Vignobles de l'abbaye des Vaux de Cernay," pp. 40–41, map.

95. Ibid., pp. 51–52.

96. Archives départementales: Yonne, G 941: the entries cited here may be found in the first three unfoliated leaves of the account. Most of the entries are not problematic: where I translate "homestead," the text uses *masura* ("messuage" might be a more technical rendering); where I talk about grain carriage, the manuscript has *herchia*, whose semantic field is somewhat wider.

97. Ibid., fol. 3r.

98. Racinet, *Maisons de l'ordre de Cluny*, pp. 65–68.

99. Ibid., pp. 68–70.

100. Ibid., pp. 65–66, 70–77.

101. Blary, *Domaine de Chaalis*, p. 8.

102. Higounet, *Grange de Vaulerent*, pp. 49–50. Blary, *Domaine de Chaalis*, p. 107.

103. Blary, *Domaine de Chaalis*, pp. 218.

104. Platelle, "Evolution du temporel de l'abbaye de St-Amand," p. 248; Platelle, *Temporel de l'abbaye de Saint-Amand*, pp. 215–41.

105. Wauters, *Table chronologique*, 8:745.

106. "Significarunt nobis quod ipsi tam pro refectione quam plurimorum domorum et grangiarum suarum per Flamingos, occasione guerrarum nostrarum, ignis incendio non solum semel, sed pluries devastatarum, quam etiam pro pluribus et diversis oneribus, gravaminibus atque injuriis, que pro dictis guerris Flandrie hactenus sustinuerunt, necnon propter sterilitatem fructuum possessionum suarum plurium preteritorum annorum, oportuit ipsos . . . plures redditus vendere nonnullis personis ad vitam, ratione quorum reddituum ad vitam in tantum sunt oppressi quod fructus, exitus, proventus dicti monasterii et pertinentiarum ejusdem vix sufficere possunt ad solutionem eorumdem; ipsosque necessario oportuit in nonnullis pecuniarum summis pluribus creditoribus obligare; que persone et creditores religiosos ipsos . . . inquietari faciunt multipliciter et vexari"; quoted in Platelle, *Temporel de l'abbaye de Saint-Amand*, p. 223 n. 41.

107. Dupont, *Registre de l'Officialité*, pp. 35–36, nos. 26a–26c.

108. Ibid., pp. 44–45, no. 41a.

109. Ibid., p. 58, no. 64a.

110. The full text of Jacques's missive is published in Valois, "Plaidoyer du XIVe siècle," pp. 352–68; the comments on the wars in Flanders and the Crusade are at pp. 365–67. Excerpts and a discussion may be found in King, *Finances of the Cistercian Order*, pp. 94–95.

111. King, *Finances of the Cistercian Order*, p. 62.

112. Valois, "Plaidoyer du XIVe siècle," pp. 366–67; King, *Finances of the Cistercian Order*, pp. 94–95.

113. Further on credit as well as Cistercian charity, below, chapter 5, text to nn. 141–44, and chapter 6, text to n. 11.

114. Valois, "Plaidoyer du XIVe siècle," p. 366; King, *Finances of the Cistercian Order*, pp. 94–95.

115. Kershaw, "Great Famine," p. 34.

116. Britnell, "Minor Landlords in England," pp. 243–44; also Day, *Medieval Market Economy*, p. 188.

117. Mate, "Coping with Inflation," pp. 95–106, especially p. 101, table 1.

118. Ibid., p. 101, table 1.

119. Ibid., p. 100.

120. On rents in kind, see Mate, "Labour and Labour Services," p. 59.

121. Mate, "Coping with Inflation," pp. 100–102.

122. Ibid., p. 102. In 1982 Mate reversed herself and argued that the increase in expenditures for wine was an attempt to maintain the lifestyle of the monks themselves. It is possible that both factors—the need for wine for clerical pilgrims and the desire to maintain lifestyle—explain the increase in expenditures. Cf. Mate, "Impact of War," p. 771.

123. Mate, "Coping with Inflation," p. 102.

124. Mate, "Impact of War," p. 771.

125. Mate, "Coping with Inflation," pp. 102–3.

126. Mate, "Agrarian Economy of South-East England," p. 89.

127. Ibid., pp. 79–80.

128. Saul, *Knights and Esquires*, p. 229; the reference is to Gloucestershire sources.

129. Cf. Farmer, "Two Wiltshire Manors and Their Markets," p. 7.

130. Bailey, *Marginal Economy*, pp. 201–2.

131. Kershaw, *Bolton Priory*, pp. 135–36. See also above, text to n. 53, and below (for some urban examples), chapter 8, text to nn. 12–18.

132. Jordan, *Women and Credit*, pp. 64–66.

133. Williams, *Welsh Cistercians*, 1:168, and below, text to n. 176, for additional details on the impact of the war on this abbey.

134. Kershaw, *Bolton Priory*, pp. 52–54; Dyer, *Standards of Living*, pp. 66, 266.

135. Goose, "Wage Labour on a Kentish Manor," pp. 211–12.

136. Kershaw, *Bolton Priory*, p. 50.

137. Jones, "Harvest Customs . . . : Hay Harvest," p. 106; Platts, *Land and People in Medieval Lincolnshire*, p. 65.

138. The occasional waiver of entry fines (initial payments made by those taking up holdings) on the Winchester estates during the famine has been interpreted now and then as a device to compensate for migration abandonment or, rather, to attract tenants who would do the work the stewards expected would need doing or to pay the rents they needed paid to make ends meet; cf. Day, *Medieval Market Economy*, p. 188. For other possible exceptions (high wages near London), see below, chapter 5, text to n. 107.

139. Hybel, *Crisis or Change*, pp. 237–39, sums up scholarly opinion on the rates. See also Stacey, *Politics, Policy and Finance*, p. 83; and Contamine, *Economie médiévale*, p. 296.

140. Lomas, "Priory of Durham," pp. 342–43.

141. Kershaw, *Bolton Priory*, pp. 46, 75, 77, 122–23.

142. Ibid., p. 14.

143. Franklin, *Cartulary of Daventry Priory*, p. xlix and nos. 35–37, 99–100,

163–69, 171–75, 189, 191–95, 218–24, 232–34, 303–5, 317, 412–14, 428, 466–68, 515–20, 559–60, 611, 613, 618, 720–21, 806, 846, 872–73, 902, 965, 971, 974–75. Except for the usual salvation formulas, the charters themselves are conventionally reticent about the reasons for the conveyances, etc.; I find no references to the "great hunger," as one might find in a list of entry fines or on a rent roll.

144. Cf. Prestwich, "Currency and the Economy," pp. 50–51, whose impression that there was no pattern to high farming may derive from the varied timetables of change: at different times for different lords with different resources.

145. Raban, *Mortmain Legislation*; Henneman, *Royal Taxation*, index, s.v. "amortissement."

146. Gervers, *Cartulary of the Knights of St. John*, pp. xlvi–xlvii.

147. But cf. Schein, "*Fideles crucis,*" pp. 112–39, which sums up the different currents of opinion concerning the Crusades and the crusading orders after the fall of Acre. Cf. also Menache, "Templar Order," pp. 1–10.

148. On the suppression of the Temple and the technical arrangements, see, most recently, Schein, "*Fideles crucis,*" pp. 240–46 (though some of her remarks must be treated cautiously). See also Barber, *Trial of the Templars*.

149. Gervers, *Cartulary of the Knights of St. John*, pp. xlvii–xlix.

150. Walsh, "Knights of the Temple," pp. 17–18.

151. Cowan, *Knights of St John of Jerusalem*, p. xxvi (cf. also pp. 47–48, no. 5).

152. Reynolds, *Registers of Roger Martival*, nos. 6, 67, 91, 99, 196, 324, 344 ("hiis annis sterilibus"; "pur defaltes des bleedz"; "precipue ex grossorum animalium mortalitate").

153. Postles, "Manorial Accountancy of God's House," pp. 38–40.

154. On the issue of the discernment of profit, Postles, "Perception of Profit," pp. 12–28. On markets, above, chapter 3, text to nn. 11–54. The De Lacy material is provided in Atkin, "Land Use and Management," p. 19.

155. Above, text to n. 64.

156. Tillotson, *Marrick Priory*, pp. 4, 38 n. 28; Bain, *Calendar of Documents Relating to Scotland*, 3:117, no. 619.

157. Tillotson, *Marrick Priory*, pp. 18, 46 n. 124.

158. Bain, *Calendar of Documents Relating to Scotland*, 3:102, 111, 117, nos. 529, 578, 619.

159. Cf. Kershaw, "Great Famine," p. 30.

160. Bain, *Calendar of Documents Relating to Scotland*, 3:86–87, no. 461, dated 23 December 1315.

161. Kershaw, *Bolton Priory*, pp. 22–25; see also Kershaw, "Great Famine," pp. 30–31.

162. Kershaw, *Bolton Priory*, p. 17.

163. Tillotson, *Marrick Priory*, p. 38 n. 27. The female religious of Yorkshire were notoriously underendowed; see Burton, *Yorkshire Nunneries*, p. 25.

164. Ormrod, "Crown and the English Economy," pp. 149–83. Cf. also Bolton, *Medieval English Economy*, p. 183.

165. Waugh, "Profits of Violence," pp. 843–69. See also Wright, "Barton Blount," p. 149.

166. On Welsh bondmen and their butter rents, see Owen, "Tenurial and Economic Developments in North Wales," p. 118 n. 6.

167. Above, chapter 3, text to n. 146.

168. For the references to all these matters, Hopkins, *Medieval Neath*, pp. 73–80, 85–92.

169. Simpson and Galbraith, *Calendar of Documents Relating to Scotland*, 5:252, no. 682.

170. Hopkins, *Medieval Neath*, pp. 89–90, 93–96. For "potters" Hopkins would probably prefer "woodworkers," in which case *disci*, their product, whose production had fallen, would be wooden dishes.

171. Hopkins, *Medieval Neath*, pp. 73–76, with references to the hiring of a boat for transporting oats for the war effort and to the sale of cows, bulls, bull calves, and an assortment of carcasses. There is also a reference to wine "sold in the war."

172. Hopkins, *Medieval Neath*, p. 66.

173. Williams, *Welsh Cistercians*, 1:47, 148.

174. Ibid., 2:275.

175. Ibid., 1:47 (this was the monks' explanation for their failure to meet the obligation of an ecclesiastical tenth).

176. Quoted in ibid., 1:47; 2:219.

177. Smith, "Edward II and the Allegiance of Wales," pp. 152–53.

178. Williams, *Welsh Cistercians*, 2:232.

179. Cf. the data and their complications in Soulsby, *Towns of Medieval Wales*, pp. 73, 106, 117, 121, 127, 150, etc.

180. Carr, *Medieval Anglesey*, p. 301.

CHAPTER 5
THE COST-OF-LIVING CRISIS: RUSTICS

1. Curschmann, *Hungersnöte*, p. 211: "creverat penuria et caristia."

2. Ibid., p. 215: "pauperes prae penuria et fame carnes mortuorum pecorum certatim comedebant."

3. Ibid., p. 216: "penuria et fames maxima"; "penuria maxima."

4. *Agrarian History*, 2:777, graph 7.11; Farmer, "Crop Yields," p. 142.

5. Above, chapter 4, text to nn. 10–11.

6. Valuable discussions of the secular history of freedom (and servility) in the Middle Ages may be found in two books by Hilton, *Decline of Serfdom* and *Bond Men Made Free*. See also *Histoire de la France rurale*, 1:366, 478–82. Old but still useful on France is Avenel, *Histoire économique de la propriété*, 1:159–86.

7. On degrees of freedom, cf. Platts, *Land and People in Medieval Lincolnshire*, pp. 59–62.

8. Dockès, *Medieval Slavery and Liberation*; Bonnassie, *From Slavery to Feudalism*. For detailed criticisms, see my review of each work (the full references may be found in the bibliography).

9. Jordan, *From Servitude to Freedom*, pp. 27–28.

10. Musset, "Quelques observations sur esclavage et servage," p. 339.

11. Cf. Owen, "Tenurial and Economic Developments in North Wales," pp. 117–20, 126–30.

12. *Ministerialitäten im Mittelrheinraum*; Arnold, *German Knighthood*.

13. The most comprehensive work on England is Hyams, *King, Lords and Peasants*. For France one can consult Bloch, "Liberté et servitude personelles," pp. 286–355.

14. Richter, "Kulturlandschaft und Wirtschaft," p. 129.

15. Platts, *Land and People in Medieval Lincolnshire*, pp. 53–62.

16. The debate is summed up by Genicot, *Rural Communities*, pp. 68–69, who allies himself with the school that diminishes the importance of juridical status. Partly the debate, specifically that part of it which addresses the emotional impact of juridical status, turns on questions of language. If obligations imposed on "serfs" used the same language or were functionally equivalent to obligations borne by people of great wealth or property, why should juridical status in itself have been felt to be degrading? What was the difference, it might be said, between mainmort (a servile due) and relief (a vassalic due), if they both functioned as inheritance taxes? Why was a *taille* (on this word, see Dubled, "Taille et 'Umgeld,'" pp. 32–47) imposed on a rustic more degrading than one imposed on a burgher, when both were taxes paid to overlords? For the other side of the debate, see Jordan, *From Servitude to Freedom*. See also Howell, *Land, Family and Inheritance*, pp. 35–36.

17. Platts, *Land and People in Medieval Lincolnshire*, p. 66.

18. Contamine, *Economie médiévale*, p. 180.

19. Cf. TeBrake, *Medieval Frontier*, pp. 200, 202, on the reclamation of the Dutch Rhineland "peat-bog wilderness."

20. Cf. Sivéry, "Variété des paysages ruraux dans le Hainaut," p. 17; Musset, "Peuplement en bourgage et bourgs ruraux," p. 205; Blaschke, *GeschichteSachsens im Mittelalter*, p. 225.

21. Schröder and Schwarz, *Die ländlichen Siedlungsformen in Mitteleuropa*, pp. 24–25; Bierwirth, *Siedlung und Wirtschaft im Lande Hadeln*, p. 16; Weinrich, "Urkunde in der Übersetzung," p. 34; Prange, *Siedlungsgeschichte des Landes Lauenburg*, pp. 253–75. Cf. the career of David de la Forest discussed in Lefèvre, "Entrepreneur de défrichements," 77–83.

22. Herrmann, "Cölln und Berlin," p. 25.

23. On the regularity of village planning, Meibeyer, "Rundling—eine koloniale Siedlungsform," p. 44, and cf. Gardiner, "Planned Medieval Land Division," pp. 109–14. The "egalitarianism" of distribution in the original assarts is doubted by some very good scholars; cf. McCloskey, "Open Fields of England," p. 33.

24. On "bourgs" as rural centers from which assarting teams operated without creating new villages, see Latouche, "Aspect de la vie rurale dans le Maine," p. 61.

25. Cf. Contamine, *Economie médiévale*, p. 167, on so-called old open-field villages.

26. One example is Géronsarts near Frasne in Flanders (the element -*sart* indicates an assarted village); Sevrin, "Comparaison des paysages issus des défrichements médiévaux," p. 186. (The element -*sart* is seen in many other place names

such as Robert*sart*, *Sars*-Baras, etc.; Sivéry, "Variété des paysages ruraux dans le Hainaut," p. 15.) Cf. Arnoux, "Métiers de férons dans la Normandie médiévale," p. 335, on other metallurgical communities attached to settlements.

27. Philippe, "Chantier ou atelier," pp. 246–47.

28. Sivéry, "Passage de l'élevage extensif à l'élevage intensif," pp. 172–76; Sivéry, "Variété des paysages ruraux dans le Hainaut," pp. 28–36; Winter, *Entwicklung der Landwirtschaft und Kulturlandschaft des monschauer Landes*, pp. 53, 55 (note the villages with names carrying the element *rod* or its variants, indicating assarts, from German *roden*, to root out: Vroenrot, Sementrot).

29. For Flemish and Brabantine examples, see Verhoeve, "Motte féodale et l'habitat dispersé," pp. 123–27; and Vermeesch, "Oppida en Brabant," pp. 31–46. On the continuing evolution of forms of settlement in Germany, see Meibeyer, "Rundling—eine koloniale Siedlungsform," p. 45.

30. The debate on the origins of the open fields (or common fields) and the explanation for scattering is very old and associated with great names, like Paul Vinogradoff, H. L. Gray, and C. S. Orwin in the late nineteenth and early twentieth centuries. The debate was reopened by Joan Thirsk ("Common Fields," pp. 3–25) in 1964 and joined by Jan Titow the next year ("Medieval England and the Open-Field System," pp. 86–102; rejoinder by Thirsk, "Origin of the Common Fields," pp. 142–47). See also Hopcroft, "Origins of Regular Open-Field Systems," pp. 563–80. In the text I am following McCloskey's recent discussion, "Open Fields of England," pp. 34–48: if scattering is inefficient (and McCloskey claims, pp. 12–25, that about a 10 percent loss of output results from scattering), then it demands a powerful explanation, for our rustics appear in almost all contexts to be very prudent (pp. 50–51, and cf. McCloskey, "Prudent Peasant," pp. 343–55). McCloskey's explanation makes sense. But the debate goes on. For two among many alternative or supplementary explanations for the apparent peculiarities of open-field farming, see, first, Fenoaltea, "Transaction Costs," pp. 171–240; he suggests that scattering was efficient in that it inhibited shirking by forcing cooperative and, therefore, mutually observable labor. There is some support for his argument in the extraordinary medieval diatribes against shirkers ("wastoures," in Middle English); see Kaske, "Character Hunger in *Piers Plowman*," pp. 187–97, and Trower, "Figure of Hunger in *Piers Plowman*," pp. 238–60. A second explanation, which tries to take the focus off scattering per se, highlights the mix (and the implicit negotiation between lords and tenants/laborers) of methods of exploitation: direct exploitation (of demesne and/or family holdings), corvée, and wage labor. The mix (including scattering, of course), it is argued, lessened risk on both sides—the seigneur's and the farmer's; see Cosgel's very schematic model sketched in "Risk Sharing in Medieval Agriculture," pp. 99–110.

31. Herrmann, "Cölln und Berlin," p. 25; Lefèvre, "Entrepreneur de défrichements," pp. 77–83.

32. In general on community sentiments in rural settlements, see Fossier, "Communes rurales," pp. 235–76 (with extensive bibliography of local studies), but note that he is not particularly concerned with assarted villages.

33. On sharing and cooperation in plowing, co-aration, see, for example, Rösener, *Bauern im Mittelalter*, p. 151. It has sometimes been felt that co-aration

was the motive or sustaining force for scattering. This is dubious; see McCloskey, "Open Fields of England," p. 26.

34. The fundamental studies are by Ault, *Open-Field Husbandry* and "Vill in Medieval England," pp. 188–211.

35. For an example, see Hogan, "Clays, *Culturae*, and the Cultivator's Wisdom," pp. 117–31.

36. Cf. Fossier, "Communes rurales," pp. 240–41.

37. The best treatment of the political economy of mill construction and milling in England, which by 1300 had 10,000 to 12,000 mills, is Holt, *Mills of Medieval England*. For France, where the number was 49,000 (almost all of which originated from seigneurial initiative), see Philippe, "Premiers Moulins à vent," pp. 99–116. And for Germany, see, among other studies, Bachmann, "Zur Entwicklung des Mühlenrechts," pp. 721–24.

38. Nash, "Size of Open Field Strips," pp. 32–40; Nash, "Customary Measure and Open Field Strip Size," pp. 109–17.

39. On the utility of the court records, see Titow, *English Rural Society*, p. 32. Much of the information in Hanawalt's panoramic view of rural family life in England (*Ties That Bound*) comes from these court rolls, supplemented by coroners' inquests.

40. DeWindt, *Land and People in Holywell-cum-Needingworth*, pp. 162, 242–75.

41. On the vexing question of whether initial residence in assarted settlements implied freedom, see Asch, "Grundherrschaft und Freiheit," pp. 107–92, especially pp. 120–21; Blaschke, *Geschichte Sachsens im Mittelalter*, p. 252.

42. Cf. Kosminsky, *Studies in the Agrarian History of England*, p. 350; Blaschke, *Geschichte Sachsens im Mittelalter*, p. 253.

43. On the bewildering variability of inheritance, even within small regions, see Campbell, "Extent and Layout of Commonfields," p. 20.

44. Small, "Grain for the Countess," pp. 56–61.

45. Hilton, *Bond Men Made Free*, p. 35.

46. For an exhaustive look at occupations in one thirteenth-century village, see Hogan, "Labor of Their Days," pp. 75–186. See also Platts, *Land and People in Medieval Lincolnshire*, p. 81; Vanja, "Frauen im Dorf," pp. 147–59; Holt, *Mills of Medieval England*, pp. 90–106. Cf. Hilton, "Towns in English Feudal Society," pp. 3–20, and "Lords, Burgesses and Hucksters," pp. 3–15, both of which, despite their titles, provide a great deal of useful information on the occupations available in what we would call rural market towns.

47. Cf. Ribbe, "Anfänge von Berlin/Cölln," p. 7.

48. Campbell, "Extent and Layout of Commonfields," p. 16.

49. Cf. Mate, "Agrarian Economy of South-East England," p. 80.

50. Cf. Kosminsky, *Studies in the Agrarian History of England*, pp. 249, 252.

51. Blum, *End of the Old Order*, pp. 104–9.

52. McDonnell, *Inland Fisheries*, pp. 18–19.

53. Birrell, "Common Rights in the Medieval Forest," p. 49; Birrell, "Un Bois convoité," p. 78. See also McDonnell, "Pressures on Yorkshire Woodland," pp. 110–25, who steers a middle course but certainly sees increasing pressure on,

if not deforestation of, woodlands from livestock grazing, charcoaling, etc., in this period.

54. Below, chapter 6, text to nn. 74–76, 88, 92, 95–97, 99–104.

55. Birrell, "Common Rights in the Medieval Forest," p. 49.

56. On Lorraine, see Lalanne, "Domaine des Prémontrés de Belval," p. 305: "défendant leurs [the monks'] intérêts de propriétaires menacés par la progression des conquêtes paysannes sur la forêt . . . tout au long du XIII siècle." On the northern Netherlands, see Slicher van Bath, "Histoire des forêts dans les Pays-Bas septentrionaux," pp. 96–99.

57. Zadora-Rio, "Parcs à gibier et garennes à lapins," p. 134. The intense competition explains another situation that troubled Xavier Halard in his study of the wolf population of Normandy. More wolves were taken in the early fourteenth century than after the demographic collapse of the later Middle Ages. It seemed to Halard that the wolf population should have been at its lowest about 1300 when human population was at its height, but the evidence of bounties (and similar evidence) seemed to point in the opposite direction. He invoked otherwise undocumented fourteenth-century pack migrations to explain the discrepancy; Halard, "Loup aux XIVe et XVe siècles," p. 190. But the explanation is simpler: the intense exploitation of the woodlands led to widespread slaughter of wolves by 1300, so reducing the density of the wolf population that it could not recover after 1350. The situation is similar to that in regions where the wolf once ran wild in America.

58. Zadora-Rio, "Parcs à gibier et garennes à lapins," pp. 133–34.

59. Bois, *Crisis of Feudalism*.

60. Above, chapter 3, text to n. 55.

61. Bois, *Crisis of Feudalism*, p. 270.

62. For example, Biddick, "Missing Links," pp. 277–98.

63. Bois, *Crisis of Feudalism*, p. 270.

64. Derville, "Hôpital Saint-Julien de Cambrai," pp. 314–15.

65. Delumeau and Lequin, *Malheurs des temps*, p. 152.

66. Bois, *Crisis of Feudalism*, pp. 270–75.

67. For a partial and inadequate critique, see Newman et al., "Agricultural Intensification," pp. 115–16.

68. Day, *Medieval Market Economy*, pp. 97–98.

69. Kosminsky, *Studies in the Agrarian History of England*, pp. 230–40; Birrell, "Peasant Craftsmen in the Medieval Forest," pp. 105–6; Britton, *Community of the Vill*, pp. 157–63; Dyer, *Lords and Peasants in a Changing Society*, pp. 90, 110; Harvey, *Peasant Land Market*, p. 165; Platts, *Land and People in Medieval Lincolnshire*, p. 81.

70. So, too, the work of May, "Index of Thirteenth-Century Peasant Impoverishment," pp. 389–402, which concludes that the peasantry was near destitution on the eve of the famine; the evidence is that of manor fines from the Winchester estates and the English holdings of the Norman abbey of Bec.

71. Continental scholars, because of the fragmentary and limited nature of the evidence available to them on villages, routinely see rustic life in its regional context. Not so for the English, where the survival of manorial court records and estate fiscalia has produced a rich but very narrowly focused kind of scholarship

that distorts our understanding of the regional perspectives of the typical rustic. DeWindt, "Redefining the Peasant Community," pp. 163–207, argues effectively in favor of a shift in the English tradition.

72. The study of settlement abandonment in Norway, where rural life was lived around the farmstead rather than the village, takes its inspiration, however, from Continental studies of village abandonments. Unfortunately, the evidence on Norwegian patterns of abandonment in the first half of the fourteenth century appears to me to be too thin to be of value in the discussion here; cf. Salvesen, "Strength of Tradition," pp. 107, 112.

73. Curschmann, *Hungersnöte*, p. 216. The assertion would be repeated in subsequent chronicles; see, for example, Diemar, *Chroniken des Wigand Gerstenberg*, p. 238: "auch vile dorffere lange tzyt wuste verpleben." Local historians in the nineteenth century accepted these assertions readily; Dochnal, *Chronik von Neustadt*, p. 39: "ganze Dörfer aussterben."

74. Cf. Garnsey, *Famine and Food Supply*, pp. 3, 31 (for an earlier example).

75. Below, chapter 6, text to nn. 27–34.

76. Hall et al., "Medieval Agriculture and Settlement," p. 23.

77. Cf. Barry, "People of the country . . . ," p. 350.

78. Hall et al., "Medieval Agriculture and Settlement," pp. 19, 22.

79. The two works by Robin Frame, "Bruces in Ireland," pp. 3–37, and *English Lordship in Ireland*, pp. 132–39, trace the vicissitudes in English control, including the modest recovery of the 1320s.

80. Crawford, "William Wilde's Table of Irish Famines," p. 6.

81. On English vicissitudes in Ulster and eastern Ireland in general to 1324, see Otway-Ruthven, *History of Medieval Ireland*, pp. 224–43.

82. Cf. Kissock, "Origins of Medieval Nucleated Rural Settlements in Glamorgan," pp. 31–49.

83. Which is not to say that the situation in Wales was an easy one; above, chapter 1, text to nn. 103–7, and chapter 4, text to nn. 166–80.

84. Abel, *Wüstungen des ausgehenden Mittelalters*, pp. 74–75. (There are still scholars who see the few abandonments documented in this period by Abel as the beginning of the huge wave of abandonments that occurred in the later fourteenth century; cf. Gerking, *Die mittelalterlichen Siedlungen*, pp. 19–20.)

85. Aerts and Van Cauwenberghe, "Grafschaft Flandern," p. 96; Verhaeghe, "Late Medieval 'Crisis' in the Low Countries," pp. 151–52.

86. Kühlhorn, *Untersuchungen zur Topographie mittelalterlicher Dörfer*, p. 43, chart; Lob and Mahr, "Beiträge zur Wüstungforschung," pp. 65–84 (only two in a list of seventy-seven abandoned settlements in Lob and Mahr's study can more or less securely be dated to the famine—Eiringshausen [perhaps 1320] and Reichtal [about 1321]; and at most only two others might be candidates for abandonment during the famine—Bischofswinden and Sommerberg; pp. 65, 67, 78, 80). See also Staerk, *Wüstungen des Saarlandes*, p. 62.

87. Dyer, *Standards of Living*, p. 266. Also Kershaw, "Great Famine," pp. 43–46.

88. Verhaeghe, "Late Medieval 'Crisis' in the Low Countries," pp. 152–56.

89. "Chronicon comitum Flandrensium," p. 180 (the reference is to the year 1321; the chronicle is more or less contemporary, pp. xxx–xxxi).

90. Wauters, *Table chronologique*, 9:26–27.

91. Ibid., p. 35.

92. Cf. Nicholson, *Scotland: The Later Middle Ages*, p. 107.

93. Cf. above, chapter 4, text to n. 106.

94. Cf. Piletta, "Bourgs du sud du pays d'Auge," p. 211.

95. McDonnell, "Medieval Assarting Hamlets," pp. 272, 275–76, 279.

96. Cf. Platts, *Land and People in Medieval Lincolnshire*, pp. 152–54, 161.

97. Thomas and Dowdell, "Shrunken Medieval Village at Barry," p. 97.

98. Brosius, *Urkundenbuch des Klosters Scharnebeck*, pp. 125–27, nos. 179, 181. On the interpretation of *coloni* as new homesteaders (German: *Neusiedler*) in the relevant documents, see Weinrich, "Urkunde in der Übersetzung," pp. 32–33.

99. See, for example, the evidence of two villages, Avendorf and Tespe, which seem to have undergone such shifting settlement patterns along the border of the so-called Elbmarsch in the early fourteenth century; cf. Prange, *Siedlungsgeschichte des Landes Lauenburg*, pp. 282, 313.

100. Of two *villae* "in supercilio montis Salberg," one with six homesteads ("cum . . . sex mansis") was deserted ("hoc est deserta") by 20 May 1319. Kloster Pforte, hoping to repopulate it, purchased it on 11 November 1319 from the nuns of Quedlinburg. See Weirauch, "Grundbesitz des Stiftes Quedlinburg," pp. 225–26, 232, 236; and Weirauch, "Güterpolitik des Stiftes Quedlinburg," p. 173. On Ropperode, see Grodde-Braun, "Töpfereiwüstung Ropperode," pp. 62, 82. (Note the element -*rode* in the village name; cf. n. 28 above.) Local knightly violence appears to have been the proximate cause of its abandonment.

101. Dyer, *Standards of Living*, p. 267.

102. Curschmann, *Hungersnöte*, p. 208: "plurimis haereditates suas propter inopiam victualium vendentibus et ob hoc ad summam paupertatem devolutis."

103. Campbell, "Population Pressure," pp. 112–14. Hallam (*Rural England*, p. 44) attempts to undermine the significance of these conclusions. Though he acknowledges a very significant decline of stored wheat in 1315/1316 because of the poor wheat harvest (surely evidence of something like an agrarian crisis), he seems determined not to see famine conditions in eastern England. His arguments are misplaced and contradictory (cf. the persuasive critique of Dyer, *Standards of Living*, p. 267).

104. Mate, "Agrarian Economy of South-East England," pp. 79–80.

105. Above, chapter 4, text to nn. 96, 129.

106. Further, below, chapter 9, text to nn. 18–19.

107. Mate, "Labour and Labour Services," p. 59.

108. Hatcher, *Rural Economy and Society*, p. 85.

109. Howell, *Land, Family and Inheritance*, pp. 40, 43, 48. Howell's material is very fragmentary. Her suggestion that the arrears point to "a high level of mortality" seems hasty.

110. Wright, "Barton Blount," p. 149.

111. Smith, "Families and Their Land," pp. 152, 160–61.

112. Cf. Barth, *Human Resources*, pp. 59–60, on precisely parallel behavior in the agricultural regimes of "traditional" Africa. I owe this reference to Professor David Nirenberg.

113. Ravensdale, "Population Changes," p. 207.

114. Harvey, "Introduction," pp. 14–16, summarizes several studies.

115. Raftis, "Land Market at Godmanchester," pp. 311–32; Raban, *Estates of Thorney and Crowland*, p. 64; Hockey, *Quarr Abbey and Its Lands*, pp. 67, 91; Pollock and Maitland, *History of English Law*, 2:12–13.

116. Slota, "Law, Land Transfer, and Lordship," pp. 119–38; Smith, "Some Thoughts on 'Hereditary' and 'Proprietary' Rights in Land," pp. 95–128; Hyams, *King, Lords and Peasants*, pp. 44, 108; King, *Peterborough Abbey*, pp. 110–15.

117. Cf. Dyer, *Standards of Living*, p. 266; *Agrarian History*, 2:599–600; Hallam, *Rural England*, p. 70.

118. Hudson, "Prior of Norwich's Manor of Hindolveston," pp. 179–214.

119. Ibid., pp. 202, 211–13.

120. Bachmann, "Zur Entwicklung des Mühlenrechts," pp. 723–24; Holt, *Mills of Medieval England*, pp. 78–79.

121. Cf. Barbé, "Aménagement des étangs en Berry," pp. 47–48. With perhaps as many as ten thousand water mills in England alone by 1300 and almost 50,000 in France (above, n. 37), fish harvested from millponds represented no minor resource.

122. On salters as payers of fixed rents, see Hiegel, "Sel en Lorraine," pp. 35–36. The richer record of the political economy of modern famines shows an even wider variety of similar behaviors among peasants; cf. Prakash, *Bonded Histories*, p. 126.

123. Cf. Kershaw, "Great Famine," pp. 37–41.

124. Wauters, *Table chronologique*, 8:615.

125. On the technique, cf. Dyer, *Lords and Peasants in a Changing Society*, p. 56; for its use in a variety of crises, see Jordan, *From Servitude to Freedom*, pp. 31, 78; King, *Peterborough Abbey*, pp. 121–22; Hockey, *Quarr Abbey and Its Lands*, p. 91.

126. "Possint reemere infra triennium" (Meinardus, *Urkundenbuch des Stiftes und der Stadt Hameln*, pp. 130–31, 136, nos. 190 and 200; the records are dated 1319–1323).

127. Kershaw, "Great Famine," p. 38, with evidence of attempts at reconsolidation in 1321–1322.

128. Bailey, *Marginal Economy*, p. 201; Smith, "Families and Their Land," pp. 152–53, 158–59, 176.

129. For the quotation, see Hallam, *Rural England*, p. 47.

130. On the waiving of entry fees, cf. Day, *Medieval Market Economy*, p. 188.

131. Smith, "Families and Their Land," p. 194.

132. Ravensdale, "Population Changes," p. 207. See also Kershaw, "Great Famine," p. 37.

133. Faith, "Peasant Families and Inheritance Customs," pp. 77–95.

134. Weber, *Entwicklung der nördlichen Weinbaugrenze in Europa*, pp. 55–58.

135. Lefèvre, "Contrats de plantation et l'extension du vignoble," pp. 29–35.

136. Jordan, *From Servitude to Freedom*, pp. 50, 114 n. 64.

137. Delafosse, "Notes d'histoire sociale: Les Vignerons," p. 15 n. 2.

138. Hoebanx, "Documents des XIIIe et XIVe siècles," p. 54 n. 5: "cara tempora fuerint et gravia"; "de pacientia ipsius ecclesie Nivellensis."

139. McGuire, *Cistercians in Denmark*, p. 197.

140. Ibid., pp. 197, 248.

141. Ibid., pp. 213–15.

142. Schneider, "Güter- und Gelddepositen in Zisterzienserklöstern," p. 111.

143. Rees, *Cartulary of Haughmond Abbey*, p. 13.

144. Cf. Martin-Lorber, "Communauté d'habitants dans une seigneurie de Cîteaux," p. 19, for the *effondrement* of the peasants as the explanation for Cîteaux's actions. She acknowledges, however, that the fragmentary state of the evidence makes this only a plausible, not a certain, explanation.

CHAPTER 6
THE STRUGGLE FOR SURVIVAL

1. Genicot, *Rural Communities*, pp. 57–61.

2. It may have been Saint-Faron, which seems to have been having internal problems (*Gallia Christiana*, 8:1694), that initiated the negotiations leading to confraternal practices. For the formal agreement, see Archives départementales: Yonne, H 6, MS 1. This formal agreement of 1324 presumes the prior existence of the spiritual union, which, I am suggesting, probably dates from the famine years immediately preceding. On the practice of spiritual union in general, cf. Johnson, *Equal in Monastic Profession*, p. 98.

3. *Monasticon belge*, 1:235.

4. Ibid., p. 260.

5. "Continuatio Chronici Guillelmi de Nangiaco," p. 614; "Chronicon Girardi de Fracheto," p. 44; "Prima vita Johannis XXII," in Baluze, *Vitae paparum*, 1:112–13. See also Lucas, "Great European Famine," p. 359.

6. Weiler, *Urkundenbuch des Stiftes Xanten*, 1:309–11, nos. 462–63.

7. Fourquin, *Anatomy of Popular Rebellion*, p. 88.

8. Hallam, *Rural England*, p. 44.

9. Kershaw, *Bolton Priory*, pp. 143–44; Dyer, *Standards of Living*, pp. 240–41.

10. Cf. Curschmann, *Hungersnöte*, pp. 210, 212, 214, 216.

11. Valois, "Plaidoyer du XIVe siècle," p. 366; King, *Finances of the Cistercian Order*, pp. 94–95.

12. Curschmann, *Hungersnöte*, p. 212: "Fuit enim in domo elemosinarii . . . fornax constructus"; also p. 216 on the use of a hospital.

13. Brugmans, "De Kroniek van het Klooster Aduard," p. 54: "Temporibus cujus facta est fames valida per omnes inferiores terras, ita ut inopia plerique deficerent. Quod considerans benignus pater [Abbot Eylard, 1305–1329] ollam mire magnitudinis conflari fecit anno Domini MCCCXV, in quo olla quotidie pulmentaria sive legumina pro pauperibus coquebantur, ne fame miserabiliter interirent. In cujus rei testimonium usque hodie [the sixteenth century] reservatur et multis ostenditur." The later history of what may have been the same pot is recorded on p. 54 n. 4 of this edition of the "Kroniek."

14. Ravensdale, "Population Changes," p. 207.

15. Jordan, *Women and Credit*, pp. 19, 24–25.

16. Ibid., pp. 25–26.

17. Suspicion and hatred of the creditor middleman, especially the middleman of a different religious or ethnic background, are expressed repeatedly down the centuries, particularly in famine times. See, for example, Simonsohn, *History of the Jews in the Duchy of Mantua*, pp. 222, 231; Zenner, *Minorities in the Middle*, pp. 46–60; and Albier, *De l'organisation du crédit*, pp. 68–69. Albier's words on Algerian Muslim outrage with Jewish moneylenders during the Algerian famine of 1867 are worth quoting: "La haine des indigènes à leur endroit est vivace. L'Arabe déteste le Juif. . . . [I]l le hait du fond de l'âme et le méprise profondément."

18. Lascombes, *Chronik der Stadt Luxemburg*, p. 148.

19. Fischer, *Aschaffenburg im Mittelalter*, p. 268.

20. I have treated the issue of the Jews' return to France and their business dealings during the famine in a paper entitled "Home Again: The Jews in the Kingdom of France, 1315–1322."

21. Dyer, *Standards of Living*, p. 266.

22. Bennett, *Women in the Medieval English Countryside*, pp. 13–14, 218, 292 n. 18.

23. Gauthier, *Lombards dans les Deux-Bourgognes*, pp. 167–68.

24. Curschmann, *Hungersnöte*, pp. 211–13, 216; Kershaw, "Great Famine," p. 11 n. 52.

25. Crawford, "William Wilde's Table of Irish Famines," p. 6.

26. "Epicedium: De Erico Sudermanniae et Valdemaro Finlandiae Duce," p. 172: ". . . Rustici depauperantur / Intra fines Sueciae."

27. Curschmann, *Hungersnöte*, pp. 64, 214.

28. Thiel, *Urkundenbuch des Stifts St. Peter und Alexander zu Aschaffenburg*, 1:493–94, no. 240.

29. Curschmann, *Hungersnöte*, pp. 63, 216.

30. Bartlett, *Making of Europe*, pp. 135–36 (referring to migration from Germany to Poland in 1264 when there were local shortages in the former).

31. On the question of desertion, cf. Bohm, "Zum Stand der Wüstungsforschung in Brandenburg," pp. 301–2. On the enormous size of new eastern holdings, see Bartlett, *Making of Europe*, pp. 126–27.

32. On the franchises, the peak after 1315, and their location, see Berdecka, "Lokacje miast małopolskich za Władysława Łokietka (1306–1333)," pp. 335–44.

33. Cf. Jaritz and Müller, *Migration in der Feudalgesellschaft*, for a collection rich in theoretical insights into the problem of mass migration.

34. Diemar, *Chroniken des Wigand Gerstenberg*, p. 238: " Vile husssessener . . . gingen in fremmede lande."

35. Dyer, *Standards of Living*, p. 181, 266–67 (citing Hanawalt). See also Kershaw, "Great Famine," pp. 12–13. Cf. Walter and Wrightson, "Death and the Social Order," p. 24, for similar patterns in other famines.

36. Piecha, *Kamp-Lintfort im Spiegel der Geschichte*, p. 84.

37. *Ordonnances*, 1:636–37 (order to the bailli of Meaux to curb crime in his district but with acknowledgment that the problem is universal).

38. Platts, *Land and People in Medieval Lincolnshire*, p. 242.

39. Britton, *Community of the Vill*, p. 162, also pp. 115 and 271 n. 94.

40. Dyer, *Standards of Living*, pp. 266–67.

41. Dupont, *Registre de l'Officialité*, pp. 47–48, nos. 44, 45a.

42. Cf. Lucas, "Great European Famine," pp. 359–60: "Murder became very frequent in Ireland." On the utility of the Annals, a valuable source when used very, very cautiously, see Cosgrove, *New History of Ireland*, p. 285; and Lyons, "Weather," p. 62.

43. Below, chapter 9, text to nn. 20–24.

44. On the persistence of "the Slavic element" even in areas of heavy German settlement, Schich, "Zum Verhältnis von slawischer und hochmittelalterlicher Siedlung," pp. 53–85, and Gehrmann, "Mittelalterliche Besiedlung des Teltows," pp. 18–21. See, again, for a comparative perspective in other famine times on the presence of state power in towns, Walter and Wrightson, "Death and the Social Order," p. 27.

45. Above, chapter 4, text to nn. 89, 91.

46. Cf. Bartlett, *Making of Europe*, pp. 236, 238–39, who points to texts in the half century from 1323 onward.

47. Cf. ibid., pp. 155–56.

48. Cosgrove, *New History of Ireland*, p. 285. Also, Crawford, "William Wilde's Table of Irish Famines," p. 6; Lyons, "Weather," p. 63.

49. Below, chapter 7, text to nn. 210–32.

50. Above, chapter 1, text to nn. 98–102.

51. Rivers, "Nutritional Biology of Famine," p. 59.

52. In rural society, many, probably most, medieval corpses, except those of aristocrats or prelates, were buried not in coffins but solely in burial shrouds (shroud pins are routinely excavated with no signs of coffin nails); cf. Durand, "Terroir médiéval de Champlieu," p. 75, and Olsen, "St. Jørgensbjærg Kirke," p. 71. In coffin burials sometimes rich cloths, like silks, were used to shroud the deceased. On these facts and the presence of jewelry and coins in typical medieval rural burials (of the thirteenth and fourteenth centuries), see Aubert, *Hôpitaux de Langres*, pp. 41–43, 216–17; James, "Excavations at the Augustinian Priory of St. John and St. Teulyddog," p. 142; Durand, "Terroir médiéval de Champlieu," p. 72. Cf. Johnson, *Equal in Monastic Profession*, p. 189.

53. See the report of the cemetery at Deux-Jumelles in Normandy on how "porci sepe fodiunt et exterrare nituntur corpora mortuorum, quod est aborrendum"; Dupont, *Registre de l'Officialité*, p. 36, no. 26b.

54. Curschmann, *Hungersnöte*, p. 213: "plerique pauperes, (si fas est dicere,) cadavera pecorum sicuti canes cruda corroderent, et gramina pratorum sicuti boves incocte commederent." This striking passage became a staple in later chroniclers' reports. See Sweerts, "Ioannis Geerbrandi Leydensis, Carmelitani, Chronicon," p. 249; Sweerts, "Reneri Snoi . . . De Rebus batavicis," p. 114.

55. Rivers, "Nutritional Biology of Famine," p. 59.

56. Ibid.

57. Ibid., p. 63.

58. Below, chapter 7, text to nn. 142–47, 152–53.

59. Rivers, "Nutritional Biology of Famine," p. 63.

60. Cf. Schmitz-Cliever, "Pest und pestilenzialische Krankheiten," p. 115.

61. Cf. Rivers, "Nutritional Biology of Famine," pp. 63, 77–80; Crawford, "Subsistence Crises and Famines," pp. 199, 201.

62. Cf. Schmitz, *Faktoren der Preisbildung*, pp. 33–37.

63. On all these matters, Rivers, "Nutritional Biology of Famine," pp. 58–59, 61–62, 80, 90–91, is comprehensive and accessible.

64. Cf. below, chapter 7, text to nn. 165–68, on mortality among vagabonds.

65. Most modern historians of medieval famines are inadequate on the biology of famine, death by disease and death by starvation being treated as equal factors in the mortality; cf. Curschmann, *Hungersnöte*, p. 60; Lucas, "Great European Famine," p. 358; Van Werveke, "Famine de l'an 1316," pp. 11–12; Carpentier, "Autour de la Peste noire," p. 1081; Kershaw, "Great Famine," p. 11; Rösener, *Bauern im Mittelalter*, p. 137.

66. For example, in the hinterland of Nuremberg, see Müllner, *Annalen der Reichstadt Nürnberg*, 1:368; and near Xanten, see Weiler, *Urkundenbuch des Stiftes Xanten*, 1:310–11, no. 463.

67. Cosgrove, *New History of Ireland*, p. 285 (also Crawford, "William Wilde's Table of Irish Famines," p. 5; Lyons, "Weather," p. 62).

68. Crawford, "William Wilde's Table of Irish Famines," pp. 1–30; Lyons, "Weather," pp. 32–35. Equally often, of course, epitomizers of earlier chronicles suppress clinical while retaining picturesque details; cf. Diemar, *Die Chroniken des Wigand Gerstenberg*, p. 238 (ca. 1500; man-eat-man, dog-eat-dog); Wendt, *Geschichte des Welfenfürstentums Grubenhagen*, p. 428 (mid–seventeenth century; "eine hefftige Pestilenz folgete, über das fiel Viel Hauffenweiss dahin").

69. The chronicle evidence is cited above, chapter 1, n. 119. The interpretation of this "sign" had a long future; cf. Nathaniel Hawthorne's observation in *The Scarlet Letter* that in seventeenth-century New England "pestilence was known to have been foreboded by a shower of crimson light" (p. 174).

70. Hardy, *Register of Richard de Kellawe*, 2:1118–20.

71. Hull, *Cartulary of Launceston Priory*, nos. 593, 336.

72. For examples of such disputes arising at other times from this cause in England and on the Continent, see Dohar, *Black Death*, pp. 82–83; Jordan, *From Servitude to Freedom*, p. 51. Cf. below, chapter 7, text to nn. 167–68, 176, on authorizations in towns for mass burials during the Great Famine.

73. Orme, "Medieval Almshouse for the Clergy," pp. 5, 9–10.

74. The complexity of this source has been well discussed in Smith, "Demographic Developments in Rural England," pp. 53–57.

75. *Agrarian History*, 2:726; Bois, *Crisis of Feudalism*, pp. 271–75.

76. Smith, "Demographic Developments in Rural England," pp. 38–45; Dyer, *Standards of Living*, pp. 140, 267, 270; Poos, "Population Turnover in Medieval Essex," p. 9; Razi, *Life, Marriage and Death*, p. 40.

77. Dyer, *Lords and Peasants in a Changing Society*, p. 111.

78. Bennett, *Women in the Medieval English Countryside*, p. 13. Below, epilogue, text to nn. 24–26, on the residual effects of severe famine.

79. Nash, "Mortality Pattern of the Wiltshire Lords," p. 40.

80. Hallam, *Rural England*, pp. 44–45.

81. *Agrarian History*, 2:537.

82. Above, chapter 4, text to nn. 130, 165.

83. Above, chapter 2, text to nn. 69–70.

84. For sharp criticisms of Hallam's often contradictory conclusions, see Smith, "Demographic Developments in Rural England," pp. 41, 55.

85. Campbell, "Population Pressure," pp. 98–99, 127.

86. Bailey, *Marginal Economy*, p. 201. Further on East Anglian mortality, Smith, "Demographic Developments in Rural England," pp. 55–56.

87. For example, "Fragment d'une Chronique Anonyme," p. 151. See also "E Chronico Anonymi Cadomensis," p. 26.

88. "Continuatio Chronici Guillelmi de Nangiaco," p. 616: "Hoc anno fuit magna mortalitas hominum et maxime pauperum, quorum multi famis inediâ perierunt." See also "Chroniques de Saint-Denis," p. 698; and "Chronicon Girardi de Fracheto," p. 46.

89. "E Chronico Anonymi Cadomensis," p. 26.

90. Bois, *Crisis of Feudalism*, pp. 271–75.

91. Fourquin, *Campagnes de la région parisienne*, pp. 191–94; but cf. Bois, *Crisis of Feudalism*, pp. 271–75. On the Flemish towns, below, chapter 7, text to nn. 162–64, 171–75, 195–209.

92. Martin-Lorber, "Communauté d'habitants dans une seigneurie de Cîteaux," pp. 16, 18.

93. Fossier, "Peuplement de la France du nord," p. 69.

94. Sax, *Annales Eyderstadiensium*, p. 41: "in diesen Nordlanden auch ein grawsame Pest gefolget, dass der dritte theil der Menschen darmit aufgegangen."

95. Weiler, *Urkundenbuch des Stiftes Xanten*, 1:310–11, no. 463.

96. Meister, "Niederdeutsche Chroniken," p. 51.

97. Weiler, *Urkundenbuch des Stiftes Xanten*, 1:309–10, no. 462.

98. Above, text to n. 73.

99. For the evidence, see Hüffer, *Bronnen voor de Geschiedenis der Abdij Rijnsburg*, 1:4 (including n. 4), 10; Ada Van Leyden died either at the very end of 1316 or perhaps as late as 27 January 1317. In a separate study of the abbey, Hüffer concluded that the evidence probably pointed to epidemic disease associated with the famine; *De Adellijke Vrouwenabdij van Rijnsburg*, p. 76.

100. *Monasticon belge*, 1:260, 301.

101. Ibid., p. 400; 4:801.

102. Ibid., 2:206; 5:311.

103. Ibid., 4:477–78. If a forged charter of the sixteenth century (purporting to be of 22 November 1315) were genuine or repeats evidence from a genuine original, there might be two deaths of abbesses in the famine years, that of Abbess Marie after 21 August 1315 and before 22 November 1315 and that of an otherwise unattested Agnès de Souveris, after 22 November 1315 and before 4 April 1317; Despy and Uyttebrouck, *Inventaire des archives de l'abbaye de La Ramée*, p. 199, no. 122.

104. All references in the list are to volume and page numbers of the *Monasticon belge*.

105. Sax, *Annales Eyderstadiensium*, p. 41; Sax, *Nova, totius Frisiae septentrionalis, Descriptio*, p. 155.

106. Cf. Smith, "Demographic Developments in Rural England," p. 63.

107. Cf. Rivers, "Nutritional Biology of Famine," pp. 79–80.

108. Ibid.; Hugo, "Demographic Impact of Famine," pp. 19–21.

109. Above, text to nn. 27–34.

110. Valois, "Plaidoyer du XIVe siècle," p. 366—but the text here has been "improved" by the editor.

111. Ravensdale, "Population Changes," p. 211.

112. Hugo, "Demographic Impact of Famine," pp. 19–21.

113. Dyer, *Standards of Living*, p. 267.

CHAPTER 7
URBAN DEMOGRAPHY AND ECONOMY

1. This is a rough estimate, to be sure. Some regions like Flanders (below, text to nn. 22–26) and southwestern Germany had a far smaller proportion of rural dwellers than this (on the German case, see Sydow, *Städte im deutschen Südwesten*, p. 148). Others (like Scandinavia, Scotland, Ireland, northern England, and Wales) had far larger proportions.

2. Above, chapter 3, text to nn. 24–25, 28, 33, 39, 43, 48.

3. Contamine, *Economie médiévale*, p. 214.

4. Sydow, "Die Klein- und Mittelstadt," pp. 9–38, especially p. 12; Sydow, *Städte im deutschen Südwesten*, p. 148.

5. See, for example, Looz-Corswarem, "Zur Wirtschafts- und Sozialgeschichte Wesels," pp. 154–55.

6. This is the "orthodox" view and is associated with traditional economic historians like Pirenne (*Economic and Social History*) and Cipolla (*Before the Industrial Revolution*). For the last twenty years it has been losing favor but is now making a comeback: see Harvey, "Introduction," pp. 11–12, who sums up the arguments surrounding the work of John Day, an outstanding recent proponent of the orthodox view.

7. Below, text to nn. 58–59.

8. The adverb *relatively* is meant as a caution against exaggeration and to recall the far greater sophistication of the urban economies of northern Italy; cf. Contamine, *Economie médiévale*, pp. 237, 240.

9. Schmidt, "*Societas christiana in civitate*," pp. 297, 324–26.

10. Catane, "Monde intellectuel de Rashi," pp. 64–65.

11. Mate, "Agrarian Economy of South-East England," p. 89.

12. Below, text to nn. 130–34.

13. For traditional estimates of London's size, see Herlihy, "Demography," p. 141; and Reyerson, "Urbanism, Western European," p. 316.

14. The progress report "Centre for Metropolitan History," p. 68, estimates 90,000 to 100,000 (the project is described on pp. 68–69). Keene, "Medieval London and Its Region," p. 107, uses 100,000 as his gross estimate.

15. Smith, "Demographic Developments in Rural England," p. 50; Hilton, *English and French Towns*, p. 51 n. 41; Mundy, *Europe in the High Middle Ages*, p. 86; Britnell, *Commercialisation of English Society*, p. 87. See also Campbell and Overton, "A New Perspective," p. 103; Campbell, "Measuring the Commer-

cialisation of Seigneurial Agriculture," p. 137; Contamine, *Economie méñiévale*, p. 272.

16. Smith, "Demographic Developments in Rural England," pp. 50–51; Platt, "Southampton," p. 13; Contamine, *Economie médiévale*, p. 272.

17. For various estimates (and a tendentious debate on their worth and the worth of the scholars making them), see Helle, "Norway in the High Middle Ages," p. 172; and Lunden, "Views and Nonviews on Medieval Norway," p. 166.

18. Sawyer and Sawyer, *Medieval Scandinavia*, p. 159.

19. Helle, "Norway in the High Middle Ages," p. 172.

20. Sawyer and Sawyer, *Medieval Scandinavia*, p. 159.

21. For example, Lödöse, whose population in the year 1300 is estimated at 1,200–1,500; Ekre, "Lödöse im Wandel vom 12. zum 13. Jahrhundert," p. 215. See also Sawyer and Sawyer, *Medieval Scandinavia*, p. 159.

22. On the proportional estimates, see Persson, "Labour Productivity in Medieval Agriculture," p. 132; Herlihy, "Demography," p. 141; and Reyerson, "Urbanism, Western European," p. 315. Sivéry, *Economie du royaume de France*, p. 14, and Contamine, *Economie médiévale*, p. 272, give the absolute figure of 180,000 urban residents for Flanders/Artois.

23. Persson, "Labour Productivity in Medieval Agriculture," p. 131; Russell, "Population in Europe," p. 34; Herlihy, "Demography," p. 141; Mundy, *Europe in the High Middle Ages*, p. 86; Contamine, *Economie médiévale*, p. 336. Cf. also Seberich, "Einwohnerzahl Würzburgs," p. 68.

24. Herlihy, "Demography," p. 141; Cipolla, *Before the Industrial Revolution*, p. 304; Mundy, *Europe in the High Middle Ages*, p. 86; Persson, "Labour Productivity in Medieval Agriculture," p. 131. See also Seberich, "Einwohnerzahl Würzburgs," p. 68.

25. Herlihy, "Demography," p. 141. Mundy, *Europe in the High Middle Ages*, p. 86, places Ypres rather in the 15,000–20,000 range; Nicholas, *Medieval Flanders*, p. 305, assesses its population at 20,000–30,000 in 1311, while Persson, "Labour Productivity in Medieval Agriculture," p. 131, favors the latter. See also *Algemene Geschiedenis der Nederlanden*, 3:1.

26. Wyffels, "Hanse, grands marchands et patriciens," p. 256. Again, Persson, "Labour Productivity in Medieval Agriculture," p. 131, interpreting Derville, favors a higher estimate, 30,000, for Arras.

27. Russell, "Population in Europe," p. 40; Mundy, *Europe in the High Middle Ages*, p. 86. For an enormous amount of information on the administration of German towns, see the essays collected in Rausch, *Stadt und Stadtherr*.

28. Ennen, "Aachen im Mittelalter," p. 473; Jakobi, "Bevölkerungsentwicklung," p. 494.

29. Sydow, "Die Klein- und Mittelstadt," p. 27: "Die grosse Stadtgründungswelle ging um 1300 bzw. bald nach 1300 ziemlich abrupt zu Ende." Drawing on a great deal of work, Sydow elsewhere estimates that central Europe as a whole saw the foundation of 1,500 new towns from the eleventh century to 1250 and 1,500 more from 1250 to 1300; *Städte im deutschen Südwesten*, p. 50.

30. Liessem, "Zur Architektur der mittelalterlichen Bauwerke," p. 383.

31. Sydow, "Die Klein- und Mittelstadt," p. 15.

32. For these estimates, some of which are based on surface area and two (Memmingen's and Nördlingen's) on figures for the period after recovery from the Black Death, see Schich, *Würzburg im Mittelalter*, pp. 208, 210; Seberich, "Einwohnerzahl Würzburgs," pp. 51, 68; Kiessling, *Die Stadt und ihr Land*, pp. 26, 267; Blaschke, *Geschichte Sachsens im Mittelalter*, p. 227; Schrammek, *Verkehrs- und Baugeschichte der Stadt Bautzen*, p. 95, graph.

33. Blaschke, *Geschichte Sachsens im Mittelalter*, p. 227. Cf. the graph in Schrammek, *Verkehrs- und Baugeschichte der Stadt Bautzen*, p. 95, for Bautzen and Dresden. For Marburg (3,500–4,000), see Dähne, "Marburg im Mittelalter," p. 25, graph; Fowler and Klein, "Bürger und Stadt," p. 69.

34. Many of the estimates are in part based on relative surface area (cf. the estimate of Marburg's population, above, n. 33) and then an informed guess about density. This is why the estimates can differ so markedly. See Seberich, "Einwohnerzahl Würzburgs," pp. 67–68; Richter, "Hamburgs Frühzeit bis 1300," pp. 78–79, 110; and, most recently, Hoffmann, "Lübeck im Hoch- und Spätmittelalter," p. 306. I do not know why Sawyer and Sawyer, *Medieval Scandinavia*, p. 159, posit a 40,000 figure for Lübeck.

35. Willert, *Anfänge und frühe Entwicklung der Städte Kiel, Oldesloe und Plön*, pp. 85, 223, 307.

36. Witte, "Geschichte Mecklenburgs," p. 15: 12.7 percent of Rostock's inhabitants were from Westphalia; 11 percent of Wismar's. In the towns of nearer Pomerania, 20.2 percent of residents were from the Rhineland and East- and Westphalia; Witte, "Geschichte Vorpommerns," p. 44.

37. Richter, "Städte," p. 109.

38. So Herlihy, "Demography," p. 141 (and Keene of the London project would agree that Paris was about twice London's size). See also Reyerson, "Urbanism, Western European," p. 316; Contamine, *Economie médiévale*, pp. 214, 272. Sivéry, *Economie du royaume de France*, p. 14, estimates that by 1250 Paris's population was 150,000, a date on which it was entering a period of spectacular growth. Older estimates (in the 80,000–100,000 range) are repeated in Cipolla, *Before the Industrial Revolution*, p. 303, and amazingly in Mundy, *Europe in the High Middle Ages*, p. 86; the latter selectively accepts Keene's or Keene's group's higher estimate of London but silently rejects the same historian's estimate of Paris, preferring the least of the ancient figures, 80,000. The result is that in Mundy's list London becomes the largest city of northern Europe!

39. Contamine, *Economie médiévale*, p. 272, suggests that Lille had more than 6,000 houses or hearths and that these were "en général occupées par une seule famille." See also Persson, "Labour Productivity in Medieval Agriculture," p. 131.

40. Contamine, *Economie médiévale*, p. 284.

41. According to Contamine (ibid., p. 272) Reims had in excess of 3,700 houses around 1300. He ventures a guess of 20,000 inhabitants in the late thirteenth century (p. 336).

42. For example, Lübeck; Hammel, "Häusermarkt und wirtschaftliche Wechsellagen in Lübeck," p. 91.

43. Cf. Samsonowicz, "Verhältnis zum Raum bei den hansischen Bürgern," p. 35.

44. Cf. Bund, "Frankfurt am Main," pp. 54–55.

45. Slicher van Bath, "Economic and Social Conditions in the Frisian Districts," p. 129.

46. For the assertions in this paragraph I have drawn selectively on the work of Ennen, *Medieval Town*; Petit-Dutaillis, *Communes françaises*; Reynolds, *History of English Medieval Towns*; Hilton, *English and French Towns*; and a number of older works.

47. Jordan, *From Servitude to Freedom*, p. 40 (on Sens).

48. McIntosh, "Money Lending on the Periphery of London," pp. 557–71; Cassard, "Premiers immigrés," pp. 85–94.

49. Lefèvre, "Contrats de plantation et l'extension du vignoble," pp. 35–36; Kleindienst, "Topographie et l'exploitation des 'Marais de Paris,'" pp. 80–99.

50. Cf. Tout, *Beginnings of a Modern Capital*.

51. Jordan, *Louis IX*, pp. 171–81; Serper, "Administration royale de Paris," pp. 123–39.

52. Jordan, "Communal Administration in France," pp. 292–313.

53. Nicholas, "Economic Reorientation and Social Change," pp. 3–29.

54. Munro, "Industrial Transformations in the North-West European Textile Trades," pp. 110–43.

55. On the Flemish uprisings, see Lalou, "Révoltes contre le pouvoir," pp. 170–80.

56. Joosen, "De Arbeidersvertegenwoordiging in de Mechelse Stadsraad," pp. 49–63.

57. Below, text to nn. 162–64, 171–75, 195–209.

58. Britnell, *Commercialisation of English Society*, pp. 87–88.

59. London's reach has been estimated conservatively at sixty miles along the coast; Campbell, "Measuring the Commercialisation of Seigneurial Agriculture," p. 137. Below, also, on Exeter, text to nn. 63–65.

60. Below, on Bruges, chapter 8, text to nn. 68–89.

61. Schich, "Entstehung des Städtewesens im Havelland," pp. 347–81; Johanek, "Handel und Gewerbe," pp. 661–62; Manske, "Ambergs Lage im Strassennetz der Oberpfalz," pp. 9–10, 17–23; Schrammek, *Verkehrs- und Baugeschichte der Stadt Bautzen*, pp. 84–119; Schwarzmaier, *Geschichte der Stadt Eberbach*, p. 80, map; Dettling, *700 Jahre Mühlbach*, pp. 94–102; Prinz, *Mimigernaford-Münster*, pp. 4–32 and appendix, map 1.

62. Bautier, "Circulation fluviale dans la France médiévale," p. 24, attributed the improvement of the navigability of the Durtain in Champagne to the need to serve the town of Provins and its fair (above, chapter 3, text to n. 4). The marshy district of Hadeln was converted to arable under the sponsorship of lords, but drainage and clearance were sustained in part by metropolitan pull from Hamburg; cf. Bierwirth, *Siedlung und Wirtschaft im Lande Hadeln*, pp. 16, 33. Examples like these could be multiplied.

63. Kowaleski, "Grain Trade." On alternative methods of measuring hinterlands, below, n. 67.

64. Campbell accepts that a grain hinterland with a radius of ten to twenty miles was normal only for a town twice as large as Exeter; "Measuring the Commercialisation of Seigneurial Agriculture," p. 137.

65. Kowaleski, "Grain Trade."

66. Kiessling, *Die Stadt und ihr Land*, p. 88, map.

67. Collette, *Foires et marchés*, p. 37 (my rough estimate after plotting Collette's topographical data). This is not the only way to estimate the size of economic hinterlands, but it may be better than most. An alternative method, which probably underestimates hinterland reach, extrapolates from the radius covered by monopolies, such as the ban of wine; cf. Ginsburger, *Inventaire-sommaire des archives municipales de la ville de Guebwiller*, p. 41, FF 1. In Dijon that extended only five kilometers; Gouvenain and Vallée, *Inventaire-sommaire des archives communales . . . Dijon*, 3:56, I.48. See also Morlet, "Tarifs de péage et de vente à Dijon," p. 123, map. Another possible method looks at the concentration of places of origins of new immigrants. This would give Soest, a town estimated at about 10,000 souls (which seems high to me), a hinterland with a radius of 15 to 25 kms. depending on what one thinks is the appropriate cutoff level in density; cf. Ditt, "Bevölkerungseinzug und Raumbeziehungen," p. 49 and maps following pp. 48, 52. One method that can wildly overestimate the size of hinterlands would be to identify them with areas where a metropolitan coinage dominated as a medium of exchange. Thus the town of Constance (say, 4,000 to 5,000 inhabitants around the year 1300) could be said to have had a hinterland largely to its northwest (where the Constance penny was most successful) of 3,000 to 4,000 kms. square. (I have based this estimate on the remarks and maps in Maurer, *Konstanz im Mittelalter*, pp. 151–52, 189, 191.)

68. The terrible mortality in Metz during the famine (cf. below, n. 187) strongly affected agrarian markets in Luxembourg, 60 kms. distant; see Lascombes, *Chronik der Stadt Luxemburg*, p. 148.

69. Cf. Stevens, "Three Lime Burning Pits," pp. 73–87.

70. Philippe, "Chantier ou atelier," pp. 239–57.

71. This is an underlying theme in Howell's *Women, Production and Patriarchy*.

72. For the denseness of social services and especially of the hospital network in Bruges, for example, see the aptly titled study of Maréchal, *De sociale en politieke Gebondenheid van het Brugse Hospitaalwezen*.

73. These are fundamental themes of Maréchal's study; see especially ibid., pp. 157–76, 288–91.

74. Delcambre, "Chronique Valenciennoise," p. 61; Borgnet and Bormans, "Geste de Liège," pp. 663–64; and the *récit* of Jan Boendale, cited and translated in Nicholas, *Medieval Flanders*, p. 207. Making reference to the Antwerp prices became a common pastime for later Low Country chroniclers. See "Chronijcke van Nederlant," p. 19; "Chronycke van Nederlant," p. 72.

75. Ilgenstein, "Handels- und Gewerbegeschichte der Stadt Magdeburg," 44:51.

76. Müllner, *Annalen der Reichstadt Nürnberg*, 1:373.

77. Baier, "Bruchstücke einer stralsundischen Chronik," p. 66.

78. "Chroniques de Saint-Denis," p. 698.

79. Jean de Jandun, "Deux éloges de la ville de Paris," p. 59.

80. "Continuatio Chronici Guillelmi de Nangiaco," p. 615; "Chroniques de Saint-Denis," p. 698; "Chronicon Girardi de Fracheto," p. 45.

81. John of Trokelowe, *Annales*, pp. 89–90, 92–93; "Vita Edwardi secundi,"

pp. 59, 69; *Flores historiarum*, 3:341; *French Chronicle of London*, p. 39; "Annales Paulini," pp. 278–79; "Annales Londonienses," p. 236; *Anonimalle Chronicle*, pp. 90–91; Higden, *Polychronicon*, 9:308.

82. Richter, *Untersuchungen zur Hamburger Wirtschafts- und Sozialgeschichte*, p. 82.

83. Van Werveke, "Famine de l'an 1316," p. 10.

84. Derville, "Hôpital Saint-Julien de Cambrai," p. 303.

85. Delcambre, "Chronique Valenciennoise," pp. 61–62: "En l'an mil trois cens et vingt, fu li bled sy bas que l'uittel ne vally que xxvi deniers à Valenchiennes ne ailleurs à l'avenant des mesurez."

86. Above, n. 85.

87. Sivéry, *Structures agraires et vie rurale dans le Hainaut*, 2:409–10. See also Nicholas, *Medieval Flanders*, p. 207.

88. Lodewijk Van Velthem provides the figures (unit prices, per *mudde*) in his contemporary *Voortzetting van den Spiegel Historiael*, 3:217. The editors mistakenly refer the Easter price to 1315, but all the scholars who have incorporated the data have calculated the dates as I have: see Henne and Wauters, *Histoire de la ville de Bruxelles*, 1:94; Lucas, "Great European Famine," pp. 353–54; Nicholas, *Medieval Flanders*, p. 207.

89. Abel, *Agricultural Fluctuations*, p. 39.

90. These conclusions are extrapolated from the graph in Anhang 2 of Göttmann, "Die Strahlenberger, der Pfalzgraf und die Kessler," p. 68 (see also p. 55 where, for his general conclusions, Göttmann depends on Curschmann, *Hungersnöte*).

91. Above, chapter 3, text to nn. 90–91.

92. Prims, *Geschiedenis van Antwerpen*, vol. 4, pt. 1, p. 140.

93. Sharpe, *Calendar of Letter-Books*, p. 44.

94. Ibid., pp. 56–57.

95. Kowaleski, "Grain Trade."

96. Borgnet and Bormans, *Ly Myreur des histors*, 6:222, and above, chapter 3, text to n. 64.

97. Sweerts, "Ioannis Geerbrandi Leydensis, Carmelitani, Chronicon," p. 249; Sweerts, "Reneri Snoi . . . De Rebus batavicis," p. 114.

98. Sweerts, "Ioannis Geerbrandi Leydensis, Carmelitani, Chronicon," pp. 249–50.

99. *Ordonnances*, 1:606–8 (information for Paris from a royal decree of 25 September 1315). For the English case, see "Annales Londonienses," p. 238.

100. "Chroniques de Saint-Denis," p. 698: "Et en cest an [1315] à Paris fu si grant chierté de sel que nul aage ne remembre ne ne treuve len en escript si grand chierté de sel à Paris avoir veue; car le boissel en fu vendu x. s. et plus par forte monnoie en ycest an decourant." On "strong money" and the manipulation of the coinage in France, see the references above, chapter 3, n. 56.

101. Ferger, *Lüneburg: Eine siedlungsgeographische Untersuchung*, p. 85; Saul, "Herring Industry at Great Yarmouth," pp. 33, 37.

102. Rogers, *History of Agriculture and Prices*, 1:609, 637, 641.

103. Saul, "Herring Industry at Great Yarmouth," p. 43 n. 48.

104. Cf., for example, the inventory of the accounts of Dijon; Gouvenain

and Vallée, *Inventaire-sommaire des archives communales . . . Dijon*, 3:92, L.31, and Vallée, *Inventaire-sommaire des archives communales . . . Dijon*, p. 16, M.46*bis*.

105. See, for example, Bohmbach and Hucker, *Urkundenbuch zur Geschichte der Stadt Bremerhaven*, 1:36; Fritze, "Entstehung, Aufstieg und Blüte der Hansestadt Stralsund," p. 57.

106. Reincke, "Bevölkerungsprobleme der Hansestädte," p. 14.

107. Richter, *Untersuchungen zur Hamburger Wirtschafts- und Sozialgeschichte*, p. 84. The misleading aggregate figures are available in Reincke, "Bevölkerungsprobleme der Hansestädte," p. 14.

108. Below, text to nn. 196–97.

109. Nicholas, *Town and Countryside*, p. 228.

110. For the relatively low level of admissions in Bruges, see ibid., p. 229. On the lesser severity of the demographic crisis in Bruges and its more effective control of prices, see below, text to nn. 200–202, and chapter 8, text to nn. 101–4.

111. Much information on these issues can be found below in the text to nn. 135–209.

112. *Histoire de Lille*, 1:209–10.

113. Winchester, "Medieval Cockermouth," p. 112.

114. Simms, "Medieval Dublin," p. 38.

115. Quoted in ibid.

116. Horrox, *Selected Rentals and Accounts of Medieval Hull*, p. 5.

117. Ibid., appendix 4, pp. 145–49. In this and subsequent references to the documents of Hull, I have counted each "plot" (*placea*; p. 2 n. 6a) as a unit. Occasionally the documents do not mention plots but land areas (acres, roods, etc.) or, very rarely, specific kinds of tenurial rights, like tolls. Where any of these seems to represent a unitary holding, I have incorporated it into my counting as a single plot.

118. Ibid., p. 5.

119. Ibid., appendix 5, pp. 150–55. I have used the same method of counting here as described above, but my figures—43 empty plots of 133 total—ignore those parts of this list that are highly defective, namely, the rentals on Marketgate Street, and the entries following the sections on Bedfordlane and Bishopgate. The data from these defective parts still manage to reveal a high rate of decayed rents.

120. Ibid., pp. 31–51.

121. Ibid., p. 6.

122. Ibid, appendix 6, pp. 156–57.

123. Britnell, *Growth and Decline in Colchester*, p. 16.

124. Britnell, "Fields and Pastures of Colchester," pp. 159–65: "In the early fourteenth century rights of common, whether over woods and heaths or over arable lands, were a burning issue for the burgesses of Colchester, who were apparently facing a shortage of pasture more critical than that at any other recorded time during the Middle Ages" (p. 163).

125. In general on the drainage of the *marais* (not equivalent to the present district) and its exploitation, see Kleindienst, "Topographie et l'exploitation des 'Marais de Paris,'" pp. 65–99, 105–6. Exploitation was limited to cropping; building was rare since the area remained subject to flooding from the Seine and

was not very salubrious (pp. 135, 154–57). The resentment over the loss of common rights is described at p. 160.

126. Britnell, *Growth and Decline in Colchester*, p. 20.

127. Ibid., pp. 20–21.

128. Ibid., p. 21.

129. For the case of Dresden, for example, see Butte, *Geschichte Dresdens*, p. 61; for that of Antwerp after disasters from 1315 to 1317, see Prims, *Geschiedenis van Antwerpen*, vol. 4, pt. 1, pp. 126, 140, 157, 163.

130. The problem is that before the data become good again, the Black Death intervenes; cf. Britnell, *Growth and Decline in Colchester*, pp. 22, 204–5.

131. Blockmans and Prevenier, "Poverty in Flanders and Brabant," p. 26.

132. Stralsund is one exception, recovering rapidly despite the legacy of war after a dismal two years (1315–1316); Fritze, "Entstehung, Aufstieg und Blüte der Hansestadt Stralsund," p. 57.

133. Hoffmann, "Lübeck im Hoch- und Spätmittelalter," p. 181.

134. I refer to the remarks of the sixteenth-century chronicler Heinrich Piel who, drawing on earlier sources, briefly rehearses these events and draws the lesson; Krieg, *Chronicon domesticum*, p. 60. I wish to thank Professor Michael Curschmann for helping me translate Piel's sixteenth-century German.

135. Curschmann, *Hungersnöte*, p. 211 (Lemaître, *Chronique et Annales de Gilles le Muisit*, pp. 89–90): "Et populus coepit in multis locis parum de pane comedere, quia non habebant."

136. The observations of Jan Boendale in Antwerp, translated in Nicholas, *Medieval Flanders*, p. 207. (On the point of view of Boendale's work, see, most recently, Stein, "Jan van Boendales Brabantsche Yeesten," pp. 185–97; "Yeesten" is the flemishing of the Latin *Gesta*.) See also Lodewijk Van Velthem, *Voortzetting van den Spiegel Historiael*, 3:211–12.

137. Curschmann, *Hungersnöte*, p. 216.

138. Above, chapter 2, text to nn. 69–70.

139. Curschmann, *Hungersnöte*, p. 211 (Lemaître, *Chronique et Annales de Gilles le Muisit*, pp. 89–90).

140. "Annales monasterii de Bermundeseia," p. 470. Further on the Bermondsey annalist, below, text to nn. 217, 221.

141. On the variety of foods raised in and around towns in our period, see Van Haaster, "Umwelt und Nahrungswirtschaft," pp. 206–9, 219 (his illustration comes from Lübeck). On the question of the access of the urban underclass to this variety, see p. 210 of the same article. With regard to the composition of the urban underclass at Lübeck—especially its Slavic minority, distinguished by low-status occupations, linguistic separateness, endogamy, and (allegedly) somatic differences—see Boenisch, "Anthropologischer Vergleich zwischen der mittelalterlichen und frühneuzeitlichen Bevölkerung Lübecks," pp. 87–93.

142. Rivers, "Nutritional Biology of Famine," pp. 63, 77, 80.

143. Curschmann, *Hungersnöte*, p. 214.

144. Rivers, "Nutritional Biology of Famine," pp. 77–78.

145. Wright, *Political Songs*, p. 341, line 397.

146. Rivers, "Nutritional Biology of Famine," pp. 77–80; Crawford, "Subsistence Crises and Famines," pp. 199, 201.

147. John of Trokelowe, *Annales*, p. 94. Cf. Walsingham, *Historia Anglicana*, 1:147. See also Lucas, "Great European Famine," p. 357.

148. Rivers, "Nutritional Biology of Famine," pp. 87–90.

149. The quotation is from Ebendorfer, *Chronica Austriae*, pp. 238–39, though the year is uncertain. The author, writing in the fifteenth century, is probably referring to the Great Famine, but he may be recording information on a local famine of 1313. See also above on the bizarrely harsh winters of the famine years, chapter 1, text following n. 57, and text to nn. 62, 68, 73–75, 81–82.

150. The connection between the dearness and the increase in sickness and mortality was noted by the eyewitness Lodewijk Van Velthem, *Voortzetting van den Spiegel Historiael*, 3:218–19. His modern editors suggest that the sickness he referred to was typhus.

151. A wide variety of texts is assembled in Curschmann, *Hungersnöte*, pp. 209–17, and Lucas, "Great European Famine," p. 357.

152. Curschmann, *Hungersnöte*, pp. 210–11 (Lemaître, *Chronique et Annales de Gilles le Muisit*, p. 89); Nicholas, *Medieval Flanders*, p. 207. See also Diemar, *Die Chroniken des Wigand Gerstenberg*, p. 238.

153. Lucas, "Great European Famine," p. 357 n. 4.

154. "Propter tempestates, grandines et pestilentias communes"; Schmitz-Cliever, "Pest und pestilenzialische Krankheiten," p. 115.

155. Vincent, *Histoire des famines à Paris*, p. 38.

156. Ibid., pp. 9–10.

157. "Excerpta e Memoriali Historiarum," p. 662; "Chronique Rimée attribuée à Geoffroi de Paris," p. 162. See also Lucas, "Great European Famine," p. 357.

158. Curschmann, *Hungersnöte*, pp. 212–14; the Latin of the last quotation is "mortifera pestis inhorruit."

159. Ibid., pp. 209–11. Later chroniclers incorporating earlier, sometimes otherwise lost, reports are also useful here; cf. "Brabandsche Kronijk," p. 50; "Korte chronijcke van Nederland," p. 64; "Chronijcke van Nederlant," p. 20.

160. See, for example, the descriptions of Nantois famines (1513/1514, 1532, 1546) cited in Blanchard, *Inventaire sommaire des archives communales . . . Nantes*, 3:66, 76, 202.

161. Fossier, *Peasant Life in the Medieval West*, p. 80. The most recent famine that was more than regional in the north was one that affected northern France and England in 1257–1258. It had important consequences; Mayhew, "Money and Prices in England," pp. 127, 130; Jordan, *From Servitude to Freedom*, pp. 50–51; Maddicott, *English Peasantry*, p. 69. Yet most people alive in 1315 were not yet born in 1257.

162. Delcambre, "Chronique Valenciennoise," p. 61: "fu li grans mortollez."

163. "Morteque non caruit"; "mortalitas atrocissima ac saevissima"; "lacrimosa mors hominum"; "fuit que gentium imortalitas inenarrabilis"; "[plagae] plus quam triennium miserabiliter duraverunt" (Curschmann, *Hungersnöte*, pp. 209–11, 215; Delcambre, "Chronique Valenciennoise," p. 61).

164. Wright, *Political Songs*, p. 341, lines 3399–3401.

165. Above, chapter 6, n. 54.

166. Curschmann, *Hungersnöte*, p. 213: "mendicantes absque numero mo-

rerentur in campis, sylvis sive nemoribus, et eorum corpora sine catholicis exequiis sepulturae traderentur in locis agrestibus."

167. Ibid., p. 215; Nicholas, *Medieval Flanders*, p. 207.

168. Curschmann, *Hungersnöte*, pp. 210–11: "corpora . . . in stratis publicis inveniebantur, et a pluribus civitatibus magnae generales foveae in cimiterium consecratae parabantur, et pretia statuebantur, ut ipsa cadavera sepulturae traderentur"; "tanta copia pauperum mendicantium in vicis moriebantur super fimis et ubique, quod per consilarios civitatis fuit ordinatum et commissum certis personis, ut corpora pauperum sic morientium portarent . . . , et pro qualibet persona habebant taxatum salarium." (Also Lemaître, *Chronique et Annales de Gilles le Muisit*, pp. 89–90.)

169. Garnsey, *Famine and Food Supply*, pp. 4–5, 28–29, 32.

170. Lex, *Inventaire sommaire des archives communales de Fontaines*, p. 16.

171. Lodewijk Van Velthem, *Voortzetting van den Spiegel Historiael*, 3:220, 222.

172. D'Haenens, "Une Oeuvre à restituer à Gilles Li Muisis," p. 9: "Et fu li anee dou mortoire qui fu l'an [13]16." Curschmann, *Hungersnöte*, p. 211: "Et testificor, quod in Tornaco tam viri quam mulieres de potentibus, de mediis et de mediocribus, senibus et juvenibus, divitibus et pauperibus, tanta copia moriebatur quotidie, quod aër erat quasi totus corruptus" (also Lemaître, *Chronique et Annales de Gilles le Muisit*, pp. 89–90).

173. Borgnet and Bormans, *Ly Myreur des histors*, p. 222 (a later-fourteenth-century report based on earlier sources).

174. "Descriptio de origine conventus, postea abbatiae Trunchiniensis," p. 615; under the year 1315, "Fames maxima Gandavi, ita ut pluries inedia absumpti. Tanta pestilentia ac fames hoc anno ut tertiam hominum partem memorent historici." On the date of the *Descriptio*, see p. xxxiv.

175. Dherent, "Maladies et mortalités à Douai," pp. 82–83. Douai's population was perhaps as high as 30,000 (Persson, "Labour Productivity in Medieval Agriculture," p. 131), but it would be absurd to extrapolate from the proportion of aldermanic deaths.

176. Curschmann, *Hungersnöte*, 211–12 (also Lemaître, *Chronique et Annales de Gilles le Muisit*, pp. 89–90); Nicholas, *Medieval Flanders*, p. 207; Lodewijk Van Velthem, *Voortzetting van den Spiegel Historiael*, 3:220.

177. Musset, "Observations sur le rôle social de la sépulture," pp. 373–74.

178. Curschmann, *Hungersnöte*, p. 211 (also Lemaître, *Chronique et Annales de Gilles le Muisit*, pp. 89–90): "et quod presbyteri parochiales saepe qua parte uti nesciebant."

179. Curschmann, *Hungersnöte*, p. 209 (also Kurth, *Chronique de Jean de Hocsem*, p. 162 and, for the editorial matter summarized hereafter, pp. xv, xvii, xxvii, xxxviii): "biga bis, vel ter in die onerata sex vel octo cadaveribus mortuorum, extra villam in nouo facto caemiterio, miseranda corpuscula continuo deportabat." Jean de Hocsem, a cleric in Liège, whose work Curschmann excerpted from an old edition and Kurth later published in extenso, was a contemporary who also traveled through Hainaut and France in 1321. He began writing his chronicle in 1334. He died during the Black Death on 2 October 1348.

180. Richter, *Untersuchungen zur Hamburger Wirtschafts- und Sozial-geschichte*, pp. 82–83 n. 101.

181. Curschmann, *Hungersnöte*, p. 216: "gruben . . . wurdent alle vol mit doten gefullet."

182. Henne and Wauters, *Histoire de la ville de Bruxelles*, 1:94 n. 3.

183. Verniers, *Millénaire d'histoire de Bruxelles*, p. 114.

184. Curschmann, *Hungersnöte*, p. 214: "innumerabilia cadavera mortuo-rum." See also Diemar, *Chroniken des Wigand Gerstenberg*, p. 238.

185. Curschmann, *Hungersnöte*, p. 217: "ibidem ecclesiam ad honorem cor-poris Christi edificaverunt."

186. Richter, *Untersuchungen zur Hamburger Wirtschafts- und Sozial-geschichte*, p. 82; Curschmann, *Hungersnöte*, p. 216.

187. Curschmann, *Hungersnöte*, pp. 61–62. See also Lascombes, *Chronik der Stadt Luxemburg*, p. 148.

188. Below, chapter 8, text to nn. 93–100, 106.

189. Rivers, "Nutritional Biology of Famine," p. 63.

190. Curschmann, *Hungersnöte*, p. 217: "cibo salvati et recreati suffocati sunt." There is a slightly different transcription of the cited text in the version published in the *Silesiacarum rerum scriptores*; see "Sigismundi Rositzii Chro-nica," p. 69.

191. Since until the 1970s the belief prevailed in prescientific and scientific guise that protein deficiencies were at the center of the high mortality in famines, it was standard to turn to foods rich in proteins, like milk, to nourish the weakest famine victims. When many died anyway, it was characteristic to attribute the cause to the victim's preexisting weakness ("we just got to her too late") rather than to the nature of the treatment. In the 1950s and 1960s such treatment "prob-ably cost hundreds of thousands of lives"; Rivers, "Nutritional Biology of Fam-ine," pp. 63, 85–86.

192. Above, text to nn. 52–57.

193. Nicholas, "Economic Reorientation and Social Change," p. 5.

194. Aerts and Van Cauwenberghe, "Grafschaft Flandern," p. 95.

195. Above, n. 25.

196. Van Werveke, "Famine de l'an 1316," pp. 6–7. Blockmans, "Nieder-lande vor und nach 1400," pp. 119, 123, estimates Ypres's population at only 20,000 before the great mortality. In any case, all scholars depend on and cite the Ypres figure: Day, *Medieval Market Economy*, p. 186; Lucas, "Great European Famine," pp. 367–69; Nicholas, *Medieval Flanders*, p. 208.

197. Des Marez and De Sagher, *Comptes de la ville d'Ypres*, 1:607–12 ("Le brief de faire fouir les mors").

198. It has been argued strongly that the burials were chiefly of poor people; cf. Van Werveke, "Famine de l'an 1316," pp. 9–12.

199. See Des Marez and De Sagher, *Comptes de la ville d'Ypres*, 1:607, for the use of the phrase "pour faire porter et quillir les mors aval les rues," but this or similar phrases are used throughout the account.

200. Van Werveke, "Bronnenmateriaal uit de Brugse Stadsrekeningen," pp. 437–40.

201. Ibid., p. 440: "Boudine Berbise, van tween scrinen met vallen, daer men de dode lieden vorseid in droech. 20 s."

202. Van Werveke, "Famine de l'an 1316," pp. 7–8; Blockmans, "Niederlande vor und nach 1400," p. 123; Nicholas, *Medieval Flanders*, p. 207.

203. Hocquet, "Table des testaments," pp. 81–148. I believe this figure is accurate. I have counted all testaments, even if a few times this meant counting an item twice where a person revised his or hers the same year. Occasionally I have had to modify Hocquet's dating for obvious misprints.

204. The years 1367 and 1368 seem to be the only ones noticeably underrepresented.

205. I have found no really solid figures on the death rate during the Black Death in Tournai, but there is no doubt that its hinterland was profoundly ravaged by the plague. The usual movements of flagellants, murderous outrages against Jews, and widespread appeals to the supernatural in 1349 in the region are well recorded by the contemporary Gilles Le Muisit, the abbot of Saint Martin of Tournai. See Lemaître, *Chroniques et Annales de Gilles le Muisit*, pp. 222–42; and also "Chronicon Aegidii Li Muisis . . . alterum," pp. 344–46, for sections left out of Lemaître's edition of the "Annales."

206. For suggestive evidence of high mortality in the rural areas of the Low Countries, see above, chapter 6, text to nn. 99–104.

207. Below, chapter 8, text to nn. 68–69, 93–100.

208. The references, except for those on Speyer and Düsseldorf, have already been cited. For Speyer, see Voltmer, "Von der Bischofsstadt zur Reichsstadt," p. 323, interpreting various snippets of evidence. For Düsseldorf, see Wisplinghoff, "Vom Mittelalter bis zum Ende des Jülich-Klevischen Erbstreits," p. 282, interpreting the *Chronicon Campense.*

209. For example, Struick, "Utrechts Beziehungen zum flachen Land," p. 5, does not believe that Utrecht suffered any noticeable population loss in this period.

210. Curschmann, *Hungersnöte*, pp. 59–60; Lucas, "Great European Famine," pp. 355–56. See also Diemar, *Chroniken des Wigand Gerstenberg*, p. 238 (man ate man and dog ate dog).

211. Above, chapter 6, text to n. 48.

212. Curschmann, *Hungersnöte*, p. 217: "plures etiam carnes de suspensis cadaveribus comederunt" (available, with slight differences, also in "Sigismundi Rositzii Chronica," p. 69).

213. John of Trokelowe, *Annales*, p. 95.

214. Curschmann, *Hungersnöte*, p. 210: "dicitur, quod quidam . . . propter famem nimiam devoraverunt proprios suos pueros."

215. Ibid.: "matres filiis vescebantur." Schultz, *Das höfische Leben*, 1:140.

216. Curschmann, *Hungersnöte*, p. 217: "pluribus in locis parentes filios et filii parentes necantes devoraverunt" (available, with slight differences, also in "Sigismundi Rositzii Chronica," p. 69).

217. "Annales monasterii de Bermundeseia," p. 470.

218. See, for example, "Excerpta ex Nicolai Henelii . . . Chronico," p. 152; and "Nicolai Henelii ab Henenfeld . . . Annales," p. 273.

219. Lucas, "Great European Famine," pp. 355–56.

220. Cf. Garnsey (*Famine and Food Supply*, pp. 4, 28), for example, on the allegations of cannibalism in the famine in Edessa, ca. A.D. 500.

221. See, for example, 2 (4) Kings 6.24–29. The old translations refer to the sale of "dove's dung" as food during a famine; the Hebrew is now believed to denote wild onions. I was greatly aided in my understanding of the cannibalism motif by a brilliant paper of Julia Marvin, a graduate student in English at Princeton University. It will appear under the title "Cannibalism as an Aspect of Famine."

222. Diemar, *Chroniken des Wigand Gerstenberg*, p. 238.

223. Kershaw, "Great Famine," pp. 9–10. More generally, Arnold, *Famine*, pp. 15, 19, who specifically censures Duby and Slicher van Bath for their dismissive views. Both Kershaw and Arnold use the phrase "stark horror," perhaps the most common locution in famine studies.

224. Sorokin, *Hunger as a Factor in Human Affairs*, pp. 61–87.

225. Camporesi, *Bread of Dreams*; the reference to self-devouring is at pp. 40–41.

226. Arnold, *Famine*, pp. 73–74.

227. Cf. the report published in the *New York Times* (15 June 1992) of the scenes reported by Soviet bureaucrats investigating famine-stricken households in the 1930s.

228. On the lanterns, see Höck, "Zu mittelalterlichen Totenlaternen," pp. 115–22. On the objects and good linen shrouds found in urban graves, see Ruffier, "Note sur les pratiques funéraires médiévales," pp. 29, 32; Aubert, *Hôpitaux de Langres*, pp. 41–43, 216–17.

229. For this burial custom as followed among certain classes in northern France and Denmark, see Madsen, "A French Connection: Danish Funerary Pots," pp. 171–83.

230. Above, chapter 6, text to n. 48.

231. Arnold, *Famine*, p. 86.

232. Curschmann, *Hungersnöte*, pp. 213–14. See also Diemar, *Chroniken des Wigand Gerstenberg*, p. 238, though the date is in error in this late source.

CHAPTER 8
COPING IN TOWNS

1. On the distribution of rights in the salt markets, see Kiessling, "Augsburgs Wirtschaft," p. 171; Jaitner, *Urkundenbuch des Klosters Ebstorf*, p. 5 (for Lüneburg); Hiegel, "Sel en Lorraine," p. 24; Willert, *Anfänge und frühe Entwicklung der Städte Kiel, Oldesloe und Plön*, pp. 234–35 (for Lübeckers in Oldesloe). On marketing and distribution from eastern Baltic towns like Danzig, Elbing, Königsberg, Riga, Visby, and Reval, see Witthöft, "Mass- und Gewichtsnormen im hansischen Salzhandel," p. 39.

2. Ennen and Höroldt, *Vom Römerkastell zur Bundeshauptstadt*, p. 78: "Wein . . . wichtigstes Bonner Handelsgut."

3. Above, chapter 3, text to nn. 94–96.

4. But see below, chapter 9, text to nn. 10, 25, on efforts at price controls.

5. The diplomas are inventoried in Nessel, *Inventaire-sommaire des archives communales . . . Haguenau*, p. 3, AA.11, AA.12.

6. The charters are inventoried in Brucker, *Inventaire sommaire des archives communales . . . Strasbourg*, pt. 1, p. 2, AA.2.

7. Stoob, "Hansische Westpolitik," p. 8.

8. Wriedt, "Annales Lubicenses," p. 560; Stoob, "Hansische Westpolitik," p. 8.

9. Wauters, *Table chronologique*, 8:597.

10. Ibid., pp. 701, 716–17.

11. Gautier and Lesort, *Ville de Cambrai*, HH5, for a reference to "Poursuites exercées contre les Cambrésiens, à la requête des 'Gardes des foires de Champagne et de Brie' pour défaut de paiement de leur loyer aux dites foires (1313–1316)."

12. Rübel, *Dortmunder Urkundenbuch*, 1:244–45, no. 349: "considerata utilitate civitatis nostre."

13. See, for example, the case of a burgher of Bruges active in the annuity market of the town of Ardenbourg in the spring of 1319: Saint-Génois, *Inventaire analytique des chartes des comtes de Flandre*, p. 391, no. 1364.

14. Cf. Gautier and Lesort, *Ville de Cambrai*, p. 86 n. 1. The damaged folios of the town accounts of Cambrai summarized here are very fragmentary; according to Gautier and Lesort, the relevant passage reads, "à Huon Lelarge de Rains, pour vies arrérages de l'acort fait l'an mil iii^c et xv de vii^{xx} con li devoit paier à trois termes, au behourdie [*first Sunday of Lent*] l'an xvviij [recte: xviij], à l'Ascension l'an xix et à le saint Pierre, l'an xix."

15. Baum, "Annuities in Late Medieval Hanse Towns," pp. 24–48.

16. Ibid., p. 40 and n. 75.

17. Heinemann, *Pommersches Urkundenbuch*, 5:271, no. 3023.

18. Richter, *Untersuchungen zur Hamburger Wirtschafts- und Sozialgeschichte*, pp. 83–85 and tables 7, 9, 11, 13. Cf. Gabrielson, "Die Zeit der Hanse," p. 177.

19. Above, text to n. 7. See also Hoffmann, "Lübeck im Hoch-und Spätmittelalter," pp. 180–81.

20. Heinemann, *Pommersches Urkundenbuch*, 5:258–59, 348–49, 353, 358, nos. 3004, 3138, 3146, 3154. The examples date from 1316, 1317, and 1318. For the case of Greifswald, another town that utilized this method of raising cash, see pp. 261–62, no. 3008.

21. Baum, "Annuities in Late Medieval Hanse Towns," pp. 43–44.

22. See, for example, Hänselmann and Mack, *Urkundenbuch der Stadt Braunschweig*, 2:507–11, no. 872 (a list of rents with buyout options, dated ca. 1320).

23. Ibid., pp. 458, 470–71, nos. 806, 826; 4:479, no. 313 (with emendation at 4:xiii).

24. Rübel, *Dortmunder Urkundenbuch*, 1:245–46, no. 351.

25. See, for example, May, "Der Eschenauer Ortsadel," pp. 75–76, for a case in 1316 in which the widow of a Limburger patrician put off redeeming her country mill at Eschenau, probably as a result of the persistent rains.

26. Heinemann, *Pommersches Urkundenbuch*, 5:258–59, 261–62, nos. 3004 and 3008.

27. Huiskes, *Andernach im Mittelalter*, p. 146.

28. Ibid., pp. 205, 207.

29. Cf. Hammel, "Hauseigentum im spätmittelalterlichen Lübeck," pp. 246–47, which argues for significant variations. Bohmbach's "Umfang und Struktur des Braunschweiger Rentenmarktes 1300–1350," pp. 119–33, by its silence on the period 1300–1320 may suggest the same thing.

30. On credit and annuities in later medieval Germany, cf. Duggan, "Zur Bedeutung des spätmittelalterlichen Kreditsystems," pp. 203–8.

31. Wauters, *Table chronologique*, 8:725, 775 (also published in Miraei and Foppens, *Opera diplomatica*, 1:597).

32. Above, chapter 4, text to nn. 145–51.

33. De Spiegeler, *Hôpitaux et l'assistance à Liège*, p. 81.

34. Brouwers, "Documents relatifs à l'Hôpital St-Julien de Liége," pp. 39–40; De Spiegeler, *Hôpitaux et l'assistance à Liège*, p. 81. (The different accents of Liége/Liège are accurate; around 1942 standard usage seems to have changed from the acute to the grave accent: Brouwers published in 1906; De Spiegeler in 1987.)

35. Saint-Génois, *Inventaire analytique des chartes des comtes de Flandres*, p. 385, no. 1336; examples include the collegial church of Saint-Omer and the abbey of Saint-Bertin of the same town.

36. Richter, *Untersuchungen zur Hamburger Wirtschafts- und Sozialgeschichte*, p. 88: "ut eas pauperes consolentur."

37. Curschmann, *Hungersnöte*, p. 215. For some revealing exchanges, etc., involving *Korn*, cf. Wagner, *Regesten der Zisterzienserabtei Bildhausen*, pp. 141–42, nos. 137–38 (January and May 1316).

38. Wagner, *Regesten der Zisterzienserabtei Bildhausen*, pp. 142–43, no. 139.

39. Ibid., p. 147, no. 145.

40. Cf. ibid., p. 107, no. 65; p. 131, no. 116 (years 1294, 1309).

41. Buck, *Politics, Finance and the Church*, p. 106 n. 53.

42. See, e.g., Ciscato, *Gli Ebrei in Padova*, pp. 35–38.

43. See, for example, Kiessling, "Augsburgs Wirtschaft," p. 172; Schich, "Entstehung des Städtewesens im Havelland," p. 373.

44. Below, chapter 9, text to n. 22.

45. Rübel, *Dortmunder Urkundenbuch*, 1:277–79, no. 390. The municipal accounts recording this information note that some of these debts were transferred from the late Count Conrad of Dortmund to the municipality as a result of the arrangements surrounding succession to his property. Conrad III's death childless in 1316 precipitated a long and difficult inheritance struggle; Meininghaus, *Grafen von Dortmund*, pp. 99–100.

46. Jordan, "Home Again: The Jews in the Kingdom of France."

47. Jan Boendale's chronicle dealing with Antwerp, cited and translated in Nicholas, *Medieval Flanders*, p. 207.

48. See, e.g., Curschmann, *Hungersnöte*, p. 214 (the example is Bremen in 1316).

49. Bynum, *Holy Feast and Holy Fast*, pp. 68–69.

50. "Continuatio Chronici Guillelmi de Nangiaco," p. 614: "et ob maxime toto mense julio vel quasi [anno 1315], facta sunt processiones devotae à clero et populo. Vidimus namque per quindecim dies continuos apud ecclesiam sancti martyris [Dionysii] maximam utriusque sexûs multitudinem unà cum clero non tantùm de prope, immo etiam à quinque leucis et ampliùs, etiam nudis pedibus, quin immo exceptis mulieribus totis nudis corporibus processionaliter confluentem, ibique deferebatur corpora sanctorum devote, et aliae reliquiae venerandae"; Lucas, "Great European Famine," p. 359. See also "Chronicon Girardi de Fracheto," p. 44; "Excerpta e Memoriali Historiarum," p. 661; "Chronique Rimée attribuée à Geoffroi de Paris," p. 160.

51. "Annales Paulini," p. 278. Cf. "Vita Edwardi secundi," p. 64. See also Kershaw, "Great Famine," p. 7.

52. *Geschichte der Stadt Magdeburg*, p. 58.

53. Curschmann, *Hungersnöte*, p. 77.

54. Marx, *Development of Charity in Medieval Louvain*, pp. 50–52, 57.

55. On Robert, see Hanawalt, *Growing Up in Medieval London*, p. 35; on Michael, *Propago sacri ordinis cartusiensis*, pp. 170–77.

56. Franz, "Alter und neuer Besitz des Würzburger Bürgerspitals," p. 12. See also above on Ludwig IV's foundations, chapter 4, text to n. 23.

57. Cf., for example, above, chapter 6, text to nn. 12–13.

58. Wauters, *Table chronologique*, 8:635 (also published in Van Lokeren, *Chartes et documents*, 2:23–24, no. 1061).

59. Devillers, *Description analytique*, 8:232, 239–40, nos. 121, 124. For further evidence on the distribution of charity and assistance to the poor and sick in Mons in the period from mid-1315 through 1321, see 8:230–54, nos. 118–139.

60. Verniers, *Millénaire d'histoire de Bruxelles*, p. 119, discusses the foundation, which probably housed about a dozen and perhaps catered principally to aged men. Bloemardinne, presumably a play on her name, would evoke the image of a delicate flower.

61. Bruchet, *Inventaire sommaire des archives communales . . . Lille*, p. 119, AA197.

62. Dherent, "Maladies et mortalités à Douai," p. 83.

63. Nicholas, "Economic Reorientation and Social Change," pp. 7–8. A somewhat similar situation obtained for Exeter, a town much smaller than the Flemish towns we will be discussing at length, but in its environs agriculture was skewed toward oats. When wheat crops failed, imports over rather vast distances were necessitated. The whole matter is very nicely discussed in Kowaleski, "Grain Trade."

64. Naudé, *Getreidehandelspolitik*, 1:17–18. That Naudé may exaggerate, cf. Britnell, *Commercialisation of English Society*, pp. 92–93, on the rather weak municipal supply policies in England.

65. See, for example, the records of Béthune inventoried in Travers, *Inventaire-sommaire des archives communales . . . Béthune*, pp. 1–2, AA.2–AA.4, and evidence from Magdeburg summarized in the *Geschichte der Stadt Magdeburg*, p. 58. See also below, text to nn. 68, 90, 106.

66. Derville, "Chapelains de Saint-Géry de Cambrai," p. 278; Naudé, *Getrei-*

dehandelspolitik, 1:220; Nicholas, *Medieval Flanders*, p. 292; Richter, "Hamburgs Frühzeit bis 1300," pp. 90–91.

67. Above, chapter 1, text to nn. 90–93, and below, chapter 9, text to nn. 11–14, 17.

68. On the identification of the agents as foreigners from Mediterranean lands, the evidence is sometimes firm; cf. Van Werveke, "Bronnenmateriaal uit de Brugse Stadtsrekeningen," pp. 469, 474, 485. At other times, it is less so, being based on the non-Flemish names that appear in the accounts; cf., in the same collection, pp. 455, 479, 508 (Spanish); 456, 489, 508 (Italian). See also Van Houtte, *Geschiedenis van Brugge*, p. 110.

69. Van Werveke, "Famine de l'an 1316," pp. 12–13.

70. Blum, *End of the Old Order*, pp. 183–84.

71. Arnold, *Famine*, p. 105; Carpentier, "Autour de la Peste noire," p. 1077. Nicholas, *Medieval Flanders*, p. 264, makes the same assertion but is more cautious on p. 207, where he talks about Italian handling of grain shipments (see below, text to n. 76).

72. Below, chapter 9, text to nn. 40, 44–46.

73. Technological advances were making the passage safer, but it was still far easier to sail into the Mediterranean from the Atlantic than the reverse; the latter remained rare. Cf. Lewis, "Northern European Sea Power," pp. 151, 156–57; Bartlett, *Making of Europe*, pp. 190–91.

74. Schaube, "Anfänge der Venezianischer Galeerenfahrten," pp. 49–55. Prims suggested that they carried wine, but this is not provable and seems unlikely to me, particularly after the partial recovery of grape production from 1317 on; *Geschiedenis van Antwerpen*, vol. 4, pt. 1, pp. 133, 167–68. See also Contamine, *Economie médiévale*, pp. 289–90.

75. Dochnal (*Chronik von Neustadt*, p. 39), in the mid–nineteenth century, may have come across records indicating imports to Neustadt on the Hardt (about one hundred kilometers northeast of Strasbourg) from Sicily; under 1316, he wrote, "Man holt Getreide aus Sicilien."

76. Cassard, "Marins bretons à Bordeaux," pp. 381, 389; Lucas, "Great European Famine," pp. 357, 371–72; Prestwich, *Three Edwards*, p. 247; Contamine, *Economie médiévale*, p. 290.

77. Cassard, "Marins bretons à Bordeaux," p. 383.

78. For evidence of the expectation of Flemish imports of southern wine (presumably by sea), see Wauters, *Table chronologique*, 8:606. Records documenting Strassburgers' (or Strasbourgeois') concerns in the fourteenth century "sur les quantités de vin importé en ville, des prix d'achat et de vente" are inventoried in Raeuber, *Inventaire des archives . . . de Strasbourg*, p. 143, H.4.101.

79. Larenaudie, "Famines en Languedoc," p. 28.

80. Cf. ibid.

81. Ibid., pp. 28, 39.

82. Ibid., p. 28; Ruiz, *Crisis and Continuity*, p. 22.

83. On England, below, chapter 9, text to nn. 48–49.

84. For example, "Excerpta e Memoriali Historiarum," p. 662.

85. Cf. Derville, "Draperies flamandes et artésiennes," p. 361 n. 68.

86. Schich, "Das mittelalterliche Berlin," pp. 216, 242; Ahrens, "Verfassung der Stadt Berlin," p. 87.

87. When southern France suffered natural or artificial grain scarcities, importers turned to Catalonia, Sicily, and, to a lesser extent, Provence; Larenaudie, "Famines en Languedoc," pp. 36–37.

88. But cf. Rösener, *Bauern im Mittelalter*, pp. 144–45.

89. *Bad Year Economics*, p. 65.

90. Huiskes, *Andernach im Mittelalter*, pp. 213–14.

91. Van Werveke, "Famine de l'an 1316," p. 11.

92. Above, chapter 7, text to nn. 196, 202, and text following n. 205.

93. That the curves of mortality were different (cf. Van Houtte, *Geschiedenis van Brugge*, p. 109) is not decisive on this point one way or the other.

94. Verbruggen, "De Getalsterkte van de Ambachten in het Brugse Gemeentleger," pp. 470–71.

95. On the French embargoes of shipments from Languedoc to Flanders in late 1315, see Wauters, *Table chronologique*, 8:606, 610–11; on piracy against carriers of Ypres, Ghent, Ecluse, and other towns that took place along the French Atlantic coast and in ports of call from 1315 through 1321, see "Excerpta e Memoriali Historiarum," pp. 662, 665; Wauters, *Table chronologique*, 8:721, 730, 751–52, and 9:31. Sturler, *Relations politiques*, pp. 239–40, suggests that incidents of this sort, at least involving the goods and business of Brabantine merchants in this period, were "accidental" interruptions to an otherwise fairly stable seaborne commerce; the passages read like special pleading.

96. Above, text to nn. 91–92.

97. Further on hoarding, speculation, and piracy, see below, chapter 9, text to nn. 5–10, 31–33, 50–52, 60–64, 68.

98. Curschmann, *Hungersnöte*, pp. 44, 51. Cf. Marx, *Development of Charity in Medieval Louvain*, p. 5; Nicholas, *Medieval Flanders*, p. 207.

99. Van Werveke, "Famine de l'an 1316," p. 11; Van Houtte, *Geschiedenis van Brugge*, p. 110.

100. See also Carpentier, "Autour de la Peste noire," p. 1076.

101. See Lütge's discussion of the general factors affecting municipal price regulations: "Preispolitik in München im hohen Mittelalter," p. 167. See also Britnell, *Commercialisation of English Society*, pp. 91–92. Cf. Sen's theory of (legal) entitlement as an explanation here: *Poverty and Famines*, pp. 45–51.

102. Cf. Bynum, *Holy Feast and Holy Fast*, pp. 32, 36, 82, 216, 322 n. 25.

103. Cf. Maréchal, *De sociale en politieke Gebondenheid van het Brugse Hospitaalwezen*, pp. 290–91.

104. The implementation of policies like this was in part predicated on the relative ease of controlling the baking industry, which was often spatially concentrated around a central municipal or guild oven and building with shop stalls. For example, this was the case in Göttingen in 1316; Last, "Topographie der Stadt," p. 92. The larger the town, however, the more dispersed (and therefore less controllable) the industry. Cf. below, text to n. 107, on Paris.

105. Van Werveke, "Famine de l'an 1316," pp. 12–14. Cf. Nicholas, *Medieval Flanders*, p. 207.

106. Van Werveke, "Famine de l'an 1316," p. 14 n. 2.

107. "Excerpta e Memoriali Historiarum," p. 663; Lucas, "Great European Famine," p. 361 n. 5. See also "Chronique Rimée attribuée à Geoffroi de Paris," p. 163.

108. John of Trokelowe, *Annales*, p. 93. Cf. Walsingham, *Historia Anglicana*, 1:150, 248. See also, above, chapter 6, text to nn. 35–41 (on rural crime); and below, chapter 9, text to nn. 50–52, 60–64, 68 (on princely anticrime policies).

109. Bartlett, *Making of Europe*, pp. 236, 238–39, and more generally, pp. 197–242.

110. Heinemann, *Pommersches Urkundenbuch*, 5:248–49, no. 2992: "propter morticinia et spolia, que per mortificatores et spoliatores in aggere seu dammo Snellemarket committebantur, ad securitatem uniuscuiusque mercatoris et probi hominis et pro utilitate terre" (12 January 1316).

111. For attacks on burghers of Kiel and Rostock, for example, in the appropriate years, see Willert, *Anfänge und frühe Entwicklung der Städte Kiel, Oldesloe und Plön*, pp. 113, 120; and Meyer-Wittenberge, "Die Rostocker Stadtverfassung," p. 105.

112. The document exists in several editions. See, for example, Wolters, *Codex diplomaticus lossensis*, pp. 217–21, for the relevant section: "chacun [lord and urban government] est tenu, selon son estat, de laburier et d'aider a son povoir, que la choese comune soit en tele manier ordinee et maintenue, que chacun puisse vivre paisiblement, et que ly malfaiteurs soient corrigies de leurs meffais." Lejeune, who invokes the significance of the famine to the establishment of the Peace, cautions about exaggerating the constitutional character of the document; contrary to Gustave Kurth, it did not establish "parliamentary" government. See Lejeune, *Liège et son pays*, pp. 333, 337.

113. At the Trinity Term (midyear) 1318, the English courts adjudicated such a case. Although the motives of the thieves are unknown, they may have been trying to capitalize on the high price of the product in London at the time. See Arnold, *Select Cases of Trespass*, 1:38.

114. Gilliodts-Van Severen, *Cartulaire de l'ancienne estaple de Bruges*, 1:142, no. 202.

115. The earliest mention of the Butter Warehouse in the town accounts is in 1282; ibid., 6:274–75.

116. Ibid., p. 277.

117. Curschmann, *Hungersnöte*, p. 214: they suffered "van smachte."

118. Ibid., p. 210: "quidam famelici vivi intraverunt sepulcra in quibusdam locis darent finem poenis suis."

119. For various incidents, see Lodewijk Van Velthem, *Voortzetting van den Spiegel Historiael*, 3:220; and Hanawalt, *Growing Up in Medieval London*, pp. 18, 66.

120. Curschmann, *Hungersnöte*, pp. 213–14.

121. Ross, "On the Evil Times of Edward II," p. 189, lines 271–75.

122. On the sect and the appropriate documents, see Patschovsky, "Waldenserverfolgung in Schweidnitz," pp. 137–62.

123. Patschovsky, "Strasburger Beginenverfolgungen," pp. 92–109.

124. The texts are edited and published in ibid., pp. 127–61.

125. Ibid., pp. 134, 140, 142.

126. I want to thank Professor Michael Curschmann for clarifying the probable meaning of the phrase for me.

127. Lodewijk Van Velthem, *Voortzetting van den Spiegel Historiael*, 3:219.

128. Borgnet and Bormans, *Ly Myreur des histors*, 6:222.

129. Uitz, "Der Kampf um kommunale Autonomie in Magdeburg," p. 320.

130. *Geschichte der Stadt Magdeburg*, p. 58.

131. According to Labande and Vernier who published their catalog of the available records in 1891, *Inventaire sommaire des archives communales . . . Verdun*, pp. xxxiv–xxxvi.

132. Prou and d'Auriac, *Actes et comptes*, p. 245.

133. Lalou, "Révoltes contre le pouvoir," pp. 170–80.

134. Diegerick, *Inventaire analytique*, 7:53, no. 2203.

135. Giry, *Histoire de la ville de Saint-Omer*, p. 462, no. 82.

136. Espinas, *Vie urbaine de Douai*, 2:38–40.

137. Above, text to n. 62.

138. The information that follows comes from the records of the adjudication of the uprising published in Espinas, *Vie urbaine de Douai*, 4:150–53, no. 1006.

CHAPTER 9
THE POLICIES OF PRINCES

1. The use of the word *state* is merely shorthand for duchy, principality, kingdom, or empire, as the case may be, and is not meant to imply any strong Weberian definition of state or indeed any strict similarity to the more complex governments of later periods.

2. Above, chapter 5, text to nn. 52–57.

3. Zadora-Rio, "Parcs à gibier et garennes à lapins," p. 134.

4. Duplès-Agier, "Ordonnances inédites de Philippe le Bel et de Philippe le Long," pp. 54–55.

5. See, for example, "Chronique Rimée attribuée à Geoffroi de Paris," p. 163; and below, text to nn. 7, 9–10.

6. *Ordonnances*, 1:606–8.

7. Schmitz, *Faktoren der Preisbildung*, pp. 41–42.

8. Above, chapter 3, text to n. 64.

9. Cf. for ancient interventions of a similar nature, Garnsey, *Famine and Food Supply*, pp. 74–78.

10. *Ordonnances*, 1:606–8.

11. Ibid., pp. 605–6 (7 August 1315).

12. Sneller and Unger, *Bronnen tot de Geschiedenis van den Handel met Frankrijk*, pp. 6–7, nos. 14, 17 (also Wauters, *Table chronologique*, 8:606, 610–11).

13. Wauters, *Table chronologique*, 8:622.

14. *Ordonnances*, 1:619–20.

15. Wauters, *Table chronologique*, 8:637.

16. Ibid., p. 641.

17. Lalou, "Maître Pierre de Chalon," p. 103 n. 41 (cited from an unpublished manuscript, Paris, Bibliothèque nationale fr. 2833, fol. 105).

18. *Ordonnances*, 1:608–9.

19. Ibid., p. 641, cap. 11.

20. My description of the Pastoureaux draws on information assembled in Jordan, *French Monarchy and the Jews*, pp. 243–45; and Barber, "Pastoureaux of 1320," pp. 143–66. An anonymous fourteenth-century chronicler of Valenciennes records that discontent among the shepherds broke out as early as 1316, and this may point to seething rural hostility in the worst year of mortality, but his report is complicated by a number of other apparently erroneous comments on the unrest. For the text see Delcambre, "Chronique Valenciennoise," p. 61; on the complications, see the editor's remarks, n. 6, on the same page.

21. Above, chapter 6, text to n. 20.

22. "Chronique Rimée attribuée à Geoffroi de Paris," p. 162. See also Artonne, *Mouvement de 1314*, pp. 74, 91, 182–84.

23. The observations on the leper scare are drawn from materials discussed in Jordan, *French Monarchy and the Jews*, pp. 245–46, and Jordan, "Home Again: The Jews in the Kingdom of France."

24. Cf. Jeanne's "Société rurale face à la lèpre," pp. 91–106, a thin article but one that makes a plausible case for tying even more generalized persecution of lepers to the bad times beginning in 1315 (his case study is based on Norman records). Baehrel, "Haine de classe en temps d'épidémie," pp. 351–60, documented a similar tendency to imagine poisoning plots in the great cholera epidemic of 1831–1832.

25. Cf. Rogers, *History of Agriculture and Prices*, 1:197.

26. Mate, "High Prices in Early Fourteenth-Century England," p. 10.

27. Above, chapter 1, text to n. 61.

28. The argument here is based on modern observations of the effect of weather on traditionally raised sheep (above, chapter 1, text to n. 62, and chapter 2, text to nn. 107–8).

29. Sharpe, *Calendar of Letter Books*, pp. 71–73; John of Trokelowe, *Annales*, pp. 92–93, 96–98; *Anonimalle Chronicle*, pp. 88–91; "Annales Londonienses," pp. 233, 237, 240–41. Cf. Walsingham, *Historia Anglicana*, 1:144–45, 147, 248. See also Lucas, "Great European Famine," pp. 346, 370–71; Prestwich, *Three Edwards*, p. 247

30. Schmitz, *Faktoren der Preisbildung*, p. 54. See also with respect to this attitude in towns, above, chapter 8, text to nn. 101–2.

31. Schmitz, *Faktoren der Preisbildung*, pp. 41–42.

32. Hardy, *Register of Richard de Kellawe*, 2:1118–20; Reynolds, *Registers of Roger Martival*, no. 40.

33. Reynolds, *Registers of Roger Martival*, no. 40.

34. The tradition was of ancient pedigree; cf. Garnsey, *Famine and Food Supply*, pp. 70–74.

35. Below, text to nn. 89–95.

36. Sadourny, "Transports sur la Seine," pp. 240–42.

37. *Olim*, vol. 3, pt. 1, pp. 193–94. The scoundrels, including a not unimportant royal functionary who may have known the government's intentions, were discovered; administrative housecleaning occurred in the wake of the discovery. For another take on the importance of the grain trade in Rouen, see Lillich, *Armor*

of Light, pp. 71–72, where she discusses local depictions in stained glass of Rouen longshoremen tackling grain shipments.

38. Kershaw, "Great Famine," p. 9.

39. Bain, *Calendar of Documents Relating to Scotland*, 3:99, no. 519.

40. Villani, *Historie Fiorentine*, as cited in Lucas, "Great European Famine," p. 372. Scholars like Lucas also draw on the English administrative records, such as the *Patent Rolls*, in this case those for 1313–1317, pp. 466, 501–2, 571–72. Naudé, *Getreidehandelspolitik*, 1:71; Arnold, *Famine*, p. 105.

41. Above, chapter 8, text to n. 71.

42. Cassard, "Marins bretons à Bordeaux," pp. 381, 383, 389, estimates that 20–25 percent of all carriage from Girondin ports as a whole in the first decade of the fourteenth century was in Breton hands, with Normans playing an important part; English carriers, however, dominated at Bordeaux itself. See also on English carriers, Lucas, "Great European Famine," pp. 357, 371–72; Prestwich, *Three Edwards*, p. 247.

43. Bain, *Calendar of Documents Relating to Scotland*, 3:104–5, nos. 542, 544; p. 110, no. 575; p. 112, no. 588.

44. Schaube, "Anfänge der Venezianischer Galeerenfahrten," pp. 46, 49–55 (citing the *Patent Rolls* for 1313–1317, p. 510).

45. Bain, *Calendar of Documents Relating to Scotland*, 3:105, no. 544.

46. Above, chapter 8, text to n. 73.

47. Above, chapter 8, text to nn. 79–85.

48. Platt, "Southampton," p. 16.

49. Ruiz, *Crisis and Continuity*, p. 27 n. 16, p. 311 n. 8.

50. Wauters, *Table chronologique*, 8:604–5.

51. Lucas, "Great European Famine," p. 360, summarizes the incidents and the royal response. Cf. Prestwich, *Three Edwards*, p. 248.

52. Lucas, "Great European Famine," p. 360.

53. Cf. Carr, *Medieval Anglesey*, p. 301.

54. On the war, see Nicholson, *Scotland: The Later Middle Ages*, pp. 91–106.

55. Bain, *Calendar of Documents Relating to Scotland*, 3:81, no. 430. Many of the documents cited here and in subsequent notes from the collection edited by Joseph Bain in 1887 have been published elsewhere, but they are conveniently accessible all together in Bain's work. Subsequent editing by Simpson and Galbraith added to the store of relevant records; Simpson and Galbraith also corrected Bain where they thought necessary, but none of the records I am citing needed such correction.

56. Bain, *Calendar of Documents Relating to Scotland*, 3:84–85, no. 452.

57. Ibid., pp. 85–86, no. 455; and below, n. 60.

58. Ibid., pp. 89–90, no. 470.

59. Ibid., pp. 90–91, nos. 473, 477.

60. Simpson and Galbraith, *Calendar of Documents Relating to Scotland*, 5:242–43, nos. 618, 620; Bain, *Calendar of Documents Relating to Scotland*, 3:93, no. 486.

61. Cf. Bain, *Calendar of Documents Relating to Scotland*, 3:105, no. 544; p. 99, no. 519; pp. 104–5, no. 542; p. 110, no. 575; p. 112, no. 588.

62. Ibid., p. 97, no. 511; Simpson and Galbraith, *Calendar of Documents*

Relating to Scotland, 5:244–47, nos. 632, 634, 636–37, 648. (Many of these and related records about the North Sea and Baltic trade and the role of the Hanse, drawn from English archives, are also published in German and Dutch collections, such as Heinemann, *Pommersches Urkundenbuch*, 5:272–73, 287, 290, nos. 3025–26, 3042, 3045; and Smit, *Bronnen tot de Geschiedenis van den Handel*, 1:155–84.) See also Friedland, "Hansische Handelspolitik," p. 91; Platt, "Southampton," p. 13; Bartlett, *Making of Europe*, p. 191.

63. Bain, *Calendar of Documents Relating to Scotland*, 3:104, no. 537; p. 129, no. 679.

64. Cf. Lloyd, *England and the German Hanse*, pp. 26–29.

65. Bain, *Calendar of Documents Relating to Scotland*, 3:99, no. 522; pp. 106–7, no. 553.

66. I am arguing back from information that the elite's concerns rose after 1317 about butchers who had become burghers yet continued to "soil their hands with the offal of animals" and of "the king's *nativi* lurking in the burgh"; Nicholson, *Scotland*, p. 109.

67. Bain, *Calendar of Documents Relating to Scotland*, 3:113, no. 593.

68. Ibid., p. 113, nos. 596–97; p. 115, no. 607.

69. "Annales Londonienses," p. 231.

70. Cf. the evidence inventoried in Saint-Génois, *Inventaire analytique des chartes des comtes de Flandre*, pp. 393–94, 397, 399, nos. 1371–74, 1382, 1384, 1389–90, on injuries suffered by burghers of various Flemish towns, including Ostend, Dunkirk, Ghent, Ecluse, to goods and crews on ships operating in the North Sea and along the English coast.

71. Lucas, "Great European Famine," pp. 372–73. Masschaele, "Transport Costs in Medieval England," pp. 266–79, appears to believe that purveyors sought out the lowest market prices for goods and transport, not that they set prices or confiscated goods without compensation. In his formulation they were "price-takers," not "price-makers" (p. 273). I remain unconvinced, particularly since the "precise nature of the accounting procedure" of the sheriffs' purveyance accounts, on which he bases his argument, "has yet to be established" (p. 268 n. 9). Indeed, if instead of being price-takers, the purveyors were price-makers, then Masschaele's more general (and counterintuitive) conclusion in his article— namely, that land transport costs were relatively less in the thirteenth and fourteenth centuries than in the eighteenth—would fail.

72. See, for example, Michael Prestwich's remarks on an attack on a northern delegation including two cardinals on 1 September 1317, which he terms "in part the result of the confused and lawless state of the north of England, ravaged by Scottish raids and afflicted by poor harvests followed by famine. It also had roots in the disaffection of a group of northern knights in the king's service. The atmosphere in Edward's household was embittered and overheated, and the events at Rushyford [where the attack took place] illustrate the consequences of factional disputes in an unhappy court" (Prestwich, "Gilbert de Middleton," p. 194).

73. Donnelly, "Thomas of Coldingham," p. 120.

74. Maddicott, *English Peasantry*, p. 7.

75. Fraser, *Northern Petitions*, pp. 135–36. See also Kershaw, *Bolton Priory*, pp. 14–16.

76. Maddicott, *English Peasantry*, p. 14, 73. His basis of comparison is the entire period from 1294 to the late 1330s.

77. But cf. Arnold, *Famine*, p. 84, who raises questions about this generalization (which he attributes to Slicher van Bath).

78. Above, chapter 5, text to nn. 59–66.

79. Maddicott, *English Peasantry*, pp. 15, 69–71, 75. Cf. Kershaw, "Great Famine," p. 47; Ormrod, "Crown and the English Economy," pp. 149–83.

80. Donnelly, "Thomas of Coldingham," p. 120.

81. The explanation for the decline of customs income is in dispute and, given the imprecise and fragmentary character of the data, cannot, I think, be resolved at present. See, most recently, Ormrod, "Crown and the English Economy," p. 171. Cf. Lloyd, "Overseas Trade and the English Money Supply," pp. 103–5; Kershaw, "Great Famine," pp. 22–24; Baker, *English Customs Service*, p. 59.

82. Ormrod, "Political Theory in Practice," pp. 207, 210. Further on these and similar measures, especially with regard to the crown's policy toward Hanse traders, see Peters, *Hansekaufleute als Gläubiger*, pp. 82–86.

83. Cf. Smith, "History, Typology and Homily," pp. 152–54.

84. Ibid., p. 152, on criticism of taxes on the clergy during the famine in England; the ancient pharaoh had not taxed the lands of the priests to provide reserves for the biblical famine.

85. Maillefer, "Front pionnier aux marges septentrionales," pp. 330–32.

86. "Chronica Erici Olai, Decani Upsaliensis," p. 92: "post multas angustias et afflictiones bellorum et oppressionum, talliarum et graviminum."

87. Above, chapter 1, text to nn. 83–84, and chapter 6, text to n. 26.

88. Helle, "Neuste norwegische Forschungen über deutsche Kaufleute," pp. 29, 32.

89. For background on the Baltic trade in the late thirteenth and early fourteenth centuries, see Kehn, "Der Oderraum und seine Beziehungen zur Hanse," pp. 89–109.

90. Ditchburn, "Trade with Northern Europe," pp. 162, 165.

91. Hamburg's exports of rye and timber were already strongly inclined toward Flanders by the end of the thirteenth century (Richter, "Hamburgs Frühzeit bis 1300," pp. 90–91), but on the general point, see Naudé, *Getreidehandelspolitik*, 1:208, 233–36.

92. Naudé, *Getreidehandelspolitik*, 1:213.

93. Cf. ibid.

94. Ibid., p. 70.

95. Cf. Gras, *Evolution of the English Corn Market*, pp. 59–61.

96. Naudé, *Getreidehandelspolitik*, 1:232; Stoob, "Hansische Westpolitik," p. 8.

97. Cf. Hoffmann, "Lübeck im Hoch- und Spätmittelalter," pp. 188–216.

98. Ślaski, "Die dänisch-polnischen Beziehungen," p. 83.

99. Ibid. For a more extensive treatment of the events culminating in this invasion—that is, of the foreign policy initiatives of the Danish king, Erik VI Menved—see Andersson, *Erik Menved och Venden*.

100. Above, chapter 1, text to n. 10.

101. Rennkamp, *Studien zum deutsch-russischen Handel*, pp. 171, 247. Even Hamburg, though far to the west, participated in the eastern Baltic trade; Brandt, "Hamburger Kaufleute," pp. 1–28.

102. For the general point, see Naudé, *Getreidehandelspolitik*, 1:211, 213, 228–30, 241. But Magdeburg, for example, yielded pride of place in the eastern Baltic trade to Lübeck and consequently was oriented more westerly (toward Bruges) and southwesterly; *Geschichte der Stadt Magdeburg*, p. 45. See also above on the marketing of Berlin rye, also in a westerly direction, chapter 3, text to n. 53.

103. Naudé, *Getreidehandelspolitik*, 1:208.

104. The debate raged in the 1970s and 1980s with Nedkvitne in a series of articles stressing dependence ("Omfanget av Tørrfiskeksporten," pp. 340–55; "Stapelreguleringer, Handelsveier og Varekvanta," pp. 53–92) and Lunden demurring, to the point of rejection ("Tørrfiskeksporten frå Bergen," pp. 245–88; "Kornavl og Pest," pp. 399–413).

105. Helle, "Anglo-Norwegian Relations," pp. 103–4; Schreiner, "Bemerkungen zum Hanse-Norwegen-Problem," p. 67.

106. Gelsinger, "Norwegian Jurisdiction over Lübeck," pp. 242–57; Gelsinger, "A Thirteenth-Century Norwegian-Castilian Alliance," pp. 55–80.

107. Above, text to n. 85.

108. Helle, "Neuste norwegische Forschungen über deutsche Kaufleute," p. 35.

109. Gelsinger, "A Thirteenth-Century Norwegian-Castilian Alliance," p. 68; cf. Naudé, *Getreidehandelspolitik*, 1:208–10.

110. Naudé, *Getreidehandelspolitik*, 1:241.

111. Ibid., p. 210; Abel, *Agricultural Fluctuations*, p.39 (citing Naudé); Nedkvitne, "Omfanget av Tørrfiskeksporten," p. 348. Cf. Jongman and Dekker, "Public Intervention in the Food Supply," p. 118.

112. Richter, "Hamburgs Frühzeit bis 1300," p. 92; *Geschichte der Stadt Magdeburg*, p. 45.

113. Richter, *Untersuchungen zur Hamburger Wirtschafts- und Sozialgeschichte*, pp. 85–86.

EPILOGUE

1. Ravensdale, "Population Changes," pp. 206–7.

2. Maddicott, "Poems of Social Protest," p. 142, analyzes the poem. Editions are available in Wright, *Political Songs*, pp. 32–45, and Ross, "On the Evil Times of Edward II," pp. 173–93.

3. Maddicott, "Poems of Social Protest," p. 144.

4. Ross, "On the Evil Times of Edward II," p. 173.

5. Although it is disputed, I accept the attribution to Langland; see Donaldson, "Langland, William," p. 330.

6. For a convenient list of editions of the various versions, see ibid., p. 337.

7. Pearsall, "Poverty and Poor People in *Piers Plowman*," pp. 167–85.

8. Kaske, "Character of Hunger in *Piers Plowman*," pp. 187–97; Trower,

"Figure of Hunger in *Piers Plowman*," p. 242; Du Boulay, *The England of "Piers Plowman,"* pp. 42–43.

9. Kaske, "Character of Hunger in *Piers Plowman*," pp. 187–97.

10. Trower, "Figure of Hunger in *Piers Plowman*," pp. 239 n. 3, 255.

11. Cf. ibid., p. 240.

12. "His wreche and his lore," Wright, *Political Songs*, pp. 341–42, lines 402–8.

13. Düll, *Die Inschriften der Stadt Oppenheim*, p. 7, no. 7 (see also the photographs appended to Düll's compilation). An early-twentieth-century local scholar inexplicably referred the stone to the year 1313. I do not know on what basis, other than a simple error. Düll and other scholars read and accept the 1317 date, as I do on the basis of my examination of the photograph supplied by Düll; see also Azzola and Azzola, "Eine Rillung aussen an der Katherinenkirche zu Oppenheim," p. 154.

14. See the reference to Polius in Düll, *Die Inschriften der Stadt Oppenheim*, p. 7, no. 7.

15. Raftis, *Estates of Ramsey Abbey*, p. 146.

16. Mate, "Estates of Canterbury Priory," pp. 1–30.

17. Hatcher, *Rural Economy and Society*, p. 85.

18. *Agrarian History*, 2:511; Hallam, *Rural England*, p. 16. Cf. Day, *Medieval Market Economy*, p. 188.

19. Saul, *Knights and Esquires*, p. 229.

20. Dyer, "Changes in Diet in the Late Middle Ages," pp. 21–37. Whether by modern nutritional or general medical standards this constituted improvement is not the point—even if we could tell (which we cannot); pp. 36–37.

21. Above, chapter 7.

22. Butte, *Geschichte Dresdens*, p. 61.

23. Above, chapter 7, text to nn. 106–7, 134.

24. Because "energy cost of growth [in all animals] is high"; Rivers, "Nutritional Biology of Famine," p. 61.

25. Ibid., p. 62.

26. Ibid.

27. The best work on the Black Death is Biraben's *Les Hommes et la peste*. Ziegler, *Black Death*, can also be consulted with profit. The relatively low rates of mortality in Flanders during the Black Death have always puzzled scholars. Even if my suggestion is correct, the case of (putatively) high mortality in Tournai in 1316 *and* in the Black Death (chapter 7, text to nn. 203–5) would remain difficult to explain.

28. Blum, *End of the Old Order*, p. 243.

29. Arnold, *Famine*, p. 130.

30. Carlyle, *Sartor Resartus*, p. 172.

31. Dickens, *A Christmas Carol*, pp. 117–20.

32. Jamie Weiss, "I Know It Can," a contemporary famine poem, in *Poets for Africa*, p. 139.

BIBLIOGRAPHY

PRIMARY SOURCES: MANUSCRIPT

Full references to manuscripts (locations, descriptions, and shelf numbers) are provided in the appropriate notes when the manuscripts are cited for the first time.

PRIMARY SOURCES (INCLUDING INVENTORIES): PRINTED

Acht, Peter, ed. *Regesten Kaiser Ludwigs des Bayern (1314–1347)*. Cologne, Weimar, and Vienna, 1991.

Anemüller, Ernst, ed. *Urkundenbuch des Klosters Paulinzelle*. Vol. 2, *1314–1534*. Thüringische Geschichtsquellen, 4. Jena, 1905.

"Annales Londonienses." In *Chronicles of the Reigns of Edward I and Edward II*, edited by W. Stubbs, 1:1–251. 2 vols. Rolls Series. London, 1882–1883.

"Annales monasterii de Bermundeseia." In *Annales monastici*, edited by H. Luard, vol. 3. Rolls Series. London, 1866.

"Annales Paulini." In *Chronicles of the Reigns of Edward I and Edward II*, edited by W. Stubbs, 1:253–370. 2 vols. Rolls Series. London, 1882–1883.

Annales suecici medii aevi. Edited by G. Paulsson. Bibliotheca Historica Lundensis. Lund, 1974.

The Anonimalle Chronicle, 1307–1334. Edited by W. Childs and J. Taylor. Yorkshire Archaeological Society Record Series, 147. Leeds, 1991.

"Anonymi Archi-Diaconi Gneznensis Brevior Chronica Cracovie." In *Silesiacarum rerum scriptores*, pt. 2, pp. 78–155. Leipzig, 1729–1732.

Arnold, Morris, ed. *Select Cases of Trespass from the King's Courts, 1307–1399*. 2 vols. London, 1984–1987.

Baier, Rudolf, ed. "Bruchstücke einer stralsundischen Chronik." *Pommersche Jahrbücher* 1 (1900): 51–76.

Bain, Joseph, ed. *Calendar of Documents Relating to Scotland*. Vol. 3, *1307–1357*. Edinburgh, 1887.

Baluze, Etienne. *Vitae paparum avenionensium*. Vol. 1. Edited by G. Mollat. Paris, 1914.

Baur, Ludwig, ed. *Hessische Urkunden*. 5 vols. Darmstadt, 1860–1873. Vol. 6, index, 1979.

Blanchard, René, Ed. *Inventaire sommaire des archives communales antérieures à 1790: Ville de Nantes*. Vol. 3. Nantes, 1919.

Bock, Friedrich, Ed. "Studien zur Registrierung der politischen Briefe und der allgemeinen Verwaltungssachen Johanns XXII." *Quellen und Forschungen aus italienischen Archiven und Bibliotheken* 30 (1940): 137–88.

Bohmbach, Jürgen, and Bernd-Ulrich Hucker, eds. *Urkundenbuch zur Geschichte der Stadt Bremerhaven*. Vol. 1, *Lehe und Vieland im Mittelalter 1072–1500*. Bremerhaven, 1982.

Borgnet, A., and Stanislas Bormans, eds. "La Geste de Liège." In *Ly Myreur des histors, chronique de Jean des Preis dit d'Outremeuse*. 7 vols. Brussels, 1864–1887.

———. *Ly Myreur des histors, chronique de Jean des Preis dit d'Outremeuse*. 7 vols. Brussels, 1864–1887.

"Brabandsche Kronijk." In *Chroniques de Brabant et de Flandre*, edited by C. Piot, pp. 49–62. Brussels, 1879.

Brosius, Dieter, ed. *Urkundenbuch des Klosters Scharnebeck*. Hildesheim, 1979.

Brouette, Emile, ed. "Chartes et documents de l'abbaye d'Argenton à Lonzée." *Académie royale de Belgique: Bulletin de la Commission royale d'histoire* 115 (1950): 297–381.

Brouwers, D.-D., ed. "Documents relatifs à l'Hôpital St-Julien de Liége." *Chronique archéologique du Pays de Liége* 1 (1906): 37–40.

Bruchet, Max, ed. *Inventaire sommaire des archives communales antérieures à 1790: Ville de Lille*. Lille, 1926.

Brucker, Jean-Charles, ed. *Inventaire sommaire des archives communales de la ville de Strasbourg antérieures à 1790: Série AA*. Pt. 1. Strasbourg, 1878.

Brugmans, H., ed. "De Kroniek van het Klooster Aduard." *Bijdragen en Mededeellingen van het Historisch Genootschap* 23 (1902): 1–188.

"Chronica Aegidii li Muisis." In *Recueil des chroniques de Flandre*, edited by J.-J. De Smet, 2:93–293. 4 vols. Brussels, 1837–1865.

"Chronica de gestis principum." In *Monumenta Germaniae Historica, Scriptores rerum germanicarum: Chronicae bavaricae saeculi XIV*, pp. 1–104. Hanover and Leipzig, 1918.

"Chronica Erici Olai, Decani Upsaliensis." In *Scriptores rerum svecicarum medii aevi*, edited by Ericus Fant et al., vol. 2, pt. 1, pp. 1–166. 3 vols. Upsala, 1818–1876.

"Chronica Laurentii Petri, Archiepiscopi Upsaliensis." In *Scriptores rerum svecicarum medii aevi*, edited by Ericus Fant et al., vol. 2, pt. 2, pp. 1–160. 3 vols. Upsala, 1818–1876.

"Chronica Ludovici imperatoris quarti." In *Monumenta Germaniae Historica, Scriptores rerum germanicarum: Chronicae bavaricae saeculi XIV*, pp. 105–38. Hanover and Leipzig, 1918.

"Chronicon Aegidii Li Muisis, abbatis Sancti-Martini Tornacensis, alterum." In *Recueil des chroniques de Flandre*, edited by J.-J. De Smet, 2:305–448. 4 vols. Brussels, 1837–1865.

"Chronicon comitum Flandrensium." In *Recueil des chroniques de Flandre*, edited by J.-J. De Smet, 1:34–257. 4 vols. Brussels, 1837–1865.

"Chronicon Girardi de Fracheto et Anonyma ejusdem Operis Continuatio." In *Recueil des historiens des Gaules et de la France*, edited by M. Bouquet et al., 21:1–70. 24 vols. Paris, 1738–1904.

"Chronicon Jacobi Muevin." In *Recueil des chroniques de Flandre*, edited by J.-J. De Smet, 2:449–71. 4 vols. Brussels, 1837–1865.

"Chronijcke van Nederlant, van den jaere 1027 tot den jaere 1525." In *Chroniques de Brabant et de Flandre*, edited by C. Piot, pp. 1–48. Brussels, 1879.

"Chronique Abrégée de Guillaume de Nangis." In *Recueil des historiens des Gaules et de la France*, edited by M. Bouquet et al., 20:649–53. 24 vols. Paris, 1738–1904.

Chronique de Robert de Torigni. Edited by L. Delisle. 2 vols. Rouen, 1872–1873.

"Chronique des Pays-Bas, d'Angleterre et de Tournai." In *Recueil des chroniques de Flandre,* edited by J.-J. De Smet, 3:111–570. 4 vols. Brussels, 1837–1865.

"Chronique Rimée attribuée à Geoffroi de Paris." In *Recueil des historiens des Gaules et de la France,* edited by M. Bouquet et al., 22:87–166. 24 vols. Paris, 1738–1904.

"Chroniques de Saint-Denis." In *Recueil des historiens des Gaules et de la France,* edited by M. Bouquet et al., 20:654–724. 24 vols. Paris, 1738–1904.

"Chronologia ab anno 266 ad 1430." In *Scriptores rerum svecicarum medii aevi,* edited by Ericus Fant et al., vol. 1, pt. 1, pp. 22–32. 3 vols. Upsala, 1818–1876.

"Chronologia Vetusta ab anno 1298 ad ann. 1473." In *Scriptores rerum svecicarum medii aevi,* edited by Ericus Fant et al., vol. 1, pt. 1, pp. 92–99. 3 vols. Upsala, 1818–1876.

"Chronycke van Nederlant, besonderlyck der stadt Antwerpen, sedert den jaere 1097 tot den jaere 1565." In *Chroniques de Brabant et de Flandre,* edited by C. Piot, pp. 71–172. Brussels, 1879.

Clanchy, Michael, ed. *The Roll and Writ File of the Berkshire Eyre of 1248.* London, 1973.

"Continuatio Chronici Guillelmi de Nangiaco." In *Recueil des historiens des Gaules et de la France,* edited by M. Bouquet et al., 20:583–646. 24 vols. Paris, 1738–1904.

Cowan, Ian, et al., eds. *The Knights of St John of Jerusalem in Scotland.* Edinburgh, 1983.

Cronica et cartularium monasterii de Dunis. Bruges, 1864.

Curschmann, Fritz, comp. *Hungersnöte im Mittelalter. Ein Beitrag zur deutschen Wirtschaftsgeschichte des 8. bis 13. Jahrhunderts.* Leipziger Studien aus dem Gebiet der Geschichte, 6. Leipzig, 1900.

De Dynter, Edmond. "Breve chronicon Brabantinum." In *Chronique des ducs de Brabant,* edited by P. De Ram, 1:55–60. 3 vols. Brussels, 1854–1860.

Delcambre, Etienne, ed. "Une Chronique Valenciennoise inédite." *Académie royale de Belgique: Bulletin de la Commission royale d'histoire* 94 (1930): 1–102.

De Ram, P., ed. *Joannis Molani in Academia lovaniensi s. theologiae doctoris et professoris Historiae lovanensium, libri XIV.* 2 vols. Brussels, 1861.

"Descriptio de origine conventus, postea abbatiae Trunchiniensis." In *Recueil des chroniques de Flandre,* edited by J.-J. De Smet, 1:589–700. 4 vols. Brussels, 1837–1865.

Des Marez, Guillaume, and E. De Sagher. *Comptes de la ville d'Ypres de 1267 à 1329.* 2 vols. Brussels, 1909–1913.

Despy, Georges, and André Uyttebrouck, eds. *Inventaire des archives de l'abbaye de La Ramée à Jauchelette.* Brussels, 1970.

Devillers, Léopold, ed. *Description analytique de cartulaires et de chartriers accompagnée du texte de documents utiles à l'histoire du Hainaut.* 8 vols. Mons, 1865–1878.

D'Haenens, Albert, ed. "Une Oeuvre à restituer à Gilles Li Muisis: La Chronique dite de Jacques Muevin." *Académie royale de Belgique: Bulletin de la Commission royale d'histoire* 127 (1961): 1–32.

Diegerick, I., ed. *Inventaire analytique et chronologique des chartes et documents appartenant aux Archives de la ville d'Ypres.* 7 vols. Bruges, 1853–1868.

Diemar, Hermann, ed. *Die Chroniken des Wigand Gerstenberg von Frankenberg.* Marburg, 1909.

Düll, Siegrid, ed. *Die Inschriften der Stadt Oppenheim.* Deutschen Inschriften, 23. Wiesbaden, 1984.

Duplès-Agier, H., ed. "Ordonnances inédites de Philippe le Bel et de Philippe le Long, sur la police de la pêche fluviale." *Bibliothèque de l'Ecole de Chartes* 14 (1853): 43–55.

Dupont, Gustave, ed. *Le Registre de l'Officialité de l'abbaye de Cerisy.* Caen, 1880.

Ebendorfer, Thomas. *Chronica Austriae.* Edited by A. Lhotsky. Berlin and Zurich, 1967.

"E Chronici Rotomagensis Continuatione." In *Recueil des historiens des Gaules et de la France,* edited by M. Bouquet et al., 23:343–50. 24 vols. Paris, 1738–1904.

"E Chronico Anonymi Cadomensis." In *Recueil des historiens des Gaules et de la France,* edited by M. Bouquet et al., 22:22–26. 24 vols. Paris, 1738–1904.

Emmius, Ubbo. *Friesische Geschichte.* Translated by E. von Reeken. 7 vols. Frankfurt-am-Main, 1981–1986.

Engel, Franz, and Heinrich Lathwesen, eds. *Urkundenbuch des Klosters Möllenbeck bei Rinteln.* 2 vols. in 3 pts. Rinteln, 1965–1969.

"Epicedium: De Erico Sudermanniae et Valdemaro Finlandiae Duce." In *Scriptores rerum svecicarum medii aevi,* edited by Ericus Fant et al., vol. 2, pt. 2, p. 172. 3 vols. Upsala, 1818–1876.

"Ex Anonymo Regum Franciae Chronico." In *Recueil des historiens des Gaules et de la France,* edited by M. Bouquet et al., 22:16–21. 24 vols. Paris, 1738–1904.

"Excerpta e Memoriali Historiarum, auctore Johanne Parisiensi." In *Recueil des historiens des Gaules et de la France,* edited by M. Bouquet et al., 21:630–76. 24 vols. Paris, 1738–1904.

"Excerpta ex Nicolai Henelii ab Hennenfeld . . . Chronico Ducatus Monsterbergensis." In *Silesiacarum rerum scriptores,* pt. 1, pp. 114–256. Leipzig, 1729–1732.

"Ex Chronico Sancti Stephani Cadomensis." In *Recueil des historiens des Gaules et de la France,* edited by M. Bouquet et al., 23:491–93. 24 vols. Paris, 1738–1904.

"Extrait d'une Chronique Anonyme." In *Recueil des historiens des Gaules et de la France,* edited by M. Bouquet et al., 21:123–30. 24 vols. Paris, 1738–1904.

"Extraits de la Chronique attribuée à Jean Desnouelles." In *Recueil des historiens des Gaules et de la France,* edited by M. Bouquet et al., 21:181–98. 24 vols. Paris, 1738–1904.

"Extraits d'une Chronique Anonyme intitulée Anciennes Chroniques de Flandre." In *Recueil des historiens des Gaules et de la France,* edited by M. Bouquet et al., 22:329–429. 24 vols. Paris, 1738–1904.

"Ex Uticensis Monasterii Annalibus." In *Recueil des historiens des Gaules et de la France,* edited by M. Bouquet et al., 23:480–84. 24 vols. Paris, 1738–1904.

Flores historiarum. Edited by H. Luard. 3 vols. Rolls Series. London, 1890.

"Fragment d'une Chronique Anonyme." In *Recueil des historiens des Gaules et de la France*, edited by M. Bouquet et al., 21:146–58. 24 vols. Paris, 1738–1904.

Franklin, M. J., ed. *The Cartulary of Daventry Priory*. Northampton, 1988.

Fraser, C. M., ed. *Northern Petitions Illustrative of Life in Berwick, Cumbria and Durham in the Fourteenth Century*. Surtees Society, 194. 1981.

The French Chronicle of London. Edited by H. Riley. London, 1863.

Gallia christiana in provincias ecclesiasticas distributa. 16 vols. Paris, 1715–1865.

Gautier, Edouard, and André Lesort, eds. *Ville de Cambrai: Inventaire sommaire des archives communales antérieures à 1790*. Cambrai, 1907.

Gervers, Michael, ed. *The Cartulary of the Knights of St. John of Jerusalem in England*. Oxford, 1982.

Gilliodts-Van Severen, Louis, ed. *Cartulaire de l'ancienne estaple de Bruges*. 6 vols. Bruges, 1904–1909.

Ginsburger, Moses, ed. *Inventaire-sommaire des archives municipales de la ville de Guebwiller antérieures à 1790*. Guebwiller, 1928.

Goffinet, Hippolyte, ed. *Cartulaire de l'abbaye d'Orval*. Brussels, 1879.

Gouvenain, Louis de, and Philippe Vallée, eds. *Inventaire-sommaire des archives communales antérieures à 1790: Ville de Dijon*. Vol. 3. Dijon, 1892.

Hänselmann, Ludwig, and Heinrich Mack, eds. *Urkundenbuch der Stadt Braunschweig*. 4 vols. Braunschweig, 1873–1912. Reprint, Osnabrück, 1975.

Hardy, Thomas, ed. *The Register of Richard de Kellawe, Lord Palatine and Bishop of Durham*. 4 vols. London, 1873–1878.

Harvey, P.D.A., ed. *Manorial Court Records of Cuxham, Oxfordshire, circa 1200–1359*. London, 1976.

Hasse, P., ed. *Schleswig-Holstein-Lauenburgische Regesten und Urkunden*. Vol. 3, *1301–1340*. Hamburg and Leipzig, 1896.

Heinemann, Otto, ed. *Pommersches Urkundenbuch*. Vol. 5, *1311–1320*. Stettin (Szczecin), 1905.

Higden, Ranulf. *Polychronicon*. Edited by C. Babington and J. Lumby. 9 vols. Rolls Series. London, 1865–1886.

Hilton, Rodney, ed. *The Stoneleigh Leger Book*. Oxford, 1960.

Hocquet, Adolphe, comp. "Table des testaments, comptes de tutelle et d'exécution testamentaire reposant aux Archives de Tournai . . . XIVe siècle." *Annales de la Société historique et archéologique de Tournai* 6 (1902): 81–161.

Hoebanx, J.-J., ed. "Documents des XIIIe et XIV siècles concernant les possessions nivelloises dans le bassin du Rhin moyen." *Académie royale de Belgique: Bulletin de la Commission royale d'histoire* 123 (1958): 11–83.

Hopkins, Anthony, ed. *Medieval Neath: Minsters' Accounts 1262–1316*. Gwent, 1988.

Horrox, Rosemary, ed. *Selected Rentals and Accounts of Medieval Hull, 1293–1528*. Leeds, 1983.

Hüffer, Maria, ed. *Bronnen voor de Geschiedenis der Abdij Rijnsburg*. 2 vols. The Hague, 1951.

Hull, P. L., ed. *The Cartulary of Launceston Priory (Lambeth Palace MS. 719): A Calendar*. Devon and Cornwall Record Society 30 (1987).

Inventaire-sommaire des archives communales antérieures à 1790: Mairie de Bergheim. Colmar, 1866.

Jaeger, Julius, ed. *Urkundenbuch der Stadt Duderstadt bis zum Jahre 1500.* Hildesheim, 1885. Reprint, Osnabrück, 1977.

Jaitner, Klaus, ed. *Urkundenbuch des Klosters Ebstorf.* Hildesheim, 1985.

Jean de Jandun. "Deux éloges de la ville de Paris." In *Paris et ses historiens aux XIVe et XVe siècles*, edited by Le Roux de Lincy and L. Tisserand, pp. 1–79. Paris, 1867.

John of Trokelowe. *Annales.* Edited by H. Riley. Rolls Series. London, 1866.

Jordan, William, ed. "Jewish-Christian Relations in Mid-Thirteenth Century France: An Unpublished *Enquête* from Picardy." *Revue des Etudes juives* 138 (1979): 47–55.

Kervyn de Lettenhove, J.-B.-M.-C., ed. "Chronique anonyme conservée dans la Bibliothèque de la ville de Berne." In *Istore et croniques de Flandres*, 1:423–606. Brussels, 1879.

———. *Codex Dunensis sive Diplomatum et chartarum medii aevi amplissima collectio.* Brussels, 1875.

———. *Istore et croniques de Flandres.* 1:1–419. Brussels, 1879.

"Korte Chronijcke van Nederland van den jaere 1285 tot 1436." In *Chroniques de Brabant et de Flandre*, edited by C. Piot, pp. 63–70. Brussels, 1879.

Krieg, Martin, ed. *Das "Chronicon domesticum et gentile" des Heinrich Piel.* Geschichtsquellen des Fürstentums Minden, 4. Münster, 1981.

Kurth, Godefroid, ed. *La Chronique de Jean de Hocsem.* Brussels, 1927.

Labande, Léon-Honoré, and Jules-Joseph Vernier, eds. *Inventaire sommaire des archives communales antérieures à 1790: Ville de Verdun.* Verdun, 1891.

La Nicollière-Teijeiro, Stephane de, ed. *Inventaire sommaire des archives communales antérieures à 1790: Ville de Nantes.* Vol. 1. Nantes, 1888.

Lass, Johannes. *Sammelung einiger Husumischen Nachrichten von anno 1089 bis anno 1700, inclusiue, aus unterschiedenen Manuscripten und Documenten etc.* Holwein, 1750–1753. Reprint, St. Peter-Ording, 1981.

Leidinger, Georg, ed. *Veit Arnpeck: Sämtliche Chroniken.* Quellen und Erörterungen zur bayerischen und deutschen Geschichte, 3. Munich, 1915.

Lemaître, Henri, ed. *Chronique et Annales de Gilles le Muisit, abbé de Saint-Martin de Tournai (1272–1352).* Paris, 1906.

Lex, Léonce, ed. *Inventaire sommaire des archives communales de Fontaines antérieures à 1790.* Mâcon, 1892.

Lodewijk Van Velthem. *Voortzetting van den Spiegel Historiael.* Edited by H. Vander Linden et al. 3 vols. Brussels, 1906–1938.

Mackay, William, ed. *Chronicles of the Frasers.* Edinburgh, 1905.

"Mårkvårdiga Håndelser i Sverige ifrån 1220 till 1552." In *Scriptores rerum svecicarum medii aevi*, edited by Ericus Fant et al., vol. 1, pt. 1, pp. 90–91. 3 vols. Upsala, 1818–1876.

Meinardus, Otto, ed. *Urkundenbuch des Stiftes und der Stadt Hameln bis zum Jahre 1407.* Hannover, 1887. Reprint, Osnabrück, 1977.

Meister, Al, ed. "Niederdeutsche Chroniken aus dem XV. Jahrhundert." *Annalen des historischen Vereins für den Niederrhein* 70 (1901): 43–64.

Menzel, K., and W. Sauer, eds. *Codex Diplomaticus Nassoicus (Nassauisches Urkundenbuch)*. Vol. 1, pt. 3. Wiesbaden, 1887.

Miraei, Aubertus, and Joannes Foppens, eds. *Opera diplomatica et historica* (vols. 1–2) and *Supplementum* (vols. 3–4). 2d ed. Louvain and Brussels, 1723–1748.

Molinier, Auguste, and Emile Molinier, eds. *Chronique normande du XIVe siècle*. Paris, 1882.

Monasticon belge. Edited by U. Berlière et al. Maredsous and elsewhere, 1890–.

Müllner, Johannes. *Die Annalen der Reichstadt Nürnberg von 1623*. Edited by Gerhard Hirschmann. 2 vols. Nuremberg, 1972–1984.

Nessel, Xavier, ed. *Inventaire-sommaire des archives communales antérieures à 1790: Ville de Haguenau*. Haguenau, 1865.

"Nicolai Henelii ab Hennenfeld . . . Annales Silesiae." In *Silesiacarum rerum scriptores*, pt. 2, pp. 197–484. Leipzig, 1729–1732.

"Olai Petri Svenska Chronica." In *Scriptores rerum svecicarum medii aevi*, edited by Ericus Fant et al., vol. 1, pt. 1, pp. 216–348. 3 vols. Upsala, 1818–1876.

Les "Olim" ou Registres des arrêts rendu par la cour du roi, edited by Arthur Beugnot. 3 vols. in 4 parts. Paris, 1839–1848.

Ordonnances des rois de France de la troisième race. 21 vols. Edited by E.-J. Laurière et al. Paris, 1723–1849.

Prou, Maurice, and Jules d'Auriac, eds. *Actes et comptes de la communauté de Provins de l'an 1271 à l'an 1330*. Provins, 1933.

Raeuber, Eugène, ed. *Inventaire des archives de la ville de Strasbourg antérieures à 1790*. Typescript. Paris, Bibliothèque Nationale; Strasbourg, 1949.

Redik, Annelies, ed. *Regesten des Herzogtums Steiermark*. 2 vols. Graz, 1976.

Rees, Una, ed. *The Cartulary of Haughmond Abbey*. Cardiff, 1985.

Reynolds, Susan, ed. *The Registers of Roger Martival, Bishop of Salisbury 1315–1330*. Vol. 3, *Royal Writs*. Torquay, 1965.

Ross, Thomas, ed. "On the Evil Times of Edward II: A New Version from MS Bodley 48." *Anglia* 75 (1957): 173–93.

Rübel, Karl, ed. *Dortmunder Urkundenbuch*. Vol. 1, *899–1340*. Dortmund, 1881.

Ruser, Konrad, ed. *Die Urkunden und Akten der oberdeutschen Städtebünde vom 13. Jahrhundert bis 1549*. Vol. 1, *Vom 13. Jahrhundert bis 1347*. Göttingen, 1979.

"Rymkronyk van Vlaenderen." In *Recueil des chroniques de Flandre*, edited by J.-J. De Smet, 4:587–896. 4 vols. Brussels, 1837–1865.

Saint-Génois, Jules de, ed. *Inventaire analytique des chartes des comtes de Flandre*. Ghent, 1843–1846.

Salimbene de Adam. *The Chronicle of Salimbene de Adam*. Translated by L. Baud et al. Binghamton, N.Y., 1986.

———. *Cronica*. Edited by G. de Scalia. 2 vols. Bari, 1966.

Sax, Peter. *Annales Eyderstadiensium*. Edited by A. Panten. Werke zur Geschichte Nordfrieslands und Dithmarschens, 2. St. Peter-Ording, 1985.

———. *Nova, totius Frisiae septentrionalis, Descriptio*. Edited by A. Panten. Werke zur Geschichte Nordfrieslands und Dithmarschens, 1. St.-Peter-Ording, 1986.

Schmidt, Gustav, ed. *Urkundenbuch des Hochstifts Halberstadt und seiner Bischöfe.* 4 vols. Leipzig, 1883–1889.

Sharpe, Reginald, ed. *Calendar of Letter-Books Preserved among the Archives of the Corporation of the City of London at the Guildhall: Letter Book E.* London, 1903.

"Sigismundi Rositzii Chronica." In *Silesiacarum rerum scriptores,* pt. 1, pp. 64–98 Leipzig, 1729–1732.

Simpson, Grant, and James Galbraith, eds. *Calendar of Documents Relating to Scotland.* Vol. 5, *(Supplementary) A.D. 1108–1516.* [Edinburgh], n.d.

Smit, H. J., ed. *Bronnen tot de Geschiedenis van den Handel met Engeland, Schotland en Ierland.* Vol. 1, *1150–1485.* The Hague, 1928.

———, ed. *De Rekeningen der Graven en Gravinnen uit het Henegouwsche Huis.* 3 vols. Amsterdam and Utrecht, 1924–1939.

Sneller, Zeger, and W. Unger, eds. *Bronnen tot de Geschiedenis van den Handel met Frankrijk.* The Hague, 1930.

Summerson, Henry, ed. *Crown Pleas of the Devon Eyre of 1238. Devon and Cornwall Record Society* 28 (1985).

Sweerts, Franciscus, ed. "Annales belgici Aegidii de Roya." In *Rerum belgicarum annales, chronici et historici,* vol. 1. Frankfurt, 1620.

———, ed. "Ioannis Geerbrandi Leydensis, Carmelitani, Chronicon Hollandiae comitum et episcoporum Ultraiectensium." In *Rerum belgicarum annales, chronici et historici,* vol. 1. Frankfurt, 1620.

———, ed. "Reneri Snoi, Goudani archiatri, De Rebus batavicis." In *Rerum belgicarum annales, chronici et historici,* vol. 1. Frankfurt, 1620.

Thiel, Matthias, ed. *Urkundenbuch des Stifts St. Peter und Alexander zu Aschaffenburg.* Vol. 1, *861–1325.* Aschaffenburg, 1986.

Travers, Emile, ed. *Inventaire-sommaire des archives communales antérieures à 1790: Ville de Béthune.* Béthune, 1878.

Turner, G. J., ed. *Select Pleas of the Forest.* London, 1899.

Vallée, Philippe, ed. *Inventaire-sommaire des archives communales antérieures à 1790: Ville de Dijon.* Dijon, 1900.

Valois, Noël, ed. "Un Plaidoyer du XIVe siècle en faveur des Cisterciens." *Bibliothèque de l'Ecole de chartes* 69 (1908): 352–68.

Van Lokeren, A., ed. *Chartes et documents de l'abbaye de Saint Pierre au Mont Blandin à Gand.* 2 vols. Ghent, 1868–1871.

Van Werveke, Hans, ed. "Bronnenmateriaal uit de Brugse Stadsrekeningen betreffende de Hongersnood van 1316." *Académie royale de Belgique: Bulletin de la Commission royale d'histoire* (Volume jubilaire / Jubileumband) 125 (1959): 431–510.

"Vita Edwardi secundi." In *Chronicles of the Reigns of Edward I and Edward II.* Edited by W. Stubbs. 2 vols. Rolls Series. London, 1882–1883.

"Vriessche Aenteyckening." In *Kleine Oudfriese Kronieken,* edited by P. Gerbenzon, pp. 44–67. Rijksuniversiteit te Utrecht, Teksten en Documenten, 4. Groningen, 1965.

Wagner, Heinrich, ed. *Regesten der Zisterzienserabtei Bildhausen 1158–1525.* Würzburg, 1987.

Walsingham, Thomas. *Historia Anglicana*. Edited by H. Riley. 2 vols. Rolls Series. London, 1863–1864.

Wauters, Alphonse, ed. *Table chronologique des chartes et diplômes imprimés concernant l'histoire de la Belgique*. Vols. 8 and 9. Brussels, 1892–1896.

Weiler, Peter, ed. *Urkundenbuch des Stiftes Xanten*. Vol. 1, *(Vor 590)–1359*. Bonn, 1935.

Wendt, Heinrich. *Geschichte des Welfenfürstentums Grubenhagen, des Amtes und der Stadt Osterode*. Edited by Jörg Leuschner. Hildesheim and elsewhere, 1988.

Westfälisches Urkunden-Buch (or *Urkundenbuch*). Edited by R. Krumbholtz and J. Prinz. Vols. 8 and 9. Münster, 1913–1982.

Wielant, Philippe. "Recueil des antiquités de Flandre." In *Recueil des chroniques de Flandre*, edited by J.-J. De Smet, 4:1–442. 4 vols. Brussels, 1837–1865.

Williams, John, comp. *Observations of Comets from 611 B.C. to A.D. 1640*. 1871. Reprint, Hornchurch, Essex, 1987.

Wisplinghoff, Erich, ed. *Urkunden und Quellen zur Geschichte von Stadt und Abtei Siegburg*. 2 vols. Siegburg, 1985.

Wolters, M., ed. *Codex diplomaticus lossensis ou Recueil et analyse de chartes servant de preuves à l'histoire de l'ancien comté de Looz*. Ghent, 1849.

Wright, Thomas, ed. *The Political Songs of England, from the Reign of John to That of Edward II*. 1839. Reprint, New York and London, 1968.

SECONDARY SOURCES

Abel, Wilhelm. *Agricultural Fluctuations in Europe: From the Thirteenth to the Twentieth Centuries*. Translated by O. Ordish. London, 1980.

———. *Die Wüstungen des ausgehenden Mittelalters*. 2d ed. Stuttgart, 1955.

Aerts, Erik, and Eddy Van Cauwenberghe. "Die Grafschaft Flandern und die sogenannte spätmittelalterliche Depression." In *Europa 1400: Die Krise des Spätmittelalters*, edited by E. Seibt and W. Eberhard, pp. 95–116. Stuttgart, 1984.

Agrarian History of England and Wales. Vol. 2, *1042–1350*. Edited by H. Hallam. Cambridge, 1988.

Ahrens, Karl-Heinz. "Die Verfassung der Stadt Berlin im Mittelalter." In *Bürger, Bauer, Edelmann: Berlin im Mittelalter*, pp. 72–93. Berlin, 1987.

Albier, A. *De l'organisation du crédit en Algérie*. Paris, 1901.

Alexandre, Pierre. *Le Climat en Europe au moyen âge*. Paris, 1987.

Algemene Geschiedenis der Nederlanden. Edited by J. Van Houtte et al. Vol. 3. Utrecht, 1951.

Allen, David. "Excavations at Bierton, 1979." *Records of Buckinghamshire* 28 (1986): 1–120.

Anderlik, Heidemarie. "Entstehung und frühe Entwicklung der havelländischen Kleinstädte." In *Das Havelland im Mittelalter*, edited by W. Ribbe, pp. 383–402. Berliner Historische Studien, 13. Berlin, 1987.

Andersson, Ingvor. *Erik Menved och Venden: Studier i Dansk Utrikespolitik, 1300–1319* (with German summary). Lund, 1954.

Antonow, Alexander. *Burgen des südwestdeutschen Raums im 13. und 14. Jahrhundert unter besonderer Berücksichtigung der Schildmauer.* Veröffentlichung des Alemannischen Instituts Freiburg i. Br., 40. Baden, 1977.

Appleby, Andrew. *Famine in Tudor and Stuart England.* Stanford, 1978.

Arnold, Benjamin. *German Knighthood, 1050–1300.* Oxford, 1985.

Arnold, David. *Famine: Social Crisis and Historical Change.* Oxford, 1988.

Arnoux, M. "Les Métiers de férons dans la Normandie médiévale." *Annales de Normandie* 38 (1988): 334–36.

Artonne, André. *Le Mouvement de 1314 et les chartes provinciales de 1315.* Paris, 1912.

Asch, Jürgen. "Grundherrschaft und Freiheit: Entstehung und Entwicklung der Hägergerichte in Südniedersachsen." *Niedersachsisches Jahrbuch für Landesgeschichte* 50 (1978): 107–92.

Atkin, M. A. "Land Use and Management in the Upland Demesne of the De Lacy Estate of Blackburnshire c. 1300." *Agricultural History Review* 42 (1994): 1–19.

Aubert, Louis. *Les Hôpitaux de Langres: Essai historique des origines à la Revolution.* Dijon, 1913.

Ault, Warren. *Open-Field Husbandry and the Village Community.* Transactions of the American Philosophical Society. Philadelphia, 1965.

———. "The Vill in Medieval England." *Proceedings of the American Philosophical Society* 126 (1982): 188–211.

Avenel, Georges d'. *Histoire economique de la propriété, des salaires, des denrées et de tous les prix en général depuis l'an 1200 jusqu'en l'an 1800.* 4 vols. Paris, 1894–1898.

Azzola, Juliane, and Friedrich Azzola. "Eine Rillung aussen an der Katherinenkirche zu Oppenheim und ihre Deutung als historische Töpferschiene." *Alzeyer Geschichtsblätter* 21 (1986): 154–69.

Bachmann, Christoph. "Zur Entwicklung des Mühlenrechts in Altbayern." *Zeitschrift für bayerische Landesgeschichte* 51 (1988): 719–65.

Bad Year Economics: Cultural Responses to Risk and Uncertainty. Edited by P. Halstead and J. O'Shea. Cambridge, 1989.

Baehrel, René. "La Haine de classe en temps d'épidémie." *Annales: ESC* 7 (1952): 351–60.

Bailey, Mark. "The Concept of the Margin in the Medieval English Economy." *Economic History Review* 42 (1989): 1–17.

———. *A Marginal Economy? East Anglian Breckland in the Later Middle Ages.* Cambridge, 1989.

———. "*Per impetum maris*: Natural Disaster and Economic Decline in Eastern England, 1275–1350." In *Before the Black Death: Studies in the "Crisis" of the Early Fourteenth Century*, edited by B. Campbell, pp. 184–208. Manchester and New York, 1991.

Baker, Alan. "Evidence in the 'Nonarum Inquisitiones' of Contracting Arable Lands during the Early Fourteenth Century." *Economic History Review* 19 (1966): 518–32.

———. "Observations of the Open Fields: The Present Position of Studies in British Field Systems." *Journal of Historical Geography* 5 (1979): 315–23.

Baker, Robert. *The English Customs Service, 1307–1343: A Study of Medieval Administration.* Transactions of the American Philosophical Society. Philadelphia, 1961.

Baldwin, John. *Masters, Princes, and Merchants: The Social Views of Peter the Chanter and His Circle.* 2 vols. Princeton, 1970.

Barbé, Hervé. "L'Aménagement des étangs en Berry (XIII–XVIIIes siècles)." *Cahiers d'archéologie et d'histoire du Berry,* no. 101 (March 1990): 43–48.

Barber, Malcolm. "The Pastoureaux of 1320." *Journal of Ecclesiastical History* 32 (1981): 143–66.

———. *The Trial of the Templars.* Cambridge, 1978.

Barry, T. B. " 'The People of the country . . . dwell scattered': The Pattern of Rural Settlement in Ireland in the Later Middle Ages." In *Settlement in Medieval Ireland: Studies Presented to F. X. Martin, O.S.A.,* edited by J. Bradley, pp. 345–60. Kilkenny, 1988.

Barth, Fredrik. *Human Resources: Social and Cultural Features of the Jebel Marra Project Area.* Bergen, 1988.

Bartlett, Robert. *The Making of Europe: Conquest, Colonization, and Cultural Change 950–1350.* Princeton, 1993.

Baum, Hans-Peter. "Annuities in Late Medieval Hanse Towns." *Business History Review* 59 (1985): 24–48.

Bautier, Robert-Henri. "La Circulation fluviale dans la France médiévale." *Actes du 112e Congrès national des Sociétés savantes: Histoire médiévale et philologie,* 1987, pp. 7–36.

Benker, Gertrud. *Ludwig der Bayer: Ein Wittelsbacher auf dem Kaiserthron, 1282–1347.* Munich, 1980.

Bennett, Judith. *Women in the Medieval English Countryside: Gender and Household in Brigstock before the Plague.* New York and Oxford, 1987.

Bentele, Günther. "Bietigheim im Mittelalter. Von der ersten Nennung 789 bis zur Einführung der Amstverfassung 1506." In *Beiträge zur Geschichte von Siedlung, Dorf und Stadt Bietigheim 789–1989,* pp. 111–216. Schriftenreihe des Archivs der Stadt Bietigheim-Bissingen, 3. Bietigheim-Bissingen, 1989.

Berdecka, Anna. "Lokacje miast małopolskich za Władysława Łokietka (1306–1333): Problematyka i stan badań." *Kawartalnik Historii Kultury Materialnej* 31 (1983): 335–44.

Berman, Constance. "Land Acquisition and the Use of the Mortgage Contract by the Cistercians of Berdoues." *Speculum* 57 (1982): 250–66.

Berner, Rolf. *Siedlungs-, Wirtschafts- und Sozialgeschichte des Artlandes bis zum Ausgang des Mittelalters.* Quakenbrück, 1965.

Biddick, Kathleen. "Missing Links: Taxable Wealth, Markets, and Stratification among Medieval English Peasants." *Journal of Interdisciplinary History* 18 (1987): 277–98.

———. *The Other Economy: Pastoral Husbandry on a Medieval Estate.* Berkeley, 1989.

Biddick, Kathleen, and Catrien Bijleveld. "Agrarian Productivity on the Estates of the Bishopric of Winchester in the Early Thirteenth Century: A Managerial Perspective." In *Land, Labour and Livestock: Historical Studies in European*

Agricultural Productivity, edited by B. Campbell and M. Overton, pp. 95–123. Manchester and New York, 1991.

Bierwirth, Lore. *Siedlung und Wirtschaft im Lande Hadeln: Eine kulturgeographische Untersuchung*. Forschungen zur deutschen Landeskunde, 164. Bad Godesberg, 1967.

Biraben, J.-N. *Les Hommes et la peste en France*. 2 vols. Paris and the Hague, 1975.

Birrell, Jean. "Un Bois convoité: Essington, en Staffordshire, vers 1300." In *Histoire et société: Melanges offerts à Georges Duby*, vol. 2, *Le Tenancier, le fidèle et le citoyen*, pp. 71–79. Aix-en-Provence, 1992.

———. "Common Rights in the Medieval Forest: Disputes and Conflicts in the Thirteenth Century." *Past & Present*, no. 117 (November 1987): 22–49.

———. "Peasant Craftsmen in the Medieval Forest." *Agricultural History Review* 17 (1969): 91–107.

Bishop, M. W. "Burials from the Cemetery of the Hospital of St. Leonard, Newark, Nottinghamshire." *Transactions of the Thoroton Society of Nottinghamshire* 87 (1983): 23–35.

Bittmann, Markus. *Kreditwirtschaft und Finanzierungsmethoden: Studien zu den wirtschaftlichen Verhältnissen des Adels im westlichen Bodenseeraum, 1300–1500*. Vierteljahrschrift für Sozial- und Wirtschaftsgeschichte, Beihefte, 29. Stuttgart, 1991.

Blary, François. *Le Domaine de Chaalis, XIIe–XIVe siècles: Approches archéologiques des établissements agricoles et industriels d'une abbaye cistercienne*. Mémoires de la Section d'Archéologie et d'Histoire de l'Art, 3. Paris, 1989.

Blaschke, Karlheinz. *Geschichte Sachsens im Mittelalter*. Munich, 1990.

Bloch, Marc. *French Rural History*. Translated by J. Sondheimer. Berkeley and Los Angeles, 1966.

———. "Liberté et servitude personelles au moyen âge, particulièrement en France." In *Mélanges historiques*, pp. 286–355. Paris, 1963.

———. *Seigneurie française et manoir anglais*. Paris, 1960.

Blockmans, Wim. "Die Niederlande vor und nach 1400: Eine Gesellschaft in der Krise?" In *Europa 1400: Die Krise des Spätmittelalters*, edited by F. Seibt and W. Eberhard, pp. 117–32. Stuttgart, 1984.

Blockmans, Wim, and W. Prevenier. "Poverty in Flanders and Brabant from the Fourteenth to the Mid–Sixteenth Century: Sources and Problems." *Acta historiae neerlandicae* 10 (1978): 20–57.

Blum, Jerome. *The End of the Old Order in Rural Europe*. Princeton, 1978.

Bockhorst, Wolfgang. *Geschichte des Niederstifts Münster bis 1400*. Veröffentlichungen der Historischen Kommission für Westfalen, 22 / Geschichtliche Arbeiten zur westfälischen Landesforschung. Münster, 1985.

Boenisch, Gerhard. "Anthropologischer Vergleich zwischen der mittelalterlichen und frühneuzeitlichen Bevölkerung Lübecks sowie anderen Populationen Europas." *Lübecker Schriften zur Archäologie und Kulturgeschichte* 21 (1991): 57–142.

Bohm, Eberhard. "Zum Stand der Wüstungsforschung in Brandenburg zwischen Elbe und Oder." *Jahrbuch für die Geschichte Mittel- und Ostdeutschlands* 18 (1969): 289–318.

Bohmbach, Jürgen. "Umfang und Struktur des Braunschweiger Rentenmarktes 1300–1350." *Niedersachsisches Jahrbuch für Landesgeschichte* 41 (1969): 119–33.

Bois, Guy. *The Crisis of Feudalism: Economy and Society in Eastern Normandy c. 1300–1550.* Cambridge, 1984.

Bolton, J. L. *The Medieval English Economy 1150–1500.* London and Totowa, N.J., 1980.

Bond, James. "Rabbits: The Case for Their Medieval Introduction to Britain." *Local Historian* 18 (1988): 53–57.

Bonnassie, Pierre. *From Slavery to Feudalism in South-Western Europe.* Translated by Jean Birrell. Cambridge, 1991.

Bourde de la Rogerie, Henri. "Les Fondations de villes et de bourgs en Bretagne du XIe au XIIIe siècle." *Mémoires de la Société d'histoire et d'archéologie de Bretagne* 9 (1928): 69–106.

Brandt, Ahasver von. "Hamburger Kaufleute in Ostseehandel des 14. Jahrhunderts (bis 1363) nach dem Lübecker Niederstadtbuch." *Zeitschrift des Vereins für Hamburgische Geschichte* 49/50 (1964): 1–28.

Brenner, Robert. "Agrarian Class Structure and Economic Development in Pre-Industrial Europe." *Past & Present*, no. 70 (February 1976): 30–75.

Britnell, R. H. "Commercialisation and Economic Development in England, 1000–1300." In *A Commercialising Economy: England 1086 to c. 1300*, edited by R. Britnell and B. Campbell, pp. 7–26. Manchester and New York, 1995.

———. *The Commercialisation of English Society, 1000–1500.* Cambridge, 1993.

———. "English Markets and Royal Administration before 1200." *Economic History Review* 31 (1978): 183–96.

———. "Essex Markets before 1350." *Essex Archaeology and History* 13 (1981): 15–21.

———. "The Fields and Pastures of Colchester, 1280–1350." *Essex Archaeology and History* 19 (1988): 159–65.

———. *Growth and Decline in Colchester, 1300–1525.* Cambridge, 1986.

———. "King John's Early Grants of Markets and Fairs." *English Historical Review* 94 (1979): 90–96.

———. "Minor Landlords in England and Medieval Agrarian Capitalism." In *Landlords, Peasants and Politics in Medieval England*, edited by T. Aston, pp. 227–46. Cambridge, 1987.

———. "The Proliferation of Markets in England, 1200–1349." *Economic History Review* 34 (1981): 209–21.

Britton, Edward. *The Community of the Vill: A Study in the History of the Family and Village Life in Fourteenth-Century England.* Toronto, 1977.

Buck, Mark. *Politics, Finance and the Church in the Reign of Edward II: Walter Stapledon, Treasurer of England.* Cambridge, 1983.

Bund, Konrad. "Frankfurt am Main im Spätmittelalter 1311–1519." In *Frankfurt am Main: Die Geschichte der Stadt in neun Beiträgen*, pp. 53–149. Veröffentlichungen der Frankfurter historischen Kommission, 17. Sigmaringen, 1991.

Burton, Janet. *The Yorkshire Nunneries in the Twelfth and Thirteenth Centuries.* Borthwick Papers, no. 56. York, 1979.

Butler, L.A.S., and D. H. Evans. "The Cistercian Abbey of Aberconway at Maenan, Gynedd: Excavations in 1968." *Archaeologia Cambrensis* 129 (1980): 37–63.

Butte, Heinrich. *Geschichte Dresdens bis zur Reformationszeit.* Cologne and Graz, 1967.

Bynum, Caroline. *Holy Feast and Holy Fast: The Religious Significance of Food to Medieval Women.* Berkeley and elsewhere, 1987.

Campbell, Bruce. "Agricultural Progress in Medieval England: Some Evidence from Eastern Norfolk." *Economic History Review* 36 (1983): 26–46.

———. "The Diffusion of Vetches in Medieval England." *Economic History Review* 41 (1988): 193–208.

———. "The Extent and Layout of Commonfields in Eastern Norfolk." *Norfolk Archaeology* 38 (1981): 5–32.

———. "Land, Labour, Livestock, and Productivity Trends in English Seignorial Agriculture, 1208–1450." In *Land, Labour and Livestock: Historical Studies in European Agricultural Productivity*, edited by B. Campbell and M. Overton, pp. 144–82. Manchester and New York, 1991.

———. "Measuring the Commercialisation of Seigneurial Agriculture c. 1300." In *A Commercialising Economy: England 1086 to c. 1300*, edited by R. Britnell and B. Campbell, pp. 132–93. Manchester and New York, 1995.

———. "Population Pressure, Inheritance and the Land Market in a Fourteenth-Century Peasant Community." In *Land, Kinship and Life-Cycle*, edited by R. Smith, pp. 87–134. Cambridge, 1984.

Campbell, Bruce, and Mark Overton. "A New Perspective on Medieval and Early Modern Agriculture: Six Centuries of Norfolk Farming, c. 1250–c. 1850." *Past & Present*, no. 141 (November 1993): 38–105.

Camporesi, Piero. *Bread of Dreams: Food and Fantasy in Early Modern Europe.* Translated by D. Gentilcore. Cambridge, 1989.

Carlye, Thomas. *Sartor Resartus.* Edited by K. McSweeney and P. Sabor. Oxford and New York, 1987.

Carpenter, David. "Was There a Crisis of the Knightly Class in the Thirteenth Century? The Oxfordshire Evidence." *English Historical Review* 95 (1980): 721–52.

Carpentier, Elizabeth. "Autour de la Peste noire: Famines et épidémies au XIVe siècle." *Annales: ESC* 17 (1962): 1062–92.

Carr, A. D. *Medieval Anglesey.* Llangefni, 1982.

Cassard, J.-C. "Les Marins bretons à Bordeaux au début du XIVe siècle." *Annales de Bretagne* 86 (1979): 379–97.

———. "Les Premiers immigrés." *Médiévales*, no. 6 (1984): 85–94.

Catane, Moché. "Le Monde intellectuel de Rashi." In *Les Juifs au regard de l'histoire: Mélanges en l'honneur de Bernhard Blumenkranz*, edited by G. Dahan, pp. 63–85. Paris, 1985.

"The Centre for Metropolitan History: A Progress Report." *London Journal* 14 (1989): 68–70.

Chédeville, André. *Chartres et ses campagnes (XIe–XIIIe s.).* Paris, 1973.

Chickering, Roger. "Young Lamprecht: An Essay in Biography and Historiography." *History and Theory* 28 (1989): 198–214.

Cipolla, Carlo. *Before the Industrial Revolution*. 2d ed. New York, 1980.

Ciscato, Antonio. *Gli Ebrei in Padova (1300–1800)*. Padua, 1901.

Clark, Elaine. "Debt Litigation in a Late Medieval English Vill." In *Pathways to Medieval Peasants*, edited by J. Raftis, pp. 247–79. Toronto, 1981.

Clark, Gregory. "The Economics of Exhaustion, the Postan Thesis, and the Agricultural Revolution." *Journal of Economic History* 52 (1992): 61–84.

Cohen, Esther. "Patterns of Crime in Fourteenth-Century Paris." *French Historical Studies* 11 (1980): 307–27.

Coleman, M. Clare. *Downham-in-the-Isle: A Study of an Ecclesiastical Manor in the Thirteenth and Fourteenth Centuries*. Woodbridge, Suffolk, 1984.

Collette, Emile. *Les Foires et marchés à Dijon*. Dijon, 1905.

Contamine, Philippe, et al. *L'Economie médiévale*. Paris, 1993.

Cosgel, Metin. "Risk Sharing in Medieval Agriculture." *Journal of European Economic History* 21 (1992): 99–110.

Cosgrove, Art, ed. *A New History of Ireland*. Vol. 2, *Medieval Ireland 1169–1534*. Oxford, 1987.

Coster, H. P. *De Kroniek van Johannes de Beka: Haar Bronnen en haar eerste Redactie*. Bijdragen van het Instituut voor Middeleeuwsche Geschiedenis der Rijks-Universiteit te Utrecht, 2. Utrecht, 1914.

Crawford, E. Margaret. "Subsistence Crises and Famines in Ireland: A Nutritionist's Views." In *Famine: The Irish Experience 900–1900: Subsistence Crises and Famines in Ireland*, edited by E. Crawford, pp. 198–219. Edinburgh, 1989.

———, ed. "William Wilde's Table of Irish Famines 900–1850." In *Famine: The Irish Experience 900–1900: Subsistence Crises and Famines in Ireland*, edited by E. Crawford, pp. 1–30. Edinburgh, 1989.

Currie, Christopher. "The Early History of the Carp and Its Economic Significance in England." *Agricultural History Review* 39 (1991): 97–107.

———. "Early Vetches in Medieval England: A Note." *Economic History Review* 41 (1988): 114–16.

Dadant, C. P. *First Lessons in Beekeeping*. Rev. ed. Hamilton, Ill., 1946.

Dähne, Eberhard. "Marburg im Mittelalter." In *Marburg: Eine illustrierte Stadtgeschichte*, pp. 9–30. Marburg, 1985.

Davies, Wendy. *Small Worlds: The Village Community in Early Medieval Brittany*. Berkeley and Los Angeles, 1988.

Day, John. *The Medieval Market Economy*. Oxford, 1987.

Decq, Edouard. "L'Administration des eaux et forêts dans le domaine royal en France aux XIVe et XVe siècles" (pts. 1 and 2). *Bibliothèque de l'Ecole de Chartes* 83 (1922): 65–110, 331–61.

Delacour, Jean. *The Waterfowl of the World*. Vol. 1. London, 1954.

Delafosse, Marcel. "Notes d'histoire sociale: Les Vignerons d'Auxerrois (XIVe–XVIe siècles)." *Annales de Bourgogne* 20 (1948): 7–41.

Delisle, Léopold. *Etudes sur la condition de la classe agricole et l'état de l'agriculture en Normandie au moyen-âge*. Paris, 1903.

Delumeau, Jean, and Yves Lequin, eds. *Malheurs des temps: Histoire des fléaux et des calamités en France*. Paris, 1987.

Deppe, Hans-Joachim. "Frühe Spuren der Stadtbildung in Mecklenburg." *Jahrbuch für die Geschichte Mittel- und Ostdeutschlands* 40 (1991): 145–67.

Derville, Alain. "Les Chapelains de Saint-Géry de Cambrai au XIVe siècle." *Le Moyen Age* 95 (1989): 256–78.

———. "Les Draperies flamandes et artésiennes vers 1250–1350." *Revue du Nord* 54 (1972): 353–70.

———. "L'Hôpital Saint-Julien de Cambrai au XIVe siècle: Etude économique." *Revue du Nord* 70 (1988): 285–318.

———. "La Première Révolution des transports continentaux (c. 1000–c. 1300)" *Annales de Bretagne* 85 (1978): 181–205.

———. "Rivières et canaux du Nord/Pas-de-Calais aux époques médiévale et moderne." *Revue du Nord* 72 (1990): 5–22.

De Spiegeler, Pierre. *Les Hôpitaux et l'assistance à Liège (Xe–XVe siècles): Aspects institutionnels et sociaux.* Paris, 1987.

Despy, Georges. "La 'Grande Peste Noire de 1348' a-t-elle touché le roman pays de Brabant?" In *Centenaire du Séminaire d'histoire médiévale de l'Université libre de Bruxelles, 1876–1976,* pp. 195–217. Brussels, 1977.

Detsicas, A. P. "A Salt-Panning Site at Funton Creek." *Archaeologia Cantiana* 101 (1984): 165–68.

Dettling, Karl. *700 Jahre Mühlbach 1290–1990.* Eppinger stadtgeschichtliche Veröffentlichungen, 2. Eppingen, 1990.

DeWindt, Anne. "Redefining the Peasant Community in Medieval England: The Regional Perspective." *Journal of British Studies* 26 (1987): 163–207.

DeWindt, Edwin. *Land and People in Holywell-cum-Needingworth.* Toronto, 1972.

D'Haenens, Albert. *L'Abbaye Saint-Martin de Tournai de 1290 à 1350: Origines, évolution et dénouement d'une crise.* Louvain, 1961.

———. "La Crise des abbayes bénédictines au bas moyen âge: Saint-Martin de Tournai de 1290 à 1350." *Le Moyen Age* 65 (1959): 75–95.

Dherent, Catherine. "Maladies et mortalités à Douai au XIVe siècle." *Actes du 110e Congrès national des Sociétés savantes: Histoire médiévale et philologie,* 1985, pp. 81–92.

Dickens, Charles. *A Christmas Carol.* New York, 1956.

Ditchburn, David. "Trade with Northern Europe, 1297–1540." In *The Scottish Medieval Town,* edited by M. Lynch et al., pp. 161–79. Edinburgh, 1988.

Ditt, Hildegard. "Bevölkerungseinzug und Raumbeziehungen der Stadt Soest in Mittelalter und Neuzeit." In *Soest: Stadt-Territorium-Reich,* edited by G. Köhn, pp. 35–84. Soester Zeitschrift, 92/93; Soester Beiträge, 41. Soest, 1981.

Dochnal, Friedrich. *Chronik von Neustadt an der Haardt.* Meisenheim, 1974.

Dockès, Pierre. *Medieval Slavery and Liberation.* Translated by Arthur Goldhammer. Chicago, 1982.

Dohar, William. *The Black Death and Pastoral Leadership: The Diocese of Hereford in the Fourteenth Century.* Philadelphia, 1995.

Donaldson, E. Talbot. "Langland, William." In *Dictionary of the Middle Ages,* edited by Joseph Strayer, 7:329–37. New York, 1986.

Donnelly, J. "Thomas of Coldingham, Merchant and Burgess of Berwick upon Tweed (died 1316)." *Scottish Historical Review* 59 (1980): 105–25.

Driesch, Angela von den, and Mostefa Kokabi. "Tierknochen aus einem Brunnen der mittelalterlichen Wüstung 'Altstadt' in Villingen." *Fundberichte aus Baden-Württemberg* 4 (1979): 371–90.

Dubled, Henri. "Taille et 'Umgeld' en Alsace au XIIIe siècle." *Vierteljahrschrift für Sozial- und Wirtschaftsgeschichte* 47 (1960): 32–47.

Dubois, Henri. "Techniques et coûts des transports terrestres dans l'espace bourguignon aux XIVe et XVe siècles." *Annales de Bourgogne* 52 (1980): 65–82.

Du Boulay, F.R.H. *The England of "Piers Plowman": William Langland and the Vision of the Fourteenth Century.* Cambridge, 1991.

Duby, Georges. *Rural Economy and Country Life in the Medieval West.* Translated by C. Postan. London, 1968.

Duggan, Lawrence. "Zur Bedeutung des spätmittelalterlichen Kreditsystems für die früneuzeitliche deutsche Geschichte." In *Stände und Gesellschaft im alten Reich*, edited by Georg Schmidt, pp. 201–9. Stuttgart, 1989.

Durand, Marc. "Le Terroir médiéval de Champlieu: Contribution archéologique." *Revue archéologique de Picardie*, nos. 1/2 (1986): 37–94.

Dury, G. H. "Crop Failures on the Winchester Manors, 1232–1349." *Transactions of the Institute of British Geographers* 9 (1984): 401–18.

———. "Crop Failures on the Winchester Manors, 1232–1349: Pseudo-Controversy as Unnecessary." *Transactions of the Institute of British Geographers* 10 (1985): 501–3.

Dyer, Christopher. "Changes in Diet in the Late Middle Ages: The Case of Harvest Workers." *Agricultural History Review* 36 (1988): 21–37.

———. "The Hidden Trade of the Middle Ages: Evidence from the West Midlands of England." *Journal of Historical Geography* 18 (1992): 141–57.

———. *Lords and Peasants in a Changing Society: The Estates of the Bishopric of Worcester 680–1540.* Cambridge, 1980.

———. *Standards of Living in the Later Middle Ages: Social Change in England c. 1200–1520.* Cambridge, 1989.

Eberl, Immo. "Die Stadt Blaubeuren im Spätmittelalter: Zur Entwicklung einer landesherrlichen Kleinstadt." In *Blaubeuren: Die Entwicklung einer Siedlung in Südwestdeutschland*, edited by H. Decker-Hauff and I. Eberl, pp. 177–219. Sigmaringen, 1986.

Edwards, J. F., and B. P. Hindle. "Comment: Inland Water Transportation in Medieval England." *Journal of Historical Geography* 19 (1993): 12–14.

———. "The Transportation System of Medieval England and Wales." *Journal of Historical Geography* 17 (1991): 123–34.

Ekre, Rune. "Lödöse im Wandel vom 12. zum 13. Jahrhundert." *Lübecker Schriften zur Archäologie und Kulturgeschichte* 7 (1983): 213–18.

English, Barbara. *The Lords of Holderness 1086–1260: A Study in Feudal Society.* Oxford, 1979.

Ennen, Edith. "Aachen im Mittelalter: Sitz des Reiches—Ziel der Wallfahrt—Werk der Bürger." *Zeitschrift des Aachener Geschichtsvereins* 86/87 (1979/1980): 457–87.

———. *The Medieval Town.* Translated by N. Fryde. Amsterdam and New York, 1979.

Ennen, Edith, and Dietrich Höroldt. *Vom Römerkastell zur Bundeshauptstadt: Kleine Geschichte der Stadt Bonn.* 3d ed. Bonn, 1976.

Espinas, Georges. *La Vie urbaine de Douai au moyen âge.* 4 vols. Paris, 1913.

Ewan, Elizabeth. *Townlife in Fourteenth-Century Scotland.* Edinburgh, 1990.

Faith, Rosamond. "Peasant Families and Inheritance Customs in Medieval England." *Agricultural History Review* 14 (1966): 77–95.

Fanchamps, M. L. "Etude sur les tonlieux de la Meuse moyenne du VIIIe au milieu du XIVe siècle." *Le Moyen Age* 70 (1964): 205–64.

Farmer, David. "Crop Yields, Prices and Wages in Medieval England." *Studies in Medieval and Renaissance History* 6 (1983): 115–55.

———. "Grain Yields on Westminster Abbey Manors, 1271–1410." *Canadian Journal of History* 18 (1983): 331–48.

———. "Two Wiltshire Manors and Their Markets." *Agricultural History Review* 37 (1989): 1–11.

Fenoaltea, Stefano. "Transaction Costs, Whig History, and the Common Fields." *Politics & Society* 16 (1988): 171–240.

Ferger, Imme. *Lüneburg: Eine siedlungsgeographische Untersuchung.* Forschungen zur deutschen Landeskunde, 173. Bonn and Bad Godesberg, 1969.

Finnemore, T. J. "A Saltway across Arden." *Birmingham and Warwickshire Archaeological Society, Transactions* 88 (1976–1977): 128–30.

Fischer, Roman. *Aschaffenburg im Mittelalter: Studien zur Geschichte der Stadt von den Anfängen bis zum Beginn der Neuzeit.* Aschaffenburg, 1989.

Fossier, Robert. "Les 'Communes rurales' au moyen âge." *Journal des Savants,* July–December 1992, pp. 235–76.

———. "Land, Castle, Money and Family in the Formation of the Seigneuries." In *Medieval Settlement,* edited by P. Sawyer, pp. 159–68. London, 1976.

———. *Peasant Life in the Medieval West.* Translated by Juliet Vale. Oxford, 1988.

———. "Peuplement de la France du nord entre le Xe et le XVIe siècles." *Annales de démographie historique,* 1979, pp. 59–97.

Fourquin, Guy. *The Anatomy of Popular Rebellion in the Middle Ages.* Translated by A. Chesters. Amsterdam and elsewhere, 1978.

———. *Les Campagnes de la région parisienne à la fin du moyen âge.* Paris, 1964.

———. *Lordship and Feudalism in the Middle Ages.* Translated by I. and A. Lytton Sells. Torquay, 1975.

Fowler, Angus, and Ulrich Klein. "Bürger und Stadt—die Entwicklung der kommunalen Verwaltung im Mittelalter." In *Marburg: Eine illustrierte Stadtgeschichte,* pp. 68–78. Marburg, 1985.

Frame, Robin. "The Bruces in Ireland, 1315–18." *Irish Historical Studies* 73 (1974): 3–37.

———. *English Lordship in Ireland.* Oxford, 1982.

Franklin, Peter. "Peasant Widows' 'Liberation' and Remarriage before the Black Death." *Economic History Review* 39 (1986): 186–204.

Franz, Albert. "Alter und neuer Besitz des Würzburger Bürgerspitals vor dem Steigerwald." *Mainfränkisches Jahrbuch für Geschichte und Kunst* 12 (1960): 12–48.

Friedland, Klaus. "Hansische Handelspolitik und hansisches Wirtschaftssystem im 14. und 15. Jahrhundert." In *Frühformen englisch-deutscher Handelspartnerschaft,* pp. 87–99. Quellen und Darstellungen zur hansischen Geschichte, 23. Cologne and Vienna, 1976.

Fritze, Konrad. "Entstehung, Aufstieg und Blüte der Hansestadt Stralsund." In *Geschichte der Stadt Stralsund*, edited by H. Ewe, pp. 9–102. Veröffentlichungen des Stadtarchivs Stralsund, 10. Weimar, 1984.

Fritze, Wolfgang. "Entstehung und Anfänge von Berlin." In *Bürger, Bauer, Edelmann: Berlin im Mittelalter*, pp. 11–19. Berlin, 1987.

Fussell, G. E. *The English Dairy Farmer, 1500–1900*. London, 1966.

Gabrielson, Peter. "Die Zeit der Hanse, 1300–1517." In *Hamburg: Geschichte der Stadt und ihrer Bewohner*, vol. 1, *Von den Anfängen bis zur Reichsgründung*, edited by H.-D. Loose, pp. 101–90. Hamburg, 1982.

Gardiner, Mark. "Planned Medieval Land Division in Withyham, East Sussex." *Sussex Archaeological Collections* 123 (1985): 109–14.

Garnsey, Peter. *Famine and Food Supply in the Graeco-Roman World: Responses to Risk and Crisis*. Cambridge, 1988.

Gauthier, Léon. *Les Lombards dans les Deux-Bourgognes*. Paris, 1907.

Gehrmann, Johannes. "Die mittelalterliche Besiedlung des Teltows zwischen 1150 und 1300: Eine Bestandsaufnahme der archäologischen Forschungsergebnisse." *Jahrbuch für die Geschichte Mittel- und Ostdeutschlands* 24 (1975): 1–59.

Gelsinger, Bruce. "Norwegian Jurisdiction over Lübeck: Background to an Unredeemed Offer." *Mediaeval Scandinavia* 11 (1978–1979): 242–57.

———. "A Thirteenth-Century Norwegian-Castilian Alliance." *Medievalia et Humanistica* 10 (1981): 55–80.

Genicot, Léopold. *Rural Communities in the Medieval West*. Baltimore, 1990.

George, Alain. "Les Vignobles de l'abbaye des Vaux de Cernay." *Mémoires de la Fédération des sociétés historiques et archéologiques de Paris et de l'Ile-de-France* 35 (1984): 37–68.

Gerking, Willy. *Die mittelalterlichen Siedlungen der Grossgemeinde Lügde*. Schriften des Lippischen Landesmuseums, 2. Detmold, 1986.

Geschichte der Stadt Magdeburg. Edited by Helmut Asmus. 2d ed. Berlin, 1974.

Giry, Arthur. *Histoire de la ville de Saint-Omer et de ses institutions jusqu'au XIV siècle*. Paris, 1877.

Gissel, Svend. "Agrarian Decline in Scandinavia." *Scandinavian Journal of History* 1 (1976): 43–54.

Given, James. "The Economic Consequences of the English Conquest of Gwynedd." *Speculum* 64 (1989): 11–45.

Goodfellow, Peter. "Medieval Bridges in Northamptonshire." *Northamptonshire Past and Present* 7 (1985–1986): 143–58.

———. "Medieval Markets in Northamptonshire." *Northamptonshire Past and Present* 7 (1987–1988): 305–23.

Goose, Nigel. "Wage Labour on a Kentish Manor: Meopham 1307–75." *Archaeologia Cantiana* 92 (1976): 203–23.

Göttmann, Frank. "Die Strahlenberger, der Pfalzgraf und die Kessler: Zum Übergang des Kesslerschutzes an Kurpfalz im 14. Jh." *Alzeyer Geschichtsblätter* 18 (1983): 48–70.

Götzelmann, Ambrosius. *Hainstadt in Baden: Ein Beitrag zur Staats- und Kirchengeschichte Ostfrankens*. Würzburg, 1922.

Graham, B. J. "The Definition and Classification of Medieval Irish Towns." *Irish Geography* 21 (1988): 20–32.

Gras, Norman. *The Evolution of the English Corn Market from the Twelfth to the Eighteenth Century.* 1915. Reprint, New York, 1967.

Grégoire, Paul-Christian. "L'Abbaye d'Orval à l'aube de la sidérurgie industrielle." *Le Pays lorrain* 68 (1987): 51–87.

Grodde-Braun, Brigitte. "Die Töpfereiwüstung Ropperode: Eine archäologisch-historische Untersuchung." *Plesse-Archiv* 4 (1969): 55–87.

Gross, Caroline. "Les Colombiers bourguignons: Typologie." In *Hommage à Geneviève Chevrier et Alain Geslan: Etudes médiévales*, pp. 57–62. Chantiers d'Etudes Mediévales, 13. Colmar and elsewhere, 1975.

Guérin, Isabelle. *La Vie rurale en Sologne aux XIVe et XVe siècles.* Paris, 1960.

Gühne, Arndt. "Nennewitz—Eine Wüstung des hohen Mittelalters im Wermsdorfer Forst, Kr. Oschatz." In *Archäologische Feldforschungen in Sachsen: Fünfzig Jahre Landesmuseum für Vorgeschichte Dresden*, pp. 421–24. Arbeits- und Forschungsberichte zur sächsischen Bodendenkmalpflege, 18. Berlin, 1988.

Haase, Carl. *Die Entstehung der westfälische Städte.* 4th ed. Veröffentlichungen des Provinzialinstituts für westfälische Landes- und Volksforschung des Landschaftsverbandes Westfallen-Lippe, ser. 1, 11. Münster, 1984.

Hahn, Peter-Michael. *Fürstliche Territorialhoheit und lokale Adelsgewalt: Die herrschaftliche Durchdringung des ländlichen Raumes zwischen Elbe und Aller (1300–1700).* Berlin and New York, 1989.

Halard, Xavier. "Le Loup aux XIVe et XVe siècles en Normandie." *Annales de Normandie* 33 (1983): 189–97.

Hall, D. N., et al. "Medieval Agriculture and Settlement in Oughterard and Castlewarden, Co. Kildare." *Irish Geography* 18 (1985): 16–25.

Hallam, H. E. "The Climate of Eastern England 1250–1350." *Agricultural History Review* 32 (1984): 124–32.

———. *Rural England, 1066–1348.* Brighton and Atlantic Highlands, N.J., 1981.

Hammel, Rolf. "Hauseigentum im spätmittelalterlichen Lübeck: Methoden zur sozial- und wirtschaftsgeschichtlichen Auswertung der Lübecker Oberstadtbuchregesten." *Lübecker Schriften zur Archäologie und Kulturgeschichte* 10 (1987): 85–300.

———. "Häusermarkt und wirtschaftliche Wechsellagen in Lübeck von 1284 bis 1700." *Hansische Geschichtsblätter* 106 (1988): 41–107.

Hanawalt, Barbara. *Growing Up in Medieval London: The Experience of Childhood in History.* New York and Oxford, 1993.

———. *The Ties That Bound: Peasant Families in Medieval England.* New York and Oxford, 1986.

Harman, Mary, and Bob Wilson. "A Medieval Graveyard beside Faringdon Road, Abingdon." *Oxoniensia* 46 (1981): 59–61.

Harrison, D. F. "Bridges and Economic Development, 1300–1800." *Economic History Review* 45 (1992): 240–61.

Harvey, Barbara. "Introduction: The 'Crisis' of the Early Fourteenth Century." In *Before the Black Death: Studies in the "Crisis" of the Early Fourteenth Century*, edited by B. Campbell, pp. 1–24. Manchester and New York, 1991.

———. *Westminster Abbey and Its Estates in the Middle Ages.* Oxford, 1977.

Harvey, P.D.A. *A Medieval Oxfordshire Village: Cuxham, 1240 to 1400.* Oxford, 1965.

———, ed. *The Peasant Land Market in Medieval England.* Oxford, 1984.

Hatcher, John. *Rural Economy and Society in the Duchy of Cornwall.* Cambridge, 1970.

Hauschild, Ursula. *Studien zu Löhnen und Preisen in Rostock im Spätmittelalter.* Quellen und Darstellungen zur hansischen Geschichte, 19. Cologne and Vienna, 1973.

Hawthorne, Nathaniel. *The Scarlet Letter: A Romance.* New York, 1983.

Heidinga, H. *Medieval Settlement and Economy North of the Lower Rhine: Archeology and History of Kootwijk and the Veluwe (the Netherlands).* Assen and elsewhere, 1987.

Helle, Knut. "Anglo-Norwegian Relations in the Reign of Håkon Håkonsson (1217–1263)." *Mediaeval Scandinavia* 1 (1968): 101–14.

———. "Neuste norwegische Forschungen über deutsche Kaufleute in Norwegen und ihre Rolle im norwegischen Aussenhandel im 12. bis 14. Jahrhundert." *Hansische Geschichtsblätter* 98 (1980): 23–38.

———. "Norway in the High Middle Ages." *Scandinavian Journal of History* 6 (1981): 161–89.

Henne, Alexandre, and Alphonse Wauters. *Histoire de la ville de Bruxelles.* Vol. 1. Brussels, 1968.

Hennell, Thomas. *The Old Farm.* Salem, N.H., 1984.

Henneman, John. *Royal Taxation in Fourteenth Century France.* Princeton, 1971.

Herlihy, David. "Demography." In *Dictionary of the Middle Ages*, edited by J. Strayer, 4:136–48. New York, 1984.

———. *Opera Muliebria: Women and Work in Medieval Europe.* New York and elsewhere, 1990.

Herrmann, Joachim. "Cölln und Berlin: Bäuerliche Rodungsarbeit und landesherrliche Territorialpolitik im Umfeld der Stadtgründung." *Jahrbuch für Geschichte* 35 (1987): 9–57.

Hiegel, Charles. "Le Sel en Lorraine du VIIIe au XIIIe siècle." *Annales de l'Est* 33 (1981): 3–48.

Higounet, Charles. *La Grange de Vaulerent: Structure et exploitation d'un terroir cistercien de la plaine de France.* Paris, 1965.

Hilton, Rodney. *Bond Men Made Free: Medieval Peasant Movements and the English Rising of 1381.* London, 1973.

———. *The Decline of Serfdom in Medieval England.* London and elsewhere, 1969.

———. *English and French Towns in Feudal Society: A Comparative Study.* Cambridge, 1992.

———. *The English Peasantry in the Later Middle Ages.* Oxford, 1975.

———. "Lords, Burgesses and Hucksters." *Past & Present,* no. 97 (1982): 3–15.

———. "Towns in English Feudal Society." *Review* 3 (1979): 3–20.

———, ed. *Peasants, Knights and Heretics.* Cambridge, 1976.

Histoire de la France rurale. Vol. 1, *La Formation des campagnes françaises des origines au XIVe siècle.* Edited by G. Duby. Paris, 1975.

Histoire de Lille. Vol. 1, *Des origines à l'avènement de Charles Quint.* Lille, [1970].

Höck, Alfred. "Zu mittelalterlichen Totenlaternen und Lichthäuschen in Hessen." *Zeitschrift des Vereins für hessische Geschichte und Landeskunde* 73 (1962): 115–22.

Hockey, S. F. *Quarr Abbey and Its Lands 1132–1631.* Leicester, 1970.

Hodder, M. A. "Excavations at Sandwell Priory and Hall 1982–1988." *South Staffordshire Archaeological and Historical Society Transactions* 31 (1991): 1–227.

Hodges, Richard. *Primitive and Peasant Markets.* Oxford, 1988.

Hoffmann, Erich. "Lübeck im Hoch- und Spätmittelalter: Die grosse Zeit Lübecks." In *Lübeckische Geschichte,* edited by Antjekathrin Grassmann, pp. 79–339. Lübeck, 1988.

Hoffmann, Hartmut. "Das Braunschweiger Umland in der Agrarkrise des 14. Jahrhunderts." *Deutsches Archiv* 37 (1981): 162–286.

Hofmeister, Adolf. *Seehausen und Hasenbüren im Mittelalter: Bauer und Herrschaft im Bremer Vieland.* Veröffentlichungen aus dem Staatsarchiv der freien Hansestadt Bremen, 54. Bremen, 1987.

Hogan, M. Patricia. "Clays, *Culturae* and the Cultivator's Wisdom: Management Efficiency at Fourteenth-Century Wistow." *Agricultural History Review* 36 (1988): 117–31.

———. "The Labor of Their Days: Work in the Medieval Village." *Studies in Medieval and Renaissance History* 8 (1986): 75–186.

Höhl, Gudrun. *Fränkische Städte und Märkte in geographischem Vergleich.* Forschungen zur deutschen Landeskunde, 139. Bad Godesberg, 1963.

Holden, E. W., and T. P. Hudson. "Salt-Making in the Adur Valley, Sussex." *Sussex Archaeological Collections* 119 (1981): 117–48.

Holt, Richard. *The Mills of Medieval England.* Oxford, 1988.

Hopcroft, Rosemary. "The Origins of Regular Open-Field Systems in Pre-Industrial Europe." *Journal of European Economic History* 23 (1994): 563–80.

Hørby, Kai. "The Fate of the Descendants of Christoffer I: Aspects of Danish Politics 1252–1319." *Scandinavian Journal of History* 4 (1979): 207–29.

Howell, Cicely. *Land, Family and Inheritance in Transition: Kibworth Harcourt 1280–1700.* Cambridge, 1983.

Howell, Martha. *Women, Production, and Patriarchy in Late Medieval Cities.* Chicago and London, 1986.

Huber, Alexander. *Das Verhältnis Ludwigs des Bayern zu den Erzkanzlern von Mainz, Köln und Trier (1314–1347).* Kallmünz, 1983.

Hudson, William. "The Prior of Norwich's Manor of Hindolveston: Its Early Organization and the Right of the Customary Tenants to Alienate Their Strips of Land." *Norfolk Archeology* 20 (1921): 179–214.

Hüffer, Maria. *De Adellijke Vrouwenabdij van Rijnsburg. 1133–1574.* Nijmegen and Utrecht, 1922.

Hugo, Graeme. "The Demographic Impact of Famine: A Review." In *Famine as a Geographical Phenomenon,* edited by B. Currey and G. Hugo, pp. 7–31. Dordrecht, Boston, and Lancaster, 1984.

Huiskes, Manfred. *Andernach im Mittelalter: Von den Anfängen bis zum Ende des 14. Jahrhunderts.* Rheinisches Archiv, 111. Bonn, 1980.

Hüster, Heidemarie. *Untersuchungen an Skelettresten von Rindern, Schafen, Ziegen und Schweinen aus dem mittelalterlichen Schleswig.* Ausgrabungen in Schleswig, Berichte und Studien, 8. Neumünster, 1990.

Hyams, Paul. *King, Lords and Peasants in Medieval England: The Common Law of Villeinage in the Twelfth and Thirteenth Centuries.* Oxford, 1980.

Hybel, Nils. *Crisis or Change: The Concept of Crisis in the Light of Agrarian Structural Reorganization in Late Medieval England.* Aarhus, 1988.

Ilgenstein, Ernst. "Handels- und Gewerbegeschichte der Stadt Magdeburg im Mittelalter bis zum Beginn der Zunftherrschaft (1330)." *Geschichts-Blätter für Stadt und Land Magdeburg* 43 (1908): 1–77; 44 (1909): 48–83.

Isenmann, Eberhard. *Die deutsche Stadt im Spätmittelalter.* Stuttgart, 1988.

Jakobi, Franz-Josef. "Bevölkerungsentwicklung und Bevölkerungsstruktur im Mittelalter und in der frühen Neuzeit." In *Geschichte der Stadt Münster,* edited by Franz-Josef Jakobi, 1:485–534. Münster, 1993.

James, Heather. "Excavations in Wootton Wawen Churchyard, 1974 and 1975." *Birmingham and Warwickshire Archaeological Society, Transactions* 90 (1980): 37–48.

James, Terrence. "Excavations at the Augustinian Priory of St. John and St. Teulyddog, Carmathen, 1979." *Archaeologia Cambrensis* 134 (1985): 120–61.

Jansen, Henrik. "Svendborg in the Middle Ages—An Interdisciplinary Investigation." *Journal of Danish Archaeology* 6 (1987): 198–219.

Jaritz, Gerhard, and Albert Müller, eds. *Migration in der Feudalgesellschaft.* Frankfurt-am-Main, 1988.

Jaubert, Anne. "The Royal Castles during the Reign of Erik Menved (1286–1319)." *Journal of Danish Archaeology* 7 (1988): 216–24.

Jeanne, Damien. "La Société rurale face à la lèpre à travers le registre de l'Officialité de Cerisy de 1314 à 1377." *Annales de Normandie* 43 (1993): 91–106.

Johanek, Peter. "Handel und Gewerbe." In *Geschichte der Stadt Münster,* edited by Franz-Josef Jakobi, 1:635–81. Münster, 1993.

Johnson, Penelope. *Equal in Monastic Profession: Religious Women in Medieval France.* Chicago, 1991.

Jones, Andrew. "Harvest Customs and Labourers' Perquisites in Southern England, 1150–1350: The Corn Harvest." *Agricultural History Review* 25 (1977): 14–22.

———. "Harvest Customs and Labourers' Perquisites in Southern England, 1150–1350: The Hay Harvest." *Agricultural History Review* 25 (1977): 98–107.

———. "Land Measurement in England, 1150–1350." *Agricultural History Review* 27 (1979): 10–18.

Jones, S.R.H. "Transaction Costs, Institutional Change, and the Emergence of a Market Economy in Later Anglo-Saxon England." *Economic History Review* 46 (1993): 658–78.

Jongman, Willem, and Rudolf Dekker. "Public Intervention in the Food Supply in Pre-Industrial Europe." In *Bad Year Economics: Cultural Responses to Risk and Uncertainty,* edited by P. Halstead and J. O'Shea, pp. 114–22. Cambridge, 1989.

Joosen, Henry. "De Arbeidsvertegenwoordiging in de Mechelse Stadsraad in de XIIe en XIVe eeuwen." *Anciens pays et assemblées d'états / Standen en Landen* 22 (1961): 49–63.

Jordan, William. "Communal Administration in France, 1257–1270: Problems Discovered and Solutions Imposed." *Revue belge de philologie et d'histoire* 59 (1981): 292–313.

———. *The French Monarchy and the Jews from Philip Augustus to the Last Capetians.* Philadelphia, 1989.

———. *From Servitude to Freedom: Manumission in the Sénonais in the Thirteenth Century.* Philadelphia, 1986.

———. "Home Again: The Jews in the Kingdom of France, 1315–1322." Paper presented at the conference on Strangers in Medieval Society, University of Minnesota, 25–26 February 1994. Forthcoming.

———. *Louis IX and the Challenge of the Crusade: A Study in Rulership.* Princeton, 1979.

———. *Women and Credit in Pre-Industrial and Developing Societies.* Philadelphia, 1993.

———. Review of *From Slavery to Feudalism in South-Western Europe,* by Pierre Bonnassie. *Slavery & Abolition: A Journal of Comparative Studies* 13 (1992): 97–102.

———. Review of *Medieval Slavery and Liberation,* by Pierre Dockès. *Journal of Interdisciplinary History* 14 (1983): 162–63.

Jung, Alfred. *Halver und Schalksmühle: Untersuchungen und Gedanken zur Siedlungsgeschichte des Amtes Halver, eines alten Kirchspiels im sächsisch-fränkischen Grenzraum.* Altenaer Beiträge, 13. Altena, 1978.

Kaske, Robert. "The Character Hunger in *Piers Plowman.*" In *Medieval English Studies Presented to George Kane,* edited by E. Kennedy et al., pp. 187–97. Wolfeboro, N.H., 1988.

Kealey, Edward. *Harvesting the Air: Windmill Pioneers in Twelfth-Century England.* Berkeley, 1987.

Keene, Derek. "Medieval London and Its Region." *London Journal* 14 (1989): 99–111.

Kehn, Wolfgang. "Der Oderraum und seine Beziehungen zur Hanse im 13. und 14. Jahrhundert." In *Pommern und Mecklenburg: Beiträge zur mittelalterlichen Städtegeschichte,* edited by R. Schmidt, pp. 89–109. Cologne and Vienna, 1981.

Kershaw, Ian. *Bolton Priory: The Economy of a Northern Monastery, 1286–1325.* Oxford, 1973.

———. "The Great Famine and Agrarian Crisis in England 1315–1322)." *Past & Present,* no. 59 (May 1973): pp. 3–50.

Kiessling, Rolf. "Augsburgs Wirtschaft im 14. und 15. Jahrhundert." In *Geschichte der Stadt Augsburg: 2000 Jahre von der Römerzeit bis zur Gegenwart,* edited by G. Gottlieb et al., pp. 171–81. Stuttgart, 1984.

———. *Die Stadt und ihr Land: Umlandpolitik, Bürgerbesitz und Wirt-*

schaftsgefüge in Ostschwaben vom 14. bis ins 16. Jahrhundert. Cologne and Vienna, 1989.

Kimball, Elisabeth. *Serjeanty Tenure in Medieval England.* New Haven and London, 1936.

King, Edmund. *Peterborough Abbey, 1086–1310: A Study in the Land Market.* Cambridge, 1973.

King, Peter. *The Finances of the Cistercian Order in the Fourteenth Century.* Kalamazoo, 1985.

Kissock, Jonathan. "The Origins of Medieval Nucleated Rural Settlements in Glamorgan: A Conjectural Model." *Morgannwg: The Journal of Glamorgan History* 35 (1991): 31–49.

Kleindienst, Thérèse. "La Topographie et l'exploitation des 'Marais de Paris' du XIIe au XVIIe siècle." *Mémoires de la Fédération des sociétés historiques et archéologiques de Paris et de l'Ile-de-France* 14 (1963): 7–167.

Komlos, John, and Richard Landes. "Alice to the Red Queen: Imperious Econometrics." *Economic History Review* 44 (1991): 133–36.

———. "Anachronistic Economics: Grain Storage in Medieval England." *Economic History Review* 44 (1991): 36–45.

Kosminsky, E. A. *Studies in the Agrarian History of England in the Thirteenth Century.* Edited by R. Hilton. Translated by R. Kisch. Oxford, 1956.

Kowaleski, Maryanne. "The Grain Trade in Fourteenth-Century Exeter." Forthcoming.

Krings, Bruno. *Das Prämonstratenserstift Arnstein a. d. Lahn im Mittelalter (1139–1527).* Wiesbaden, 1990.

Kühlhorn, Erhard. *Untersuchungen zur Topographie mittelalterlicher Dörfer in Südniedersachsen.* Forschungen zur deutschen Landeskunde, 148. Bad Godesberg, 1964.

Lalanne, Jean-Michel. "Le Domaine des Prémontrés de Belval aux XIIe et XIIIe siècles." *Annales de l'Est* 36 (1984): 287–305.

Lalou, Elisabeth. "Maître Pierre de Chalon, surintendant des ports et passages: 1297–1345." *Actes du 112e Congrès national des Sociétés savantes: Histoire médiévale et philologie,* 1987, pp. 95–117.

———. "Les Révoltes contre le pouvoir à la fin du XIIIe et au début du XIVe siècle." *Actes du 114e Congrès national des Sociétés savantes: Histoire médiévale et philologie,* 1989, pp. 159–83.

Lamb, Hubert. *Climate, History and the Modern World.* London and New York, 1982.

———. *Weather, Climate and Human Affairs: A Book of Essays and Other Papers.* London and New York, 1988.

Lamprecht, Karl. *Deutsches Wirtschaftsleben im Mittelalter: Untersuchungen über die Entwicklung der materiellen Kultur des Platten Landes auf Grund der Quellen zunächst des Mosellandes.* 4 vols. Leipzig, 1886.

Langdon, John. "The Economics of Horses and Oxen in Medieval England." *Agricultural History Review* 30 (1982): 31–40.

———. "Horse Hauling: A Revolution in Vehicle Transport in Twelfth-and Thirteenth-Century England?" *Past & Present,* no. 103 (May 1984): 37–66.

Langdon, John. "Inland Water Transport in Medieval England." *Journal of Historical Geography* 19 (1993): 1–11.

———. "Water-Mills and Windmills in the West Midlands, 1086–1500." *Economic History Review* 44 (1991): 424–44.

Larenaudie, Marie-Josèphe. "Les Famines en Languedoc aux XIVe et XVe siècles." *Annales du Midi* 64 (1952): 27–39.

Laschinger, Johannes. "Das Spital in Amberg." In *Amberg 1034–1984: Aus tausend Jahren Stadtgeschichte*, pp. 153–64. Amberg, 1984.

Lascombes, François. *Chronik der Stadt Luxemburg, 963–1443.* Luxembourg, 1968.

Last, Martin. "Die Topographie der Stadt vom 13. bis zum 16. Jahrhundert." In *Göttingen: Geschichte einer Universitätsstadt*, vol. 1, *Von den Anfängen bis zum Ende des Dreissigjährigen Krieges*, edited by D. Denecke and H.-M. Kühn, pp. 70–106. Göttingen, 1987.

Latouche, Robert. "Un Aspect de la vie rurale dans le Maine au XIe et au XIIe siècle: L'Etablissement des bourgs." *Le Moyen Age* 47 (1937): 44–64.

Le Bacon, René. "Le Vignoble d'Issy." *Mémoires de la Fédération des sociétés historiques et archéologiques de Paris et de l'Ile-de-France* 35 (1984): 109–23.

Le Duc, Placide. *Histoire de l'abbaye de Sainte-Croix de Quimperlé.* Quimperlé, [1882?].

Lefèvre, Simone. "Les Contrats de plantation et l'extension du vignoble en Ile-de-France (Xe-XIIIe s.)." *Mémoires de la Fédération des sociétés historiques et archéologiques de Paris et de l'Ile-de-France* 35 (1984): 29–36.

———. "Un Entrepreneur de défrichements au XIIe siècle: David de la Forest." *Mémoires de la Fédération des sociétés historiques et archéologiques de Paris et de l'Ile-de-France* 28 (1977): 77–83.

Legras-Martin, A. "La Culture maraichère de Saint-Omer." *Hommes et terres du Nord*, 1970, pp. 25–31.

Lejeune, Jean. *Liège et son pays: Naissance d'une patrie (XIIIe–XIVe siècles).* Bibliothèque de la Faculté de philosophie et lettres de l'Université de Liège, 112. Liège, 1948.

Lepiksaar, Johannes. "Restes d'animaux provenant du Grand Besle." *Meddelanden från Lunds Universitets Historiska Museum*, 1966–1968, pp. 85–116.

Le Roy Ladurie, Emmanuel. *Histoire du climat depuis l'an mil.* Paris, 1967.

Lewald, Ursula. "Karl Lamprecht und die rheinische Geschichtsforschung." *Rheinische Vierteljahrsblätter* 21 (1956): 279–304.

Lewis, Archibald. "Northern European Sea Power and the Straits of Gibraltar, 1031–1350 A.D." In *Order and Innovation in the Middle Ages: Essays in Honor of Joseph R. Strayer*, edited by W. Jordan et al., pp. 139–64. Princeton, 1976.

Liessem, Udo. "Zur Architektur der mittelalterlichen Bauwerke." In *Geschichte der Stadt Koblenz von den Anfangen bis zum Ende der kurfürstlichen Zeit*, edited by Ingrid Bátori et al., pp. 383–408. Stuttgart, 1992.

Lillich, Meredith. *The Armor of Light: Stained Glass in Western France, 1250–1325.* Berkeley, 1994.

Lloyd, T. H. *England and the German Hanse, 1157–1611.* Cambridge, 1991.

————. "Overseas Trade and the English Money Supply in the Fourteenth Century." *British Archaeological Reports* 36 (1977): 96–124.

Lob, Reinhold, and Walter Mahr. "Beiträge zur Wüstungforschung im nördlichen Unterfranken." *Mainfränkisches Jahrbuch für Geschichte und Kunst* 24 (1972): 61–95.

Lomas, R. A. "The Priory of Durham and Its Demesnes in the Fourteenth and Fifteenth Centuries." *Economic History Review* 31 (1978): 339–53.

Long, W. Harwood. "The Low Yields of Corn in Medieval England." *Economic History Review* 32 (1979): 459–69.

Looz-Corswarem, Clemens von. "Zur Wirtschafts- und Sozialgeschichte Wesels. Von den Anfängen bis 1609." In *Geschichte der Stadt Wesel*, 2:148–202. Düsseldorf, 1991.

Lorcin, Marie-Thérèse. *Les Campagnes de la région lyonnaise aux XIVe et XVe siècles.* Lyon, 1974.

Lucas, Henry. "The Great European Famine of 1315, 1316, and 1317." *Speculum* 5 (1930): 343–77.

Lunden, Kåre. "Gardar, Bruk og Menneske i Høgmellomalderen." *Historisk Tidsskrift* (Norway) 58 (1979): 111–58 (with English summary).

————. "Kornavl og Pest i Norge i Sigdal, 1349–1667." *Historisk Tidsskrift* (Norway) 67 (1988): 399–413 (with English summary).

————. "Korntienda etter Biskop Eysteins Jordebok, i lys av Norske og Engelske kornprisar." *Historisk Tidsskrift* (Norway) 47 (1968): 189–212 (with English summary).

————. "Øydegardsprosjektet—Metodar og resultat." *Historisk Tidsskrift* (Norway) 60 (1981): 26–49 (with English summary).

————. "Tørrfiskeksporten frå Bergen på 1300-talet ein gong til." *Historisk Tidsskrift* (Norway) 56 (1977): 245–88 (with English summary).

————. "Views and Nonviews on Medieval Norway." *Scandinavian Journal of History* 7 (1982): 165–71.

Lütge, Friedrich. "Die Preispolitik in München im hohen Mittelalter: Ein Beitrag zum Streit über das Problem 'Nahrungsprinzip' oder 'Erwerbsstreben.'" *Jahrbücher für Nationalökonomie und Statistik* 153 (1941): 162–202.

Lyons, Mary. "Weather, Famine, Pestilence and Plague in Ireland, 900–1500." In *Famine: The Irish Experience 900–1900: Subsistence Crises and Famines in Ireland*, edited by E. Crawford, pp. 31–74. Edinburgh, 1989.

McCloskey, Donald. "Conditional Economic History." *Economic History Review* 44 (1991): 128–32.

————. "The Open Fields of England: Rent, Risk, and the Rate of Interest, 1300–1815." In *Markets in History: Economic Studies of the Past*, edited by D. Galenson, pp. 5–51. Cambridge, 1989.

————. "The Prudent Peasant: New Findings on Open Fields." *Journal of Economic History* 51 (1991): 343–55.

McDonnell, John. *Inland Fisheries in Medieval Yorkshire 1066–1300.* Borthwick Papers, no. 60. York, 1981.

————. "Medieval Assarting Hamlets in Bilsdale, North-East Yorkshire." *Northern History* 22 (1986): 269–79.

McDonnell, John. "Pressures on Yorkshire Woodland in the Later Middle Ages." *Northern History* 28 (1992): 110–25.

McGuire, Brian. *The Cistercians in Denmark.* Kalamazoo, 1982.

McIntosh, Marjorie. "Money Lending on the Periphery of London, 1300–1600." *Albion* 20 (1988): 557–71.

Maddicott, J. R. *The English Peasantry and the Demands of the Crown, 1294–1341. Past & Present,* Supplement no. 1, 1975.

———. "Poems of Social Protest in Early Fourteenth-Century England." In *England in the Fourteenth Century: Proceedings of the 1985 Harlaxton Symposium,* edited by W. Ormrod, pp. 130–44. Woodbridge, Suffolk, 1986.

Madsen, Per. "A French Connection: Danish Funerary Pots—A Group of Medieval Pottery." *Journal of Danish Archaeology* 2 (1983): 171–83.

Maillefer, Jean-Marie. "Un Front pionnier aux marges septentrionales de l'occident médiéval: Le Norrland suédois au XIVe siècle." *Revue du Nord* 70 (1988): 319–32.

Manske, Dietrich. "Ambergs Lage im Strassennetz der Oberpfalz während des Mittelalters und der Neuzeit. Ein Beitrag zur historischen und Verkehrsgeographie." In *Ein Jahrtausend Amberg,* edited by H. Bungert and F. Prechtl, pp. 9–45. Regensburg, 1985.

Maréchal, Griet. *De sociale en politieke Gebondenheid van het Brugse Hospitaalwezen in de Middeleeuwen.* Anciens pays et assemblées d'états / Standen en Landen; 73 (1978).

Martin-Lorber, Odile. "Une Communauté d'habitants dans une seigneurie de Cîteaux aux XIIIe et XIVe siècles." *Annales de Bourgogne* 30 (1958): 7–36.

Marvin, Julia. "Cannibalism as an Aspect of Famine in Two English Chronicles." In *Food and Eating in Medieval Society,* edited by Joel T. Rosenthal. Binghamton, N.Y. Forthcoming.

Marx, Walter. *The Development of Charity in Medieval Louvain.* Yonkers, 1936.

Masschaele, James. "The Multiplicity of Medieval Markets Reconsidered." *Journal of Historical Geography* 20 (1994): 255–71.

———. "Transport Costs in Medieval England." *Economic History Review* 46 (1993): 266–79.

Mate, Mavis. "The Agrarian Economy of South-East England before the Black Death: Depressed or Buoyant?" In *Before the Black Death: Studies in the "Crisis" of the Early Fourteenth Century,* edited by B. Campbell, pp. 79–109. Manchester and New York, 1991.

———. "Coping with Inflation: A Fourteenth-Century Example." *Journal of Medieval History* 4 (1978): 95–106.

———. "The Estates of Canterbury Priory before the Black Death, 1315–1348." *Studies in Medieval and Renaissance History* 8 (1986): 1–30.

———. "The Farming Out of Manors: A New Look at the Evidence from Canterbury Cathedral Priory." *Journal of Medieval History* 9 (1983): 331–43.

———. "High Prices in Early Fourteenth-Century England: Causes and Consequences." *Economic History Review* 28 (1975): 1–16.

———. "The Impact of War on the Economy of Canterbury Cathedral Priory, 1294–1340." *Speculum* 57 (1982): 761–78.

————. "The Indebtedness of Canterbury Cathedral Priory, 1215–1295." *Economic History Review* 26 (1973): 183–97.

————. "Labour and Labour Services on the Estates of Canterbury Cathedral Priory in the Fourteenth Century." *Southern History: A Review of the History of Southern England* 7 (1985): 55–67.

————. "Medieval Agrarian Practices: The Determining Factors." *Agricultural History Review* 33 (1985): 22–31.

————. "Property Investment by Canterbury Cathedral Priory 1250–1400." *Journal of British Studies* 23 (1984): 1–21.

Maurer, Helmut. *Konstanz im Mittelalter.* Vol. 1, *Von Anfängen bis zum Konzil.* Constance, 1989.

May, Alfred. "An Index of Thirteenth-Century Peasant Impoverishment? Manor Court Fines." *Economic History Review* 26 (1973): 389–402.

May, Karl. "Der Eschenauer Ortsadel und die nach ihm benannten Limburger Patrizier." *Nassauische Annalen* 86 (1975): 73–97.

Mayhew, Nicholas. "Modelling Medieval Monetisation." In *A Commercialising Economy: England 1086 to c. 1300,* edited by R. Britnell and B. Campbell, pp. 55–77. Manchester and New York, 1995.

————. "Money and Prices in England from Henry II to Edward III." *Agricultural History Review* 35 (1987): 121–32.

Mazerand, Michel. "Histoire de l'abbaye de Sainte-Marie-au-Bois." *Le Pays lorrain* 67 (1986): 111–27.

Meibeyer, Wolfgang. "Der Rundling—eine koloniale Siedlungsform des hohen Mittelalters." *Niedersachsisches Jahrbuch für Landesgeschichte* 44 (1972): 27–49.

Meininghaus, August. *Die Grafen von Dortmund: Ein Beitrag zur Geschichte Dortmunds.* Dortmund, 1905.

Menache, Sophia. "The Templar Order: A Failed Ideal?" *Catholic Historical Review* 79 (1993): 1–21.

Meyer-Wittenberge, Paul. "Die Rostocker Stadtverfassung bis zur Ausbildung der bürgerlichen Selbstverwaltung (um 1325)." *Jahrbücher des Vereins für Mecklenburgische Geschichte und Altertumskunde* 93 (1929): 37–114.

Miller, Edward, and John Hatcher. *Medieval England—Rural Society and Economic Change 1086–1348.* London and New York, 1978.

Ministerialitäten im Mittelrheinraum. Geschichtliche Landeskunde, 17. Wiesbaden, 1978.

Monahan, W. Gregory. *Year of Sorrows: The Great Famine of 1709 in Lyon.* Columbus, Ohio, 1993.

Moore, Ellen. *The Fairs of Medieval England: An Introductory Study.* Toronto, 1985.

Moraw, Peter. "Das späte Mittelalter." In *Das Werden Hessens,* edited by W. Heinemeyer, pp. 195–223. Marburg, 1986.

Morgan, Richard. "The Barony of Powys, 1275–1360." *Welsh History Review* 10 (1980): 1–42.

Morlet, Marie-Thérèse. "Tarifs de péage et de vente à Dijon aux XIIIe et XIVe siècles." *Actes du 112e Congrès national des Sociétés savantes: Histoire médiévale et philologie,* 1987, pp. 119–47.

Mundy, John. *Europe in the High Middle Ages, 1150–1309.* 2d ed. London and New York, 1991.

Munro, John. "Industrial Transformations in the North-West European Textile Trades, c. 1290–c. 1340: Economic Progress or Economic Crisis?" In *Before the Black Death: Studies in the "Crisis" of the Early Fourteenth Century,* edited by B. Campbell, pp. 110–48. Manchester and New York, 1991.

Musset, Lucien. "L'Ancienne Foire rurale de Saint-Georges-en-Auge (XII–XVe siècles)." *Annales de Normandie* 43 (1993): 85–90.

———. "Foires et marchés en Normandie à l'époque ducale." *Annales de Normandie* 26 (1976): 3–23.

———. "Observations sur le rôle social de la sépulture et des cimetières (VIIIe–XIIe siècles)." *Annales de Normandie* 37 (1987): 373–74.

———. "Peuplement en bourgage et bourgs ruraux en Normandie du Xe au XIIIe siècle." *Cahiers de civilisation médiévale* 9 (1966): 177–205.

———. "Quelques observations sur esclavage et servage dans la Normandie ducale." *Annales de Normandie* 36 (1986): 339.

———. "Voie publique et chemin du roi en Normandie du XIe au XIIIe siècle." *Annales de Normandie* 30 (1980): 320–21.

Nash, Alan. "Customary Measure and Open Field Strip Size in Sussex." *Sussex Archaeological Collections* 121 (1983): 109–17.

———. "The Mortality Pattern of the Wiltshire Lords of the Manor, 1242–1377." *Southern History: A Review of the History of Southern England* 2 (1980): 31–43.

———. "The Size of Open Field Strips: A Reinterpretation." *Agricultural History Review* 33 (1985): 32–40.

Nau, Elisabeth. "Währungsverhältnisse am oberen Neckar in der Zeit von ca. 1180 bis ca. 1330." *Zeitschrift für Württembergische Landesgeschichte* 12 (1953): 190–220 and maps following p. 430.

Naudé, W. *Die Getreidehandelspolitik der europäischen Staaten vom 13. bis zum 18. Jahrhundert, als Einleitung in die preussische Getreidehandelspolitik.* Vol. 1. Berlin, 1896.

Nedkvitne, Arnved. "Omfanget av Tørrfiskeksporten fra Bergen." *Historisk Tidsskrift* (Norway) 55 (1976): 340–55.

———. "Stapelreguleringer, Handelsveier og Varekvanta i Bergenshandeln i Seinmiddelalderen." *Historisk Tidsskrift* (Norway) 57 (1978): 53–92 (with English summary).

Neveux, Hugues. "Bonnes et mauvaises récoltes du XIVe au XIXe siècle." *Revue d'histoire économique et sociale* 53 (1975): 179–92.

Newman, Lucille, et al. "Agricultural Intensification, Urbanization, and Hierarchy." In *Hunger in History: Food Shortage, Poverty, and Deprivation,* edited by L. Newman, pp. 101–25. Cambridge and Oxford, 1990.

Nicholas, David. "Economic Reorientation and Social Change in Fourteenth-Century Flanders." *Past & Present,* no. 70 (February 1976): 3–29.

———. *Medieval Flanders.* London and New York, 1992.

———. *Town and Countryside: Social, Economic, and Political Tensions in Fourteenth-Century Flanders.* Bruges, 1971.

Nicholson, Ranald. *Scotland: The Later Middle Ages.* Edinburgh, 1974.

Nordic Archaeological Abstracts 1975. Viborg, 1976.

Norlind, Arnold. *Einige Bemerkungen über das Klima der historischen Zeit*. Lunds Universitets Årsskrift. N. F. AFD. 1. Bd. 10. Nr. 1. Lund and Leipzig, 1914.

Oexle, Judith. "Mittelalterliche Stadtarchäologie in Baden-Württemberg." In *Archäologie in Württemberg*, edited by D. Planck, pp. 381–411. Stuttgart, 1988.

Olsen, Olaf. "St. Jørgensbjærg Kirke: Arkæologiske undersøgelser: Murværk og guev." *Aarbøger for Nordisk Oldkyndighed og Historie*, 1960, pp. 1–71 (with English summary).

Orme, Nicholas. "A Medieval Almshouse for the Clergy: Clyst Gabriel Hospital near Exeter." *Journal of Ecclesiastical History* 39 (1988): 1–15.

Ormrod, W. M. "The Crown and the English Economy, 1290–1348." In *Before the Black Death: Studies in the "Crisis" of the Early Fourteenth Century*, edited by B. Campbell, pp. 149–83. Manchester and New York, 1991.

———. "Political Theory in Practice: The Forced Loan on English Overseas Trade of 1317–18." *Bulletin of the Institute of Historical Research* 64 (1991): 204–15.

O'Shea, J. M. "The Role of Wild Resources in Small-Scale Agricultural Systems: Tales from the Lakes and the Plains." In *Bad Year Economics: Cultural Responses to Risk and Uncertainty*, edited by P. Halstead and J. O'Shea, pp. 57–67. Cambridge, 1989.

Osmaston, Henry. "Crop Failures on the Winchester Manors, 1232–1349 A.D.: Some Comments." *Transactions of the Institute of British Geographers* 10 (1985): 495–500.

Osten, Gerhard. "Siedlungsbild und mittelalterliche Agrarverfassung im nordöstlichen Niedersachsen." *Niedersachsisches Jahrbuch für Landesgeschichte* 41 (1969): 1–49.

Österreichisches Städtebuch. Edited by A. Hoffmann. Vienna, 1968–.

Otway-Ruthven, A. J. *A History of Medieval Ireland*. London and New York, 1968.

Owen, D. Huw. "Tenurial and Economic Developments in North Wales in the Twelfth and Thirteenth Centuries." *Welsh History Review* 6 (1972): 117–35.

Palermo, Luciano. "Carestie e cronisti nel Trecento: Roma e Firenze nel racconto dell'Anonimo e di Giovanni Villani." *Archivio Storico Italiano* 142 (1984): 343–75.

Patschovsky, Alexander. "Strasburger Beginenverfolgungen im 14. Jahrhundert." *Deutsches Archiv* 30 (1974): 56–198.

———. "Waldenserverfolgung in Schweidnitz 1315." *Deutsches Archiv* 36 (1980): 137–62.

Paulmier-Foucart, Monique. "Histoire ecclésiastique et histoire universelle: le *Memoriale temporum*." In *Vincent de Beauvais: Intentions et réceptions d'une oeuvre encyclopédique au moyen âge*, edited by M. Paulmier-Foucart et al., pp. 87–110. Saint-Laurent, Quebec, and Paris, 1990.

Pearsall, Derek. "Poverty and Poor People in *Piers Plowman*." In *Medieval English Studies Presented to George Kane*, edited by E. Kennedy et al., pp. 167–85. Wolfsboro, N.H., 1988.

Penn, Simon. "Female Wage-Earners in Late Fourteenth-Century England." *Agricultural History Review* 35 (1987): 1–15.

Perroy, Edouard. *La Terre et les paysans en France aux XIIe et XIIIe siècles.* Paris, 1973.

Persson, K. Gunnar. "Labour Productivity in Medieval Agriculture: Tuscany and the 'Low Countries.'" In *Land, Labour and Livestock: Historical Studies in European Agricultural Productivity*, edited by B. Campbell and M. Overton, pp. 124–43. Manchester and New York, 1991.

Peters, Inge-Maren. *Hansekaufleute als Gläubiger der englischen Krone (1294–1350).* Quellen und Darstellungen zur hansischen Geschichte, 24. Cologne and Vienna, 1978.

Petit-Dutaillis, Charles. *Les Communes françaises.* Paris, 1947.

Philippe, Michel. "Chantier ou atelier: Aspects de la verrerie normande aux XIVe et XVe siècles." *Annales de Normandie* 42 (1992): 239–57.

Philippe, Robert. "Les Premiers Moulins à vent." *Annales de Normandie* 32 (1982): 99–116.

Piecha, E. Günter. *Kamp-Lintfort im Spiegel der Geschichte: Vom Enstehen und Werden einer jungen Stadt.* Cologne, 1978.

Piekarczyk, Stanislaw. "Some Notes on the Social and Economic Situation of the Swedish Tenants in the XIIIth Century." *Scandia* 27 (1961): 192–216.

Piletta, Françoise. "Les Bourgs du sud du pays d'Auge du milieu du XIe au milieu du XIVe siècle." *Annales de Normandie* 30 (1980): 211–30.

Pirenne, Henri. *Economic and Social History of Medieval Europe.* Translated by I. Clegg. New York, 1937.

Piskozub, Andrzej. "Czynnik Tradycji w Rozmieszczeniu Sieci Komunikacyjnej Polski." *Gdańskie Zeszyty Humanistyczne* 24 (1985): 19–40 (with English and Russian summaries).

Platelle, Henri. "L'Evolution du temporel de l'abbaye de St-Amand." *Bulletin de la Société des antiquaires de Picardie*, 1962, pp. 247–49.

———. *Le Temporel de l'abbaye de Saint-Amand des origines à 1340.* Paris, 1962.

Platt, Colin. "Southampton, 1000–1600 A.D.: Wealth and Settlement Patterns in a Major Medieval Seaport." *Hansische Geschichtsblätter* 91 (1973): 12–23.

Platts, Graham. *Land and People in Medieval Lincolnshire.* Lincoln, 1985.

Poets for Africa: An International Anthology for Hunger Relief. Edited by S. Flammang. Las Vegas, Nev., 1986.

Pollock, Frederick, and Frederic Maitland. *The History of English Law before the Time of Edward I.* 2d ed. 2 vols. Cambridge, 1968.

Poncelet, Edouard. "Herstal et Vivegnis. Souveraineté territoriale, règlements de seigneurie, chartes d'affranchissements." *Académie royale de Belgique: Bulletin de la Commission royale d'histoire* 102 (1937): 77–139.

Poos, L. R. "Population Turnover in Medieval Essex: The Evidence of Some Early-Fourteenth-Century Tithing Lists." In *The World We Have Gained*, edited by L. Bonfield et al., pp. 1–22. Oxford and New York, 1986.

Portet, Pierre. "Les Mesures du vin en France aux XIIIe et XIVe siècles d'après les mémoriaux de la Chambre des comptes de Paris." *Bibliothèque de l'Ecole de Chartes* 149 (1991): 435–46.

Post, John. *Food Shortage, Climatic Variability, and Epidemic Disease in Preindustrial Europe: The Mortality Peak in the Early 1740s.* Ithaca and London, 1985.

Postan, Michael. *The Medieval Economy and Society.* London, 1972.

Postles, David. "Cleaning the Medieval Arable." *Agricultural History Review* 37 (1989): 130–43.

————. "Manorial Accountancy of God's House, Southampton." *Archives* 18 (1987): 36–41.

————. "The Perception of Profit before the Leasing of Demesnes." *Agricultural History Review* 34 (1986): 12–28.

————. "Rural Economy on the Grits and Sandstones of the South Yorkshire Pennines, 1086–1348." *Northern History: A Review of the History of the North of England* 15 (1979): 1–23.

Prakash, Gyan. *Bonded Histories: Genealogies of Labor Servitude in Colonial India.* Cambridge, 1990.

Prange, Wolfgang. *Siedlungsgeschichte des Landes Lauenburg im Mittelalter.* Quelle und Forschungen zur Geschichte Schleswig-Holstein, 41. Neumünster, 1960.

Prestwich, Michael. "Currency and the Economy of Early Fourteenth Century England." *British Archaeological Reports* 36 (1977): 45–58.

————. "Gilbert de Middleton and the Attack on the Cardinals, 1317." In *Warriors and Churchmen in the High Middle Ages: Essays Presented to Karl Leyser,* edited by T. Reuter, pp. 179–94. London and Rio Grande, Ohio, 1992.

————. *The Three Edwards.* New York, 1980.

Prévôt, Jacques. "Le Grand Hautmont, l'abbaye de sa fondation à la Revolution: Son domaine et son rayonnement." *Mémoires de la Société archéologique et historique de l'arrondissement d'Avesnes* 25 (1974): 3–326.

Prims, Floris. *Geschiedenis van Antwerpen.* Vol. 4, *Onder Hertog Jan den Derde (1312–1355),* pt. 1, *Politische en economische Orde.* Antwerp, 1933.

Prinz, Joseph. *Mimigernaford-Münster: Die Enstehungsgeschichte einer Stadt.* 3d ed. Veröffentlichungen der Historischen Kommission Westfalens, 22; Geschichtliche Arbeiten zur westfälischen Landesforschung, 4. Münster, 1981.

Propago sacri ordinis cartusiensis de provinciis Burgundiae, Franciae, Picardiae, Teutoniae, et Angliae . . . Dom Georgius Schwengel. Analecta Cartusiana, 90:2. Salzburg, 1981.

Raban, Sandra. *The Estates of Thorney and Crowland: A Study in Medieval Monastic Land Tenure.* University of Cambridge, Department of Land Economy, Occasional Paper, no. 7. 1977.

————. *Mortmain Legislation and the English Church, 1279–1500.* Cambridge, 1982.

Racinet, Philippe. *Les Maisons de l'ordre de Cluny au moyen âge: Evolution et permanence d'un ancien ordre bénédictin au nord de Paris.* Louvain, 1990.

Raftis, J. Ambrose. *The Estates of Ramsey Abbey.* Toronto, 1957.

————. "The Land Market at Godmanchester c. 1300." *Mediaeval Studies* 50 (1988): 311–32.

————. *Tenure and Mobility: Studies in the Social History of the Mediaeval English Village.* Toronto, 1964.

Raftis, J. Ambrose. *Warboys: Two Hundred Years in the Life of an English Mediaeval Village.* Toronto, 1974.

———. "Western Monasticism and Economic Organization." *Comparative Studies in Society and History* 3 (1960–1961): 452–69.

Rausch, Wilhelm, ed. *Stadt und Stadtherr im 14. Jahrhundert: Entwicklungen und Funktionen.* Beiträge zur Geschichte der Städte Mitteleuropas, 2. Linz, 1972.

Ravallion, Martin. *Markets and Famines.* Oxford, 1987.

Ravensdale, Jack. "Population Changes and the Transfer of Customary Land on a Cambridgeshire Manor in the Fourteenth Century." In *Land, Kinship and Life-Cycle*, edited by R. Smith, pp. 197–225. Cambridge, 1984.

Razi, Zvi. *Life, Marriage and Death in a Medieval Parish: Economy, Society and Demography in Halesowen 1270–1400.* Cambridge, 1980.

———. "The Toronto School's Reconstitution of Medieval Peasant Society: A Critical View." *Past & Present*, no. 85 (November 1979): 141–57.

Reed, C. G., and T. L. Anderson. "An Economic Explanation of English Agricultural Organization in the Twelfth and Thirteenth Centuries." *Economic History Review* 26 (1973): 134–37.

Reincke, Heinrich. "Bevölkerungsprobleme der Hansestädte." *Hansische Geschichtsblätter* 70 (1951): 1–33.

Rennkamp, Walter. *Studien zum deutsch-russischen Handel bis zum Ende des 13. Jahrhunderts: Nowgorod und Dünagebiet.* Bochum, 1977.

Reyerson, Kathryn. "Urbanism, Western European." In *Dictionary of the Middle Ages*, edited by J. Strayer, 12:311–20. New York, 1989.

Reynolds, Susan. *An Introduction to the History of English Medieval Towns.* Oxford, 1977.

Ribbe, Wolfgang. "Die Anfänge von Berlin/Cölln als Forschungsproblem." *Jahrbuch für die Geschichte Mittel- und Ostdeutschlands* 34 (1985): 1–9.

Richard, Jean. "Passages de Saône aux XIIe et XIIIe siècles." *Annales de Bourgogne* 22 (1950): 245–74.

Richter, Gerold. "Kulturlandschaft und Wirtschaft." In *Mecklenburg/Vorpommern: Historische Landeskunde Mitteldeutschlands*, edited by H. Heckmann, pp. 127–58. Würzburg, 1989.

———. "Städte." In *Mecklenburg/Vorpommern: Historische Landeskunde Mitteldeutschlands*, edited by H. Heckmann, pp. 109–16. Würzburg, 1989.

Richter, Klaus. "Hamburgs Frühzeit bis 1300." In *Hamburg: Geschichte der Stadt und ihrer Bewohner*, vol. 1, *Von den Anfängen bis zur Reichsgründung*, edited by H.-D. Loose, pp. 17–100. Hamburg, 1982.

———. *Untersuchungen zur Hamburger Wirtschafts- und Sozialgeschichte um 1300 unter besonderer Berücksichtigung der städtischen Rentengeschäfte 1291–1330.* Hamburg, 1971.

Rivers, J.P.W. "The Nutritional Biology of Famine." In *Famine*, edited by G. A. Harrison, pp. 57–106. Oxford, 1988.

Rogers, James. *A History of Agriculture and Prices in England.* 7 vols. in 8 parts. Oxford, 1866–1902.

Romhányi, Beatrix. "The Role of the Cistercians in Medieval Hungary: Political Activity or Internal Colonization." *Annual of Medieval Studies of the Central European University* (1993–1994): 180–204.

Rösener, Werner. *Bauern im Mittelalter.* Munich, 1985.

———. *Grundherrschaft im Wandel: Untersuchungen zur Entwicklung geistlicher Grundherrschaften im südwestdeutschen Raum vom 9. bis 14. Jahrhundert.* Veröffentlichungen des Max-Planck-Instituts für Geschichte, 102. Göttingen, 1991.

Rosenthal, Jean-Laurent. "Rural Credit Markets and Aggregate Shocks: The Experience of Nuits St. Georges, 1756–76." *Journal of Economic History* 54 (1994): 288–306.

Rotberg, Robert, and Theodore Rabb, eds. *Hunger and History: The Impact of Changing Food Production and Consumption Patterns on Society.* Cambridge, Mass., 1985.

Rubner, Heinrich. *Untersuchungen zur Forstverfassung des mittelalterlichen Frankreichs.* Wiesbaden, 1965.

Ruffier, Olivier. "Note sur les pratiques funéraires médiévales à Bourges." *Cahiers d'archéologie et d'histoire du Berry,* no. 91 (December 1987): 29–34.

Ruiz, Teofilo. *Crisis and Continuity: Land and Town in Late Medieval Castile.* Philadelphia, 1994.

Russell, Josiah. "Population in Europe 500–1500." In *Fontana Economic History of Europe: The Middle Ages,* edited by C. Cipolla, pp. 25–70. London and Glasgow, 1972.

Ryder, M. L. "Medieval Sheep and Wool Types." *Agricultural History Review* 32 (1984): 14–28.

Sadourny, Alain. "Les Transports sur la Seine aux XIIIe et XIVe siècles." *Annales de Bretagne et des pays de l'ouest* 85 (1978): 231–44.

Salvesen, Helge. "The Strength of Tradition: A Historiographical Analysis of Research into Norwegian Agrarian History during the Late Middle Ages and the Early Modern Period." *Scandinavian Journal of History* 7 (1982): 75–133.

Samsonowicz, Henryk. "Das Verhältnis zum Raum bei den hansischen Bürgern im Mittelalter." *Hansische Geschichtsblätter* 95 (1977): 27–37.

Sandnes, Jørn. "Ødegårdsprosjektet og Tallet på Gårdsbruk i Norge i Høgmiddelalderen." *Historisk Tidsskrift* (Norway) 58 (1979): 397–410 (with English summary).

Santiard, M.-Th. "Un Aspect du commerce des porcs en Bourgogne au XIVe siècle." *Annales de Bourgogne* 48 (1976): 100–106.

Sarrazin, Jean-Luc. "Le Littoral poitevin (XIe–XIIIe siècles): Conquête et aménagement (2e partie)." *Annales de Bretagne et des pays de l'ouest* 99 (1992): 117–30.

———. "Maîtrise de l'eau et société en marais poitevin (vers 1190–1283)." *Annales de Bretagne et des pays de l'ouest* 92 (1985): 333–54.

Saul, A. "The Herring Industry at Great Yarmouth c. 1280–c. 1400." *Norfolk Archaeology* 38 (1981): 33–43.

Saul, Nigel. *Knights and Esquires: The Gloucestershire Gentry in the Fourteenth Century.* Oxford, 1981.

Sawyer, Birgit, and Peter Sawyer. *Medieval Scandinavia: From Conversion to Reformation, circa 800–1500.* Nordic Series, 17. Minneapolis and London, 1993.

Schaube, Adolf. "Die Anfänge der Venezianischer Galeerenfahrten nach der Nordsee." *Historische Zeitschrift* 101 (1908): 28–89.

Schein, Sylvia. *"Fideles Crucis": The Papacy, the West, and the Recovery of the Holy Land 1274–1314.* Oxford, 1991.

Schich, Winfried. "Die Entstehung Berlins im Urbanisierungsprozess innerhalb der *Germania Slavica.*" *Jahrbuch für die Geschichte Mittel- und Ostdeutschlands* 34 (1985): 10–20.

———. "Die Entstehung des Städtewesens im Havelland: Die grossen Städte." In *Das Havelland im Mittelalter,* edited by W. Ribbe, pp. 341–81. Berliner Historische Studien, 13. Berlin, 1987.

———. "Das mittelalterliche Berlin (1237–1411)." In *Geschichte Berlins,* vol. 1, *Von der Frühgeschichte bis zur Industrialisierung,* edited by W. Ribbe, pp. 137–248. Munich, 1987.

———. *Würzburg im Mittelalter: Studien zum Verhältnis von Topographie und Bevölkerungsstruktur.* Städteforschung: Veröffentlichungen des Instituts für vergleichende Städtegeschichte in Münster, Reihe A, Darstellung, 3. Cologne and Vienna, 1977.

———. "Zum Verhältnis von slawischer und hochmittelalterlicher Siedlung in den brandenburgischen Landschaften Zauche und Teltow." *Jahrbuch für die Geschichte Mittel- und Ostdeutschlands* 26 (1977): 53–85.

Schmidt, Hans-Joachim. "*Societas christiana in civitate*: Städtekritik und Städtelob im 12. und 13. Jahrhundert." *Historische Zeitschrift* 257 (1993): 297–354.

Schmitz, Hans-Jürgen. *Faktoren der Preisbildung für Getreide und Wein in der Zeit von 800 bis 1350.* Stuttgart, 1968.

Schmitz-Cliever, Egon. "Pest und pestilenzialische Krankheiten in der Geschichte der Reichsstadt Aachen." *Zeitschrift des Aachener Geschichtsvereins* 66/67 (1954/1955): 108–68.

Schneider, Reinhard. "Güter- und Gelddepositen in Zisterziensererklöstern." *Zisterzienser-Studien* 1 (1975): 97–126.

Schöller, P. "Der Markt als Zentralisationsphänomen. Das Grundprinzip und seine Wandlungen in Zeit und Raum." *Westfälische Forschungen* 15 (1962): 85–92.

Scholz, Klaus. "Das Spätmittelalter." In *Westfälische Geschichte,* edited by W. Kohl, 1:403–68. Düsseldorf, 1983.

Schorn-Schütte, Luise. *Karl Lamprecht: Kulturgeschichtsschreibung zwischen Wissenschaft und Politik.* Göttingen, 1984.

Schrammek, Rochus. *Verkehrs- und Baugeschichte der Stadt Bautzen.* Bautzen, 1984.

Schreiner, Johan. "Bemerkungen zum Hanse-Norwegen-Problem." *Hansische Geschichtsblätter* 72 (1954): 64–77.

Schröder, Karl, and Gabriele Schwarz. *Die ländlichen Siedlungsformen in Mitteleuropa: Grundzüge und Probleme ihrer Entwicklung.* Forschungen zur deutschen Landeskunde, 175. Bad Godesberg, 1969.

Schultz, Alwin. *Das höfische Leben zur Zeit des Minnesinger.* 2d ed. 2 vols. Leipzig, 1889.

Schulze, Hans. "Die Besiedlung der Mark Brandenburg im hohen und späten Mittelalter." *Jahrbuch für die Geschichte Mittel- und Ostdeutschlands* 28 (1979): 42–178.

Schumann, Gail. *Plant Diseases: Their Biology and Social Impact.* Saint Paul, Minn., 1991.

Schwarzmaier, Hansmartin. *Geschichte der Stadt Eberbach am Neckar bis zur Einführung der Reformation 1556.* Sigmaringen, 1986.

Seavoy, Ronald E. *Famine in East Africa: Food Production and Food Policies.* Westport, Conn., 1989.

————. *Famine in Peasant Societies.* New York, 1986.

Seberich, Franz. "Die Einwohnerzahl Würzburgs in alter und neuer Zeit." *Mainfränkisches Jahrbuch für Geschichte und Kunst* 12 (1960): 49–68.

Sée, Henri. *Les Classes rurales et le régime domanial en France au moyen âge.* Paris, 1901.

Sen, Amartya. *Poverty and Famines: An Essay on Entitlement and Deprivation.* Oxford, 1981.

Serper, Arié. "L'Administration royale de Paris au temps de Louis IX." *Francia* 7 (1979): 123–39.

Sevrin, Robert. "Comparaison des paysages issus des défrichements médiévaux (Géronsarts), de la deuxième moitié du XVIIIe siècle (Tournaisis-Pévèle) et du XIXe siècle (forêts des princes de Chimay)." *Hommes et terres du Nord,* 1986, pp. 186–89.

Shiel, Robert. "Improving Soil Productivity in the Pre-Fertilizer Era." In *Land, Labour and Livestock: Historical Studies in European Agricultural Productivity,* edited by B. Campbell and M. Overton, pp. 51–77. Manchester and New York, 1991.

Simms, Anngret. "Medieval Dublin: A Topographical Analysis." *Irish Geography* 12 (1979): 25–41.

Simonsohn, Shlomo. *History of the Jews in the Duchy of Mantua.* Jerusalem, 1977.

Sivéry, Gérard. *L'Economie du royaume de France au siècle de saint Louis.* Lille, 1984.

————. "Le Passage de l'élevage extensif à l'élevage intensif et l'évolution des paysages forestièrs dans le sud-est du Hainaut à la fin du moyen âge." *Hommes et terres du Nord,* 1986, pp. 172–76.

————. *Structures agraires et vie rurale dans le Hainaut à la fin du moyen-âge.* 2 vols. Villeneuve d'Ascq, 1977–1980.

————. *Terroirs et communautés rurales dans l'Europe occidentale au moyen âge.* Lille, 1990.

————. "La Variété des paysages ruraux dans le Hainaut à la fin du moyen-âge." *Mémoires de la Société archéologique et historique de l'arrondissement d'Avesnes* 26 (1977): 15–48.

Ślaski, Kasimiers. "Die dänisch-polnischen Beziehungen von dem Tode Valdemars II. bis zum Entstehen der Kalmarer Union." *Mediaeval Scandinavia* 4 (1971): 80–90.

Slicher van Bath, B. H. *The Agrarian History of Western Europe, A.D. 500–1850.* Translated by Olive Ordish. London, 1963.

————. "The Economic and Social Conditions in the Frisian Districts from 900 to 1500." *Afdeling agrarische Geschiedenis, Landbouwhogeschool Wageningen* 13 (1965): 97–133.

Slicher van Bath, B. H. "L'Histoire des forêts dans les Pays-Bas septentrionaux." *Afdeling agrarische Geschiedenis Landbouwhogeschool Wageningen* 14 (1967): 91–104.

———. *Yield Ratios, 810–1820. Afdeling agrarische Geschiedenis, Landbouwhogeschool Wageningen* 10 (1963).

———. "The Yields of Different Crops (Mainly Cereals) in Relation to the Seed c. 810–1820." *Acta historiae neerlandicae* 2 (1967): 26–106.

Slota, Leon. "Law, Land Transfer, and Lordship on the Estates of St. Albans Abbey in the Thirteenth and Fourteenth Centuries." *Law and History Review* 6 (1988): 119–38.

Small, Carola. "Grain for the Countess: The 'Hidden Costs' of Cereal Production in Fourteenth-Century Artois." *Proceedings of the Annual Meeting of the Western Society for French History* 17 (1990): 56–63.

Smith, G. H. "The Excavation of the Hospital of St. Mary of Ospringe, Commonly Called Maison Dieu." *Archaeologia Cantiana* 95 (1979): 81–184.

Smith, J. Beverley. "Edward II and the Allegiance of Wales." *Welsh History Review* 8 (1976): 139–71.

Smith, Kathryn. "History, Typology and Homily: The Joseph Cycle in the Queen Mary Psalter." *Gesta* 32 (1993): 147–59.

Smith, Richard. "Demographic Developments in Rural England, 1300–48: A Survey." In *Before the Black Death: Studies in the "Crisis" of the Early Fourteenth Century*, edited by B. Campbell, pp. 25–77. Manchester and New York, 1991.

———. "Families and Their Land in an Area of Partible Inheritance: Redgrave, Suffolk 1260–1320." In *Land, Kinship and Life-Cycle*, edited by R. Smith, pp. 135–95. Cambridge, 1984.

———. "Some Thoughts on 'Hereditary' and 'Proprietary' Rights in Land under Customary Law in Thirteenth and Fourteenth Century England." *Law and History Review* 1 (1983): 95–128.

Snooks, Graeme. "The Dynamic Role of the Market in the Anglo-Norman Economy and Beyond, 1086–1300." In *A Commercialising Economy: England 1086 to c. 1300*, edited by R. Britnell and B. Campbell, pp. 27–54. Manchester and New York, 1995.

Sorokin, Pitirim. *Hunger as a Factor in Human Affairs*. Translated by E. Sorokin. Gainesville, 1975.

Soulsby, Ian. *The Towns of Medieval Wales: A Study of Their History, Archaeology and Early Topography*. Chichester, 1983.

Spahn, Norbert. *Untersuchungen an Skelettresten von Hunden und Katzen aus dem mittelalterlichen Schleswig*. Ausgrabungen in Schleswig, Berichte und Studien, 5. Neumünster, 1986.

Spufford, Peter. *Handbook of Medieval Exchange*. Royal Historical Society Guides and Handbooks, 13. London, 1986.

Stacey, Robert. "Agricultural Investment and the Management of the Royal Demesne Manors, 1236–40." *Journal of Economic History* 46 (1986): 919–34.

———. *Politics, Policy and Finance under Henry III, 1216–1245*. Oxford, 1987.

Staerk, Dieter. *Die Wüstungen des Saarlandes: Beiträge zur Siedlungsgeschichte des Saarraumes vom Frühmittelalter bis zur französischen Revolution.*

Veröffentlichungen der Kommission für Saarländische Landesgeschichte und Volksforschung, 7. Saarbrücken, 1976.

Stein, Robert. "Jan van Boendales Brabantsche Yeesten: Antithese of Synthese." *Bijdragen en Mededelingen betreffende de Geschiedenis de Nederlanden* 106 (1991): 185–97.

Steinhausen, Josef. "Die Waldbienenwirtschaft der Rheinlande in ihrer historischen Entwicklung." *Rheinische Vierteljahrsblätter* 15/16 (1950/1951): 226–57.

Stephenson, M. J. "Wool Yields in the Medieval Economy." *Economic History Review* 41 (1988): 368–91.

Stevens, Lawrence. "Three Lime Burning Pits, Church Street, Eastbourne." *Sussex Archaeological Collections* 128 (1990): 73–87.

Stievermann, Dieter. "Biberbach im Mittelalter." In *Geschichte der Stadt Biberbach*, edited by D. Stievermann, pp. 209–54. Stuttgart, 1991.

Stoob, Heinz. "Hansische Westpolitik im frühen 14. Jahrhundert." *Hansische Geschichtsblätter* 94 (1976): 1–16.

Störmer, Wilhelm. "Die Gründung von Kleinstädten als Mittel herrschaftlichen Territorienaufbaus, gezeigt an fränkischen Beispielen." *Zeitschrift für bayerische Landesgeschichte* 36 (1973): 563–85.

Strayer, Joseph. *The Reign of Philip the Fair*. Princeton, 1980.

Struick, J. Eduard. "Utrechts Beziehungen zum flachen Land im Mittelalter." *Hansische Geschichtsblätter* 99 (1981): 1–10.

Sturler, Jan de. *Les Relations politiques et les échanges commerciaux entre le Duché de Brabant et l'Angleterre au moyen âge*. Paris, 1936.

Sydow, Jürgen. "Die Klein- und Mittelstadt in der südwestdeutschen Geschichte des Mittelalters." In *Pforzheim im Mittelalter: Studien zur Geschichte einer landesherrlichen Stadt*, edited by Hans-Peter Becht, pp. 9–38. Pforzheimer Geschichtsblätter, 6. Sigmaringen, 1983.

———. *Städte im deutschen Südwesten: Ihre Geschichte von der Römerzeit bis zur Gegenwart*. Stuttgart, 1987.

Tahon, Benoît. "L'Eglise Saint-Martin de Graçay (fin XIe/XIIe s.)." *Cahiers d'archéologie et d'histoire du Berry*, no. 98 (September 1989): 45–54.

TeBrake, William. *Medieval Frontier: Culture and Ecology in Rijnland*. College Station, Tex., 1985.

Theissen, Andrea. "Das Leben in den Städten." In *Bürger, Bauer, Edelmann: Berlin im Mittelalter*, pp. 94–114. Berlin, 1987.

Thirsk, Joan. "The Common Fields." *Past & Present*, no. 29 (December 1964): 3–25.

———. "The Origin of the Common Fields." *Past & Present*, no. 33 (April 1966): 142–47.

Thomas, Howard, and Gareth Dowdell. "A Shrunken Medieval Village at Barry, South Glamorgan." *Archaeologia Cambrensis* 136 (1987): 94–137.

Thomas, Hugh. "Subinfeudation and Alienation of Land, Economic Development, and the Wealth of Nobles on the Honor of Richmond." *Albion* 26 (1994): 397–417.

Thornton, Christopher. "The Determinants of Land Productivity on the Bishop of Winchester's Demesne of Rimpton, 1208 to 1403." In *Land, Labour and*

Livestock: Historical Studies in European Agricultural Productivity, edited by B. Campbell and M. Overton, pp. 183–210. Manchester and New York, 1991.

Thornton, Christopher. "Efficiency in Medieval Livestock Farming: The Fertility and Mortality of Herds and Flocks at Rimpton, Somerset, 1208–1349." In *Thirteenth Century England IV: Proceedings of the Newcastle upon Tyne Conference 1991*, edited by P. Coss and S. Lloyd, pp. 25–46. Woodbridge, Suffolk, 1992.

Tillotson, John. *Marrick Priory: A Nunnery in Late Medieval Yorkshire*. Borthwick Papers, no. 75. York, 1989.

Titow, Jan. *English Rural Society, 1200–1350*. London, 1969.

———. "Medieval England and the Open-Field System." *Past & Present*, no. 32 (December 1965): pp. 86–102.

Tout, Thomas. *The Beginnings of a Modern Capital: London and Westminster in the Fourteenth Century*. London, 1923.

Townsend, Robert. *The Medieval Village Economy: A Study of the Pareto Mapping in General Equilibrium Models*. Princeton, 1993.

Trower, Katherine. "The Figure of Hunger in *Piers Plowman*." *American Benedictine Review* 24 (1973): 238–60.

Tyerman, Christopher. *England and the Crusades, 1095–1588*. Chicago and London, 1988.

Uitz, Erika. "Der Kampf um kommunale Autonomie in Magdeburg bis zur Stadtverfassung von 1330." In *Stadt und Städtebürgertum in der deutschen Geschichte des 13. Jahrhunderts*, edited by Bernhard Töpfer, pp. 228–323. Berlin, 1976.

Ulsig, Erik. "Pest og Befolkningsnedgang i Danmark i det 14. Århundrede." *Historisk Tidsskrift* (Denmark) 91 (1991): 21–43 (with English summary).

Unwin, Tim. "Rural Marketing in Medieval Nottinghamshire." *Journal of Historical Geography* 7 (1981): 231–51.

Usilton, Larry. "Edward I's Exploitation of the Corrody System." *American Benedictine Review* 31 (1980): 222–36.

Vandekerckhove, Antoine. *Histoire de l'abbaye du Val-Dieu à travers les siècles, 1215–1954*. 2d ed. Dison, 1954.

Van Derveeghde, Denise. *Le Domaine du Val Saint-Lambert de 1202 à 1387*. Paris, 1955.

Van Haaster, Henk. "Umwelt und Nahrungswirtschaft in der Hansestadt Lübeck vom 12. Jahrhundert bis in die Neuzeit." *Lübecker Schriften zur Archäologie und Kulturgeschichte* 21 (1991): 203–22.

Van Houtte, J. *De Geschiedenis van Brugge*. Tielt, 1982.

Vanja, Christina. "Frauen im Dorf: Ihre Stellung unter besonderer Berücksichtgung landgräflich-hessischer Quellen des späten Mittelalters." *Zeitschrift für Agrargeschichte und Agrarsoziologie* 34 (1986): 147–59.

Van Werveke, H. "La Famine de l'an 1316 en Flandre et dans les régions voisines." *Revue du Nord* 41 (1959): 5–14.

Verbruggen, J. "De Getalsterkte van de Ambachten in het Brugse Gemeentleger." *Belgisch Tijdschrift voor Militaire Geschiedenis / Revue belge d'histoire militaire* 25 (1984): 461–80.

Verhaege, Frans. "The Late Medieval 'Crisis' in the Low Countries: The Archaeological Viewpoint." In *Europa 1400: Die Krise des Spätmittelalters*, edited by F. Seibt and W. Eberhard, pp. 146–66. Stuttgart, 1984.

Verhoeve, A. "La Motte féodale et l'habitat dispersé en Flandre." *Hommes et terres du Nord*, 1974, pp. 123–27.

Vermeesch, Albert. "Les Oppida en Brabant (1123–1355)." *Anciens pays et assemblées d'états / Standen en Landen* 22 (1961): 31–46.

Verniers, Louis. *Un Millénaire d'histoire de Bruxelles*. Brussels, 1965.

Vincent, François. *Histoire des famines à Paris*. Paris, 1946.

Volk, Otto. *Salzproduktion und Salzhandel mittelalterlicher Zisterzienserklöster*. Sigmaringen, 1984.

Voltmer, Ernst. "Von der Bischofsstadt zur Reichsstadt: Speyer im Hoch- und Spätmittelalter (10. bis Anfang 15. Jahrhundert)." In *Geschichte der Stadt Speyer*, vol. 1, edited by W. Eger, pp. 249–368. Stuttgart, 1983.

Wagner, Rudolf. "Das Heilig-Geist-Spital: Gründung, Spitalleben und Grundbesitz bis zum Dreisigjährigen Krieg." In *Aichach im Mittelalter*, edited by W. Liebhart and R. Wagner, pp. 131–57. Aichach, 1985.

Waites, Bryan. "Medieval Assessments and Agricultural Prosperity in Northeast Yorkshire: 1292–1342." *Yorkshire Archaeological Journal* 44 (1972): 134–45.

Waldow, K. "The Rise and Decline of a Saltern: Rent-Seeking at Its Best." *Journal of European Economic History* 22 (1993): 581–600.

Walsh, Thomas. "The Knights of the Temple." *Journal of the Old Wexford Society* 2 (1969): 13–18.

Walter, Friedrich von. *Kurze Geschichte von dem Prämonstratenserstifte Obermachtal*. Ehingen, 1835. Reprinted in *Aus der Geschichte des Klosters Obermachtal*. Bad Buchau, 1985.

Walter, John, and Roger Schofield, eds. *Famine, Disease and the Social Order in Early Modern Society*. Cambridge, 1989.

Walter, John, and Keith Wrightson. "Death and the Social Order in Early Modern England." *Past & Present*, no. 71 (May 1976): 22–42.

Wanderwitz, Heinrich. *Studien zum mittelalterlichen Salzwesen in Bayern*. Munich, 1984.

Wardwell, John. Review of Ronald Seavoy, *Famine in Peasant Societies*. *Contemporary Sociology* 16 (1987): 835–36.

Warry, John. "The Ancient History of Rabbits." *Local Historian* 18 (1988): 13–15.

Waschinski, Emil. *Währung, Preisentwicklung und Kaufkraft des Geldes in Schleswig-Holstein von 1226–1864*. Quellen und Forschungen zur Geschichte Schleswig-Holsteins, 26. Neumünster, 1952.

Waugh, Scott. "The Profits of Violence: The Minor Gentry in the Rebellion of 1321–1322 in Gloucestershire and Herefordshire." *Speculum* 52 (1977): 843–69.

Weber, Wilfried. *Die Entwicklung der nördlichen Weinbaugrenze in Europa: Eine historisch-geographische Untersuchung*. Forschungen zur deutschen Landeskunde, 216. Trier, 1980.

Weinrich, Lorenz. "Die Urkunde in der Übersetzung: Studien zu einer Sammlung von Ostsiedlungsurkunden." *Jahrbuch für die Geschichte Mittel- und Ostdeutschlands* 19 (1970): 1–48.

Weirauch, Hans-Erich. "Der Grundbesitz des Stiftes Quedlinburg im Mittelalter." *Sachsen und Anhalt* 14 (1938): 203–95.

———. "Die Güterpolitik des Stiftes Quedlinburg im Mittelalter,." *Sachsen und Anhalt* 13 (1937): 117–81.

Weiss, Harvey. "Early Irrigation Agriculture." *Science* 200 (1978): 1377.

Willert, Helmut. *Anfänge und frühe Entwicklung der Städte Kiel, Oldesloe und Plön.* Quellen und Forschungen zur Geschichte Schleswig-Holsteins, 96. Neumünster, 1990.

Williams, David. *The Welsh Cistercians.* 2 vols. Caldey Island, Tenby, 1984.

Winchester, Angus. "Medieval Cockermouth." *Transactions of the Cumberland and Westmorland Antiquarian and Archaeological Society* 86 (1986): 109–28.

Winter, Heinrich. *Die Entwicklung der Landwirtschaft und Kulturlandschaft des monschauer Landes unter besonderer Berücksichtigung der Rodungen.* Forschungen zur deutschen Landeskunde, 147. Bad Godesberg, 1965.

Wisplinghoff, Erich. "Beiträge zur Wirtschaftsgeschichte des Klosters St. Pantaleon in Köln." In *Aus Kölnischer und rheinischer Geschichte*, edited by H. Blum, pp. 133–62. Veröffentlichungen des Kölnischen Geschichtsvereins, 29. Cologne, 1969.

———. "Beiträge zur Wirtschafts- und Besitzgeschichte der Benediktinerabtei Siegburg." *Rheinische Vierteljahrsblätter* 33 (1969): 78–138.

———. "Vom Mittelalter bis zum Ende des Jülich-Klevischen Erbstreits (ca. 700–1614)." In *Düsseldorf: Geschichte von den Ursprüngen bis ins 20 Jahrhundert*, vol. 1, *Von der ersten Besiedlung zur frühneuzeitlichen Stadt (bis 1614)*, edited by H. Weidenhaupt, pp. 161–400. Düsseldorf, 1988.

Witte, Otto. "Geschichte Mecklenburgs." in *Mecklenburg/Vorpommern: Historische Landeskunde Mitteldeutschlands*, edited by H. Heckmann, pp. 9–38. Würzburg, 1989.

———. "Geschichte Vorpommerns." In *Mecklenburg/Vorpommern: Historische Landeskunde Mitteldeutschlands*, edited by H. Heckmann, pp. 39–55. Würzburg, 1989.

Witthöft, Harald. "Mass- und Gewichtsnormen im hansischen Salzhandel." *Hansische Geschichtsblätter* 95 (1977): 38–65.

Woolgar, C. M. *Household Accounts from Medieval England.* 2 vols. Records of Social and Economic History, n.s., 17. Oxford, 1992.

Wriedt, Klaus. "Die Annales Lubicenses und ihre Stellung in der Lübecker Geschichtsschreibung des 14. Jahrhunderts." *Deutsches Archiv* 22 (1966): 556–86.

Wright, Susan. "Barton Blount: Climatic or Economic Change?" *Medieval Archaeology* 20 (1976): 148–52.

Wyffels, Carlos. "Hanse, grands marchands et patriciens de Saint-Omer." In *Miscellanea archivistica et historica*, pp. 241–323. Brussels, 1987.

Ylikangas, Heikki. "Major Fluctuations in Crimes of Violence in Finland." *Scandinavian Journal of History* 1 (1976): 81–103.

Yrwing, Hugo. "Salt och saltförsörjning i det medeltida Sverige." *Scandia* 34 (1968): 218–42 (with German summary).

Zadora-Rio, Elisabeth. "Parcs à gibier et garennes à lapins: Contribution à une étude archéologique des territoires de chasse dans le paysage médiéval." *Hommes et terres du Nord*, 1986, pp. 133–39.

Zenner, Walter. *Minorities in the Middle: A Cross-Cultural Analysis*. Albany, 1991.

Ziegler, Philip. *The Black Death*. New York, 1971.

INDEX

About the Author

WILLIAM CHESTER JORDAN is Professor of History and Director of the Shelby Cullom Davis Center for Historical Studies at Princeton University. He is the author of *Louis IX and the Challenge of the Crusade: A Study in Rulership* (Princeton, 1979); *From Servitude to Freedom: Manumission in the Sénonais in the Thirteenth Century* (Philadelphia, 1986); *The French Monarchy and the Jews from Philip Augustus to the Last Capetians* (Philadelphia, 1989); *Women and Credit in Pre-Industrial and Developing Societies* (Philadelphia, 1993).